INTERNATIONAL ACCOUNTING AND COMPARATIVE FINANCIAL REPORTING

International Accounting and Comparative Financial Reporting

Selected Essays of Christopher Nobes

Christopher W. Nobes

Professor of Accounting, University of Reading, UK

Edward Elgar

Cheltenham, UK • Northampton, MA, USA

657.02
N74i

Published by
Edward Elgar Publishing Limited
Glensanda House
Montpellier Parade
Cheltenham
Glos GL50 1UA
UK

Edward Elgar Publishing, Inc.
136 West Street
Suite 202
Northampton
Massachusetts 01060
USA

A catalogue record for this book
is available from the British Library

Library of Congress Cataloguing in Publication Data

Nobes, Christopher W.
    International accounting and comparative financial reporting:
selected essays / of Christopher Nobes.
    Includes index.
    1. Accounting — Standards.   2. Financial statements — Standards.
3. Comparative accounting.   4. International business enterprises -
- Accounting.   I. Title.
HF5626.N63   1999   99-21907
657'.02'18—dc21   CIP

ISBN 1 85898 974 4

Printed and bound in Great Britain by Bookcraft (Bath) Ltd.

Contents

Preface

I am grateful to Edward Elgar, the eponymous publisher, for suggesting that I should collect together some of my writings on international accounting. My selection criteria are explained in the Introduction.

While working on the papers included here, I have benefited, for over twenty years, from a continual stream of encouragement, advice and, occasionally, admonishment from Bob Parker. More recently, I have come also to rely on rapid, detailed and refreshingly honest advice from Alan Roberts. These two colleagues have provided many useful ideas and have stopped me from making many errors.

Of the twenty pieces reproduced in this volume, seven have been co-authored. Graham Diggle, Lisa Evans, Margaret Lamb, Samantha Miles and Julie Norton have written, or are writing, doctoral theses under my supervision. I hope that they have gained as much from our discussions and joint work as I have. Alan Roberts is a co-author of one of the papers, but provided guidance on all the others published in the 1990s. Another recent co-author, Gerhard Mueller, was an inspiration for some of my early work, as he was for that of many others. Missing as a co-author here is Bob Parker, with whom I have written on international accounting and for academic journals but not both at once.

Many other colleagues have provided help. Those acknowledged in the original versions of the papers reproduced in this volume are listed overleaf. Many known journal editors and unknown referees have also provided invaluable advice.

Other indispensable aid, particularly for someone who still relies on the word-processing developments pioneered by László Biro, has been supplied over the years by many secretaries, reaching their acme in Carol Wright.

University of Reading
England
October 1998

Help from the following was gratefully acknowledged in the original versions of the papers reproduced here:

David Alexander
David Ashton
John Bowen-Walsh
Roberto Bruni
Rob Bryer
Adolf Coenenberg
Walther Busse von Colbe
Michel Couzigou
Judy Day
John Dyson
Don Egginton
Octavio Gastambide Fernandes
Maria Leonor Fernandes Ferreira
David Forrester
Steve Goldberg
Sir John Grenside
Nicholas Grier
Axel Haller
Jean Harris
David Hatherly
John Hegarty
Karel van Hulle
Frank Jenkins
Horst Kaminski
Liesel Knorr
Geoffrey Lee
Yannick Lemarchand
P. Lepidas
Richard Macve

Jill McKinnon
Dieter Ordelheide
Michael Page
Bob Parker
Dieter Pfaff
Brenda Porter
Michael Renshall
Alan Roberts
Fulvia Rocchi
Brian Rutherford
Etsuo Sawa
Jean-Claude Scheid
Jim Schweikart
Anne Semler
Autar Singh
Saskia Slomp
Antonio Socías Salvá
Ian Stewart
George Tridimas
Peter Walton
Tom Watts
Peter Wessel
Geoff Whittington
David Wilde
Basil Yamey
David Young
Stefano Zambon
Peter van der Zanden
Steve Zeff

Introduction

The selection
This volume was prepared at the request of the publisher, Edward Elgar. It brings together a number of published papers on international accounting. The papers have been selected using the following criteria:

1. The content of the paper is not purely descriptive, but contains analysis, a proposed model or the testing of a model.
2. The paper has not been significantly overtaken by subsequent events.

Because of the first criterion, the papers are all to be found in *refereed* journals: British, Australian, American and pan-European. This is not to imply that descriptive articles are worthless. Indeed, the production of clear and accurate descriptive material in international accounting is of great value to researchers, students and practitioners. Although the academic field of international accounting has been criticized for its concentration on description, the problem is much worse than that: the descriptions are often inaccurate, misleading or dated.

One reason for establishing the first criterion is that papers are thereby less likely to fail the second. The papers selected were written over a period of twenty years. Perhaps surprisingly, the earliest (on currency translation) seems not to break the second criterion, because its reference points are SFAS 52 and SSAP 20, which are still in force.

The papers are organized into five sections by subject matter, although naturally there are overlaps. One feature of the selection is that eight 'comment' papers have been included. I believe that comments and replies can be a useful way of advancing academic debate, and they often have the merit of brevity and incisiveness. Of course, 'comments' can only be fully understood and assessed in the context of the original papers and any replies. However, it is hoped that the comments selected for reproduction here are intelligible by themselves. In each case, a note is provided to direct readers to the related originals or replies.

My work is nearly all concerned with comparative international financial reporting, which is clearly not the whole of international accounting, although it accounts for the bulk of publications in that wider field.

The rest of this Introduction is devoted to a brief analysis of the contents of this volume, under the headings of the five sections. I acknowledge in the Preface the assistance of several co-authors and of many others in the writing of these papers.

I International origins of double-entry bookkeeping
The import and export of accounting technology (see Parker, 1989) is a constant theme (explicit or otherwise) of the papers in this volume. This international transfer did not start with double-entry bookkeeping, nor did it stop with it. However, the spread of double entry through the movement of persons and texts has been

particularly well described and analysed by several researchers (for example, Yamey, 1940; de Roover, 1978).

My amateur contributions in this area include a paper (Chapter 1) on the Gallerani account book of 1305 to 1308, which seems to comprise the oldest surviving double-entry records written in England, albeit by an Italian firm in the Tuscan language and now preserved in Flanders. The records had been examined before, but by historians and linguists. They contain references and transactions relating to interesting personages of the time, including Edward II, Piers Gaveston and the Grand Master of the Order of the Templars.

Schoolboy Latin plus my long-running attempts to establish a rudimentary grasp of modern Italian came in surprisingly useful when interpreting 700-year-old entries, although expert help was needed. It was also necessary to marshall the previous thoughts of others on how to define double entry. This paper can be seen to fit into a series on account books of the period (for example, Lee, 1977; Peragallo, 1977).

Chapter 2 is a comment on a paper (Lall Nigam, 1986) which suggested that double entry was not an invention of thirteenth-century Italian merchants but of Indians in the fourth century BC or earlier. Claims for non-Italian origin are fairly common, but most share the completely speculative nature of the paper commented on here.

Interestingly, my own comment contained some misleading remarks, as clearly pointed out by Scorgie (1990), but without damaging the main point that there was no convincing evidence to support the Indian claim.

II   Causes of international differences and classification of systems

This is a fundamental area of study within the field of comparative international financial reporting. The two issues in the above heading seem to be in the logical order. However, the papers in Part II of this volume are in the reverse order, largely for chronological reasons. The papers are mostly on classification, and they gradually led me towards the 'general model of the reasons for international differences' in the final paper (Chapter 9), which includes proposed improvements to earlier classifications.

The first paper in this Part (Chapter 3: a 'judgemental international classification') is drawn from my doctoral dissertation (examined by Bob Parker and Sid Gray, who provided much useful advice). This paper was an attempt to improve on the pioneering work of Mueller without sacrificing the essential elements of judgement in favour of the appearance of scientific methodology provided by statistics. A comment (Chapter 4) expands on this latter point, as does Nobes (1982).

The conclusions of Chapter 3 (most obviously its two-sided world of Anglo-Saxon and continental systems) have passed into many textbooks (for example, Choi and Mueller, 1992, p. 34; Radebaugh and Gray, 1997, p. 70; Walton, Haller and Raffournier, 1998, pp. 8 and 23; and, of course, Nobes and Parker, 1998, p. 58). They have also been the subject of extension (for example, Al Najjar, 1986) and of, generally supportive, empirical investigation (for example, Doupnik and Salter, 1993). However, some have criticized the classification (for example, Roberts, 1995; Cairns, 1997; Feige, 1997). On the whole, I agree with Roberts. Some of these ideas had developed from our earlier discussions and had been included in a rudimentary form in Nobes (1992, p. 95); others have been adopted in Chapter 9 here. Replies to Feige and Cairns are reproduced as Chapters 5 and 6; they add a few points to the earlier arguments in Chapters 3 and 4.

Another small contribution to the classification literature was a disagreement (Chapter 7) with a suggestion by Shoenthal (1989) that classification might be made on the basis of different competencies of recently qualified accountants.

One of the major factors associated with international accounting differences is corporate taxation. Several authors (including myself) had suggested that tax differences helped to cause accounting differences. Lamb, Nobes and Roberts (1995) suggest that this is misleading, at least for the first major split of countries into two types. In some countries, the calculation of taxable income is a prime purpose of accounting, and tax rules dominate financial reporting. In this sense, tax rules can certainly cause international accounting differences. However, in other countries there are differences between tax and financial reporting rules on many topics, so that tax rules have no effect on financial reporting *practice* in these areas. All this should be separated from the development of financial reporting *rules* over time, which interacts with the development of tax rules over time.

Chapter 8 draws on the above work to establish a method for assessing the current operational connection between tax and financial reporting practice in the UK, the US, France and Germany. One conclusion is that there is a clear distinction, especially for unconsolidated statements, between the degree of influence of tax on UK or US financial reporting practice and the degree of influence in Germany.

It is suggested above (Chapters 7 and 8) that international financial reporting differences (particularly a two-class classification) are not caused by different education or different tax systems. This leads to the examination of which factors *are* plausible. This is the subject of Chapter 9.

First, one should examine previous models. Many papers contain speculations about dozens of possible causal factors. The two best articulated models are by Gray (1988) and Doupnik and Salter (1995). It is concluded that Gray's cultural model is difficult to operationalize for this purpose and that Doupnik and Salter's contains too many overlapping factors and some unconvincing reasoning. Chapter 9 proposes a parsimonious model based on two factors: the degree of colonial influence and the strength of equity markets. It is suggested that these explain the initial two-class split of systems. Also, the idea that one should examine systems rather than countries is explored.

III   International differences and their effects
This part contains three papers on international accounting differences. They each have two international dimensions. Chapter 10 concerns a specific accounting problem of multinational companies (currency translation) and analyses the international debate leading to the current rules in the US and the UK. Chapter 11 deals with international differences in accounting for goodwill and how this affects cross-border acquisitions. Chapter 12 looks at major international accounting differences and how London-based financial institutions deal with foreign accounting data containing these differences.

Chapter 10 concludes that the US and UK argumentation in support of the closing rate method is similar and similarly unconvincing. The net investment method, which supports the closing rate, seems inconsistent with consolidation theory. This problem could largely be solved by using current values with current exchange rates.

Chapter 11 is a comment on Lee and Choi (1992), who seemed to show that accounting and tax rules gave an advantage to German and Japanese multinationals in international aquisitions. Chapter 11 suggests that the conclusions on tax cannot be correct because the analysis was based on the rules for purchased non-consolidated goodwill rather than those for goodwill on consolidation. A similar criticism of Dunne and Ndubizu (1995) is made in Nobes (1996). Elsewhere, Nobes and Norton (1996) look at international variations in accounting and tax rules, and criticize Dunne and Rollins (1992) in the process.

Choi and Lee (1997) reply to the criticism in Chapter 11 but do not dispute the main point. Dunne and Ndubizu (1996) reply to the similar criticism by suggesting that errors in the analysis of tax rules are not important because tax cash flows are the major issue. They still seem not to recognize the main point that different treatments of goodwill on consolidation do not affect tax cash flows.

Chapter 12 builds on the work of other researchers on (i) the use of UK accounting data in UK acquisitions, and (ii) the effects of international differences on analysis and investment. This paper is different from (i) as it looks at foreign accounting data. It is different from (ii) as it separates analysts from fund managers, and sector specialists from country specialists. Significant findings thereby emerge, such as that fund managers rely on analysts to adjust for accounting differences but that analysts generally make no such adjustments.

IV European harmonization

Another major topic in the accounting journals is harmonization, particularly of financial reporting. In Europe, most attention has been given to the harmonization through Directives of the European Communities. The six papers in this Part are set in that context. They concern the second, fourth, seventh and eighth company law Directives. Many of the papers concentrate on Germany and the UK, which seem to be examples of opposite accounting traditions in Europe.

Chapter 13 traces the arrival of various European (particularly German) ideas into UK law through the second and fourth Directives. Chapter 14 examines a particular issue (the prudence principle) and looks at German and British influence on the fourth Directive and then the latter's implementation in German and British law. Small differences in wording and large differences in practice are found.

Chapter 15 concerns perhaps the most famous and controversial provision of the European accounting Directives: the requirement to give a true and fair view. The paper starts with the UK formulation in the 1940s and traces this into some other countries and then into the fourth Directive, where different language versions have non-literal translations. On implementation as national laws, further linguistic complications occur. The operational effect of the requirement seems to vary from substantial to negligible in EU countries. Other papers have taken further the question of whether there is a 'European' true and fair view (for example, Alexander, 1993; Van Hulle, 1993; and several papers in *European Accounting Review*, Vol. 6, No. 4, 1997).

The mechanisms whereby a final Directive emerges are examined in Chapter 16, using the seventh Directive as a case study. Several players are involved, including accountancy professional bodies, legal bureaucrats in Brussels, national government politicians and large companies. At various stages in the life of the Directive, these players exert different degrees of influence. Also noticeable in this case is the gradual move from a German starting point towards a British conclusion.

Nervousness at the Anglo-Saxon influences on continental Europe are expressed by Hoarau (1995) for France. However, Chapter 17 comments that most of the French changes were deliberately made by France and are a sensible response in that the effects particularly relate to the consolidated statements of listed companies. Subsequent developments (for example, the law no. 98-261 of 6 April 1998, enabling complete departure from normal French rules for such statements) confirm the direction of change.

Finally, in this Part, Chapter 18 looks at harmonization of audit regulations between Germany and the UK, as driven by the eighth Directive. The conclusion is that, although changes to laws were made, only slightly greater *de jure* harmony was achieved.

V   IASC harmonization
Much literature, particularly from the mid-1980s onwards, has described the International Accounting Standards Committee and its work. Some has tried to investigate its success empirically. The two papers here are concerned with this.

Chapter 19 identifies some extra requirements of IASC standards beyond US rules and then finds, not surprisingly, that the IASC requirements seem to have had no effect on reporting by US companies. Chapter 20 casts doubt on Doupnik and Taylor (1985), who purported to show some effects of the IASC on financial reporting across time and across regions.

These papers and most others were set in a world before the IASC improved its standards in 1993 and dramatically increased its profile. Currrent empirical work would probably show major effects in several Commonwealth countries and on some large continental European companies.

Bibliography
Al Najjar, F. (1986), 'Standardization in accounting practices: a comparative international study', *International Journal of Accounting*, Spring.
Alexander, D. (1993), 'A European true and fair view?', *European Accounting Review*, Vol. 2, No. 1.
Cairns, D. (1997), 'The future shape of harmonization: a reply', *European Accounting Review*, Vol. 6, No. 2.
Choi, F.D.S. and Lee, C. (1997), 'Goodwill and merger premia: a reply', *Journal of International Financial Management and Accounting*, Vol. 8, No. 2.
Choi, F.D.S. and Mueller, G.G. (1992), *International Accounting* (2nd edition), Englewood Cliffs: Prentice-Hall.
De Roover, R. (1978), 'The development of accounting prior to Luca Pacioli according to the account books of medieval merchants', in A.C. Littleton and B.S. Yamey (eds), *Studies in the History of Accounting*, New York: Arno Press.
Doupnik, T. and Salter, S. (1995), 'External environment, culture, and accounting practice: a preliminary test of a general model of international accounting development', *International Journal of Accounting*, Vol. 30, No. 3.
Doupnik, T.S. and Salter, S.B. (1993), 'An empirical test of a judgemental international classification of financial reporting practices', *Journal of International Business Studies*, Vol. 24, No. 1.

xiv International Accounting and Comparative Financial Reporting

Doupnik, T.S. and Taylor, M.E. (1985), 'An empirical investigation of the observance of IASC standards in Western Europe', *Management International Review*, Vol. 25, No. 1.

Dunne, K.M. and Ndubizu, G.A. (1995), 'International acquisition accounting method and corporate multinationalism: evidence from foreign acquisitions', *Journal of International Business Studies*, Vol. 26, No. 2.

Dunne, K.M. and Ndubizu, G.A. (1996), 'The effects of international differences in the tax treatment of goodwill: a reply', *Journal of International Business Studies*, Vol. 27, No. 3.

Dunne, K.M. and Rollins, T.P. (1992), 'Accounting for goodwill: a case analysis of US, UK and Japan', *Journal of International Accounting, Auditing and Taxation*, Vol. 2.

Feige, P. (1997), 'How "uniform" is financial reporting in Germany? The example of foreign currency translation', *European Accounting Review*, Vol. 6, No. 1.

Gray, S.J. (1988), 'Towards a theory of cultural influence on the development of accounting systems internationally', *Abacus*, March.

Hoarau, C. (1995), 'International accounting harmonization: American hegemony or mutual recognition with benchmarks', *European Accounting Review*, Vol. 4, No. 2.

Lall Nigam,B.M. (1986), 'Bahi-Khata: the pre-Pacioli Indian double-entry system of bookkeeping', *Abacus*, September.

Lamb, M., Nobes, C.W. and Roberts, A.D. (1995), 'The influence of taxation on accounting: international variations', *Reading University Discussion Papers*, No. 46.

Lamb, M., Nobes, C.W. and Roberts, A.D. (1998), 'International variations in the connections between tax and financial reporting', *Accounting and Business Research*, Summer.

Lee, C. and Choi, F.D.S. (1992), 'Effects of alternative goodwill treatments on merger premia: further empirical evidence', *Journal of International Financial Management and Accounting*, Vol. 4, No. 3.

Lee, G.A. (1977), 'The coming of age of double entry: the Giovani Farolfi Ledger of 1299-1300', *Accounting Historians Journal*, Fall.

Nobes, C.W. (1981), 'An empirical analysis of international accounting principles: a comment', *Journal of Accounting Research*, Spring.

Nobes, C.W. (1982), 'A typology of international accounting principles and policies: a comment', *AUTA Review*, Spring.

Nobes, C.W. (1992), *International Classification of Financial Reporting*, (2nd edition), London: Routledge.

Nobes, C.W. (1996), 'The effects of international differences in the tax treatment of goodwill: a comment', *Journal of International Business Studies*, Vol. 27, No. 3.

Nobes, C.W. and Norton, J. (1996), 'International variations in the accounting and tax treatments of goodwill, and the implications for research', *Journal of International Accounting, Auditing and Taxation*, Vol. 5, No. 2.

Nobes, C.W. and Parker, R.H. (1998), *Comparative International Accounting*, (5th edition), Hemel Hempstead: Prentice-Hall.

Parker, R.H. (1989), 'Importing and exporting accounting: the British experience', in A.G. Hopwood (ed.), *International Pressures for Accounting Change*, Hemel Hempstead: Prentice-Hall.

Peragallo, E. (1977), 'The ledger of Jachomo Badoer: Constantinople September 2, 1436 to February 26, 1440', *Accounting Review*, October.

Radebaugh, L.H. and Gray, S.J. (1997), *International Accounting and Multinational Enterprises*, New York: Wiley.

Roberts, A.D. (1995), 'The very idea of classification in international accounting', *Accounting, Organizations and Society*, Vol. 20.

Scorgie, M. (1990), 'Indian imitation or invention of cash-book and algebraic double-entry', *Abacus*, March.

Shoenthal, E.R. (1989), 'Classification of accounting systems using competencies as a discriminating variable: a Great Britain-United States study', *Journal of Business Finance and Accounting*, Vol. 16, No. 4.

Van Hulle, K. (1993), 'Truth and untruth about true and fair', *European Accounting Review*, Vol. 2, No. 1.

Walton, P., Haller, A. and Raffournier, B. (1998), *International Accounting*, London: Thomson.

Yamey, B.S. (1940), 'The functional development of double-entry bookkeeping', *The Accountant*, 2 November.

Acknowledgements

The publishers wish to thank the following who have kindly given permission for the use of copyright material.

Academic Press for article: 'Compliance by US Corporations with IASC Standards', *British Accounting Review*, **22**, March 1990, 41-9.

Accounting and Business Research for articles: 'International Variations in the Connections between Tax and Financial Reporting', with Margaret Lamb and Alan Roberts, **28**(3), Summer 1998, 173-88; 'A Review of the Translation Debate', **40**, Autumn 1980, 421-31; 'The Evolution of the Harmonising Provisions of the 1980 and 1981 Companies Acts', **14**(53), Winter 1983, 43-53; 'The True and Fair View Requirement: Impact on and of the Fourth Directive', **24**(93), Winter 1993, 35-48; 'European Rule-Making in Accounting: The Seventh Directive as a Case Study', with Graham Diggle, **24**(96), Autumn 1994, 319-33.

American Accounting Association for article: 'The Gallerani Account Book of 1305-1308', *Accounting Review*, **LVII**(2), April 1982, 303-10.

Blackwell Publishers for articles: 'The Pre-Pacioli Indian Double-Entry System of Bookkeeping: A Comment', *Abacus*, **23**(2), September 1987, 182-4; 'A Judgemental International Classification of Financial Reporting Practices', *Journal of Business Finance & Accounting*, **10**(1), Spring 1983, 1-19; 'Classification of Accounting Systems Using Competencies as a Discriminating Variable: A Great Britain-United States Study: A Comment', *Journal of Business Finance & Accounting*, **19**(1), January 1992, 153-5; 'Towards a General Model of the Reasons for International Differences in Financial Reporting', *Abacus*, **34**(2), September 1998, 162-87; 'Effects of Alternative Goodwill Treatments on Merger Premia: A Comment', with Julie Norton, *Journal of International Financial Management and Accounting*, **8**(2), 1997, 137-41; 'The Use of Foreign Accounting Data in UK Financial Institutions', with Samantha Miles, *Journal of Business Finance & Accounting*, **25**(3/4), April/May 1998, 309-28.

European Accounting Review for articles: 'How "Uniform" is Financial Reporting in Germany: Some Replies', with Gerhard G. Mueller, **6**(1), 1997, 123-9; 'The Future Shape of Harmonization: Some Responses', **7**(2), 1998, 323-30; 'Some Mysteries Relating to the Prudence Principle in the Fourth Directive and in German and British Law', with Lisa Evans, **5**(2), 1996, 361-73; 'International Accounting Harmonization: A Commentary', **4**(2), 1995, 249-54; 'Harmonization of the Structure of Audit Firms: Incorporation in the UK and Germany', with Lisa Evans, **7**(1), 1998, 125-48.

PART I

INTERNATIONAL ORIGINS OF DOUBLE-ENTRY BOOKKEEPING

THE ACCOUNTING REVIEW
Vol. LVII, No. 2
April 1982

The Gallerani Account Book
of 1305–1308

Christopher W. Nobes

ABSTRACT: This paper examines the account book of an Italian firm operating in London in the early 14th century. The existence of the book is well known to accounting historians, but it has not previously been carefully studied by them. The history of the firm and of the book are discussed, followed by an examination of the treatment of cash and non-cash entries and of opening and closing procedures. The presence of accounts for joint-ventures, petty cash, expenses, profit, and capital; the use of a single monetary unit; the consistent method of recording; and the achievement of balance at the end of an accounting period are features that may justify a claim that this account book was part of a double-entry system.

THIS paper discusses the *Libro dell'Entrata e dell'Escita* of the London branch of the Gallerani company between the years 1305 and 1308. It appears that it has not been considered in detail before by an accountant. The question of whether it represents double entry is considered. The Farolfi ledger, which may be the earliest extant example of double entry, is only six years older [Lee, 1977]. This research should be of interest to those who are not accounting historians because it deals with the period when bookkeeping was developing into the Italian fifteen century double-entry system which is still the basis of accounting throughout most of the world. Further, because it is not immediately clear whether this account book uses double entry, it raises interesting questions about the exact nature of the characteristics of double entry.

History of the "Libro"

This surviving book of "entry and exit," which is written in medieval Tuscan Italian, is akin to a journal. It is at present in Belgium where it arrived with Tommaso Fini, who was a member of the Gallerani company and also a Flanders agent of Robert of Béthune. It is not clear exactly when and why the Gallerani left London, but it *is* clear that foreign merchants and bankers were in danger from the King, Edward II. De Roover [1956, p. 126] refers to the records of the flight of the Frescobaldi partners from England to escape arrest in 1311–1312. But difficulties were not confined to England, and Fini had to leave "Belgium" hurriedly in 1309, whereupon the documents were confiscated by the Count of Flanders and thereby preserved. They may now be found in the State Archives

I am very grateful to R. H. Parker for prompting the work leading to this paper; to him, G. A. Lee, B. S. Yamey, and anonymous reviewers for their many helpful comments on earlier drafts; and to R. Bruni for help with translation.

Christopher W. Nobes is a Lecturer in Accountancy, University of Exeter.

Manuscript received June 1980.
Revision received July 1981.
Accepted July 1981.

The Accounting Review, April 1982

at Ghent.[1] There they were noticed in passing by P. de Decker[2] in 1844 and subsequently transcribed by Georges Bigwood, whose work was carried on after his death in 1930 by Armand Grunzweig. The latter completed the study and published a two-volume work [Bigwood, 1961 and 1962].

The Bigwood books contain much history of the Gallerani company and its international operations, and also deal with other early fourteenth century records which relate to their Paris branch. Bigwood's transcription work is obviously of great value. However, his readers should note that it is possible to detect some errors. There are a number of simple transcription errors where the Italian date in the entry is different from that in the margin.[3] In addition, it should be mentioned that the marginal dates are sometimes the dates of the entry and, at other times, the dates of the transaction. In the present writer's opinion, there is also misinterpretation of some entries.[4]

Bigwood [1962, p. 257] suggests that the *Libro* represents "*comptabilité en partie double.*" Martinelli [1974, p. 480] quotes Bigwood in translation and does not disagree with him. However, Bigwood was not an accountant, and there is no specific backing for the claim. He was relying on a discussion with and reading of Melis [1950, p. 474], who refers to the Gallerani papers as "*partita doppia senese in piena maturita.*"[5] However, de Roover [1956, p. 123], who was consistently more skeptical about such claims, comments[6] that ". . . a cursory examination led Professor Melis to the conclusion that the Gallerani unquestionably kept their books in double entry. This is possible, but by no means established without more careful study." It appears that no accountant has given the question "more careful study" in

published form since the publication of the transcription. It is intended to do this here, after a brief digression on the London branch of the Gallerani.

THE GALLERANI IN EARLY 14TH CENTURY LONDON

The Gallerani, we are told [Bigwood, 1962, p. 5], was a Sienese merchant company of medium size. Its London branch was closely linked with that in Paris.[7] It borrowed and lent money; bought and sold horses, lead, gems, and other merchandise; and settled and collected debts relating to other branches. Most of the bookkeeping was carried out by a London partner called Biagio Aldobrandini, as the *Libro* records. It is not clear exactly where they did business, but they paid for premises at what they called "Valbrocco" (Walbrook, in the City of London) [Bigwood, 1952, p. 120].

At the beginning of the period of the *Libro*, England was ruled by Edward I (reigned 1272–1307). The Prince of Wales was the future Edward II (reigned 1307–1327) of considerable notoriety and unusually unpleasant demise, as historians and playwrights have recorded (e.g., Keen [1973]; Marlowe [1598]). Biagio went to the coronation of Edward II, as

[1] When Melis [1950, p. 475] wrote, the *Libro* was in Brussels. However, it has now returned to the Rijksarchief at Ghent, where I worked on it in May 1981.

[2] Cited in Bigwood [1962] as de Decker [1844].

[3] For example, entries 318–323, 377, 378, 394, and 395.

[4] See entry 402 quoted in text (*Dr.* fo.128 in *GL; Cr.* fo.57 in *LDC*). Bigwood thinks fo.57 in the *LDC* is a clothes account. However, why should this be *credited*? There must have been a credit to either "cash" or "Frescobaldi." I believe fo.57 contained the Frescobaldi account.

[5] "Fully developed Sienese double entry."

[6] De Roover's writing was published five years *before* the publication of the Bigwood transcription.

[7] For more details on the activities of the company and its organization, see Melis [1950, pp. 472–476] and Bigwood [1962].

entry 402[8] records:

402. (*escita*) £7.8.0d to expenses, to be given to the Frescobaldi for gold cloth and robes they bought for us for the King's coronation.

It is clear that the Gallerani dealt with the mighty: there are many entries concerning lords, knights, and cardinals. One of the characters who looms large in the history and drama relating to this period is Piers Gaveston, the favorite of Edward II. In the Gallerani records, there are two interesting entries dealing with "Piero di Ghavestona." Entry 400 notes that on August 4, 1306, Biagio spent 28 shillings and 6 pence sterling[9] on merchandise, including some for the said Piers Gaveston. More fascinating is entry 190:

190. (*entrata*) £8.13.4d charged to the Treasurer of the Prince (*LDC* fo.37) for a horse ("*sardo leardo*") received by Piers Gaveston [see 179 and 351 below].

THE NATURE OF THE "LIBRO"

The *Libro dell' Entrata e dell'Escita* (*LDE*) is a form of journal organized in two parts, as was Sienese custom [de Roover, 1956, pp. 122, 123, 127]. Each page has five or six entries which consist of narratives, amounts of money in sterling, and references to other books. Although the *Libro* is clearly related to a cash book and probably evolved from it, it would be misleading to call it by such a name, for many entries have no direct cash involvement. Folios 1–26 (including the *verso* in each case up to folio 25) contain entries concerning sterling receipts or the creation of sterling debits in some other way. At the end of each piece of narrative there is a folio reference to

another book of account, the *Grande Libro*. This book is missing, as are all others apart from the *LDE* itself. However, in all cases, the reference for the credit entry is to this *Grande Libro*. Where cash is received there is no reference to an account to be debited (clearly this implies a debit to cash); where another account is to be debited because cash has not been received, there is a folio reference to a third type of book, the *Libro dei Conti*.

Then there are blank pages from 26 v^0 to 36 v^0. The second part of the *LDE* runs between folios 37 and 54. It contains sterling payments or the creation of other sterling credits. In each case there is a narrative, a reference to an account to be debited in the *Grande Libro*, and, where the transaction is other than a cash payment, a reference to an account in the *Libro dei Conti* to be credited.

The first half of the *Libro* (*entrata*, inflow) contains entries involving either *da* (i.e., received from) or *che dieno* (or *debeno*) *avere* (i.e., who should have or should be credited). The second half (*escita* or *uscita*, outflow) contains entries involving either *a* (i.e., payment to) or *che dieno dare* (i.e., who should give or should be debited).[10] In the case of noncash entries, it is often unclear why the debit, rather than the credit, goes to the *Grande Libro*, that is, why the transaction is an *escita* rather than an *entrata*. Most accounts seem to have existed in both the *Grande Libro* and the *Libro dei Conti*.

[8] Entry numbers are those allocated by Bigwood [1961]. Narratives are the author's abbreviated translations.

[9] All of the entries are in sterling, and in the pounds (£), shillings (s), and pence (d) system adopted from the Romans, and only abandoned in England in 1971. In this case, there are 12 pence to one shilling, and 20 shillings to one pound.

[10] Similar expressions were noted by Lee [1973, p. 141] in a Florentine bank ledger of 1211.

Possibly, an attempt was made to put frequent transactions through the latter in order not to clutter the former. Alternatively, perhaps stricter security and secrecy were attached to the former.

The dates of the entries are a slight problem because, as mentioned above, some are the dates of transactions, and others are the dates of recording. Many dates are missing. The *LDE* does not follow strict chronological order, which is not unusual for "early" accounting. However, within any folio the order is mostly chronological, and the two halves of the *LDE* generally move forwards, starting from May 1305 and ending in October 1308, but with several exceptions.

As has been mentioned, the *Grande Libro* and the *Libro dei Conti* are missing. However, the accounts that they con-tained can be inferred from the many references to them in the *LDE*. Bigwood [1962, pp. 246–254] lists the accounts that must have been on the various folios in these two books. However, he omits a cash account which, judging by closing entries in the *LDE*, would have been on folio 30 of the *Grande Libro* (entry 427, see below). The accounts in the *Libro dei Conti* are transferred to the *Grande Libro* at the end of the period (entry 423, see below).

The first two entries in the *LDE* are balances brought forward at May 1, 1305 from the previous period. Entry 1 is the cash balance of £15.0s.10d; entry 2 is the excess of all other debit balances over all credit balances remaining in the previous period's *Libro dei Conti*, £109.4s.11d (detailed as the entries necessary to close the previous *Libro dei Conti*):

		Dr.	Cr.
1. (*entrata*) May 1, 1305	£15.0.10d. cash left on April 30, 1305.	(Cash)	From previous *LDC* via the *GL*.
2. (*entrata*) May 1, 1305	£109.4.11d. balance of the *Libro de' Conti* i.e. 224.17.6d to be collected and 115.12.7d to be given to others. [Thus, some entries would be the opposite of those shown on the right].	Various accounts in *LDC*.	From previous *LDC* via the *GL*.

Judging by the procedure of October 1308 (discussed below), the entries to close the previous *Libro dei Conti* had their counterparts in the *Grande Libro*. The entries are here reversed to open up the new *Libro dei Conti*. The *Grande Libro* had not been closed down. Its balance could have been used to determine profit and to draw up a balance sheet. Sadly, any evidence of either of these activities has not come to light.

Turning to the end of the period on October 31, 1308 and the end of the *LDE* (*escita* half), we have a closing cash balance of £34.1s.8d as entry 427, and a closing list of debit balances (mostly personal debtors) of £153.7s.1d as entry 423:

		Dr. in GL	Cr. in LDC
423 (*escita*) October 31, 1308	£153.7.1d, which amount remained in *LDC* on the last day of October 1308; written to the debit of accounts in the *GL* fos. 26 to 29.	fos.26–29	Various accounts in *LDC*.
427 (*escita*) October 31, 1308.	£34.1.8d. The closing cash balance held by Nicoluccio.	fo.30, Cash	Nicoluccio fo.59 in *LDC*.

Entry 423 is supported by a detailed schedule of 26 constituent balances which are to be transferred to accounts in the *Grande Libro*, which remains open.

Thus it might be hoped that, if the *Grande Libro* is to balance, then the total of the *entrata* half of the *LDE* (which creates credits in the *Grande Libro*) would be equal to the *escita* half (which creates debits). This is almost exactly the case, as will now be shown.

There is a memorandum at the end of the *LDE* written to Nicoluccio di Cante, a Paris partner, which gives totals: *Avere* (credits) £9481.8s.9d, *Resta* ("the other" or "the rest"?) £9477.16s.1d. Bigwood has noted some errors in the folio totals which help to account for the small difference above. The present writer, taking these and another I have

found[11] into account, has totaled all the *entrata* entries (£9484.12s.8d) and all the *escita* entries (£9482.19s.1d.). A degree of error of this size seems more than acceptable over a three-and-a-half-year period, particularly as many of the entries were in cumbersome Roman numerals.

SOME SPECIAL CASES

There are a few exceptions to the otherwise consistent use of the rules for the use of the *LDE* explained above. There are some non-cash *entrata* entries which create only a credit, but these are matched by *escita* entries of the same date which create only a debit.[12] This practice is especially common for the purchase of horses (a purchase: 179 and 351; the subsequent sale: 190):

		Dr.	Cr.
179. (*entrata*) June 5, 1306	£7.0.6d to be credited to Paris branch for 94.16.3d. *tournois* paid for a horse ("*sardo leardo*") bought by Biagio in Paris. Written to the horse account.		fo.102 in *GL*, Paris branch.
351. (*escita*)	£7.0.6d. debit a horse ("*sardo leardo*"), for 94.16.3d. *tournois* which Paris paid and Biagio bought from a Genoese. Credit to Paris.	fo. 24 in *GL*, Horse account.	
190. (*entrata*)	(see above)	fo.37 in *LDC*	fo.24 in *GL*.

Further, for the period June 1, 1306 to November 1, 1308, a joint venture for the trading of horses was run with the Frescobaldi company. The joint venture is set up by entry 377 and closed by entry 216:

[11] There seems to be a mistake in entry 281 of October 8, 1305:

£0.18.0d to equipment; given to Bindo di Pari of Florence; and £0.2.0d more for other small things.

The 2s. was missed when the folio was totaled, and not noticed by Bigwood.

[12] Entries 20 and 249, for example.

		Dr.	Cr.
377. (*escita*)	£133.6.8d debited to the Horse Joint Venture with the Frescobaldi.	fo.25 in *GL*, Horse J-V.	J-V account, fo.39 in *LDC*.
216. (*entrata*) Nov. 1, 1308	£156.14.10d to our capital in the Horse Joint Venture, including £23.8.2d. of profit.	Capital account in *Libro dei Cavalli*, i.e. fo.2	fo.25 in *GL*, Horse J-V.

The difference between purchase and sale prices is noted as profit.[13] It is fairly clear that the bookkeeper was initially uncertain about how to deal with the joint venture. There is a canceled entry on June 1, 1306 which mistakenly credited the Frescobaldi account in the *Grande Libro* with their contribution to the capital of the joint venture. Also, the opening entry credits an account in the *Libro dei Conti* rather than the capital account in the *Libro dei Cavalli*. This seems to have been altered by the date of the closing entry, 216.

Lastly, the penultimate and pre-penultimate entries of the *escita* half of the *LDE* are to debit the expense account in the *Grande Libro* for two petty cash accounts which have been running throughout the three-and-a-half-year period. These are the *dentro* (inside the office) and *fuore* (outside) petty cash accounts. These entries are necessary because transfers from cash to petty cash are not recorded in the *LDE* as they occur (as *Dr* Petty Cash; *Cr* Cash). Thus, at the end of the period, the closing entries are not (*Dr* Expenses; *Cr* Petty Cash) but (*Dr* Expenses; *Cr* Cash).

THE ESSENTIALS OF DOUBLE ENTRY

Before asking whether the London branch of the Gallerani was using double-entry bookkeeping in 1305, it is necessary to recognize some criteria for double entry against which to judge the Gallerani system as evidenced by the *LDE*. Here we are assisted by useful precedents set by Lee, de Roover, and Martinelli. Lee [1973, p. 154] notes that double entry requires that "there is (supposed to be) a debit for every credit, with full cross-references." In a later work, Lee [1977, pp. 85 and 90] suggests more detailed criteria, including the presence of concepts of accounting entity and proprietor's equity, the use of accounting periods and a single monetary unit, the calculation of profit and loss, and the periodic collection of balances to prove equality of debits and credits.

How well does the Gallerani accounting system measure up to these criteria? It is very clear that the Gallerani company was accounted for as an entity and that there was even a strict separation of the branches within the company.[14] For instance, there are many entries of debit or credit to the account of the Paris branch.[15] Lee's criterion of monetary homogeneity is also strictly respected. Although the narratives for many entries *refer* to other currencies, the actual entries are always recorded in sterling. For example, entry 116:

		Dr.	Cr.
116. (*entrata*)	£0.19.0d. to the credit of the Paris branch for 12.7.6d. *livres tournois* received by Nicoluccio and charged to his account in *LDC*.	Nicoluccio's account, fo.6 in *LDC*.	fo.100 *in GL*, Paris Branch.

It is apparent from the entries in the *LDE* that the London partners, including Aldobrandini, had capital accounts. Sadly, it is not possible to tell what they contained or how the profits were split up. Nevertheless, there were accounts for profits, interest, and other expenses. For example, entries 87 and 166;

---

[13] Profits of about 23 per cent for the single horse, and 18 percent for the joint venture.

[14] Melis [1950, p. 475] says: "Hence, such branches had an autonomous bookkeeping system, which must have included some accounts linking up with the central office bookkeeping."

[15] Entries 116 and 179, for example.

	Dr.	Cr. in *GL*
87. *(entrata)* £3.18.6d to the "bay horse" account. The	Expenses	fo.10,
Nov. 9, 1305 amount has been written to the lead ex-	of lead	horse
penses in the *LDC* (fo.8) because the horse	account,	account.
has become lame.[16] It has been given to	fo.8 in	
God [charity?]	*LDC*.	
166. *(entrata)* £0.12.0d to profit, gained on the purchase	(Cash)	fo.120,
August 29, and sale of gold doubloons.		profit.
1306		

There also appears to be a regard for accounting periods: the *LDE* runs for exactly three-and-a-half years. It could be argued that this period was merely the term set for the partnership or the stint of the bookkeeper. However, even if periodicity cannot be read into this one account book, the importance of perio-dicity as a prerequisite for double entry might well be questioned. Surely it is more telling that, at a point in time, there are closing entries, and the balances are collected together to prove equality of debits and credits.

De Roover [1956, p. 125] would re-quire each transaction to be recorded twice, and the existence of accounts for expenses and operating results. It has been shown that the *LDE* creates two entries for each transaction: one for the *Grande Libro* and usually one for the *Libro dei Conti*. For cash amounts, it is presumably the physical existence of the cash which acts as the record of the other entry. An actual counterpart entry is created at the end of periods when the cash is counted to establish a closing entry to the *Grande Libro*. At the same time, the *Libro dei Conti* is closed down and a total balance in the *Grande Libro* is achieved at the end of the period. It is possible that there was a separate cash book, but this seems unlikely as the *LDE* itself looks so much like a cash book which has just been adapted to include non-cash entries. As for de Roover's other point, it has been shown that there were accounts for expenses and profit.

Martinelli [1977, p. 11] would look for "the presence of two complete sets of antithetical accounts,[17] constant refer-ence for each entry to its cross-entry, and constant application of the same mone-tary unit." These requirements seem to be satisfied, except for the criterion about cross-references (also mentioned by Lee, above). It is not possible to be sure on this point because of the absence of the *Grande Libro* and the *Libro dei Conti*. However, there are full references in the *LDE*.

CONCLUSION

The *Libro dell'Entrata e dell'Escita* (*LDE*) of the London branch of the Gallerani from 1305 to 1308 was written in Italian, using typically Tuscan expres-sions and with a characteristically Sienese format. Beacuse of the clear evidence for the creation of double entries, and be-cause the two halves of the *LDE* are in almost exact balance, it seems that this bookkeeping contained, at the least, substantial elements of double entry. Incidentally, if this view is accepted, then these records represent the earliest extant accounting records using a form of double entry in the British Isles. How-ever, as the Gallerani in London was a (short-lived) branch of a foreign firm, there is no suggestion that indigenous English records were kept in this ad-vanced way either during or following its presence.

[16] Presumably, the lead expense account is debited because the horse became lame as a result of carrying too much of this heavy metal.

[17] It is supposed that Martinelli means "two complete sets of antithetical entries."

REFERENCES

Bigwood, G. (ed. A. Grunzweig) (1961), *Les Livres des Comptes des Gallerani, Book I* (the transcription) (Commission Royale d'Histoire, Brussels, 1961).

——, (ed. A. Grunzweig) (1962), *Les Livres des Comptes des Gallerani, Book II* (the commentary) (Commission Royale d'Histoire, Brussels, 1962).

de Decker, P. (1844), *Etudes historiques et critiques sur les Monts de Piété* (The Author, Brussels, 1844).

de Roover, R. (1956), "The Development of Accounting Prior to Luca Pacioli According to The Account-books of Medieval Merchants," in A. C. Littleton and B. S. Yamey, eds., *Studies in the History of Accounting* (Irwin, 1956; reprinted in 1978 by Arno Press), pp. 114–174.

Keen, M. H. (1973), *England in the Later Middle Ages* (Methuen, 1973).

Lee, G. A. (1973), "The Development of Italian Bookkeeping, 1211–1300," *Abacus* (December 1973), pp. 137–155.

—— (1977), "The Coming of Age of Double Entry: The Giovanni Farolfi Ledger of 1299–1300," *The Accounting Historians Journal* (Fall 1977), pp. 79–95.

Marlowe, C. (1598), *The Troublesome Raigne and Lamentable Death of Edward the Second* (London, 1598).

Martinelli, A. (1974), "The Origination and Evolution of Double Entry Bookkeeping to 1440" (unpublished doctoral thesis. University Microfilms, Ann Arbor, Mich., 1974).

—— (1977), "Notes on the Origin of Double Entry Bookkeeping," *Abacus* (June 1977), pp. 3–27.

Melis, F. (1950), *Storia della Ragioneria* (Zuffi, Bologna, 1950).

ABACUS, Vol. 23, No. 2, 1987

CHRISTOPHER W. NOBES

The Pre-Pacioli Indian Double-entry System of Bookkeeping: A Comment

The claims made by Lall Nigam that the Bahi-khata was a double-entry system of accounting that predated Pacioli are challenged. Evidence purporting to support Nigam's claims is dismissed as hearsay.

Key words: Accounting records; Bookkeeping; Historical cost accounting; History.

The Main Claim

The paper by Lall Nigam (1986) makes a very important claim, as its title suggests. If the paper's remarkable conclusions were true, it would revolutionize our understanding of the origins of Western accounting, as the following extracts show:

> The Bahi-khata is a double-entry system of bookkeeping that predates the 'Italian' method by many centuries. Its existence in India prior to the Greek and Roman empires suggests that Indian traders took it with them to Italy. (p. 148)
>
> . . . the development in India of a system of bookkeeping which predates and was far ahead in sophistication of its European counterpart. (p. 149)
>
> . . . the Bahi system . . . [may be expected] to have some inherent strengths which have helped it survive for thousands of years. (p. 149)
>
> . . . financial statements . . . are . . . the principal means of communicating accounting information to external parties . . . significance was well understood thousands of years before Christ. (p. 158)
>
> The Bahi-khata based on a double-entry system . . . has been used for thousands of years. (p. 160)

These bold conclusions rest on a wholly inadequate case that should not be allowed to pass without challenge.

The fundamental problem with the paper is that it contains no evidence other than hearsay. The author offers us no evidence of extant early double-entry records, as is possible for Europe from the thirteenth century (e.g., Lee, 1973a, 1973b; Peragallo, 1977, 1980; Nobes, 1982). Nor does he offer us examples of early writings concerning double entry (by analogy to Pacioli, 1494, etc.). The paper gives us the following evidence only:

> Circumstantial evidence indicates that it was introduced and used in prehistoric days. (p. 149)
>
> Alexander Hamilton, a noted orientalist, writes, 'we would remark that the Bahis of India have been for time immemorial in possession of the methods of bookkeeping by double-entry'. (p. 149)
>
> The introduction and usage of a double-entry system . . . is also evidenced by Kautilya's *Arthsastra* . . ., dating as early as the 4th century BC . . . There are detailed references to the supervising and checking of accounts, and to the distinction between capital and revenue, expenses and profits. (p. 150)

CHRISTOPHER W. NOBES is the Deloitte's Professor of Accounting, University of Reading, U.K.
The author is grateful for comments on an earlier draft from R. Macve, R. H. Parker and B. S. Yamey.

INDIAN DOUBLE-ENTRY

However, this is the sort of inexpert hearsay that has been effectively dismissed in relation to claims of double entry for Greek or Roman accounting (de Ste Croix, 1956; Macve, 1985) or for some early Italian accounting (de Roover, 1956). It is unsatisfactory here, also. First, we are not told what the circumstantial evidence in the above quotation is. Second, when Lall Nigam mentions Hamilton, he appears to be drawing on Littleton and Yamey (1956), who note that the attribution to Hamilton is not certain. Anyway, it seems unlikely that 'a noted orientalist', writing in 1798, would understand whether a set of accounting records was in double entry or that he would have seen direct evidence of what the Bahis were doing in 'time immemorial'.

Third, there is the *Arthsastra* (which other writers render as *Arthaśāstra*). Even if we can rely on the accuracy of its account, there is no necessity for use of double entry in order to distinguish between capital and revenue or to produce a form of accounts for a year (Yamey, 1940; Macve, 1985). Choudhury (1982) discusses the *Arthaśāstra's* accounting content at some length. He notes that its system was probably cash-based not accruals-based (p. 107), and he makes no suggestion that there was double entry.

The paper also offers a deduction in favour of its conclusion:

> Historians generally hold a view that Indian traders frequented European port-towns . . . but the reverse was not true . . . As such, it is fair to presume that the skill of bookkeeping more likely travelled from India to Italy, than the reverse. (p. 149)

There seem to be several problems here:

1. Surely some European traders visited the East.
2. The reasoning tells us nothing about the 'thousands of years before Christ' part of the thesis.
3. In the absence of written records in the West, the above logic would presumably argue that the idea of smoking tobacco was exported from Spain to the Americas.
4. There is evidence that double entry evolved step-by-step from more primitive forms of bookkeeping (Yamey, 1947; de Roover, 1956; Lee, 1973b). This strongly argues against the importation of a fully-formed double-entry system, particularly as the Indian system is noticeably different from European pre-double entry, early double entry and modern double entry.

The paper itself notes the lack of evidence:

> . . . unfortunately, the practice has not been accompanied by a description in the nature of *Suma* [*sic*] *de Arithmetica* (p. 150)

> It is difficult to pin down the precise period of the advent of Bahi-khata. (p. 149)

Conclusion

There is nothing that approaches convincing proof to support the resounding assertions of Lall Nigam.

REFERENCES

Choudhury, N., 'Aspects of Accounting and Internal Control—India 4th Century BC', *Accounting and Business Research*, Spring 1982.

de Roover, R., 'The Development of Accounting prior to Luca Pacioli according to the Account-Books of Medieval Merchants', in A. C. Littleton and B. S. Yamey (eds), *Studies in the History of Accounting*, Sweet and Maxwell, 1956.

de Ste Croix, G. E. M., 'Greek and Roman Accounting', in A. C. Littleton and B. S. Yamey (eds), *Studies in the History of Accounting*, Sweet and Maxwell, 1956.

Lall Nigam, B. M., 'Bahi-Khata: The Pre-Pacioli Indian Double-entry System of Bookkeeping', *Abacus*, September 1986.

Lee, G. A., 'The Florentine Bank Ledger Fragments of 1211: Some New Insights', *Journal of Accounting Research*, 1973a.

———, 'The Development of Italian Bookkeeping 1211-1300', *Abacus*, December 1973b.

Littleton, A. C. and B. S. Yamey (eds), *Studies in the History of Accounting*, Sweet and Maxwell, 1956.

Macve, R., 'Some Glosses on "Greek and Roman Accounting"', *History of Political Thought*, Spring 1985.

Nobes, C. W., 'The Gallerani Account Book of 1305-1308', *Accounting Review*, April 1982.

Pacioli, L., *Summa de Arithmetica, Geometria, Proportioni e Proportionalita*, Paganinus de Paganinis, 1494.

Peragallo, E., 'The Ledger of Jachomo Badoer: Constantinople September 2, 1436 to February 26, 1440', *The Accounting Review*, 1977.

———, 'Jachomo Badoer, Renaissance Man of Commerce and his Ledger', *Accounting and Business Research*, 1980.

Yamey, B. S., 'The Functional Development of Double-entry Bookkeeping', *The Accountant*, November 1940.

———, 'Notes on the Origin of Double-entry Bookkeeping', *The Accounting Review*, 1947.

PART II

CAUSES OF INTERNATIONAL DIFFERENCES AND CLASSIFICATION OF SYSTEMS

[3]

A JUDGEMENTAL INTERNATIONAL CLASSIFICATION OF FINANCIAL REPORTING PRACTICES

C.W. Nobes*

Much recent work and published material has concerned the classification of countries into groups by their financial reporting practices. The purpose of classification has been discussed in that material (cited below) and elsewhere (AAA, 1977). Briefly, it is seen as a fundamental step in an organised and scientific study of a population; as a method to "sharpen description and analysis" (AAA, 1977, p.97), to reveal underlying structures, and to predict the behaviour of a member of the population; and as a tool to assist in the analysis of the need for, means towards and progress of harmonisation.

The aim here is to examine the recent papers and their weaknesses, and to propose an alternative approach. After a brief survey of these papers, they are examined in greater detail by looking at the data and methodology they used. The alternative approach of this paper is proposed in the third section, which includes a detailed statement of the problem tackled. It waits until then, because the other papers surveyed have not defined the problem in such detail or with exactly the same scope.

A Brief Survey of Recent Work

International classification in accounting had been discussed many times before the late 1970s, for example by Hatfield in 1911 (Hatfield, 1966) and Mueller (1967). However, from the late 1970s, a series of papers (e.g. da Costa et al., 1978; Frank, 1979; Nair and Frank, 1980; and Goodrich, 1982) have reported on a "scientific" approach to classification, which has moved away from the earlier "subjective" studies.

These recent studies have used data on differences in practices between countries provided in the surveys of Price Waterhouse (1973, 1975 and 1979). These data have been subjected to factor analysis in order to identify important discriminating variables, and then a clustering technique has been used. This results in a number of groupings of countries: from two to six groups depending on the researchers and the survey they were using (Table 1 shows such a grouping). The intention is to produce groups of countries whose accounting characteristics are more similar to those of other members of the same group than to those of members of another group. In the case of Nair and Frank (1980), the accounting practices were split into those relating to accounting measurements and those relating to disclosure, and then two separate analyses were performed. In addition, Frank (1979) and Nair and Frank (1980) investigated whether their groupings correspond with differences in underlying environmental variables.

*The author is Professor of Accountancy and Finance at the University of Strathclyde. He wishes to express his gratitude for the comments of R.H. Parker, I.C. Stewart and an anonymous referee on earlier drafts of this paper. (Paper received March 1982, revised August 1982)

Journal of Business Finance & Accounting 10,1(1983)

The data and the general methodology for this are discussed and criticised in the next section; the detailed statistical techniques, which are neither criticised nor used in this paper, are explained in the original papers.

TABLE 1
FOUR-GROUP "MEASUREMENT" CLASSIFICATION, (NAIR AND FRANK)

Group I	Group II	Group III	Group IV
Australia	Argentina	Belgium	Canada
Bahamas	Bolivia	France	Japan
Fiji	Brazil	Germany	Mexico
Jamaica	Chile	Italy	Panama
Kenya	Colombia	Spain	Philippines
Netherlands	Ethiopia	Sweden	United States
New Zealand	India	Switzerland	
Pakistan	Paraguay	Venezuela	
Republic of Ireland	Peru		
Rhodesia	Uruguay		
Singapore			
South Africa			
Trinidad and Tobago			
United Kingdom			

Source: Nair and Frank, 1980, p.429.

Criticism of Data and Methodology
The Data

Doubts have been expressed elsewhere on the use of the Price Waterhouse data for the purpose of classification (Nobes, 1981). Four types of problem with the 1973 data were noted: (i) straightforward mistakes, (ii) misleading answers, (iii) swamping of important questions by trivial ones, and (iv) exaggeration of the differences between the USA and the UK because of the familiarity of these countries (and thus their differences) to the compilers of the survey questions. The examples from the 1973 survey will not be repeated here, but a few errors in the 1979 survey will be mentioned.

Taking consolidation practices as an example, the survey reports that, for practice 209 ("consolidated statements .... are prepared for the shareholders") the answer is "required" in France. The reason given for this is that the *Commission des Opérations de Bourse* (COB) "requires" consolidation. However, as the Annual Report of COB shows, only 305 listed companies published consolidated balance sheets and profit and loss accounts in 1979 (289 in 1978).

This is less than half of the listed companies, and a very much smaller proportion of "enterprises which issue their statements to the general public" about which the survey is said to be (Price Waterhouse, 1979, p.5). Further, one wonders whether consolidation practices in Fiji, Malaysia or Trinidad are really correctly understood by suggestions in various survey practices that Standard No.3 of the IASC is being followed.

These examples could be replicated many times over. They suggest that, at some points, the surveys report not on actual practices but on what practices might be if non-mandatory rules were obeyed or on what Price Waterhouse partners might like practices to be. This and the other types of error may suggest that the data are unsatisfactory for the purpose of classification. At the very least, it calls for substantial caution when interpreting the results.

The Methodology

All the researchers cited above use cluster analysis on the Price Waterhouse data, and appear to consider that this may be superior to previous subjective classifications. Nair and Frank state that their research is:

"aimed at empirically assessing the validity of international classifications proposed repeatedly in the accounting literature". (p.449)

This version of "empiricism" may be challenged. It does not directly test a particular hypothetical classification. It classifies a mass of data which was not collected with this purpose in mind. The use of this approach leads one set of researchers (da Costa et al., 1978, p.79) to conclude that the country least like the UK group is the USA. That is, accounting in Uruguay or Ethiopia is more like accounting in the UK than accounting in the USA is. While this may be a statistically sound result from the Price Waterhouse data, it is clearly a very inaccurate representation of the real world (Mueller, 1967; and Carsberg and Eastergard, 1981). By itself such a result is of interest, but the researchers, who were generating an hypothesis from doubtful data rather than testing one,[1] fell into the trap of taking their results seriously. This led them to the conclusion that a group of countries containing France, West Germany, Belgium and Italy among many others:

"follows the lead of the United States in dissociating themselves from practice common to the British Model."

However, it seems highly unlikely that the makers of the detailed and rigid company and tax laws that govern accounting in such countries bear in mind either that they should follow the USA or that they should dissociate themselves from the UK when legislating. The differences between the USA and continental European countries are great, and also suggest that there is no accidental or subconscious "following" of the former by the latter (Mueller, 1967; Macharzina, 1981; and Parker, 1981).

A further illustration of the unlikely results that may be obtained by these so-called "empirical" methods is the classification by Goodrich (1982) which suggests that accounting in the USA is more similar to that in Peru or Bolivia than it is to accounting in the UK (from which US accounting developed); and that Australia is in the same group as Japan and Colombia but in a different group from New Zealand and the UK, which have very similar accounting to Australia (Standish, 1981).

The problem that these two examples illustrate stems from the use of data which contains errors and which was not designed for the purpose in hand. In order to seek a way out of these difficulties, it may be useful to draw an analogy with classification in other disciplines. There have been many attempts in law, economics and politics (e.g. Kagan, 1955; David and Brierley, 1978; Neuberger and Duffy, 1976; Gregory and Stuart, 1980; Finer, 1970; and Shils, 1966). However, these have been simple compared to the recent accounting attempts. Turning to the Linnaean biological system for an analogy may be more useful. To the extent that subjectivity and empiricism can be counterposed, the life scientists use a large measure of the former. Exactly which criteria to use for classification of living things, and which weights to give them are matters of judgement.

Judgement is needed to avoid such classifications as Plato's of man as a featherless biped.[2] In fact, man is now seen to be much more closely related to most quadrupeds, and to dolphins which appear to have no feet at all. Aristotle saw this latter distinction. He referred to homologues, where organs similar in structure play different roles (e.g. human feet and dolphins' flippers), and to analogues where similar functions are performed by quite different organs (e.g. birds' wings and bees' wings). It is the homologues which indicate nearness.

David and Brierley (1978, p.19) make a similar point when discussing the classification of legal systems:

> "When endeavouring to determine the families into which different laws can be grouped, it is preferable to take into consideration these constant elements rather than the less stable rules found in the law at any given moment .... The classification of laws into families should not be made on the basis of the similarity or dissimilarity of any particular legal rules, important as they may be; this is .... inappropriate when highlighting what is truly significant in the characteristics of a given system of law."

Looking in more detail at the Linnaean biological classification, one notes that, when classifying plants or animals, biologists largely ignore the most obvious characteristics. That is, they do not carry out factor analysis on animals by weight, colour, number of legs, nature of body covering, length of life, etc. This would merely lead to a classification of those data. It would put men with ostriches, dolphins with sharks, bats with owls, and so on. In fact, by concentrating on a subjective model which involves underlying (but less obvious) characteristics, biologists classify men, dolphins and bats more closely with each other than with any of the other three types of animal. It is then found that behaviour, intelligence, reproduction and ancestry begin to fit with the classi-fication. The biological scientists, then, use a classification which is evolutionary and concentrates on underlying fundamental variables.

The analogy with classification in accounting seems clear. The danger with "empirical" classifications is that one merely classifies the Price Waterhouse data, which concentrate on differences which may be ephemeral and super-ficial (and which may not be correctly recorded). The need is apparent for a model based on the evolution of accounting practices and upon variables which have caused differences in them. This needs to be checked against carefully measured "structural" practices.

A Hypothetical Classification

Thus, it would be possible to criticise previous classifications for (i) lack of precision in the definition of what is to be classified, (ii) lack of a model to compare the statistical results with, (iii) lack of hierarchy which would add more subtlety to the portrayal of the size of differences between countries, and (iv) lack of judgement in the choice of "important" discriminating features. Can these problems be remedied?

(i) Definition

The purpose of the present research is to classify countries by the financial reporting practices of *public companies*. The countries chosen as a population are those of the *developed Western world;* the reporting practices will be those concerned with *measurement and valuation*. The date of the classification is *1980*, before the enactments in EEC countries of the Fourth Directive on Company Law.

It is public companies whose financial statements are generally available, and whose practices can be most easily discovered. It is the international differ-ences in reporting between such companies which are of interest to shareholders, creditors, auditing firms, taxation authorities, managements and harmonizing agencies (like the International Accounting Standards Committee or the EEC Commission) (Mason, 1978, ch.5). It is really only in developed Western countries that public companies exist in large numbers. It has been mentioned above that the Price Waterhouse data seem to suffer from the difficulties of holding this factor constant across their very broad coverage.

Measurement and vaulation practices have been chosen because these deter-mine the size of the figures for profit, capital, total assets, liquidity and so on. Nair and Frank (1980, pp.426 and 428) point out that it is useful to separate measurement from disclosure practices.[3] The present research deals with the former only; the latter would require an additional paper.

(ii) and (iii) A Model with a Hierarchy

The hypothetical classification shown as Table 2 was drawn up in 1979 and first published in 1980;[4] it has been slightly amended since then. It is based on the evolution of accounting, and the suggestions of many academics inter-ested in comparative accounting.[4] Some explanatory variables for differences in measurement practices were also borne in mind when drawing up this proposed classification; for example, the importance of the influence of law or of economics.[5] Some descriptions are included at the branching points in Table 2. The proposed classification which results from consideration of these background factors is designed as a "prediction" of how countries will be grouped together on consideration of their measurement practices. The testing of this is the main subject of the rest of this paper.

The number of countries is kept to 14,[6] but all these are developed Western nations; they are all included in the Price Waterhouse Surveys and thus in the results of the above researchers; and they include all the countries identified as "vital" by Mason (1978, ch.6) for the purposes of international harmonization.

Previous classifications have contained separate groups (e.g. Table 1) but no hierarchy which would indicate the comparative distances between the groups. It may well be reasonable to classify the UK and the USA in different groups, but it might be useful to demonstrate that these two groups are closely linked compared to, say, continental European countries.

The classification in Table 2 contains a hierarchy which borrows its labels from biology.

(iv) Discriminating Features

An attempt has been made to isolate those features of a county's accounting which may constitute long-run fundamental differences between countries. The exercise was made possible by having reduced the scope to 14 countries with public companies. A programme of visits, interviews and reading relating to these countries was carried out. The result was a selection of nine factors which, unlike the factors of most of the researchers above, are overt and thus available for inspection, criticism and amendment (see Table 3).

These factors are designed to operate for developed Western countries, which share certain economic features. Thus, if one wished to include developing countries or Eastern bloc countries, it would be necessary to include other discriminating factors, like degree of development of economy or nature of economic systems. Incidentally, such a process might not be sensible because there are few or no public companies in these other countries, so one would have to classify something other than published financial reporting.

Also, the nine factors do not include consideration of, for example, whether on "a sale by a parent company to its partly owned subsidiary, profit is eliminated only to the extent of the parent's interest" or whether "deferred taxes are provided on timing differences resulting from intercompany transactions." These are Practices 222 and 224 of the Price Waterhouse Survey (1979). They are perfectly legitimate for the purpose of the Survey but they (and 40 or so other consolidation practices) are trivial in comparison to Practice 210 on whether or not a country's companies present consolidated financial statements. However, in the "empirical" research using the Survey, all 40 practices were given equal weight.[7]

TABLE 2

A HYPOTHETICAL CLASSIFICATION OF FINANCIAL REPORTING MEASUREMENT PRACTICES IN DEVELOPED WESTERN COUNTRIES IN 1980

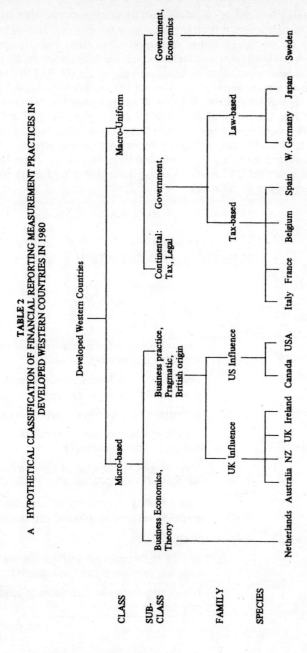

It is not straightforward to separate out measurement practices from explanatory variables. However, it is clear that at least the first two factors in Table 3 are examples of the latter. Other factors are less clear. For example, the "taxation" factor could be taken as a factor explaining differences, or, by scoring this factor on the basis of whether particular valuations are affected by tax rules, it could be seen as a measurement practice. All the factors except the first two have been taken in this latter sense, and scored using examples of practices.

This difficulty is shared by all the studies mentioned in the first section of this paper, where a number of characteristics like "conservatism" or "tax effects" were included. In this case, two separate exercises are carried out. First, factors 1, 2 and 3 are analysed as explanatory variables; then, factors 3 to 9 are analysed as measurement practices. Before this can be done, the nine factors must be measured for each of the 14 countries.

TABLE 3
FACTORS FOR DIFFERENTIATION

Factor No. and Abbreviation	*Factor Name*
1 (USER)	Type of users of the published accounts of the listed companies
2 (LAW)	Degree to which law or standards prescribe in deatil, and exclude judgement
3 (TAX)	Importance of tax rules in measurement
4 (PRU)	Conservatism/prudence (e.g. valuation of buildings, stocks, debtors)
5 (HC)	Strictness of application of historic cost (in the historic cost accounts)
6 (RC)	Susceptibility to replacement cost adjustments in main or supplementary accounts.
7 (CONS)	Consolidation
8 (PROV)	Ability to be generous with provisions (as opposed to reserves) and to smooth income
9 (UNI)	Uniformity between companies in application of rules.

The Testing

Scoring

The basis of scoring countries on factors is shown in the "morphology" of Table 4. The scores are set out in Table 5. The scoring was done on the basis of an extensive programme of reading, followed by visits to a great majority of the countries included. References for the accounting practices of countries are included in an Appendix. The author will be pleased to supply a detailed justification of the scoring on request.

TABLE 4

MORPHOLOGY BASED ON TABLE 3

Factor	0	1	2	3
1 (USER)	banks, revenue		institutions	individuals
2 (LAW)	detailed pre-scription			lack of pre-scriptions, much room for judgement
3 (TAX)*	nearly all figs. determined			no figures det-ermined
4 (PRU)**	heavy conser-vatism			dominance of accruals
5 (HC)	no exceptions			many exceptions
6 (RC)	no suscept-ibility	small experi-mentation	supplementary	used, considered for all
7 (CONS)	rare consoli-dation	some consoli-dation	domestic subsids	all subsids + assocs
8 (PROV)	considerable flexibility			no room for smoothing
9 (UNI)	compulsory accounting plan			no standardised format, rules or definitions

* Scoring on this factor (see Table 5) is carried out using particular valuation practices affected by taxation, i.e. depreciation, bad debt provisions, the valuation of buildings and the establishment of provisions for risks, contingencies, etc.

** Scoring on this factor is based on particular practices, i.e. the prevalance of provisions in the valuation of stocks and debtors, and the strength of rules against capitalisation of certain expenses.

A Judgemental International Classification   9

TABLE 5
SCORING BASED ON TABLE 4

	Australia	Belgium	Canada	France	Germany	Italy	Japan	Netherlands	New Zealand	R. of Ireland	Spain	Sweden	UK	USA
1 (USER)	3	1	3	1	0	1	0	2	3	2	1	0	2	3
2 (LAW)	3	1	2	1	0	1	1	3	3	2	1	1	2	1
3 (TAX)	3	0	3	0	0	1	0	3	3	3	1	0	3	2
4 (PRU)	2	0	2	0	0	0	0	3	2	2	0	0	2	2
5 (HC)	2	1	1	1	0	0	0	3	2	3	1	0	3	1
6 (RC)	2	1	2	1	0	0	0	3	2	2	0	1	2	2
7 (CONS)	3	1	3	1	2	0	1	3	3	3	0	2	3	3
8 (PROV)	2	1	2	1	1	1	0	2	2	2	1	0	2	3
9 (UNI)	3	0	3	0	1	2	1	3	3	3	0	1	3	3

The scale 0 to 3 was chosen on the grounds that it compromised between a smaller scale, which would have restricted differentiation, and a larger scale, which would have exaggerated the fineness with which judgement is possible. It is clear that one problem is the implied assumption of linearity. However, it is also a problem with all the previous research, and the results in the following figures may be seen to be so clear that some other reasonable assumption would not alter the classification seriously.

It may also be noted that the "direction" of the factors could be altered, that is that Factor 4 might have "heavy conservatism" with a score of "3" (see Table 4). This is dealt with by concentrating on differences or roots of squared differences, as seen below.

A further matter to consider is what weights the factors should have. The implication in all the previous research reviewed and reported here is that all practices have equal weight. This procedure is continued here, but the analysis is repeated with three of the factors being given double weight to see if the results are sensitive to such adjustments.

Finally, one might be criticised for adding different factors together as though they were measured in the same units. This is connected with the weighting problem. All previous researchers had to do this addition, which perhaps may not be so serious when dealing with the *differences* in scores, and in the light of the clear results which follow.

Analysis of Results

The final stage is to analyse these figures in order to produce a classification. Several methods are attempted.

(i) Totailing

A simple analysis is merely to total the scores. This ignores the non-linearity of the scoring system, and assumes that none of the factors is "back to front". However, the extremely clean split of the countries into two groups (as in Table 6) may reduce concern about these problems. The high-scoring countries correspond with the "micro" group of Table 2, and the low-scoring countries with the "macro" group. This split is clear both for the explanatory variables and for the measurement practices. Having established that the two point in the same direction, the rest of the analysis will proceed with measurement practices only, as it is these which are to be classified.

TABLE 6
TOTALS FROM TABLE 5

	Practices	*Explanatory*
Netherlands	20	8
United Kingdom	18	7
Ireland	18	7
Australia	17	9
New Zealand	17	9
Canada	16	8
United States	16	6
France	4	2
Italy	4	3
Belgium	4	2
Sweden	4	1
W. Germany	4	0
Spain	3	3
Japan	2	1

(ii) Totalling Differences

A somewhat more sophisticated approach is to calculate the sum of the differences on the factors, taking all possible pairs of countries. For example, using the scored morphology of Table 5, one might find the difference in the scores of Australia and Belgium on Factor 3 and add this to the difference on Factor 4, and so on. This would give a matrix of differences as shown in Table 7. The difference in scores for the pair Australia-Belgium is seen to be "13".

TABLE 7
MATRIX OF TOTAL DIFFERENCES BETWEEN COUNTRIES

	Aus	Bel	Can	Fra	Ger	Ita	Jap	NL	NZ	Ire	Spa	Swe	UK	USA
Aus	0													
Bel	13	0												
Can	1	12	0											
Fra	13	0	12	0										
Ger	13	4	12	4	0									
Ita	13	6	12	6	4	0								
Jap	15	4	14	4	2	4	0							
NL	3	16	4	16	16	16	18	0						
NZ	0	13	1	13	13	13	15	3	0					
Ire	1	14	2	14	14	14	16	2	1	0				
Spa	14	3	13	3	5	3	5	17	14	15	0			
Swe	13	4	12	4	2	6	2	16	13	14	7	0		
UK	1	14	2	14	14	14	16	2	1	0	15	14	0	
USA	3	12	2	12	12	12	14	6	3	4	13	12	4	0

This technique may be preferable to the simple totals of Table 6. First, it avoids the need to ensure that all the factors have been placed in the correct "direction". When concentrating on differences, it would not matter if, say, factor 4 had scored "heavy conservatism" as "3" and "dominance of accruals" as "0". Secondly, concentrating on differences reveals that countries with similar total scores in Table 6 may nevertheless be significantly different from each other. For example, Italy and France have identical total scores in Table 6, but these totals have somewhat different causes. Thus Italy and France are differentiated in Table 7.

12 Nobes

By inspection of the information in Table 7, particularly by focusing on one country at a time by listing out the differences between it and each other country, groupings as in Table 8 may be prepared. Again, the simple classification which results seems to fit with Table 2.

TABLE 8
GROUPS OF COUNTRIES FROM TABLE 7

"Micro"	Netherlands UK, Ireland, Australia, New Zealand, Canada USA, Canada

- -

"Macro"	France, Belgium, Spain Italy Germany, Japan, Sweden

(iii) Squaring the Differences

One may also calculate similar information involving the totals of the squares of differences and the roots of the totals of the squares of differences. This data presents a similar picture to Table 7, and thus the remarks in the previous section apply to it.

(iv) Clustering

The next approach is to use this output (in this case, the roots of the squared differences) in a systematic way to produce clusters. A computer program designed to do this was used.[8] This starts with the two countries which are nearest to each other (in this case, Belgium and France, which have identical scores). Next. it identifies another set of two or more similar countries. That is, in this case, Australia and New Zealand, which are closer together than Belgium plus France plus x. Thus, there are now twelve clusters: Australia plus New Zealand; Belgium plus France; and ten clusters of one country each. This process continues, culminating in a "two cluster solution" which, in this case, has the same groups as Tables 6, 8 and 2.

Interesting information may be obtained by noting which countries are classified last. Italy is the last to fall into the "macro" group. This seems very reasonable. Italy has seen dramatic changes in accounting in the last few years;[9] most of these have been excluded from the 1980 scoring process, but the fact that they have occurred suggests that the country must have been different from its "macro" neighbours *before* they occurred. The USA is the last to be included in the "micro" group; this seems reasonable for a group which starts off clustering around Australia and New Zealand.

The four-group cluster is shown as Table 9.[10] This seems plausible, but it illustrates one of the problems of clustering. The data used here for clustering do not suggest that Australia is more like the USA than the UK (see Table 7).

TABLE 9
FOUR-GROUP CLUSTERING

1	2	3	4
Australia	Netherlands	Belgium	Germany
Canada	Ireland	France	Japan
New Zealand	UK	Italy	Sweden
USA		Spain	

However, Table 9 does suggest this. The confusion arises because the USA is the last "micro" country to fall into a group, and it is easier for the program to get the USA into group 1 of Table 9 than to get the whole of group 2 into group 1 instead. The "problem" arises because Australia-plus-New Zealand and UK-plus-Ireland set themselves up as groups in the early stages of clustering. Once the clusters have thus been "seeded", they tend to grow and resist combination with other clusters. If the clustering process were seeded around the USA and the UK, slightly different groups would emerge. Indeed, a group consisting of Australia, New Zealand, Ireland and the UK has a considerably smaller "total internal difference" than the group: Australia, Canada, New Zealand and the USA.[11] However, the groupings are very stable even if factors 3, 4 and 5 are given double weighting or if Australia, Ireland and Belgium (which have identical scores to New Zealand, the UK and France, respectively, and thus seed immediate clusters) are omitted.

Conclusion

The scoring and testing process reported on above seems to support the hypothetical classification presented as Table 2, which was drawn up nearly two years before that process. The split between the two "classes" is very clear in Table 6. The further split into sub-classes and then families is best supported by Table 8, which draws on Table 7.

It may be noted that the classification of Nair and Frank (1980) as shown in Table 1 is also quite closely consistent with Table 2 for the relevant countries; the main difference being that the "macro" group has not been split up. However, this should probably not be seen as support for Table 2 nor for "empirical" classification using the Price Waterhouse data, because most of the other "empirical" results reported in the first part of this paper are quite different from Table 2 and from Nair and Frank's results.

Thus, this paper has proposed a classification based on evolution and "general knowledge" of background factors. This has been tested by selecting factors which are thought to be long-run and "structural", and by scoring these on the basis of detailed investigation in particular countries. Such a process of hypothesis, followed by selection and analysis of data specifically designed to test it, might be claimed to be *more* scientific and reliable than research which generates hypotheses from data which may be unreliable and unsuitable for such a purpose.

APPENDIX
References for Accounting in Some Countries Considered in the Text

France:
Mueller (1967), pp.103-108.
Beeny (1976).
Nobes and Parker (1981), ch.4.
Choi and Mueller (1978), chs.2 and 6.

West Germany:
Mueller (1967), ch.4.
Beeny (1975).
Macharzina (1981).
Choi and Mueller (1978), chs.2 and pp.191-192.

Netherlands:
Mueller (1967), ch.2.
Muis (1975).
Klaassen (1980).
Nobes and Parker (1981), ch.6.
Choi and Mueller (1978), ch.2 and pp.195-196.
Beeny and Chastney (1978).

United States:
Carsberg and Eastergard (1981).
Choi and Mueller (1978), ch.2.
Mueller (1967), ch.3.
Benston (1976).
Zeff (1972).

Canada:
Carsberg and Eastergard (1981), pp.275, 281.
Zeff (1972).

Sweden:
Choi and Mueller (1978), pp.25,38-40.113.114.218,219.
Johansson (1965).
Mueller (1967), pp.27-30,95-96,108-109,229.
Price Waterhouse (1979) on consolidation and equity method.

Japan:
Ohno et al (1975).
Dale (1979).
Katsuyama (1976).
Ballon et al (1975), chs.10 to 15.

Italy:
Stillwell (1976).

Belgium:
Pauwells and Flower (forthcoming).

Spain:
McRossin (1975).
Forrester (1981).
Donaghy and Laidler (1982).

NOTES

1   See Armstrong (1967) for a powerful exposition of the pitfalls of factor analysis used without a theoretical framework.

2   There is a useful discussion of this problem under "Classification, Biological" in *Encyclopaedia Britannica*, 15th edn. vol.4, pp.683-694. Also, see Knight (1981).

3   It is convincingly suggested that measurement practices and disclosure practices produce different classifications. Thus, to combine them would cause "interference". To study disclosure practices would involve a separate and additional research programme. The author regards the classification of measurement practices as the more difficult, useful and interesting task.

4   The author is particularly grateful to R.H. Parker for comments on the first draft of the hypothesis. It was first presented at the AUTA conference, Loughborough, April 1980, when useful suggestions were received. It has also been discussed at Staff Seminars at Monash University, University of Tasmania, University of New South Wales and the Australian National University. It was published in a tentative way in Nobes and Parker (1981, p.213).

5   The causal relationships cannot easily be proved, but many may be fairly easily demonstrated to be plausible. For example, see Nobes and Parker (1981, pp.3-6).

6   The countries were chosen as those with whose accounting the author was already familiar, or those which were "vital" and with whose accounting the author made himself familiar. It is hoped that this may be regarded as reasonable coverage of the developed Western world.

7   The da Costa, et al. (1978) work omitted some factors, because they were "uniform" across countries. It is not possible to tell which factors they refer to.

8   The programs used were "clustering by nearest neighbour" and "clustering by furthest neighbour" (see, K.V. Mardia, J.T. Kent and J.M. Bibby, *Multivariate Analysis*, Academic Press, London, 1979, pp.369-375).

9   The taxation system in Italy was reformed as from 1.1.1974. This reduced the arbitrariness of tax assessments by limiting the power of inspectors. It has resulted in the partial freeing of financial accounting from tax accounting; e.g. the greater use of the accruals convention and "fairness". In June 1974 the Stock Exchange body *(Commissione Nazionale per le Società e la Borsa)* was formed. In March 1975 a presidential decree required listed companies to have a more extensive audit (effective date: 1982 onwards). These will be carried out mainly by Anglo-American audit firms using new Accounting Standards issued by the professional accounting body from 1979. These have a strong Anglo-American flavour.

10   This grouping was produced using a computer program "clustering by furthest neighbour" with the roots of the squared differences of the data in Table 5.

11   "Total internal difference" merely sums the differences on each pair of countries, using the differences in Table 7. For Australia, New Zealand, Ireland and the UK, the total internal difference is 4; for the alternative group, as in Table 9, the difference is 10.

REFERENCES

American Accounting Association (1977), Report of the Committee on International Accounting Operations and Education, *Accounting Review Supplement,* (1977), pp.65-132.

Armstrong, J.S. (1967), "Derivation of Theory by Means of Factor Analysis", *American Statistician,* (December 1967), pp.17-21.

Ballon, et al (1976), *Financial Reporting in Japan* (Kodansha Int. Ltd., 1976).

Beeny, J.H. (1975), *European Financial Reporting – 1* (ICAEW, 1975).

───── (1976), *European Financial Reporting –11* (ICAEW, 1976).

───── and J.C. Chastney (1978), *European Financial Reporting – 4* (JCAEW, 1978), London.

Benston, G.J. (1976), "Public (US) Compared to Private (UK) Regulation of Corporate Financial Disclosure", *Accounting Review* (July 1976).

Carsberg, B. and A. Easterguard (1981), "Financial Reporting in North America" in (Nobes and Parker, 1981).

Choi, F.D.S. and G.G. Mueller (1978), *An Introduction to Multinational Accounting* (Prentice Hall, 1978).

da Costa, R.C., J.C. Bourgeois and W.M. Lawson (1978), "A Classification of International Financial Accounting Practices", *International Journal of Accounting* (Spring 1978), pp.73-85.

Dale, B. (1979), "Accounting in Japan", *Australian Accountant* (April 1979).

David, R. and J.E.C. Brierley (1978), *Major Legal Systems in the World Today* (Stevens, 1978).

Donaghy, P.J. and J. Laidler (1982), *European Financial Reporting –5* (ICAEW, 1982).

Finer, S.E. (1970), *Comparative Government* (Penguin, 1970), p45.

Forrester, D.A.R. (ed.) (1981), *Spanish Accounting in the Past and Present,* (Strathclyde Convergencies, University of Strathclyde, 1981), ch.3.

Frank, W.G. (1979), "An Empirical Analysis of International Accounting Principles", *Journal of Accounting Research* (Autumn 1979), pp.593-605.

Goodrich, P.S. (1982), "A Typology of International Accounting Principles and Policies", *AUTA Review* (1982).

Gregory, P.R. and R.C. Stuart (1980), *Comparative Government* (Praeger, 1980).

Hatfield, H.R. (1966), "Some Variations in Accounting Practices in England, France, Germany and the US", *Journal of Accounting Research* (Autumn 1966).

Johansson, S. (1965), "An Appraisal of the Swedish System of Investment Reserves", *International Journal of Accounting* (Fall 1965).

Kagan, K.K. (1955), *Three Great Systems of Jurisprudence* (Stevens, 1955).

Katsuyama, S. (1976), "Recent Problems of the Financial Accounting System in Japan", *International Journal of Accounting* (Fall 1976).

Klaassen, J. (1980), "An Accounting Court: The Impact of the Enterprise Chamber on Financial Reporting in the Netherlands", *Accounting Review* (April 1980).

Macharzina, K. (1981), "Financial Reporting in West Germany" in (Nobes and Parker, 1981).

Mason, A.K. (1978), The Development of International Reporting Standards (ICRA, 1978).

McRossin, F.M. (1975), "Spain – Country at the Crossroads", *Accountant's Magazine* (February 1975).

Mueller, G.G. (1967), *International Accounting* (Macmillan, 1967), Part 1.

Muis, J. (1975), "Current Value Accounting in the Netherlands: Fact or Fiction?", *Accountant's Magazine* (November 1975).

Nair, R.D. and W.G. Frank (1980), "The Impact of Disclosure and Measurement Practices on International Accounting Classification", *Accounting Review* (July 1980), pp.426-449.

Neuberger, E. and W. Duffy (1976), *Comparative Economic Systems,* (Allyn and Bacon, 1976) chs.6 to 9.

Nobes, C.W. (1981), "An Empirical Analysis of International Accounting Principles: A Comment", *Journal of Accounting Research* (Spring 1981), pp.268-270.

———— and R.H. Parker (1981), *Comparative International Accounting* (Philip Allan, 1981).

Ohno, et al (1975), "Recent Changes in Accounting Standards in Japan", *International Journal of Accounting* (Fall 1975).

Parker, R.H. (1981), "Financial Reporting in France" in (Nobes and Parker, 1981).

Pauwells, P.A. and J.F. Flower (forthcoming), *European Financial Reporting–6* (ICAEW, forthcoming).

Price Waterhouse (1973), *Accounting Principles and Reporting Practices* (Price Waterhouse, 1973).

———— (1975), *Accounting Principles and Reporting Practices* (P.W. 1975).

———— (1979), *International Survey of Accounting Principles and Reporting Practices,* (Butterworths, 1979).

Shils, E. (1966), *Political Development in the New States,* (Mouton, 1966).

18 Nobes

Standish, P.E.M. (1981), "Financial Reporting in Britain and Australia" in (Nobes and Parker, 1981).

Stillwell, M. (1976), *European Financial Reporting—3. Italy* (ICAEW, 1976), p.49.

Zeff, S.A. (1978), "The Rise of Economic Consequences", *Journal of Accountancy* (December 1978).

4

Journal of Accounting Research
Vol. 19 No. 1 Spring 1981
Printed in U.S.A.

An Empirical Analysis of International Accounting Principles: A Comment

C. W. NOBES*

In a recent article in this *Journal*, Frank uses data from the 1973 Price Waterhouse survey of financial accounting practices to classify countries' accounting systems into groups.[1] While the methodology seems more satisfactory and the results greatly more reasonable than those reported elsewhere using the same data,[2] neither Frank nor other researchers have investigated the reliability of these data and how appropriate they are for their statistical analyses.

I believe that the data may be questionable on three counts. First, they may contain some straightforward mistakes. These are illustrated in table 1. The easiest answers for me to check are those for the United Kingdom in the 1976 survey. Note that if such answers can be wrong for this country, would it be reasonable to rely on similar answers for Bolivia?

Second, some of the answers, although either strictly or conditionally true are misleading, particularly to a computer. Table 2 gives examples of this. The survey's impression that U.K. or U.S. accounting is as conservative as German accounting and more conservative than French accounting is surely misleading. The table hides the fact that German or French conservatism is of a wholly different order than Anglo-Saxon prudence.[3] Regarding the "clear profit figure," anyone acquainted with

---

* Lecturer, Exeter University. [Accepted for publication August 1980.]

[1] Werner G. Frank, "An Empirical Analysis of International Accounting Principles," *Journal of Accounting Research* (Autumn 1979): 593–605; Price Waterhouse and Co., *Accounting Principles and Practices: A Survey in 38 Countries* (New York, 1973).

[2] R. C. da Costa, J. C. Bourgeois, and W. M. Lawson, "A Classification of International Financial Accounting Practices," *International Journal of Accounting* (Spring 1978).

[3] See G. G. Mueller, *International Accounting* (New York: Macmillan, 1967), pt. 1; J. H. Benny, *European Financial Reporting, West Germany* (London: Institute of Chartered

268

INTERNATIONAL ACCOUNTING PRINCIPLES   269

TABLE 1
Survey Answers for the United Kingdom

Practice	Number and Score	
	1973	1976
A. "Land is shown separately from other fixed assets." *Comment:* It is normally not separated from buildings.	77, Required	40, Required
B. "Cost of inventories is determined by *FIFO.*"		93, Required
"Cost of inventories is determined by Weighted Average."		95, Not permitted
"Cost of inventories is determined by Retail Inventory." *Comment: SSAP 9* specifically allows all three (appendix, paras. 11–14).		98, Not permitted
C. There are several examples where U.K. practice is said to differ from Irish practice in 1976, even though the countries used identical Standards on the subject, e.g., 205.		
D. "Leases are capitalized by the lessee." *Comment:* This was not the case in 1973 or 1976; a forthcoming exposure draft calling for this is expected to meet criticism.	178, Majority	47, Majority

TABLE 2
1973 Survey Answers

PW Practice	Country and Score*			
	U.S.	U.K.	France	West Germany
11. Conservatism applies	5	5	4	5
201. Clear profit figure	2	5	5	5
14. Consolidated statements *only*	4	1	2	1
15. Consolidated + parent statements	1	5	2	5
16. Parent statements *only*	1	1	4	1
49. *EPS* disclosed	5	5	2	1
50. *EPS* on outstanding shares	1	5	4	1
51. *EPS* on shares and equivalents	5	1	1	1

* 1 = not permitted or not found; 2 = minority practice; 3 = followed by half of the companies; 4 = majority practice; 5 = required.

continental European financial statements knows of the greater difficulty in arriving at a figure for, say, profit after corporation tax but before extraordinary items, transfers to reserves, and payment of dividends. Moreover, in Germany, the "contrived" nature of the profit is well known.

Accountants in England and Wales, 1975), chaps. 3 and 4; J. H. Benny, *European Financial Reporting, France* (London: Institute of Chartered Accountants in England and Wales, 1976), chaps. 6–8; C. W. Nobes, "Why International Accounting Is Important," *The Accountant* (September 1977): 277–78, 312–14; and M. Lafferty, *Accounting in Europe* (Cambridge: Woodhead-Faulkner, 1975), pp. 8–21, 50–64.

Thirdly, the questions were not chosen for the purpose for which Frank and others used them. This may be illustrated by the consolidation questions in table 2 (14, 15, and 16). The most revealing of these is 16, but when all three are put into a computer with equal weight, confusion must result. Similarly, the important answers to question 49 will be diluted by 50 and 51. Finally, discriminating questions whether the accounting is designed to present a "fair" view, and about whether one finds income smoothing, secret reserves, tax-based depreciation, etc. are missing entirely. It is natural to try to avoid subjectivity in the selection of data, but the refusal to select here means that one is left with the subjective choice of several busy *PW* staff who had a different purpose in mind than do researchers who might use the data.

These problems appear not to be too serious for Frank's analysis, mainly because his results are so appealing. Whatever errors exist are probably minor and unsystematic. The one bias I personally fear is that the differences between the U.K. and the U.S. are comparatively exaggerated because of their familiarity to the question compilers who come from these countries. For example, in both the da Costa et al. and the Frank results, the classification of the U.S. with Germany and not with the U.K. seems to run heavily counter to experience in using sets of published financial statements.

I think that any future researchers who intend to use *PW* or similar data should first investigate these possible data problems or at least acknowledge them in their publications.

5

The European Accounting Review 1997, **6:1**, 123–129

How 'uniform' is financial reporting in Germany?: some replies

[1]*Christopher W. Nobes and* [2]*Gerhard G. Mueller*
[1]*University of Reading, UK and* [2]*Financial Accounting Standards Board, USA*

ABSTRACT

This paper is a reply to that by Feige in this issue which criticizes the accounting classifications of Mueller and Nobes. It is suggested here that Feige's criticisms are either already expressed in more detail elsewhere or are inaccurate or both. Feige then claims to test the classifications but is really disputing the label 'uniform' for Germany. For either purpose, Feige's test based on one atypical issue using a very small sample is not appropriate. Anyway, it turns out that Mueller did not classify post-war German accounting as uniform, and Nobes uses the word differently from Feige.

INTRODUCTION

Feige (1997) in this issue uses the topic of foreign currency translation as a way of testing aspects of classifications of accounting, particularly those by Mueller (e.g. 1968) and Nobes (1983). This present paper addresses some of Feige's general criticisms of classification and those related to particular classifications. Then the success of Feige's own empirical tests is examined.

THE TECHNIQUES OF CLASSIFICATION

Feige makes several points about classification in international accounting:

  (i) the factors used to classify are interrelated (p.110);
  (ii) the measurement of these factors is difficult (p.110);
  (iii) borrowings from other disciplines are a bad idea (pp.111 and 119);
  (iv) borrowings from other disciplines have to be treated with caution (p.119); and

---

Address for correspondence
C. W. Nobes, Coopers & Lybrand Professor of Accounting, Department of Economics, Faculty of Letters and Social Sciences, P.O. Box 218, Whiteknights, Reading, RG6 6AA, UK.

     0963–8180

(v) Mueller and Nobes were wrong to include Germany under the heading 'uniform' (Abstract, p.112 and p.119).

However, points (i) to (iv) are not new. Feige seems to add nothing because they have already been acknowledged elsewhere (see below) in greater detail.

On point (i), Feige notes (p.110) that the sources of financial reporting rules are connected to the main users of the reports. This is, of course, discussed at length by Choi and Mueller (1992, ch.2) and by Nobes and Parker (1995:11–7). Why is this a problem for classification, given that a consideration of both the sources of rules and the users of reports point in the same direction? Nobes (1983:8) and Nobes and Parker (1995:70) discuss the difficulty of separating explanatory variables from measurement practices.

On point (ii), Feige suggests (p.110) that measurement of the factors is difficult. However, he merely repeats the example of this given by Nobes and Parker (1995:17) without commenting on their conclusion that the difficulty is not fatal.

On point (iii), Feige criticizes the analogy with biological classification:

> Nobes draws an analogy with biology ... thus conveying the impression that his model provides clear-cut distinctions between the phenomena it classifies, only to subsequently qualify this analogy in a fashion which raises the question of why he has invoked the example of a 'hard' science. (p.111)

However, Nobes (1992:28, 30–2, 86) argues at length that the biological classifications are *not* clear-cut and are far from hard science, and seeks to learn lessons from this.

Again, Feige notes that Nobes' classification uses terms (e.g. 'class', 'family') borrowed from biology, and that Nobes suggests that these are 'loose labels'. Feige suggests that this is difficult to reconcile 'with the notion of "precision" which classification models, according to Nobes ..., afford in conjunction with the analysis of international accounting phenomena' (p.111). However, Nobes merely claims that 'the *activity* involved in *preparing* a classification ... *should encourage precision*' (Nobes and Parker, 1995:62, emphasis added). How can this claim be called into question because of the peripheral issue of what labels to use for the various levels of hierarchy of a classification? Nobes (1992:95–6) had already discussed the problem of labels at greater length. Feige (p.119) prefers the treatment of the classification models by Samuels *et al.* (1995), who do not refer to natural sciences. However, this is because Samuels *et al.* are *using* the models of Mueller and Nobes, rather than *constructing* them.

Is Feige saying that any attempt to classify is a bad idea? If so, does he object to the classifications in law, politics and economics (see Nobes and Parker, 1995:61–2)? Does he object to any borrowing of ideas from other disciplines in social or other sciences? This appears to be the case, given his final quotation (p.119). If so, this would make most of the world's accounting journals rather empty. Or is he merely calling for caution in the borrowings (see below)?

On point (iv), Feige advises caution, implying that there has not been any or not enough. However, the above references from Nobes (1992) and Nobes and Parker (1995) show several examples of caution. More could be offered. Feige himself in the above two quotations from his page 111 recognizes an example. Feige seems to add no new instances of why caution is necessary, nor does he add to the more detailed investigation of the problems of accounting classifications by Roberts (1995).

On point (v), Feige seems to be in error. Mueller[1] (1967) does not apply the label 'uniform' to post-war Germany; he cites France as the example. Nobes does use 'macro/uniform' for a large group of countries including Germany, but gives detailed explanations and caveats in the surrounding text (e.g. Nobes, 1992:66 and 95–7). With respect to Germany, Nobes (1992:24) suggests that:

> without a compulsory accounting plan, the same effect [i.e. aspects of uniformity] is achieved *in some areas* by detailed laws and tax regulations. (emphasis added)

So, it is not clear that Feige's criticism is reasonable (especially of Mueller). An issue of relevance here is the meaning of the word 'uniform'. Feige suggests (p.112) that it is 'self-explanatory'. This seems far from the case, which is a particular problem given that the issue is central to Feige's paper. Both Mueller and Nobes use the word in the context of charts of accounts and accounting plans. This leads them to associate Germany (particularly in the past) and France with uniformity. Feige does not mention charts or plans; and he may be using the word somewhat differently.

SUCCESS OF THE *F*-TEST

Feige suggests that the country studies of Choi and Mueller (1992) and Nobes and Parker (1995) are not detailed enough to be a 'serious test' of the classifications, so he will 'provide an empirical assessment of the "international accounting classification models" under discussion' (p.112). Remarkably, this 'empirical assessment' of classifications relating to the late 1960s (Mueller) and 1980 (Nobes) is thought to be provided by investigating *one* accounting issue for a sample of *six* companies each in *one* industry from *two* countries in *1994*. Any one of these italicized numbers would be a fatal flaw in his test; let alone all five together.

A difficulty with assessing the effectiveness of Feige's empirical work is that there is confusion about what he is testing. Although he claims to be assessing the classifications, he is really assessing the differential uniformity of German and UK accounting. His success in these two areas is examined below under five headings.

One accounting issue

It is not clear how anyone could expect to make an 'empirical assessment' of a classification using one accounting issue. The particular issue chosen (currency translation of subsidiaries' financial statements) actually offers support for the classifications. The reason why the German rule-makers are content to have lack of uniformity on this major issue is because it only affects group accounts and therefore does not affect distributable profit (connected to the protection of creditors) or taxable profit. The fact that these two matters are the drivers of financial reporting in Germany is a major factor in distinguishing Germany from the UK, as the background discussions to the classifications point out (e.g. Nobes and Parker, 1995:12–6).

Perhaps it would be fairer on Feige to ask whether this issue is a test of general German uniformity. Unfortunately, it is a bad test because translation[2] is one of those rare major issues on which the *Handelsgesetzbuch* has no rules. It is an 'outlier', presumably chosen deliberately by Feige to 'prove' a point about lack of German uniformity. Of course, as an outlier, it proves no general point. Feige suggests (p.118) that similar conclusions would follow from a consideration of other accounting issues, for example extraordinary/exceptional items and goodwill on consolidation. However, Feige offers no evidence of comparative German/UK uniformity in these areas at the time of the classifications (see below). Further, perhaps the main point is that these are also special issues in Germany because they do not affect taxation.

One industry

Feige notes the potential problem of looking at one industry. He suggests that there is a limited choice of translation methods and 'Therefore, it is quite unlikely that the chemical industry is an "outlier"' (p.113). This is a *non sequitur*. He suggests that by focusing on a single industry it is possible to demonstrate differences 'even within one and the same industry'. Of course, separate data for two industries would double the demonstration (and so on). There is no convincing justification for choosing one industry only or for the one chosen.

Two countries

It is self-evident that a study of two countries cannot be a serious 'empirical assessment' of a classification involving many countries.

Six companies

There have been many surveys of UK and German financial reporting practices, including currency translation (e.g. Treuarbeit, 1990; FEE, 1991;

ICAEW, 1992). These include larger samples than Feige's. It is not at all clear why he bothered to take a new sample given how small it was.

The 'random sample' of six German companies is most unfortunate because it includes Bayer, Schering and Hoechst. The first two of these were the first[3] German companies to prepare group accounts according to International Accounting Standards (IASs). The first year they did this was 1994, which was the very year investigated by Feige. Hoechst also moved toward IASs that year. Given the absence of German rules in the area chosen, these three companies had free rein to follow IASs. Consequently, half the German sample is an 'outlier'.

1994

As noted above, the annual accounts looked at are mostly those of 1994. This is obviously not a test of the classifications of many years earlier. Nobes and Parker (1995:71–2) point out that the classification is a historical one and that 'Nobes (1992:95–9) has suggested some refinements on his earlier model, and noted that EC harmonization may have reduced the differences in the model'.

The 1980 classification of Nobes (and, of course, the 1967 classification of Mueller) was before the implementations of the Fourth and Seventh Directives in the UK or Germany, whereas Feige's study is after those implementations. In 1980, there were no requirements in UK law or standards relating to formats of published accounts, and there were no accounting principles in law. Also, 1980 was before the UKs accounting standard (SSAP 20) on currency translation, which Feige notes was being closely followed by his UK companies in 1994. In summary, there was probably much less UK uniformity in general (and particularly on Feige's issue) at the dates of the classifications than in 1994.

Summary on the *F*-test

As an empirical test of the international accounting classification models of Mueller and Nobes, Feige's study fails because:

  (i) it looks at only one industry, for which there is no satisfactory reason;

 (ii) the sample is very small, and half the German sample is unrepresentative;

(iii) the single accounting issue chosen actually *supports* one of the key bases of the positions of Germany and the UK in the classifications;

(iv) only two countries are looked at, which cannot be a serious test of classifications involving many countries;

 (v) the data of 1994 cannot test classifications of 1980 or earlier.

Incidentally, better empirical work to test the classifications has been done by Doupnik and Salter (1993 and 1995). Of the above problems, this suffers only from (v). These researchers suggest strong support for the classification. Actually, Feige does not question the position of Germany and the UK in the classifications. He seems to approve (pp.112 and 119) of remarks on this subject by Mumford (1991) and by Samuels *et al.* (1995), which have been based on, or are consistent with, the classifications.

Feige's study is really a test of differential degrees of uniformity between Germany and the UK, and his paper's title is consistent with that. However, even for this, the above problems (i) and (ii) are very serious. Also, the issue chosen is an outlier, and therefore not a test of general German uniformity.

CONCLUSION

Feige provides criticisms which might be summarized into four types:

(a) against borrowings from other disciplines, using the example of classification in international accounting;
(b) against incautious such borrowings:
(c) against two particular classifications;
(d) against the inclusion of Germany under the label 'uniform' whereas the UK is under the label 'fair/judgement'.

Success with criticism (a) would strike at a large proportion of accounting research, but Feige only offers vague warnings. Criticism (b) offers nothing new, since the classifiers have already acknowledged all of Feige's concerns.

Feige's empirical work claims to be related to criticism (c) but is very wide of the mark for five reasons noted above. It turns out that Feige's empirical work is really related to criticism (d), but the work also fails as a test of general German uniformity for three of the reasons noted above. Anyway it turns out that it is either inaccurate or unfair to criticize the classifiers as though they had particularly chosen Germany as the exemplar of uniformity.

ACKNOWLEDGEMENTS

The authors are grateful to the editors for commissioning this comment, and to R. H. Parker and A. D. Roberts for suggestions on an earlier draft.

NOTES

1   Choi and Mueller (1992:47) describe certain aspects of earlier German practice (e.g. charts of accounts) as being uniform.

2 Rules on the treatment of unsettled foreign currency balances can be inferred from basic German principles. However, that is another issue. On the issue of the translation of foreign subsidiaries' financial statements, there are no binding rules, only a discussion of the alternatives by a committee of the *Institut der Wirtschaftsprüfer*.

3 For 1994, these two plus Heidelberger Zement did this. For 1995, Hoechst and several others joined them.

REFERENCES

Choi, F. D. S. and Mueller, G. G. (1992) *International Accounting* (2nd edn). Englewood Cliffs: Prentice-Hall.

Doupnik, T. S. and Salter, S. B. (1993) 'An empirical test of a judgmental international classification of financial reporting practices', *Journal of International Business Studies*, 24(1): 41–60.

Doupnik, T. S. and Salter, S. B. (1995) 'External environment, culture, and accounting practice: a preliminary test of a general model of international accounting development', *International Journal of Accounting*, 30(3): 189–207.

FEE (1991) *European Survey of Published Accounts*. Routledge: London.

Feige, P. (1997) 'How "uniform" is financial reporting in Germany? The example of foreign currency translation', *European Accounting Review*, 6(1): 109–22.

ICAEW (1992) *Financial Reporting*. London: ICAEW.

Mueller, G. G. (1967) *International Accounting*. New York: Macmillan.

Mueller, G. G. (1968) 'Accounting principles generally accepted in the United States versus those generally accepted elsewhere', *International Journal of Accounting*, 3(1): 91–103.

Mumford, M. (1991) 'United Kingdom', in Alexander, D. and Archer, S. (eds) *The European Accounting Guide*. London: Academic Press.

Nobes, C. W. (1983) 'A judgmental international classification of financial reporting practices', *Journal of Business Finance and Accounting*, 10(1): 1–19.

Nobes, C. W. (1992) *International Classification of Financial Reporting* (2nd edn). London: Routledge.

Nobes, C. W. and Parker, R. H. (1995) *Comparative International Accounting* (4th edn). Englewood Cliffs: Prentice-Hall.

Roberts, A. D. (1995) 'The very idea of classification in international accounting', *Accounting, Organizations and Society*, 20: 639–64.

Samuels, J. M., Brayshaw, R. E. and Craner, J. M. (1995) *Financial Statement Analysis in Europe*. London: Chapman & Hall.

Treuarbeit (1990) *Konzernabschlüsse 1989*. Düsseldorf: IDW Verlag.

6

The European Accounting Review 1998, **7:2**, 323–330

Personal view

The future shape of harmonization: some responses

Christopher Nobes
University of Reading, UK

Cairns (1997) makes some remarks about work by Flower and Nobes in a way which does not seem to be part of normal measured debate in an academic journal. Like Cairns, 'I found it difficult to know how best to reply' or, indeed, whether to ignore these attacks because readers will already have noted their tone and assessed their validity appropriately. I will leave Flower to reply to the bulk of the criticisms, and concentrate on those which concern my own work.

Incidentally, for the avoidance of doubt, Flower and I can often be found on opposite sides of arguments about EU and IASC harmonization, and my disagreement with Cairns should not be taken as support for Flower's (1997) conclusions.

In the first part of Cairns's paper, he concentrates partly on 'the distinction between Anglo-American and Continental European accounting' (p. 305). He notes that some French and German companies have adjusted their reporting towards US or international practices (pp. 307–8). He also notes that, on certain issues, the US and the UK take opposing views (p. 315). These and other arguments lead Cairns to the following six observations in the order shown here (pp. 316–17):

1 '... the distinction between Anglo-American accounting and Continental European accounting is becoming less and less relevant and more and more confused.'
2 '... those who continue to favour these classifications are ignoring what is happening in the world and how companies actually account for transactions and events.'

Address for correspondence
C. W. Nobes, Department of Economics, University of Reading, Reading RG6 6AA, UK.

0963–8180

3 'It is increasingly apparent that the different economic, social and legal considerations which have influenced national accounting do not necessarily result in different accounting ...'
4 '... there are now probably far more similarities between American and German accounting than there are between American and British accounting.'
5 'The futility of attempting to classify accounting was well demonstrated ...'
6 'In their attempts to maintain the distinction between Anglo-American and Continental European accounting, Flower and Nobes have started to clutch at straws. The[y] both make offensive attacks on the people involved in the work of the IASC.'

These statements by Cairns conflate four different issues:

(a) The usefulness of classifications in accounting (statements 2 and 5).
(b) The causes of international differences in accounting (statement 3).
(c) The appropriateness of particular classifications of 'Anglo-American' versus 'Continental European' (statements 1, 4 and 6, and perhaps 2).
(d) The accuracy of a classification of countries by compliance with international standards (statement 5).

(a) THE USEFULNESS OF CLASSIFICATIONS

In statement 5 (and perhaps statement 2), Cairns suggests that classification is pointless. Although writing in an academic journal,[1] Cairns does not comply at this point with the usual convention of referring to and taking account of previous literature. There is a large literature on the potential usefulness of classification (e.g. Mueller, 1967; AAA, 1977; Nobes, 1992; Roberts, 1995), which Cairns does not address.

Statement 5 is phrased as an attack on attempting to classify in accounting. However, the context is a particular one: a classification of countries by compliance with international accounting standards (IAS) (see section (d) below). This has nothing to do with the bulk of the literature on the classification of accounting systems. Therefore, the 'futility' of classification in accounting is *not* demonstrated. The futility of classifying countries by compliance with IAS would also not be demonstrated by one allegedly erroneous attempt.

Statement 2 is unclear. Is it an attack on classification in general or on the Anglo-American versus Continental European classification? If the former, then the previous literature is a response. If the classifications are 'ignoring what is happening in the world', then perhaps classifications need to be updated rather than abandoned. If it is an attack on the Anglo-American versus Continental European classification, then section (c) below returns to this.

One suggestion in the previous literature is important here. Roberts (1995), in a critical review of classification in accounting, proposes that classification should not consider countries but systems. That is, for example, it should not be the UK and Germany that are classified but different bundles of accounting practices ('systems') as used by companies in sets of financial statements. A classification could then allow for the possibility that the consolidated accounts of some large German companies[2] in 1998 use a different system from the 'normal' German system used in 1998 in most consolidated accounts and in nearly all individual accounts (including the parent company accounts of the groups using other than 'normal' German accounting). That is, more than one way of accounting can be used in one country and even by one company in one year. Cairns examines the consolidated accounts of a few large companies, but these are unrepresentative of most annual reports in the countries concerned.

(b) THE CAUSES OF INTERNATIONAL DIFFERENCES

Cairns (in statement 3) appears to suggest that it is pointless not only to classify but also to try to identify any underlying causes of international differences (e.g. legal or cultural), because these cannot be relied on to explain differences in practice. However, if the factors allegedly influencing accounting do not cause differences or do not explain the differences, then we must try harder to find relevant factors and better models. Perhaps part of the solution is to recognize that different influences are working on different *companies* as opposed to countries, as suggested above in the context of classification.

(c) THE APPROPRIATENESS OF PARTICULAR CLASSIFICATIONS

Although past accounting classifications have differed, classifications with either the UK and US together or several continental countries together (or both of these features) are dominant in the literature (e.g. Hatfield, 1911; Mueller, 1967; Frank, 1979; Nair and Frank, 1980; Nobes, 1983). Cairns challenges this consensus.

It is obvious that, if EU and IASC efforts and commercial forces for harmonization have succeeded at least to some extent, then international differences have become less stark, particularly for consolidated accounts. Perhaps this is the background to Cairns's statement 1. Of course, this would not prove that a two-way classification had become meaningless, merely less dramatic. Indeed, Doupnik and Salter (1995) use recent empirical data and suggest that the classification is largely still in place. Many recent papers in this journal examine the difference remaining between UK accounting and that of most companies in France, Germany or Italy (e.g. for tax effects, see Hoogendoorn, 1996).

Cairns does not explain statement 4. Perhaps he is considering such matters as the relatively small number of adjustments necessary for Daimler-Benz to reconcile from the German *Handelsgesetzbuch* (HGB) to US generally accepted accounting principles (GAAP). However, one must take account of the fact (acknowledged earlier by Cairns) that Daimler had already made a number of major changes[3] to its traditional domestic accounting with the specific purpose of minimizing the adjustments to US GAAP, and it also had to produce a Form 20-F of over 200 pages.

Cairns appears to suggest (statement 2) that the classifications (particularly the distinction between the US and Germany) are associated with the unworldly, by which he may mean academics. Perhaps the best informed *practitioners* in the world on the subject of US compared to German rules are the financial staff at Daimler-Benz, who were the first to work on published reconciliations between the two sets of rules. In the 1996 annual report, Daimler state (p. 90):[4]

> German and U.S. accounting principles are based on fundamentally different perspectives. While accounting under the German HGB emphasizes the principle of caution and creditor protection, the availability of relevant information for shareholder decision-making is the chief objective of U.S. accounting. The comparability of the financial statements – both from year to year and from company to company – and the determination of performance on an accrual basis therefore rank higher under U.S. GAAP than under the HGB.

In conclusion, Cairns has provided no evidence to support statement 4, which would overturn a great mass of literature. His reference to co-operation among standard setters (p. 316) reminds one of further evidence to counter to his conclusion. Current thinking of the US and the UK in 'G4 + 1' meetings and elsewhere shows a large measure of agreement about the definition of 'provision', the desirability of capitalizing all leases, the need to move towards the fair valuation of financial instruments, and the usefulness of expanding the present income statement. On all these major issues, Germany disagrees with the US and the UK standard setters.

Again, perhaps more clarity would be added by noting that a *few* German companies (including Deutsche Bank and Daimler) have moved their *consolidated* accounting towards both UK and US accounting. This would not undermine the general classification, although as more German consolidated reports follow this lead it will become essential to show at least two German 'systems', as noted above.

As explained below, Cairns's statement 6 is (i) a *non sequitur*, (ii) wrong and (iii) not relevant to the argument because the points are *ad hominem*. After statement 6, Cairns states (p. 317) that:

> Nobes complains that the Germans on the IASC board have been contaminated by
> lengthy exposure to Anglo-Saxon accounting . . . and that the French, German and
> Japanese representatives are atypical of their countries because they come from
> multinational companies and big six accounting firms. . . . Nobes' comments are
> remarkable for the fact that he has been one of the UK's representatives on the
> IASC board for the past four years and that his university chair is sponsored by a
> big six firm.

This statement is a *non sequitur* because the point about the IASC representatives is not designed to maintain a classification but to explain how it is possible for the IASC to operate so successfully despite large international differences in laws, practices, etc. I am not aware that any researcher has used this line of thought to propose or maintain any classification of accounting systems; classifications are based on causal factors, on laws, on practices, etc.

The statement is wrong in that it turns my remarks on their head. I do not 'complain'[5] that French, German or Japanese representatives are atypical; I celebrate it. Such representatives provide over six weeks a year of their time; they need to be able to operate for long days in English; they must deal with topics such as deferred tax and defined benefit pensions (which may not be normal domestic problems for most accountants in their countries); they have mostly been involved in international committees for several years so that they have learnt to understand other countries' problems and solutions. Also, a French representative, for example, is more likely to understand the US viewpoint if he or she is a Big Six partner rather than being a typical French sole practitioner. Why does Cairns suggest that it is an 'offensive attack' to call these representatives atypical?

The idea of atypicality was suggested to me by an IASC representative of one of these countries, and confirmed by others of them. It is surely self-evident. I hope that I am thought of as atypically British and that any purely British ideas that I once had have been 'contaminated'[6] by foreign ones. Certainly the present and former UK delegation has frequently argued and voted against current UK rules or practice. Without all the above, the IASC's great progress in reducing options in its standards in the 1990s would not have been possible.

The final *ad hominem* points of Cairns are not relevant to his arguments. Anyway, board representation or the sponsorship of a chair should not be allowed to affect what one writes, except to the extent that it improves one's knowledge.

(d) A CLASSIFICATION BY COMPLIANCE WITH IAS

In developing statement 5, Cairns refers to a classification of countries by compliance with IAS. It has been noted above that this should be separated from the issue of classification of accounting systems. In the classification by compliance with IAS, UNCTAD (1996) propose four groups of countries, *not* a two-group Anglo-American versus Continental European split as Cairns implies by placing his remarks between two paragraphs on this split. Given that the survey covered fifty-six countries, it would be unfortunate if Cairns were correct in suggesting that classification is futile. We would not then be allowed to say that the response of Germany to IAS is somewhat similar to that of France, whereas the response of Sri Lanka is somewhat similar to that of Malaysia. All countries would just be unclassifiably different. Researchers would be unable to make sense of any field which has a substantial population of items if they were not allowed to classify. It would seem reasonable to express concerns that classification can be done badly or that it can obscure by oversimplifying, but that is not the same as saying that any attempt is futile.

About this classification, Cairns notes that: '... Nobes ... concluded that compliance with International Accounting Standards was unlikely or impossible in many countries. ... The government experts from the countries knew differently ...' (p. 317). Cairns should not have referred to Nobes (who is not named as the author) but to UNCTAD who made heavy abbreviations and amendments before issuing a draft document based on an earlier draft by Nobes. More seriously, Cairns misleads the reader because he misses out several paragraphs of caveats and explanations of the 'unlikely or impossible'. The category concerned was said to include, among others,[7] several Continental European countries and Japan. The report noted that compliance *by companies*[8] in these countries was unlikely or impossible *under present rules*[9] and '*without a separate set of IAS financial statements*'. It also mentioned a series of ways in which the rule-makers or some companies in those countries were moving towards IASs and noted that 'compliance was confined to the consolidated accounts of most or a few listed companies'.

If something is neither unlikely nor impossible, presumably it is likely. By implying that no such 'unlikely or impossible' category exists, Cairns must be suggesting that in countries such as France, Germany and Japan (see note 7), it is likely that companies will, under present rules, comply with IASs in their statutory financial statements. I do not believe that this is the case.

As for the particular countries categorized, the classification was based on questionnaires returned to UNCTAD by their official contacts in the countries concerned (mostly government officials), as the report made clear. So, for each of Cairns's recollections of error suggested by a government expert, I have a contradictory written response from an official contact of the same country. Cairns gives us no explanation and no examples of error.

SUMMARY

Cairns makes a series of attacks on some fundamental research areas in international accounting and on some specific work. The attacks are jumbled up and not explained. The unrepresentative nature of the consolidated accounts of a few large companies is not acknowledged. The personal remarks are not relevant to the arguments. The attacks therefore seem to be unreasoned and unreasonable.

ACKNOWLEDGEMENTS

The author is grateful for comments on an earlier draft from Liesel Knorr (IASC), R. H. Parker (University of Exeter), Alan Roberts (University of Reading), and a referee of this journal.

NOTES

1 The paper appeared in a section of the journal called 'Personal View'. Nevertheless, there is no indication to the reader that different criteria of care apply here, and it would be unfortunate if they did. Elsewhere in Cairns's paper, he uses several references and criticizes others for poor research.
2 For example, Bayer in 1995 used IAS in its group accounts (having chosen carefully from German HGB options) but a different set of policies in its parent accounts. The Deutsche Bank in 1995 prepared two sets of group accounts, one according to the HGB and another according to IAS but not the HGB.
3 For example, Daimler moved from a version of the temporal method of currency translation to a version of the current rate method. Several other changes are noted on p. 78 of the 1993 Annual Report.
4 Of course, what an annual report states may not coincide with management's private view. Nevertheless, there seems no reason on this subject to suppose a major difference between the two.
5 I did use the word 'contaminated' in Nobes (1995) in the context of German representation on the IASC Board. However, the word was in the context of a laudatory paragraph. It was in inverted commas, and obviously intended ironically. The whole work in draft was read by the main German representative, as acknowledged in the preface.
6 See note 5.
7 Belgium, France, Germany, Greece, Italy, Japan, Spain; Czech Republic, Hungary, Poland, Romania; Brazil, Chile, Costa Rica, Mexico; China, Korea, Mali.
8 The context was *de facto* compliance, i.e. what companies actually do.
9 The context was the IASs in issue in 1995.

REFERENCES

AAA (1977) *Accounting Review, Supplement to Vol. 52.* Sarasota, FL: American Accounting Association.
Cairns, D. (1997) 'The future shape of harmonization: a reply', *European Accounting Review*, 6(2): 305–48.
Doupnik, T. S. and Salter, S. B. (1995) 'External environment, culture, and accounting practice: a preliminary test of a general model of international accounting development', *International Journal of Accounting*, 30(3): 189–207.
Flower, J. (1997) 'The future shape of harmonization: the EU versus the IASC versus the SEC', *European Accounting Review*, 6(2): 281–303.

Frank, W. G. (1979) 'An empirical analysis of international accounting principles', *Journal of Accounting Research*, Autumn: 593–605.

Hatfield, H. R. (1911) 'Some variations in accounting practices in England, France, Germany and the US', reprinted in *Journal of Accounting Research*, Autumn 1966: 169–82.

Hoogendoorn, M. (1996) 'Accounting and taxation in Europe – a comparative overview', *European Accounting Review*, Vol. 5, Supplement: 783–94.

Mueller, G. G. (1967) *International Accounting*, Part I. London: Macmillan.

Nair, R. D. and Frank, W. G. (1980) 'The impact of disclosure and measurement practices on international accounting classifications', *Accounting Review*, July: 426–50.

Nobes, C. W. (1983) 'A judgemental international classification of financial reporting practices', *Journal of Business Finance and Accounting*, 10(1): 1–19.

Nobes, C. W. (1992) *International Classification of Financial Reporting* (2nd edn), London: Routledge.

Nobes, C. W. (1995) *German Accounting Explained*. London: Financial Times Business Information, p. 43.

Roberts, A. (1995) 'The very idea of classification in international accounting', *Accounting, Organizations and Society*, 20: 639–64.

UNCTAD (1996) *Compliance with International Accounting Standards*. Geneva: United Nations Trade and Development Board.

7

Journal of Business Finance & Accounting, 19(1), January 1992, 0306 686 X $2.50

CLASSIFICATION OF ACCOUNTING SYSTEMS USING COMPETENCIES AS A DISCRIMINATING VARIABLE: A GREAT BRITAIN–UNITED STATES STUDY: A COMMENT

CHRISTOPHER NOBES*

Shoenthal (1989) reports that:

> The clustering of GB and the US into separate accounting systems, as shown in prior studies using other variables as discriminators, was evidenced by the findings of this study, using perceived competencies of newly licensed accountants. This suggests that competencies can serve as a differentiating variable among accounting systems (p. 562).

This conclusion can be challenged in several ways.

PRIOR STUDIES

Shoenthal cites several authors who put the UK and the US into different clusters, but also some who do not. Those who do, rely on Price Waterhouse (PW) data. This has been criticised by Nobes (1983) as having four types of drawback for this use:

> (i) straightforward mistakes, (ii) misleading answers, (iii) swamping of important questions by trivial ones, and (iv) exaggeration of the differences between the USA and the UK because of the familiarity of these countries (and thus their differences) to the compilers of survey questions (p. 2).

It is point (iv) which is of most relevance here. It is a truism that the cited studies produce clusters of the PW data rather than of the countries' accounting. Nevertheless, one set of researchers mentioned by Shoenthal even manage to conclude (using the PW data for 38 countries) that the US is the country least like the UK group (da Costa et al., 1978, p. 79). Shoenthal seems to accept the suggestions of such authors on the UK/US split, but it is based on data unsuitable for this purpose, and is strongly counter-intuitive (e.g. Carsberg, 1985; and Mueller, 1967).

THE COMPETENCIES MEASURED

Shoenthal's two most explanatory 'competencies' were (p. 559):

* The author is Coopers Deloitte Professor of Accounting at the University of Reading. He is grateful for comments on an earlier draft from R.H. Parker and J. McKinnon.

F2:   understanding the 'historical reasons' for 'control exerted by a central
       government unit upon large business corporations'.

F4c: understanding 'the concept of a liability'.

The newly qualified Britons were better at F2 and the newly qualified Americans
at F4c. However, does this tell us anything about professional accountancy
training, let alone about whether the two countries should be in different
clusters? The general educational systems are quite different in the two
countries, so a different answer to F2 is not surprising. One would expect a
different answer from the two populations on perceptions of causes of the First
World War, etc., etc. This would allow the countries to be discriminated but
it would be of little relevance for accounting clusters.

In particular, CPAs study accounting at university whereas most London-
based chartered accountants do not. This will probably affect answers to
questions like F4c. If the study had used Edinburgh-based accountants (who
are mostly accounting graduates) the results might have been closer to New
York than to London. This would help to put the US and Scotland in one
accounting cluster, with England in another. This would be unreasonable, and
anyway Shoenthal treats Great Britain as a single country.

CAUSALITY

There is a suggestion of causality by Shoenthal (e.g. pp. 549 and 562); the
direction being *from* differences in competencies of auditors *to* international
differences in accounting. No proof is offered for causality or its direction. It
has been noticed elsewhere that there was an inverse correlation between the
side of the road that a country's vehicles drove on and the side that they were
on as assets in its balance sheets.[1] However, no causality was suggested, let
alone the direction of it.

The papers cited by Shoenthal suggest that there are long-running causes
of accounting differences, such as ownership structures, tax systems and legal
systems. Is it not as likely that auditors are adapted to serve the different
accounting environments rather than the other way round?

DIFFERENTIATION AND CLUSTERING

Shoenthal examines only two countries but still suggests that his factors will
improve clustering. However, all he should claim is that the two sets of data
are different. There are two problems here, even if the data are measuring
something relevant for classification:

(i) The data measure multinational auditors in London and New York.

COMPETENCIES AS A DISCRIMINATING VARIABLE: A COMMENT   155

It seems possible that there would be a greater difference between Wyoming and New York; and perhaps London is more typical of the UK than New York is of the US. These points need to be addressed before this factor can be used to put the whole countries into different clusters.

(ii) London and New York will obviously be differentiable if sufficiently detailed questions are asked; any two cities would be (e.g. Chicago and New York). We would need to include France, Germany, etc. before anything could be told about ease of international clustering. Perhaps the two populations sampled by Shoenthal are very similar in a world context. I would expect so. In that case, the data would put the UK and the US into the same cluster.

CONCLUSION

Prior classification studies are not unanimous, and those whose conclusions are apparently accepted by Shoenthal can be particularly criticised for their US/UK split. The competencies isolated by Shoenthal may not be closely linked to professional education; and they may not cause differences in accounting. Even if all the above problems were found to be unimportant, the examination of only two countries can tell us nothing about clustering, merely that the two countries are different, which we knew already.

NOTE

1 The author first heard this pointed out by Steve Zeff at the EAA Conference in Barcelona, 1981. Japan was noted as one apparent exception, but they write everything back to front.

REFERENCES

Carsberg, B. (1985), 'Financial Reporting in North America', in *Comparative International Accounting*, C.W. Nobes and R.H. Parker (Philip Allan, 1985).

da Costa, R.C., J.C. Bourgeois and W.M. Lawson (1978), 'A Classification of International Financial Accounting Practices', *International Journal of Accounting*, Vol. 13, No. 2 (1978), pp. 73–85.

Mueller, G.G. (1967), *International Accounting* (Macmillan, 1967), Part I.

Nobes, C.W. (1983), 'A Judgemental International Classification of Financial Reporting Practices', *Journal of Business Finance & Accounting*, Vol. 10, No. 1 (Spring 1983), pp. 1–19.

Shoenthal, E.R. (1989), 'Classification of Accounting Systems Using Competencies as a Discriminating Variable: A Great Britain–United States Study', *Journal of Business Finance & Accounting*, Vol. 16, No. 4 (Autumn 1989), pp. 549–563.

8

Accounting and Business Research, Vol. 28. No. 3. pp. 173–188. Summer 1998

173

International Variations in the Connections Between Tax and Financial Reporting

Margaret Lamb, Christopher Nobes and Alan Roberts*

Abstract—This paper constructs a method for assessing the degree of connection between tax rules and practices and financial reporting rules and practices in a country. Five types of connection and disconnection are suggested, and 15 arenas of accounting are proposed for assessment on this basis. The method is applied to four countries, partly in order to test the claim of a clear distinction between Anglo-Saxon and continental European countries.

1. Introduction

A number of papers have begun to investigate the relationship between taxation and financial reporting in a comparative international context (e.g. Haller, 1992; Walton, 1993; Radcliffe, 1993; Quéré, 1994). Hoogendoorn (1996:793) suggests a seven-category classification of 13 European countries based on the relative independence or mutual dependence of tax and financial reporting. However, this was a brief editorial based on a summary of papers by different authors from different countries, writing without a standard approach to assessment of independence or dependence. The classification also gives equal weight to two quite separate issues: the financial reporting treatment of deferred tax and the connection between tax and financial reporting. Consequently, there remains a need for a systematic approach to assessing international variations in the connection between tax and financial reporting. This paper suggests one. It also tests the claim (e.g. Nobes and Parker, 1995, ch. 1) that there is a clear distinction between Anglo-Saxon countries[1] and some continental European countries.

*Margaret Lamb is at the University of Warwick; Christopher Nobes and Alan Roberts are at the University of Reading. They thank the following for their valuable comments on earlier drafts of this paper: Rob Bryer, Michel Couzigou, Axel Haller, Jean Harris, Liesel Knorr, Alain Le Deudé, Yannick Lemarchand, Dieter Ordelheide, Dieter Pfaff, Bernard Sauvée, Jim Schweikart, Anne Semler, Peter Walton, David Wilde, and two referees and the editor of this journal. They also thank participants in the following seminars for good discussion that has helped to clarify the analysis: the EIASM Workshop on Accounting in Europe: 4 (Geneva, June 1995); and the Fifth ICAEW Tax Research Workshop (Lancaster, September 1995). Any errors of interpretation or omission remain the responsibility of the authors. Correspondence should be addressed to Professor C.W. Nobes, Department of Economics, University of Reading, PO Box 218, Whiteknights, Reading RG6 2AA. This paper was first submitted in October 1996; the final version was accepted in March 1998.

Two aspects of this issue can be separated: taxation as an historical reason for accounting, and the degree of contemporary separation or connection between financial reporting[2] and tax for purposes of profit measurement. The first of these includes the effect of tax considerations on rule-making in financial reporting. Rule-makers and corporate taxpayers will have been alert to potential effects of financial reporting on tax liabilities. A few recent examples of this are mentioned in the text below. However, these issues are largely beyond the scope of this paper and are covered elsewhere (Lamb et al., 1995). This paper concentrates on the second aspect: connections and influences between tax and accounting practice in the

[1] 'Anglo-Saxon' is used here in its European sense to mean those countries, generally English-speaking, where accounting is seen as market-driven and where rules are made by non-governmental bodies. The UK and the US are examples.

[2] Our study considers connections between taxation and financial accounting (and its output, published financial reporting). It is beyond the scope of our study to consider connections between taxation and other functional parts of accounting practice.

[3] Radcliffe (1993:1) distinguishes 'financial conformity' from 'tax conformity': 'Financial conformity implies substantial reliance on the principle that choice of a particular accounting practice in the financial report is conclusive for tax purposes and that inclusion of particular items therein is a necessary precondition for the grant of tax relief; tax conformity implies the adoption of a general presumption that taxable profit is computed on the basis of generally accepted accounting principles'. (Radcliffe's categorisation is a broader representation of what we have referred to below as Case II and Case III connections between tax and accounting). The existence of either conformity condition is evidence of a strong link between tax and accounting. The dynamic nature of the link, as Radcliffe (1993) demonstrates through his legal study and as we discuss below, makes the observable patterns of influence reciprocal. The Haller (1992) and Ordelheide & Pfaff (1994) discussion of reverse 'congruence' (or 'authoritativeness') in the German context is a broader representation of what we have referred to below as Case IV and Case V connections.

context of existing sets of tax and financial reporting rules.

The argument proceeds as follows. First, we
suggest a method of assessing the degree of linkage
between tax and financial reporting. Then, we apply this to four countries: the UK, the US, France
and Germany. Finally, we ask whether there is a
clear distinction between the countries.

2. A method of assessing linkage

We examine here the degree of connection or conformity[3] between (i) tax rules[4] and practices and
(ii) financial reporting and practices. It is suggested
that five cases[5] of connection or disconnection for
any particular accounting 'arena' (e.g. depreciation of fixed assets) can be distinguished, as in
Table 1.

The issue here is not whether the economic
decisions of management are affected by tax. We
presume that this is the case for many decisions in
all countries. The issue is the degree to which financial reporting practice and tax practice are connected in an operational sense. The cases in Table

---

[4] 'Rules' refer to authoritative practice. By far the most common source of rules in the analyses that follow is legislation:
primary, secondary or tertiary. However, rules which govern
practice may also be drawn from case law or extra-statutory
guidance, produced by tax authorities. The key to our recognition of a 'rule' is whether or not it governs observable practice in the majority of cases. We have endeavoured to consider
the rules in effect at 1 January 1996 and to base our comparative analysis at this date. Changes in details and shifts in patterns of interrelations between tax and accounting since that
date are inevitable, and, where significant, have been noted.
[5] The classificatory scheme rests upon the authors' judgments
concerning interrelationships. For a review of methodological
issues in international accounting classification, and the importance of judgment, see Roberts (1995).

1 are presented in increasing order of the influence
of tax on financial reporting decisions (the latter
are also referred to below as accounting policy
choices). Case I is disconnection of tax rules and
practice from financial reporting rules and practice. This suggests lack of influence of tax on financial reporting decisions.

The other four cases involve various forms of
connection. Case II is where there are tax rules and
financial reporting rules without major options,
and the rules are the same. This suggests that there
is limited room for tax considerations to affect accounting policy choice by managers. In Case III,
the accounting rules are more detailed than the tax
rules, and tax practice is to follow accounting
practice. Initially, this suggests the influence of accounting on tax. However, where the accounting
rule allows choice or is vague, there may be a
'reverse effect' whereby the financial reporting
rules (or options in them) are chosen, interpreted
or shaped with the tax effect in mind. Examples
of Case III where such a reverse effect seems most
likely are shown as 'III†' in Table 2.

Cases IV and V are clearer examples of tax influence on accounting policy choice. In Case IV,
there is no precise financial reporting rule, so a tax
rule is followed for convenience or a tax option is
chosen in order to reduce tax liabilities. In Case
V, financial reporting rules are overridden.

We suggest a number of accounting arenas
which can be assessed to determine the cases of
linkage for any particular country.[8] The first col-

---

[8] More accurately, this could be applied to any particular
combination of tax system and accounting system. Some countries have more than one accounting system. For example,
group accounts may use different rules from individual
accounts.

Table 1
Cases of linkage between tax and financial reporting

Case I	Disconnection	The different tax and financial reporting rules (or different options) are followed for their different purposes.[6]
Case II	Identity	Identity between specific (or singular) tax and financial reporting rules.
Case III	Accounting leads	A financial reporting rule or option is followed for financial reporting purposes, and also for tax purposes. This is possible because of the absence of a sufficiently specific (or singular) tax rule.[7]
Case IV	Tax leads	A tax rule or option is followed for tax purposes, and also for financial reporting purposes. This is possible because of the absence of a sufficiently specific (or singular) financial reporting rule.
Case V	Tax dominates	A tax rule or option is followed for tax and financial reporting purposes instead of a conflicting financial reporting rule.

[6]Such disconnection will be recognised when distinct, independent and detailed tax and financial reporting operational rules
exist. Even if measurement outcomes are essentially the same, the particular arena may still be characterised as Case I; the
independence and completeness of the sets of rules 'disconnects' tax and accounting in an operational sense.
[7]This case may be either *de facto* identity or an instance where financial reporting is the 'leader'. It may be difficult to
distinguish between the two circumstances. However, both indicate a *prima facie* financial reporting influence on tax.

Table 2
Tax linkage in material arenas of financial reporting

Arena		Connection or disconnection case			
		UK	*US*	*France*	*Germany*
1	Fixed asset recognition and valuation	I	II (possibly IV)	II*	III, IV (and sometimes V)
2	Financial and operating leases	III†	Small operating lease payments: II Other lease payments: I	II*	IV
3	Depreciation (a) normal (b) excess	I n/a	I n/a	IV V*	IV V
4	Contingencies, provisions	I (possibly III)	I	II*	III†
5	Grants and subsidies	I	II	III	IV
6	Research and development costs	I	III	III†	III†
7	Inventory valuation: (a) flow assumptions (b) other areas	II III†	IV III†	II* II	IV IV
8	Long-term contracts	III in most cases	I (possibly IV in elements of details)	IV	III
9	Interest expense (a) capitalisation (b) other	I II	I I**	IV* III	III III
10	Foreign currency transactions	I**	I**	I	III
11	Non-consolidation purchased goodwill	I	I (IV may become the norm under new rules)	I	V
12	Pensions	I	I	IV	IV
13	Policy changes and fundamental errors	I	I	III, I	III
14	Scope of the group	I	I	I	I
15	Fines, charitable donations, entertaining expenses	I	I	I	I

Key: Cases I-V — As defined in Table 1:
* Case I is specifically allowed or required for group accounts.
** Strictly Case I, but measurements are identical in normal circumstances.
n/a Not applicable, because there is no distinction for accounting or tax between normal and excess depreciation.
† Examples of Case III where a reverse effect (i.e. tax considerations influencing financial reporting) seem particularly likely.

umn of Table 2 lists these arenas, which were chosen on the basis that they were sufficiently important[9] to warrant coverage[10] by an International Accounting Standard.

The discussion is set primarily in the context of listed companies, which encompass a large proportion of the economic activity of the four countries considered. As Walton (1993) notes, smaller companies' accounts may present information with tax users primarily in mind. In general, the comparative international issues discussed here apply to both listed and other companies. We concentrate on the rules in force in 1996.

The focus of most of our discussion is individual company financial statements, as these are the basis for tax computation[11] in each of the four countries. However, we will also highlight the relationship between taxation and financial reporting in the context of consolidated accounts. In the UK and the US, one would generally expect the same accounting policies to be used for parent and consolidated financial statements. This is not the case for some large French and German groups.

3. Application to four countries

Our classification of arenas by country into the five cases are, of course, subjective in the sense that judgment is required; first, in deciding how rules of accounting and taxation will normally be applied, and second, in deciding to which case the manner of application best corresponds. In the first sense, we are doing nothing more than replicating the application of professional judgment in practice. We have ensured the realism of our professional judgments of rule application and case classification by (i) extensive research in primary and secondary sources of tax and accounting rules; (ii) discussion among the three authors and reference to the original sources; and (iii) consultation with a minimum of two experts in each country to confirm our replication of professional judgments and subsequent case analysis. We explain the clas-

[9] This may not mean that all these differences between tax and accounting rules are material in size. This will vary by sector, country, etc. Nevertheless, we hope that this method will include most material issues.
[10] We have eliminated those International Accounting Standards (IASs) which seem irrelevant for our thesis because they do not affect the profit measurement of individual companies in the countries studied: those on disclosure (IASs 1, 7, 14, 15, 24, 30, 32 and 33); associates and joint ventures (IASs 28 and 31); IAS 26 on accounting by pension plans; and IAS 29 on hyperinflation. We have also left out IAS 12 on taxation (in order to avoid circularity) but have added the arena of fines, donations, etc. as a catch-all for tax/accounting disconnections which are common in all four countries. We use IASs as at the end of 1997.
[11] Very limited exceptions to this generalisation may apply in relation to groups of companies. However, rules of tax consolidation exist where appropriate. See Lamb (1995: 38–9) for a discussion of this aspect of group taxation.

sifications in the text below, providing references for the rules.

Given the general reliance of tax rules on accounting practice for all the countries covered by this study, it is not surprising that there are many examples of Case II and Case III conformity; to this extent, we could regard such conformity as the 'normal' state of affairs in any country. For example, on the whole, the tax rules do not specify treatments for such issues as sales, wages and most business overheads, so Case III conformity is normal.

3.1. The UK

A distinction between accounting profit and taxable profit—caused largely by definitions and distinctions incorporated into tax law—has been recognised since the late nineteenth century (Freedman, 1987; Lamb, 1996). Where there is no specific tax law to the contrary, recent UK case law has helped to clarify that modern accountancy practice will apply in normal circumstances. Despite the possibility that established legal concepts could overrule accountancy practice, a judge's ruling 'will not override a generally accepted rule of commercial accountancy which (a) applies to the situation in question[,] (b) is not one of two or more rules applicable to the situation[,] and (c) is not shown to be inconsistent with the true facts or otherwise inapt to determine the true profits or losses of the business' (Freedman, 1993:477). Therefore, net profit before taxation as shown in the published accounts of limited companies is the usual starting place for tax computations, but many adjustments in theory and in practice can be made.

An example of an unusually complex Case III relationship is the current treatment of lease accounting. The capitalisation of leases was unusual in the UK before the passage of Statement of Standard Accounting Practice (SSAP) 21 in 1984.[12] The Accounting Standards Committee (ASC) confirmed with the tax authorities that the application of SSAP 21 would not alter the tax position, i.e. rental payments under all leases[13] would remain deductible expenses for tax purposes (a Case I disconnection). However, a subsequent Inland Revenue Statement of Practice (confirmed by case law)[14] requires the tax basis to follow the accounting basis in normal circumstances (a Case III relationship). Accounting leadership is established by reference to the categorisation of leasing agreements as 'operating leases' or 'finance leases'.

[12] SSAP 21 applied to accounting periods beginning on or after 1 July 1987.
[13] Provided, in general, that the leases themselves, and the profile of payments, conformed to normal commercial practice.
[14] SP 3/91 and *Gallagher v. Jones, Threlfall v. Jones* (1993) STC 537.

Rental payments for operating leases are deductible in arriving at profit measured for financial reporting and tax purposes. In contrast, under new Inland Revenue practice 'inspectors will normally be prepared to accept that the properly computed commercial depreciation of the asset which is charged to the profit and loss account in the period' represents, together with the finance charge element of finance lease rentals, the appropriate tax deduction.[15] In principle, there are no major choices in the accounting rules. However, given the amount of judgment required to distinguish an 'operating lease' from a 'finance lease' under the terms of SSAP 21, there may be a reverse effect (as for many other Case III areas), in that the directors may wish to capitalise or not for tax purposes and therefore may seek to apply SSAP 21 in particular ways.

In the field of inventory valuation, LIFO is not acceptable for tax purposes in the UK,[16] nor generally for accounting purposes[17] (i.e. a Case II relationship). Other aspects of inventory valuation—recognition and categorisation of costs and lines of inventory—are generally subject to Case III conformity.[18] A reverse effect—application of the financial reporting rule with a tax effect in mind—may apply to such aspects of inventory valuation. Given the flexibility of SSAP 9's criteria for the use of the percentage-of-completion method, a reverse effect may also apply to long-term contract accounting. However, Case III conformity (and the scope for reverse effects) is limited by the Revenue's reluctance to accept provisions for foreseeable losses on long-term contracts as calculated in accounts; Inland Revenue guidelines[19] have been provided to deal with such provisions.

The UK treatment of provisions is an arena generally characterised by Case I disconnection. Tax law tends to distinguish between 'general provisions', which are not deductible for tax purposes, and 'specific provisions', which are. A combination of specific legislation and case law has established the clear distinction between 'general' and 'specific' in relation to provisions for bad debts[20] and repairs.[21]

The position for other sorts of provisions is less clear. In a recent case[22], Britannia Airways' provision for future aircraft engine overhaul was accepted as tax deductible, even though the costs had not been incurred, nor the time for overhaul arrived. The High Court's decision rested on the facts that (i) there was no specific tax law that dealt with this type of provision and (ii) that commercial accounting, as reflected in the company's audited accounts, accepted the provisions as accounting expenses. In other words, the Court accepted that a Case III connection existed. However, the strength of the Britannia Airways precedent for law and practice is not yet clear: the case sits somewhat uneasily with the tax treatment of other types of provisions. The extension of the Case III 'imperative' beyond the facts of the particular case is not yet clear;[23] and certain UK accounting standard setters seem unconvinced that Britannia's accounting treatment is an acceptable form of commercial accounting.[24] All in all, it is considered that Case I best characterises the current disconnection of tax and accounting rules in this arena.

Most other material arenas in UK financial reporting (see Table 2) involve quite separate rules for tax and financial reporting (Case I). Fixed assets and their depreciation provide good examples of this. It is provided in law[25] that fixed assets may be revalued in various ways, and this is common practice in the UK, particularly when property prices are rising. Revaluation (upward or downward) is ignored for tax purposes.[26] Similarly, depreciation for financial reporting purposes is controlled by company law and accounting

---

[15] SP 3/91, paragraph B 10–11.

[16] SP 3/90 and *Minister of National Revenue v. Anaconda American Brass Ltd.* (1956) AC 85.

[17] SSAP 9 suggests that LIFO will not normally give a true and fair view.

[18] 'The Revenue accepts any method of computing the value of stocks, which is recognised by the accountancy profession, so long as it does not violate the taxing statutes as interpreted by the Courts' (SP 3/90, paragraph 2).

[19] SP 3/90, paragraph 7.

[20] ICTA 1988, s. 74(1)(j); *Anderton and Halstead Ltd v. Birrell* (1931) 16 TC 200; and *Dinshaw v. Bombay Commissioner of Taxes* (1934) 13 ATC 284. Inland Revenue Interpretation,

Tax Bulletin: 12, August 1994 concerns the evidence required to justify the deduction of a bad debt provision.

[21] ICTA 1988, s.74(1)(d) for the basic legislation.

[22] *Johnston v. Britannia Airways Ltd.* (1994) STC 763.

[23] Clarification of the Revenue's views was sought by the Tax Faculty of the ICAEW in early 1995. For provisions such as warranty claims and closure costs, the Revenue made clear that normal practice would be to follow commercial accounting principles, but subject to judicial tests established by case law and in statute. The suggestion that a taxpayer might be able to claim a more prudent deduction than shown in commercial accounts was dismissed. (*Taxes*, 1995: 513–4 summarises the Inland Revenue guidance.)

[24] The Britannia Airways overhaul provision is, *prima facie*, inconsistent with the definition of 'liability' included in the ASB's draft *Statement of Principles* (see Chapter 3). Instead, the original purchase of the 'asset', the new aircraft, may in substance be better represented as the purchase of the aircraft (with a long useful life) and the purchase of a right to fly the aircraft (with a useful life that will expire after a much shorter period of flying) until the first overhaul. See Green (1995) and Whittington (1995) for summaries of these issues.

[25] CA 1985, Sch. 4, para. 31.

[26] Taxable capital gains or losses are calculated by reference to purchase cost, revaluation at particular dates and a form of indexation unrelated to financial reporting; TCGA 1992, Ss. 35, 38, 272.

standards,[27] but is not deductible against taxable income.[28] Instead, a scheme of capital allowances sets out the available tax depreciation.[29]

Case I disconnection also operates in the following arenas:

(i)   *grants and subsidies*: tax treatment starts from general tax principles to distinguish 'capital' from 'revenue',[30] rather than by using the accounting rules in SSAP 4;

(ii) *research and development expenses*: tax rules[31] specify expensing even if development expenditure is capitalised under the rules of SSAP 13;

(iii) *non-consolidation purchased goodwill*: tax rules preclude an expense for amortisation of goodwill;

(iv) *pension costs*: tax allowances are calculated on a different basis[32] from that used by SSAP 24; and

(v)   *fines, charitable donations, entertaining expenses*: tax rules very substantially restrict deduction for such expenses.

Two further Case I arenas are worth comment: foreign currency and changes in accounting policy. For foreign currency transactions, the tax rules[33] have recently been changed to bring them more into line with the financial reporting rules dealing with foreign exchange (SSAP 20).The method of this attempt to create greater conformity was to recreate a parallel set of 'commercial accounting rules' for tax purposes. Certain parts of the new legislation have been written in such a way that crucial measurement variables may be chosen in a manner that will permit compliance with both sets of rules: this is the case with Section 150, Finance Act 1993 which allows sufficient flexibility in the choice of translation rates for accounting/tax mismatches to be avoided (Muray and Small, 1995:19). Such provisions would suggest a Case III relationship between accounting and tax rules. However, the differences in detail remain so extensive that it still seems reasonable to describe this arena as Case I.[34]

---

[27] CA 1985, Sch. 4, paras. 17-19, 32; SSAP 12.
[28] Save in respect of finance lease assets capitalised in conformity with SSAP 21. See above.
[29] CAA 1990, Ss. 24, 25, 159.
[30] Accounting and tax will almost always distinguish the general nature of government grants and subsidies in the same way. There is a substantial degree of accord concerning what is 'capital' in this context. However, SSAP 4 treatment of a capital grant is irrelevant to its tax treatment which depends on the type of asset to which it relates and the tax depreciation rules, if any, that apply. Revenue grants and subsidies will effectively be treated in the same way for tax and accounting.
[31] CAA 1990, part VII.
[32] ICTA 1988, Ss. 74, 592.
[33] SP 1/87 until April 1995; then FA 1993, Ss. 125–170, Schs. 15–17 and FA 1994, Ss. 114–116, Sch. 18.
[34] The different vocabulary, definitions and statements of rules create distinct sets of references that are disconnected in

The arena of changes in accounting policy and correction of fundamental errors also provides an example of Case I. For accounting purposes (FRS 3), these items are treated as prior year adjustments (i.e. the opening balance sheet is adjusted), whereas for tax purposes prior year assessments are amended or, in the case of acceptable[35] changes in accounting policy, are absorbed in the year.[36]

Historically, another example of Case I was that the UK tax system operated on a cash basis for interest and similar receipts or payments,[37] whereas financial reporting worked on an accruals basis. However, new rules for interest introduced in 1996 better align the tax rules with the accounting rules (i.e. establish a Case II relationship). Identity of measurement rules is achieved, but the new tax rules are very detailed as far as the tax categorisation of debits and credits related to 'loan relationships' are concerned; it is not a simple matter of tax rules being required to follow the accounting requirement.[38] Capitalisation of interest on construction projects is not followed for tax purposes (Case I).

As with the other countries considered here, group structures for tax purposes (e.g. loss reliefs, ACT surrender, chargeable gains)[39] are quite different from those for financial reporting as in the Companies Act and FRS 2.

In summary, the UK has many arenas characterised by Case I disconnection, despite general

---

their detail. Although there was an intention at the time of the creation of the new tax legislation that it should recreate existing accounting rules, there is no in-built mechanism for that substantial measure of congruence to be, of necessity, maintained in the future; accounting and tax rules can develop in their own separate ways in the future. This is the characteristic structure of traditional tax rule setting in the UK. As Muray and Small (1995: 19) explain, the complexity arises because 'a modern and sophisticated tax régime had to be laid over the top of an archaic and excessively complex framework.....Without the schedular system, the distinction between [types of taxable income] would have been unnecessary and no special loss relief rules would have been needed. The extraordinary contortions demanded by the regulations dealing with deferral calculations...could have been dispensed with'. As will be discussed below in connection with the US, such complex detail of tax rules, even when intended to replicate in substance commercial accounting rules, may lead to moves over time to a Case IV relationship between accounting and tax.
[35] 'Acceptable' generally means in accordance with the law and accounting standards.
[36] *Pearce v Woodall-Duckham Limited* (1978) CA, 51 TC 271.
[37] ICTA 1988, Ss. 337–338; IR Int. 3.
[38] A company has a 'loan relationship' if it is a debtor or creditor with regard to any debt which is a loan under general law, e.g. gilt-edged securities, corporate bonds, bank loans and overdrafts. Normally amounts payable and receivable are included in the tax computation on an accruals basis. However, if the relationship has been entered into for trade purposes, then the income or expense is treated as part of taxable trading income; otherwise, the income or expense is dealt with under other tax recognition rules (Melville, 1997: 364, 427).
[39] For example, ICTA 1988, Ss. 240, 402, 413, 770; and TCGA 1992, Ss. 170, 171, 175.

principles of judicial tax law that tend toward 'tax conformity' (Radcliffe, 1993) and that emphasise the importance of commercial accounting in 'leading' tax treatment.

3.2. The US

Under the current Internal Revenue Code (IRC), there is no general requirement of conformity between taxable profit and financial statement profit. However, there is an apparently strong link between tax law and accounting in Section 446(a) IRC 1986 which states: 'taxable income shall be computed under the method of accounting on the basis of which the taxpayer regularly computes his income in keeping his books'. Most companies adopt the accruals method as their 'method of accounting' and GAAP for tax profit calculations. Relatively recent changes make clear that the phrase 'method of accounting' may be defined in such a way as to permit divergence from financial accounting in a number of circumstances.[40]

Although there is an absence of 'presumptive equivalency'[41] between accounting and tax measurement of profits, and although the opportunities for permissive disconnection of accounting and tax measurements have increased over time, US recognition of taxable profits rests on a bedrock of *de facto* conformity with commercial accounting. Therefore, we should not be surprised to find examples of Case II identity between tax and accounting rules in important areas of measurement. In most circumstances, such identity exists in the arena of fixed asset valuation (other than depreciation—see below).[42] However, as the tax rules[43] for the valuation of tangible fixed assets are often more specific and detailed than accounting GAAP,[44] a number of Case IV (tax leader) rela-

tionships may operate to support the identification and categorisation of historical costs for tax purposes. For example, uniform capitalisation rules for tax purposes[45] require direct costs and some indirect costs of fixed assets produced by the taxpayer to be capitalised, not expensed; categorisation for accounting purposes will provide *prima facie* evidence concerning the nature of costs.

Perhaps more characteristic, given the detailed nature of tax regulation, are those arenas characterised by Case III or Case IV conformity. In Case III examples, the detailed tax regulations outline a number of acceptable approaches, whereas the financial reporting rules are more constrained and will tend to be adopted for both purposes. In Case IV examples, the detailed tax guidelines will tend to be followed (or may have to be followed) rather than a more general, or an alternative, financial reporting rule.

In the arena of research and development expenditure, the accounting rule[46] is clear: research and development expenditure should be treated as an expense. The tax rules are more permissive: research and development expenditure incurred may be expensed, but if not, depreciation or amortisation over a specified period is possible.[47] Although the detailed accounting and tax rules are written without reference to one another, this arena seems characterised by a Case III relationship, without room for much reverse effect: if research and development expenses are written off in accounts in accordance with SFAS 2, then for tax purposes Section 174(a)(1) IRC 1986 will apply and will give the same treatment.

Inventory valuation is an arena where tax rules[48] state explicitly that 'best accounting practice' should be adopted to find appropriate valuation rules, provided 'income is clearly reflected'. In normal circumstances, therefore, tax and accounting valuations are identical. Both sets of rules[49] permit companies to choose a valuation method from a range of options—FIFO and LIFO are within the range of acceptable flow assumptions. However, given that the tax rules normally require conformity of flow assumption with financial reporting,[50] the tax option that has the most beneficial tax effect (e.g. LIFO in periods of rising inventory costs)

---

[40] Reg. § 1.446-1(a)(1) defines 'method of accounting' as 'not only the overall method of accounting of the taxpayer but also the accounting treatment of any item'. The taxpayer adopts an overall method of accounting and methods of accounting for particular items when first filing a tax return. The method(s) must thereafter be applied consistently, unless IRS approval is obtained for a change in overall method of accounting or for the method of accounting of a 'material item used in such overall plan' (Reg. § 1.446-1(e)(2)(ii)(a)). With some exceptions, the IRS no longer imposes 'a financial statement conformity condition on proper to proper changes in accounting method'; a year-end reconciliation is the only requirement (Godshalk, 1994: 159). Thus, financial accounts and tax computation 'methods of accounting' are permitted to diverge. Such a divergence does not apply to the LIFO choice; see footnote 50.

[41] *Thor Power Tool Co. v. CIR* (1979) 58L Ed. 2d 785.

[42] The same analysis applies to the treatment of grants and subsidies under tax and accounting rules. Neither system of rules deals with the impact of grants and subsidies on profit as an explicit subject. Instead, historical cost measurement takes this aspect into account. If grants or subsidies were not capital in nature, general principles of income recognition would apply for tax and accounting purposes.

[43] Sections 263A, 1011–1013, IRC 1986; Regs. § 1.1012–1.

[44] SEC rules and Accounting Principles Board Opinion (APBO) 6 (1965).

[45] Section 263A IRC 1986.

[46] Statement of Financial Accounting Standards (SFAS) 2 (1974).

[47] Section 174 IRC 1986.

[48] Section 471 IRC 1986; Regs. § 1.471–1; Regs. § 1.471–2.

[49] Inventory accounting is governed by Accounting Research Bulletin (ARB) 43: 4 (1953).

[50] Section 472(e) IRC 1986 requires that taxpayers who adopt LIFO methods must use the same method in their financial reports. Regs. § 1.472–2(e) deals with this LIFO 'report rule' in more detail.

will tend to be adopted for financial reporting,[51] to the exclusion of other options. Therefore, characterisation of the tax/accounting relationship as Case IV, rather than Case II, seems appropriate. The close link between accounting and tax in this arena is made clear by the requirement that taxpayers must obtain tax authority approval for any change in method of valuing inventory.[52]

In other respects, tax and accounting rules detail the types of inventory costs to be taken into account and the methods for reaching appropriate measures of cost. Despite the detail, the method of measurement advocated in each set of rules is consistent and, therefore, the financial reporting treatment normally leads the tax treatment (Case III): that this should be so seems clear from the reference to 'best accounting practice' in tax rules.

The distinct and separate purposes of tax and accounting rules (Case I) were clearly evident in the arena of long-term contracts until changes to tax law introduced in 1986: accounting rules[53] permitted the completed-contract or percentage-of-completion methods to be used (depending on the circumstances), while the tax rules required the use of the completed-contract method. The 1986 tax change[54] requires the percentage-of-completion method, defined in detail in the tax law, to apply to most long-term contracts.[55] As the choice for financial reporting does not depend on the tax rules, and *vice versa*, this remains a Case I relationship. However, when the percentage-of-completion method is applicable under both sets of rules, the more detailed tax basis of calculation is likely to be adopted, too, for financial reporting purposes. A secondary Case IV relationship may, therefore, apply to elements of measurement.

The fact that there is no presumptive equivalence in the US between tax and financial reporting, together with an institutional recognition of the separate, distinct purposes of tax accounting and financial reporting,[56] means that Case I disconnection of tax and financial reporting is likely to be an important feature of the US system. We find Case I disconnection in a number of arenas:

(i)   *Fixed asset depreciation*: The accounting rules[57] are distinct and separate from the tax rules.[58] The latter are very detailed and specify, *inter alia*, the method of depreciation to be used; guidelines for the length of useful life; salvage value should be equal to zero; and the convention of depreciation to apply in years of acquisition and disposal.

(ii) *Non-consolidation purchased goodwill*: Accounting rules[59] require amortisation over an expected useful life of no more than 40 years. Until 1993 the tax/accounting relationship was Case I because no tax deduction was available for goodwill. Under new rules introduced in 1993[60], certain non-consolidation purchased goodwill may be amortised over 15 years. The tax/accounting relationship remains, strictly, Case I but it is possible that a reverse effect will become evident to make the choice of useful life for accounting purposes tend to be at or near 15 years for reasons of simplicity.[61]

(iii) *Accounting for leases*: Accounting and tax rules are detailed and apply for their distinct purposes.[62] The accounting treatment of payments under leases depends, under SFAS 13, on whether or not the lease is classified as a capital lease. The tax rules do not recognise the concept of capital lease, but are concerned with ascertaining the permissible de-

---

[51] There is, of course, a trade-off between tax savings and reported earnings. A large literature exists concerning the implications of the choice of LIFO by management (e.g. Sunder, 1973, 1975; Ricks, 1982).

[52] Section 446(e) IRC 1986 and Regs. § 1.446–1(e). A number of other changes in method of accounting require prior Internal Revenue Service (IRS) approval. However, most of the other circumstances have greater impact on unincorporated businesses or small companies and are likely to have an impact on financial statements prepared for tax accounting purposes only. Special notice provisions apply to the adoption of LIFO.

[53] ARB 45 (1955). Both methods are acceptable, but the percentage-of-completion method is preferable when costs to completion estimates are reasonably reliable. Otherwise, the completed-contract method should be used.

[54] Bittker and Loklan (1989, ¶106.2.1) explain that the purpose of the 1986 change was to eliminate the deferral of taxable income permitted by adoption of the completed-contract method. They quote (fn. 3) a Congressional report as saying 'corporations had large deferred taxes attributable to this accounting method and low effective tax rates. Annual reports for the large defense contracts indicate extremely low (or negative) tax rates for several years due to large net operating loss deductions arising from the use of the completed-contract method' (H.R. Rep. No. 426, 99th Cong., 1st Sess. 625–26).

[55] Section 460 IRC 1986.

[56] *Thor Power Tool Co v CIR* (1979) 58L Ed. 2d 785.

[57] ARB 43, Chapter 9A (1953); ARB 44 (revised 1958).

[58] Sections 167, 168, 197 IRC; Regs. 1.167(a); Regs. 1.446–1(a). Nevertheless, the 1913 income tax law defined the depreciation rules that were then widely adopted for accounting purposes (Watts and Zimmerman, 1979).

[59] APBO 17 (1970).

[60] Section 197 IRC 1986. An 'amortisable section 197 intangible' means, broadly, purchased business 'goodwill', 'going concern value', business records (including customer lists and market intelligence), intellectual property and know-how, and 'workforce in place including its composition and terms and conditions...of its employment'. Self-created 'goodwill' will normally fall outside the definition of an 'amortisable section 197 intangible'; the exceptions are, broadly, property rights that have been legally documented (e.g., as a licence, trademark or covenant agreement). Detailed rules make clear that recognition of 'amortisable section 197 intangibles' will normally occur in connection with the purchase of assets amounting to a going concern.

[61] While a longer useful life may be justified and permissible for financial accounting purposes, equal amortisation for tax and accounting reduces the complexity of deferred tax calculations.

[62] SFAS 13 (1976); Section 467 IRC 1986; Regs. § 1.446–1(a).

duction of rent accrued under the lease for the period in question. Small operating lease payments (aggregate payments up to $250,000) will be presumed to follow the normal accounting method; other lease rentals will be deductible according to specific tax rules and calculations.

(iv) *Provisions and contingencies*: Accounting rules[63] require recognition of liabilities (and any consequential expense) where it is probable that losses have been incurred at the financial statement date and the amount can be reasonably estimated. Tax rules permit an expense deduction only when 'incurred', a concept defined by reference to specific statutory tests which take into account financial reporting treatment,[64] but must conform to a judicial test of appropriate accrual (the 'all events' test). The effect of the combined tax rules tends to make the tax concept of accrual more restricted than the accounting concept, which is defined in probabilistic terms to a far greater degree. Despite the explicit influence of the accounting treatment on the tax treatment, this remains an area best described as Case I because of the independence of the tests of judgment reserved to the distinct tax and accounting purposes.

(v) *Interest expense*: Tax rules[65] permit a deduction for interest accrued, but numerous special rules apply to deal with, *inter alia*, interest on indebtedness to fund corporate investment[66] and capitalised interest.[67]

(vi) *Foreign currency gains/losses*: Tax rules[68] will, in general, permit the gain or loss associated with accrued income and expenses to be recognised or deducted from ordinary income. Such treatment is consistent with the accounting rules[69] applicable to individual company accounts.[70] However, detailed rules exist to govern the tax treatment of foreign dividend flows.[71]

(vii) *Pension costs*: Accounting for employers' pension costs is an arena where tax and accounting rules diverge in their detail, impact on profit measurement, and intention. Ac-

counting rules[72] aim to ensure full recognition (using an actuarial method of calculation) of the pension costs and allocation to the periods in which they accrue. Tax rules[73] are more concerned to ensure that tax deductions are given for contributions made at an acceptable level to an acceptably constituted plan (e.g. a Section 401 qualified pension plan).

(viii) *Accounting policy changes and correction of fundamental errors*: The accounting rules[74] require prior year adjustment in certain cases. Tax rules require that certain accounting policy changes ('changes in accounting method' for 'material items' as defined in regulations) should be approved by the IRS in advance and, once approved, should be reflected in the year of the change.[75] Taxpayers may be able to take advantage of an option to reconstruct earlier years' calculations of taxable income to reflect the change of policy.[76] Fundamental errors will generally be corrected by adjustment of earlier years' taxable income.

(ix) *Group recognition*: The consolidated income tax return rules are defined in a manner entirely distinct from the accounting rules governing the recognition of an accounting group for consolidated accounts purposes.[77]

(x) *Fines, charitable donations, entertaining*: Accounting rules apply the general matching principle to recognise such expenses. Tax rules restrict the deductibility of these expense categories: in general, fines are disallowed; charitable contributions are restricted to 10% of a corporation's taxable income;[78] and many business entertaining expenses are disallowable or restricted by a 50% limitation.[79]

Although its volume and detail suggests the separateness of the tax accounting regime (and creates a number of Case I disconnections), US tax officials are free to observe, choose and adapt practices and rules from commercial accounting and financial reporting regulation[80] to suit tax pur-

---

[63] SFAS 5 (1975).
[64] Section 461(h)(3)(B) IRC 1986.
[65] Section 162(a) IRC 1986.
[66] Section 279 IRC 1986.
[67] Section 460 IRC 1986. Accounting rules would permit an interest deduction on an accruals basis, subject to special treatment for interest capitalised—SFAS 34 (1979).
[68] Sections 985–988 IRC 1986.
[69] SFAS 52 (1981).
[70] The translation of the results of overseas subsidiaries' accounts in consolidated group accounts has no applicability for tax purposes.
[71] The calculation of earnings and profits under Section 986 IRC 1986.

[72] SFAS 87 (1985); SFAS 88 (1985).
[73] Section 404 IRC 1986.
[74] APBO 9 (1966) and APBO 20 (1971); SFAS 16 (1977).
[75] Section 446, IRC 1986 and Regs. § 1-446–1(e).
[76] Section 481(a), IRC 1986 and Regs. § 1-481-1 and § 1-481-2.
[77] Sections 1501 and 1504 IRC 1986; ARB 51 (1959).
[78] But the excess may be carried forward.
[79] Sections 162, 170 and 274 IRC 1986 respectively.
[80] As many of the tax rules detailed above apply equally to companies that publish financial reports, companies not subject to public reporting requirements, and unincorporated businesses, detailed tax rules will define the primary accounting rules for many enterprises. It is unsurprising that tax authorities adopt sound financial reporting principles when trying comprehensively to define adequate standards of accounting.

poses. An indicator of the responsiveness of tax authorities to, and their awareness of, changing commercial accounting circumstances is the frequency and volume of changes in tax statutes and regulations.[81] Such frequency and volume constitutes part of a plausible explanation of the persistence of Case III and Case IV connections in the context of a tax accounting regime seemingly predisposed to disconnection. Further, the reliance on very detailed income tax regulations to articulate and clarify applications of primary legislation permits the tax authorities to rationalise circumstances when accounting is permitted to lead tax (Case III) and to specify those conditions when tax requirements should lead accounting (Case IV). The balance of influence in the relationship (i.e. should it be seen as Case III or Case IV?) may depend on the extent to which tax accounting detail overwhelms—for relative simplicity or to save effort—the rules in financial reporting standards.

3.3. France

A key requirement of the *Code General des Impôts* (General Tax Code—CGI)[82] is that, for tax purposes, businesses must respect the definitions set out in the *Plan Comptable Général* (General Accounting Plan—PCG) to the extent that they are not incompatible with the tax base (*l'assiette d'impôt*). This emphasises the significance of accounting for tax purposes.

The many Case II connections between tax and accounting reflect the historical development of tax and accounting rules in France (Frydlender and Pham, 1995; Mikol, 1995). Tax influence on company financial reporting can be illustrated by a consideration of the rules concerning accounting for tax-deductible or regulatory provisions (*provisions reglementées*) and the difference between economic and fiscal depreciation (*amortissements dérogatoires*).

Regulatory provisions are defined in the PCG as provisions which do not correspond to the usual object of a provision[83] and are accounted for as a result of statutory regulations. In effect, these provisions are created for purely tax reasons; they include provisions for price increases in stocks, for exchange rate fluctuations relative to stocks (until 1998), for investment arising from employee share ownership, and for allowable industry-specific provisions. If a business wishes to claim the benefits of these provisions (and fiscally-calculated depre-

ciation), the CGI[84] requires that entries must be made within the financial accounting system of the business. That is, in order to claim accelerated depreciation, the business has to charge it in the profit and loss account (i.e. Case V).

The total depreciation is split between an economic charge to operating expenses and an excess fiscal charge to extraordinary expenses. The 1983 PCG recognised this fiscal occupation of the space of financial accounting by creating a set of account codes to handle these tax requirements. The bookkeeping involves a debit to the extraordinary items caption in the profit and loss account and a credit to a regulatory provisions caption on the capital and liabilities side of the balance sheet.

For normal depreciation expenses, there is also a connection between tax and accounting. The tax rules incorporate a number of specific requirements: the use of zero disposal values; guidelines on useful lives; and pro rata charges for assets bought or sold in the year. These rules seem to be derived from generally accepted commercial practice. Now that they have become tax rules, accountants tend to follow them for convenience; thus, the treatment of normal depreciation is an example of a Case IV tax/accounting relationship.

The general rules for asset valuation in individual company accounts are a clear *de jure* connection (Case II) between tax and accounting rules. The accounting rules[85] set out the general historical cost basis for the valuation of assets, and the wording used is effectively the same in the relevant section of the CGI.[86] However, there are nuances to this general identity. For example, there is a potential divergence between tax and accounting practice in the treatment of interest on borrowings used to finance fixed assets under construction. The accounting rule[87] permits companies to capitalise such interest into the cost of the fixed asset,[88] but such financial costs are excluded for tax purposes. They are to be treated as an expense in the determination of taxable profit[89] and thus an adjustment to accounting profit would be required[90] if a company opted for capitalisation. However, capitalisation is rare in practice (Case IV).

Case II identity exists, for individual company accounts, in the field of inventory valuation. The governing accounting rule[91] allows either FIFO or

[81] There are other reasons for the frequent and detailed changes in tax statute and regulation: for example, pursuit of socio-economic incentives or broader aims; political aims; control of certain kinds of avoidance activities or multinational commercial behaviour.
[82] CGI, Ann. III, art. 38 *quater*.
[83] Defined by CNC Terminology Commission as 'precise in its nature but uncertain as to its impact'.

[84] CGI, art. 39-1-2°.
[85] C. Com. art. 12; *Décret* 83-1020, art. 7; PCG *Titre* II, *Chapitre* III, Section IA.
[86] CGI, Ann. III, art. 38 *quinquies* and *nonies*.
[87] *Décret* 83-1020, art. 7-2°.
[88] A rule extended for consolidated accounts to permit capitalisation into the cost of production of a current asset: *Décret* 86-221, art. D248-8(d).
[89] CGI, Ann. III, at. 38 *quinquies*.
[90] On form N°2058-AN.
[91] C. Comm art. 12.

weighted average cost as methods of stock valuation and these methods are also those allowed for tax purposes.[92] Other situations exist where the tax/accounting identity may be said to derive from general principles. Accounting rules for individual company accounts do not permit the capitalisation of finance leases; indeed, a whole sub-section of the PCG[93] is devoted to accounting for leases which sets out the particular accounting codes to be used. There is no explicit provision in the CGI which considers the issue of capitalisation, and lease payments would thus be classified as an expense, recognised by the PCG, to be deducted in arriving at accounting and taxable profit.[94]

A more complicated relationship exists in circumstances where both accounting rules and tax rules contain options for treatment. Accounting for research and development provides one example. The accounting rules of the Commercial Code and the PCG[95] require such costs to be expensed, although exceptionally (and under certain conditions) applied research and development may be capitalised. The option provided in the Tax Code[96] is expressed slightly differently: at the choice of the enterprise, research and development costs may be either charged against profit or capitalised and then amortised. In this case the tax treatment seems to follow the accounting treatment of the expenditure (Case III). However, the possibility of a reverse effect seems equally to result: the accounting treatment may be chosen with the tax effect in view.

Another example of the complications for the tax/accounting relationship created by options in accounting treatment is accounting for long-term contracts. The accounting rules appear to admit both the completed-contract and percentage-of-completion methods, although there are caveats. According to the general rule set out in the Commercial Code,[97] only realised profits can be recognised in the annual accounts, but a 1985 amendment to the rule[98] permits the inclusion of profit taken on work completed under certain conditions. The PCG[99] has particular accounting requirements when this percentage-of-completion method is used. The tax rules are not clear in this area. The main rule[100] appears to align taxable profit on long-term contracts with the completed-contract method; there seems to be no official consideration of the percentage-of-completion

method, which would generally accelerate tax liabilities. This appears to be a Case I. However given the indeterminacy of both sets of rules, this suggests a Case IV relationship in practice.

There are other instances that more clearly illustrate Case I in that, for tax purposes, adjustments are made to the profit declared in the company's annual accounts. One example has already been mentioned: capitalisation of interest. Similar divergences exist in the treatment of foreign exchange transactions where the provision for transaction losses arising on unsettled foreign currency debtors and creditors required by the PCG[101] is disregarded under the relevant tax rule,[102] and the unsettled transaction loss itself is included in arriving at taxable profit.

Another example which illustrates the struggle for the 'nerve centres' of accounting in France is pension provisions (Mikol, 1995). The central accounting rule contained in the Commercial Code requires pension commitment totals to be included in the notes to the annual accounts. Businesses can decide to make a provision for all or some of these commitments in the balance sheet.[103] However, the relevant provision of the CGI[104] specifically forbids the deduction of provisions relating to pensions; indeed, at one stage the tax authorities sought to bar the creation of pension provisions within company accounts (Scheid and Walton, 1992:223–4). Given the current divergence of accounting and tax rules, an adjustment for tax purposes is made to accounting profit where such provisions have been created. In practice, French companies do not generally make pension provisions in their accounts (Case IV).

The accounting treatment of changes in accounting policy or the correction of errors is to absorb the changes in the current year's income.[105] The tax treatment, however, is a little more complicated. For changes in accounting policy made in accordance with accounting law by managerial decision (*décisions de gestion régulières*) it appears that tax treatment follows accounting treatment (Case III), although it should be noted that the force of the accounting principle of the permanence of accounting methods in France[106] may, in practice, restrict the possibilities for companies to change their accounting policies. For the correction of errors, the situation is a little different. The

---

[92] D. adm. 4A-252 § 6.
[93] PCG, *Titre* II, *Chapitre* III, *Section* IIA4.
[94] CGI, art. 39-1.
[95] C. Com. art. D.19. PCG, *Titre* II, *Chapitre* III, *Section* IA (Code 203).
[96] CGI, art. 236-1.
[97] C. Com. art. 15.
[98] L85-31.
[99] PCG, *Titre* II, *Chapitre* III, *Section* IIB4.
[100] CGI, art. 38-2-*bis*.

[101] PCG, *Titre* II, *Chapitre* I, *Section* IC. The loss is shown in the balance sheet as an 'asset'.
[102] CGI, art. 38-4. Table 2058-A requires cancellation of the provision and substitution of the unsettled loss.
[103] C. com. art. 9, modified by L85-695.
[104] CGI, art. 39-1-5°.
[105] C. Com. art. 13; PCG, *Titre* II, *Chapitre* I, *Section* II. A recent CNC opinion (June 1997) has suggested that such changes and corrections should be treated as a prior period adjustment.
[106] C. com. art. 11.

impact of such corrections upon accounting profit must be eliminated in arriving at taxable profit (Case I);[107] adjustments would be made to earlier years' assessments.

For the most part the above discussion has focused on the tax/accounting relationship in French individual company accounts. However, a different kind of relationship exists for consolidated accounts. Statutory requirements for the publication of consolidated accounts only arrived in France with the enactment of the EU Seventh Directive—much later than in the UK or Germany. Although the French tax system has special tax *régimes* available for groups (e.g. *régime de l'integration fiscale*) the constitution of these groups is different from the requirements for the establishment of consolidated accounts. The French legislation enacting the Seventh Directive[108] took the opportunity to permit a flexibility of accounting rules for consolidation which removed the intimate tax/accounting relationship required for individual company accounts, and recognised the benefits for large multinational French companies of having internationally-comparable consolidated financial reports (*Gardes des Sceaux*, quoted by Corre, 1987:47).

Individual company accounts prepared according to the rules and definitions of the PCG, not consolidated accounts, are the starting point for the calculation of taxable profit. This flexibility and 'international orientation' are possible because no tax implications flow from consolidation for financial reporting purposes. Disconnections possible under the legislation are several:

(i)   tangible fixed assets and inventories may be valued at replacement cost;
(ii)   inventories may be valued using the LIFO method;
(iii) capitalised interest may be included in the cost of current assets under construction;
(iv)   finance leases may be capitalised;[109] and
(v)   unsettled gains on foreign currency monetary balances may be recognised as income.

In addition, the legislation requires the elimination of the effect of fiscal intrusions into the preparation of company annual accounts (specifically, in connection with investment grants, regulatory provisions and depreciation).[110] In practice, a number of large French groups do take advantage of these specific disconnections in order to move their groups accounts approximately or completely in accordance with US rules or international ac-

counting standards (Cauvin Angleys Saint-Pierre, 1996:177–182).

In summary, there are many examples of strong tax influences upon accounting for individual companies in France, but these influences can be substantially modified in the construction of consolidated financial reports.

3.4. Germany

As noted in the introduction, the context of this paper is largely the statutory annual accounts of individual tax-paying companies. For Germany, as for France, special comments for consolidated financial statements are relevant, and these are made at the end of this section.

The formal relationship between German tax and accounting rules is that the former rest on the latter (Ordelheide and Pfaff, 1994:81). There are many instances of this Case III conformity: for example, sales, wages, interest payments, research and development costs, and the compulsory accrual for repairs in the first three months of the following year.[111] Another example of Case III is the tax treatment of changes in accounting policy and the correction of fundamental errors. This follows the accounting treatment, which is to absorb the changes in the year's income. This conforms to the *Handelsgesetzbuch* (HGB) principle[112] that the opening balance sheet should be last year's closing balance sheet. In some arenas (e.g. long-term contracts and foreign currency transactions), the accounting rule is derived from the principles of the HGB, and then Case III follows.

However, it is also easy to find instances of Cases IV and V, where accounting practice chooses to follow tax rules for various reasons:

(a)   for simplicity, in order to have a unified tax and accounting statements (*Einheitsbilanz*);
(b)   for simplicity, to reduce the differences between the tax and accounting statements;
(c)   following an option in the HGB, in order to gain tax relief;
(d)   following a tax rule in the absence of other rules, in order to gain tax relief; or
(e)   breaking *Grundsätze ordnungsmässiger Buchführung* (GoB),[113] with the permission of the HGB, in order to gain tax relief.

Areas of practice illustrating types (a) and (b) above include asset and liability recognition options in the HGB where there is no option for tax purposes. These accounting options might be considered as examples of 'disconnections', except that in practice most German companies choose to fall under (a) and nearly all the rest choose to fall under (b) for their individual company ac-

---

[107] C.E. 17 *mai* 1982, n°23559.
[108] *Loi* 85-11, *Décret* 86-221.
[109] *Décret* 86-221, art. D248-8.
[110] *Décret* 86-221, art. D248-6(c). This specific mention in legislation of the need to correct tax intrusions into consolidated accounts reflects the provisions of Article 29(5) of the EC Seventh Directive.

[111] HGB § 249(1).
[112] HGB § 252(1)1.
[113] Principles of proper accounting.

counts. In more detail, decisions of the highest tax court, the *Bundesfinanzhof* (BFH) (in 1969) hold that various HGB options to capitalise assets must be taken for tax purposes and various options for the recognition of liabilities must not be. An example of the former is discount on a debt,[114] which must be capitalised for tax purposes. An example of the latter is accruals for repairs to be carried out between three and 12 months after the year end,[115] which cannot be recognised for tax purposes. An exception to the asset rule relates to business start-up expenses, which must be expenses for tax purposes and are therefore generally treated as expenses for accounting purposes, although they do not have to be.[116]

Similarly, in practice, many companies adhere to the tax rules for financial reporting purposes in the following areas:
(i)   use of the tax law's 15-year write-off period for non-consolidation purchased goodwill, rather than the four-year period found in commercial rules (unless a longer period can be justified);[117]
(ii)   the tax law's maximum rate of 30% for declining balance depreciation is in practice not usually exceeded for accounting purposes;
(iii) the use of inventory flow assumptions (e.g. average cost, FIFO or LIFO)[118] generally coincide for tax and accounting, although they do not have to;[119]
(iv)   the accounting option to include production overheads[120] is generally taken up following the tax requirement to include them;
(v)   the accounting option to provide for pension commitments relating to the period before 1987 is generally not taken up; and
(vi)   the tax decrees of the Ministry of Finance are followed for determining if a lease should be capitalised (Ordelheide and Pfaff, 1994:124).

An example of type (c) (following an HGB option in order to get tax relief) is the writing down of an asset below cost.[121]

Examples of type (d) (following a tax option in the absence of other rules, in order to get tax relief) include the common accounting practices of:
(i)   the use of maximum depreciation rates allowed by tax law;

(ii)   changing depreciation method[122] from reducing balance to straight-line for an asset when this would increase the expense;
(iii) expensing items that cost less than DM800;[123]
(iv)   charging six months' depreciation on assets bought in the first half of the year and a full year's depreciation on assets bought in the second half;[124]
(v)   discounting of non-interest-bearing long-term debtors;
(vi)   calculation of pension expenses on the basis of interest rates and other assumptions in tax rules (Seckler, 1992: 238–9); and
(vii) taking federal grants to income immediately because they are not taxable, whereas other grants are deducted from the related assets and therefore taken to income (and taxable income) more slowly.

Examples of type (e) (breaking GoB in order to gain tax relief) include:
(i)   the lack of re-instatement of historical cost[125] even when a previous write-down is no longer necessary; and
(ii)   using accelerated depreciation as allowed for certain assets or in certain regions.[126]

In terms of the five cases, types (a) to (d) seem to be examples of Case IV (tax rules followed instead of other acceptable financial reporting rules). However, type (e), although 'voluntary', seems to be an example of Case V (tax rule followed instead of a conflicting financial reporting rule). One could argue that the arena of lease accounting (as noted above) is another example of Case V. The HGB is unclear but the decrees of the Ministry of Finance are followed rather than the guidance of the *Institut der Wirtschaftsprüfer*. However, classification as Case V would rely on treating the *Institut*'s guidance as an accounting 'rule' which may be inappropriate. Therefore, we retain the Case IV classification.

By contrast, there are some specific disconnections between German accounting and tax rules where practice actually does diverge (Case I). These might be split into those instances where practice *sometimes* diverges and those where it *must*. The examples of types (a) to (e) above are not included here because practice tends not to diverge. However, an example where it sometimes

---

[114] HGB § 250(3).
[115] HGB § 249(1).
[116] HGB § 269.
[117] EStG § 7(1) as opposed to HGB § 255(4).
[118] HGB § 240(4) and § 256.
[119] Brooks and Mertin (1993: E13) suggest that, when prices rise, companies might use average cost for tax purposes and FIFO for financial reporting.
[120] HGB § 255(2).
[121] Allowed by HGB § 253(2) and EStG § 6.

[122] Incidentally, the BFH held in 1990 that conformity between tax and accounting was required for the method of depreciation, not merely the amount (BStBl, 1990 s. 681).
[123] See § 6, para. 2 of EStG.
[124] Art. 44, para. 2, *Einkommensteuer-Richtlinien*.
[125] With the permission of HGB § 280.
[126] There is an option to show the credit entry for this not against the asset but in a special balance sheet caption called *Sonderposten mit Rücklageanteil*, which might be interpreted as partly reserves and partly deferred tax.

does diverge is where a company feels obliged to make certain provisions which are not sufficiently concrete to be deductible for tax purposes. Instances where tax and accounting *must* diverge include expenses which are not tax deductible, including (i) certain fines, (ii) 20% of entertainment expenses, (iii) charitable and political donations above certain maxima, and (iv) half the fees of members of the supervisory board.

In summary, there are many examples of the influence of tax on accounting in Germany. However, some large companies choose to use different accounting policies in their consolidated financial statements in order to reduce this influence. Major examples of this are the annual reports of Bayer and Schering for 1994 onwards, where International Accounting Standards (IASs) have been followed by choosing appropriate options from the HGB. Other companies (e.g. Hoechst) have subsequently adopted this practice for 1995 onwards. A further development is that Deutsche Bank used IASs for a supplementary set of group accounts for 1995, and Daimler-Benz used US rules for a supplementary set in 1996.

Clearly, the choice of accounting policies for the group accounts· of certain large German companies is driven by factors which override the influence of taxation. However, in some cases, these effects are seen particularly in non-statutory supplementary accounts (e.g. Deutsche Bank, Daimler-Benz) and, in other cases, the effects are not typical of German accounting in general (e.g. Bayer, Hoechst). As in the case of France, these effects are only apparent in the group accounts of certain large companies, although (at the time of writing)[127] there is no formal mechanism in Germany for the use of different rules.

4. Comparative analysis

In the opening section of this paper we set ourselves the task of investigating the claim that there is a clear distinction between Anglo-Saxon countries and some continental European countries with respect to the degree of connection between taxation and financial reporting. In this final section, we summarise our comparative analyses of the degree of linkage between tax rules and financial reporting in our four countries, and suggest some ways in which our analysis could be applied and extended.

Cases I and II have been defined as those where tax rules or considerations do not determine financial reporting practice in the sense of accounting

[127] In 1996, draft laws were in preparation in both Germany and France to allow the group accounts of certain companies to depart from national laws in order to follow other approved rules (e.g. US or IASC principles). In early 1998, laws were passed in both cases.

policy choices by managers. The Cases are distinguishable in that Case I involves different tax and financial reporting practices whereas Case II involves the same practices. Case III (accounting leads) is less clear. Where the financial reporting rule is precise, there may be little room for tax influence, but where there is vagueness or an option, then tax considerations may dominate. Cases IV and V involve clearer tax prominence. Table 3 summarises by country the distinct Cases of linkage previously reported in detail in Table 2. There are, of course, other areas of accounting where all four countries would score III. For example, the German requirement for *Massgeblichkeit* means that Case III applies in principle.

In Table 3 we see relatively numerous Case I disconnections between tax and financial reporting in the UK and the US, and relatively numerous Case IV and Case V relationships for Germany. The suggestion is clear that the influence of tax on operational accounting policy choice is least in the UK and the US and greatest in Germany, with France in between. This is supported by more Cases II and fewer Cases III for the UK and the US than for Germany. If the uncertainty of Case III is addressed by adding it to Cases IV and V, then the conclusion remains the same. Of course, the scoring in Table 3 assumes an equal weight for the 18 arenas or sub-arenas chosen, and rests upon the particular arenas chosen. However, inspection reveals that assigning any other reasonable weightings would make little difference to the order of countries. Further, as noted above, adding more arenas would generally add more Cases III rather than more Cases I, IV or V, which are the clearest arenas of international variation. This assessment has been made at a particular point in time. Variations in the assessment over time could also be measured.

In summary, it is possible to distinguish our two Anglo-Saxon countries from our two continental European countries on the grounds of relatively low and relatively high tax influence on financial reporting in a contemporary operational sense. Consequently, we find some support for the hypothesis that it is possible to distinguish 'Anglo-Saxon' from 'continental European' countries according to the relative strength of tax influence on accounting policy choice. However, France, too may be clearly distinguished from Germany, and US and UK patterns of influence may be distinguished from one another.

This distinct modelling of tax-accounting interrelations—'Anglo-Saxon' and 'continental European'—is also in concurrence with a number of German and French commentators (e.g. Quéré, 1994:71; Haller, 1992:321; Gélard, 1990:15), that German accounting is especially tax-influenced. However, the recognition of such models should not be allowed to obscure the complex pattern of reciprocal influence between taxation practice and financial reporting practice in all four countries studied. In Section 3, we noted some examples of the changes in the relationship between tax and accounting practice over time. More examples are given in a paper which concentrates on this historical relationship (Lamb et al., 1995). More generally, focus on national models draws attention away from the richness and variety of changing patterns of tax influence.[128] Despite this caveat and the shifting nature of the relationships in the various countries, a stable pattern seems to be clear in each country and therefore comparatively.

The main change in the pattern relates to group accounting in France and Germany. Table 3 does not record the more complex position for group accounting in France and Germany. In both countries, the law allows group accounts to use different accounting policies from those used by the parent. Further, the previous section records how French law allows specific changes from individual company accounting to consolidated accounting. As a result there have been examples in France over many years of reduction of tax influence in group accounts.[129] Such an approach is clear for a few German companies from the mid-1990s.

One policy implication arising from our studies is that accounting harmonisation efforts in the world or in the EU would be more likely to succeed if focused on group accounts (cf. FEE, 1993 and Biener, 1995). The deeply entrenched links between tax and accounting and the large number of Case IV and V arenas in certain countries seem to make harmonisation more difficult for individual company accounts.

In conclusion, we suggest that it may be more fruitful to compare systems of financial accounting according to the reciprocal patterns of influence and interrelations between tax and accounting, rather than to label such systems according to national, and to some extent out-of-date, stereotypes. One thing that we have clearly observed is that the degree and nature of tax influence on accounting changes over time, as do international patterns of similarity and dissimilarity. The assessment method adopted in our analysis of the influence of taxation on accounting could be used in a historical context 'to trace patterns of divergence and convergence over time' (Roberts, 1995) and to better link 'cross-temporal and cross-spatial variance' in accounting practices (Christiansen and McLeay, 1995:7). The extension of our approach to a wider range of countries could, of course, increase the richness of the comparative analysis.

References

Biener, H. (1995). *Statement to the Board of the IASC*. Amsterdam, May.

Bittker, B. I. and Loklan, L. (1989). *Federal taxation of income, estates and gifts*. Boston: Warren, Gorham and Lamont.

Brooks, J. and Mertin, D. (1993). *Deutsches Bilanzrecht*. Düsseldorf: IDW-Verlag.

Cauvin Angleys Saint-Pierre (1996). *L'information Financière, 100 Groupes Industriels et Commerciaux*. Paris: CPC Meylan.

Christiansen, M. and McLeay, S. (1995). 'A prisoner of the state: comparative cross-national research in accounting'. Paper presented at the EAA Congress, Birmingham, May.

Corre, J. (1987). *Les Nouvelles Règles de la Consolidation des Bilans*. Paris: Dunod.

Fédération des Experts Comptables Européens (FEE) (1993). *The Seventh Directive and Harmonisation. Seventh Directive Options and Their Implementation*. London: Routledge.

Freedman, J. (1987). 'Profit and prophets—law and accountancy practice on the timing of receipts—recognition under the earnings basis (Schedule D, Cases I and II)'. *British Tax Review*, 2: 61–79; 3: 104–33.

Freedman, J. (1993). 'Ordinary principles of commercial accounting—clear guidance or a mystery tour?'. *British Tax Review*, 6: 468–78.

---

[128]Further, undue focus on models defined by reference to nations may obscure important patterns of international diffusion of practices. Christiansen and McLeay (1995: 7) argue that 'the central problem of comparative research [is] linking cross-temporal and cross-spatial variance'; 'encompassing comparisons' that allow comparative research to escape being the 'prisoner of the state' are likely to be most appropriate in their view.

[129] The survey of the practices of large French groups illustrates this. See Cauvin Angleys Saint-Pierre (1996).

Table 3
Cases of linkage in certain material arenas of financing reporting for individual companies

	UK	US	France	Germany
Case I	12	11.5	4.5	2
Case II	2	2.5	5	0
Case III	3	2	3.5	7.5
Case IV	0	1	4	6.5
Case V	0	0	1	2
N/A	1	1	0	0

Note: Each of the 18 arenas or sub-arenas is weighted as one. Therefore, the total for each country should, and does, equal 18

Frydlender, A. and Pham, D. (1996). 'Relationships between accounting and taxation in France'. *European Accounting Review*, 5, Supplement: 845–857.

Gélard, G. (1990). 'La prudence en droit comptable allemand, la notion d'actif et la possibilité d'activer des charges'. *Revue Française de la Comptabilité*, 216, October: 15.

Godshalk, R. (1994). 'Financial statement conformity no longer required in change in accounting method consent letter'. *Tax Adviser*, March: 159.

Green, S. (1995). 'Accounting standards and tax law: complexity, dynamism and divergence'. *British Tax Review*, 6: 445–51.

Haller, A. (1992). 'The relationship of financial and tax accounting in Germany: a major reason for accounting disharmony in Europe'. *International Journal of Accounting*, 27: 10–23.

Hoogendoorn, M. N. (1996). 'Accounting and taxation in Europe—a comparative overview'. *European Accounting Review*, 5, Supplement: 783–94.

Lamb, M. (1995). 'When is a group a group? Convergence of concepts of "group" in European Union corporate tax'. *European Accounting Review*, 4(1): 33–78.

Lamb, M. (1996). 'The relationship between accounting and taxation: the United Kingdom'. *European Accounting Review*, 5, Supplement: 933–49.

Lamb, M., Nobes, C. and Roberts, A. (1995). 'The influence of taxation on accounting: international variations'. University of Reading Discussion Paper, No. 46, first half.

Melville, A. (1997). *Taxation—Finance Act 1997*. London: Pitman.

Mikol, A. (1995). 'The history of financial reporting in France' in Walton, P. (ed.), *European Financial Reporting: A History*. London: Academic Press.

Muray, R. and Small, D. (1995). 'Welcoming the dawn'. *The Tax Journal*, 16 February: 18–9.

Nobes, C. W. and Parker, R. (1995). *Comparative International Accounting* (4th ed.). Hemel Hempstead: Prentice Hall.

Ordelheide, D. and Pfaff, D. (1994). *European Financial Reporting: Germany*. London: Routledge.

Quéré, B. (1994). ' Le principe allemand de préponderance du bilan commercial sur le bilan fiscal et ses effects comptable'. *Revue Française de da Comptabilité*, March: 64–71.

Radcliffe, G. (1993). 'The relationship between tax law and accounting principles in the United Kingdom and France'. *Irish Journal of Taxation*, 1: 1–20.

Ricks, W. (1982). 'The market's responses to the 1974 LIFO adoptions'. *Journal of Accounting Research*, Autumn: 367–87.

Roberts, A. (1995). 'The very idea of classification in international accounting'. *Accounting Organizations and Society*, 20, No. 7/8.

Scheid, J.-C. and Walton, P. (1992). *European Financial Reporting: France*. London: Routledge.

Seckler, G. (1992). 'Germany' in D. Alexander and S. Archer, *European Accounting Guide*. London: Academic Press.

Sunder, S. (1973). 'Relationship between accounting changes in stock prices: problems of measurement and some empirical evidence'. *Empirical Research in Accounting: Selected Studies*: 1–45.

Sunder, S. (1975). 'Stock price and risk related accounting changes in inventory valuation'. *Accounting Review*, April: 305–14.

Taxes (1995). 'Revenue provide guidance on acceptability of accounting practices'. 28 April: 513–14.

Walton, P. (1993). 'Links between financial reporting and taxation in the United Kingdom: a myth explored'. Paper presented at the EAA Congress, Turkü, April.

Watts, R. L. and Zimmerman, J. L. (1979). 'The demand for and supply of accounting theories: the market for excuses'. *Accounting Review*, April: 273–304. [Reprinted in Bloom, R. and Elgers, P. T., *Accounting Theory and Policy: A Reader*. New York: Harcourt Brace Jovanovich, 1987: 22–57].

Whittington, Geoffrey (1995). 'Tax policy and accounting standards'. *British Tax Review*, 5: 452–6.

ABACUS, Vol. 34, No. 2, 1998

CHRISTOPHER NOBES

Towards a General Model of the Reasons for International Differences in Financial Reporting

The article first examines the existing modelling literature, which contains a large number of suggested reasons for international differences in accounting. After examining terminological problems, a preliminary parsimonious model is developed to explain the initial split of accounting systems into two classes. The term 'accounting system' is used here to mean the financial reporting practices used by an enterprise. A country might exhibit the use of several such systems in any one year or over time. Consequently, it should be systems and not countries that are classified. The model proposes a two-way classification using two variables: the strengths of equity markets and the degree of cultural dominance. Implications for classifiers and rule-makers are suggested.

Key words: Classification; International accounting.

INTRODUCTION AND PREVIOUS MODELLING

Many reasons have been suggested in the literature for international differences in financial reporting. Some authors state that they are merely listing plausible reasons; few provide precise hypotheses or tests of them, as noted by Meek and Saudagaran (1990). Wallace and Gernon (1991) complain about the lack of theory in international comparative accounting. This article seeks to address this.

The literature (e.g., Choi and Mueller, 1992, ch. 2; Radebaugh and Gray, 1993, ch. 3; Belkaoui, 1995, ch. 2; Nobes and Parker, 1995, ch. 1) offers a large number of possible reasons for international differences (see Table 1) but no general theory linking the factors. Schweikart (1985) and Harrison and McKinnon (1986) provide some elements of a general theory, without specifying which factors are major explanatory variables for accounting practices. Two somewhat similar theoretical models of the reasons for accounting differences are those of Gray (1988) and of Doupnik and Salter (1995; hereafter DS). Gray suggests a model based on cultural factors, as examined later. DS provide a synthesis of previous discussions, leading to a framework, which is simplified here as in Figure 1 so that an alternative can

---

CHRISTOPHER NOBES is Coopers & Lybrand Professor of Accounting at the University of Reading.
The author is grateful for helpful comments on earlier drafts from Michael Page, Bob Parker, Alan Roberts and Autar Singh, and from the editor and the referees of this journal.

INTERNATIONAL DIFFERENCES IN FINANCIAL REPORTING

TABLE 1

REASONS PREVIOUSLY PROPOSED FOR INTERNATIONAL ACCOUNTING
DIFFERENCES

---

1   Nature of business ownership and financing system
2   Colonial inheritance
3   Invasions
4   Taxation
5   Inflation
6   Level of education
7   Age and size of accountancy profession
8   Stage of economic development
9   Legal systems
10 Culture
11 History
12 Geography
13 Language
14 Influence of theory
15 Political systems, social climate
16 Religion
17 Accidents

FIGURE 1

A SIMPLIFICATION OF DS'S MODEL OF DEVELOPMENT

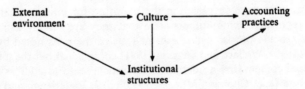

Source: Adapted from Doupnik and Salter (1995), exhibit 1.

be proposed later. One difficulty emerging from Figure 1 is that four of DS's ten variables (see Table 2) are cultural (based on Gray) and six are institutional, but culture is seen as giving rise to the institutions. This suggests the possibility of double counting. A related difficulty with DS is that there is no attempt to connect their six institutional factors to see whether they might cause each other. In particular, it is suggested later that four of the six (taxation, inflation, level of education and stage of economic development) are not necessary. DS thus have provided a mix of theories, not a general theory.

A number of terminological issues are raised by studying this literature. These need to be addressed before attempting to develop a general model.

163

TABLE 2

DS'S INDEPENDENT VARIABLES

Cultural	Institutional
Individualism	Legal system
Power distance	Capital market
Uncertainty avoidance	Tax
Masculinity	Inflation levels
	Level of education
	Level of economic development

SOME TERMINOLOGICAL ISSUES

One of the problems of identifying reasons for differences, and perhaps then classifying accounting systems, is a lack of clarity about what is being examined or classified. This article discusses accounting *practices*, using 'accounting' to mean published financial reporting. In some jurisdictions, the *rules* of financial reporting may be identical, or very similar, to the practices, but sometimes a company may depart from rules or may have to make choices in the absence of rules. The Price Waterhouse data, used by many researchers,[1] seem to contain a mix of *de facto* and *de jure* aspects 'in a perplexing way' (Rahman *et al.*, 1996).

Another difficulty concerns the word 'system' (Roberts, 1995). DS use it to cover such things as regulatory agencies. Others (e.g., Nair and Frank, 1980) have concentrated on a corpus of accounting rules or practices. This article follows the latter route, that is, an 'accounting system' is a set of practices used in a published annual report. Although this is a narrow definition, these practices will reflect the wider context in which they operate.

Another issue is whether to separate disclosure from measurement practices. Nair and Frank (1980) show that this can be important. Nobes (1983) looks at measurement practices only. DS acknowledge the distinction but add the categories together. It seems appropriate to include the presence or absence of certain key disclosures (e.g., earnings per share, cash flow statements) as elements of a system, and this is discussed later.

A further issue is to determine whose accounting practices are being examined. The Price Waterhouse data seem, in practice, to have reported on companies audited by Price Waterhouse (see Nobes, 1981). DS (p. 198) specify the measurement and disclosure practices of 'companies', which is vague, particularly for disclosure practices. Nobes (1983, p. 5) chose the measurement practices of 'public companies', which the context suggests meant those with securities which are traded publicly.

A related point is that all the researchers look at classifications of *countries* by their accounting environments or systems. Roberts (1995) highlighted this problem,

---

[1] For example, Da Costa *et al.* (1978); Frank (1979); Nair and Frank (1980).

INTERNATIONAL DIFFERENCES IN FINANCIAL REPORTING

noting that a country could have more than one system, for example, one system for companies with publicly traded securities, and another for small private companies.[2] Similarly, some large public companies may adopt very different practices from what is 'normal' for most large companies in the country. This is becoming especially obvious in continental Europe, with the use of U.S. rules or International Accounting Standards (IAS) by some very large companies. Therefore, it may be useful to refer to a country's 'dominant accounting system', which might be defined as that used by enterprises encompassing the majority[3] of the country's economic activity. Hereafter, references to a country's 'system' should be taken to mean its dominant system.

In some countries, the law requires or commercial pressures dictate that a large number of companies use the same system. For example, in the U.K., most provisions of the Companies Act 1985 and of accounting standards apply to all companies. In other countries, a particular accounting system might be legally or commercially imposed on a small minority of companies, as in the U.S. where 'generally accepted accounting principles' are legally imposed on only that small proportion of companies registered with the Securities and Exchange Commission. In both these rather different cases, there is still clearly a dominant system as defined above.

Nevertheless, as there can be more than one system in a country it would be more useful to specify accounting systems, and then to note that particular companies in particular countries at particular dates are using them. Of course, for labelling purposes, it might be useful to refer, for example, to the system used in 1998 by U.S. public companies. With labels, it will then be possible to identify separate influences on, and to show separate places in the classification for, for example, 'normal' German public companies in 1998, compared to the group accounts of such companies as Daimler-Benz, Deutsche Bank and Bayer in 1998.

Also, a country's accounting system may change dramatically over time, for example, as a result of economic or political revolutions (c.f. China, Russia, Poland, etc.). Less dramatically, accounting in a country can change quite significantly as a result of new laws (e.g., Spain from the late 1980s as a consequence of EC Directives).[4]

Lastly, companies in two countries (e.g., the U.K. and Ireland) can use extremely similar accounting practices (i.e., perhaps the same 'system'). In a similar manner to the characteristics of human individuals, the detailed elements of a company's accounting practices can differ so much that the number of different sets of practices is effectively infinite. Nevertheless, it is useful for some purposes to recognize that humans all belong to the same species. The individual members

[2]   I am grateful to my colleague, Autar Singh, for discussions that clarified my thoughts on this.

[3]   Researchers would have to decide whether to start from the smallest enterprise or from the largest. Presumably, it would make sense to start from the largest, since this would involve far fewer enterprises, and since the small enterprises would not be publishing any financial reports in most countries.

[4]   See, for example, Gonzalo and Gallizo (1992), ch. 3.

of the species are all different but have certain features in common. By analogy, a certain degree of variation among company practices may be allowed without having to abandon the idea that the companies are all using the same system.

AN INITIAL STATEMENT OF A GENERAL MODEL

The proposal here, which will be explained more fully later, is that the major reason for international differences in financial reporting is different purposes for that reporting.

Financing Systems
In particular, at a country level, it is suggested that the financing system is relevant in determining the purpose of financial reporting. Zysman (1983) distinguishes between three types of financing system: (a) *capital market based*, in which prices are established in competitive markets; (b) *credit-based system: governmental*, in which resources are administered by the government; and (c) *credit-based system: financial institutions*, in which banks and other financial institutions are dominant.

Zysman suggested that the U.K. and the U.S.A. have a type (a) system; France and Japan a type (b) system; and Germany a type (c) system. According to Zysman, in all systems companies rely considerably on their own profits for capital but their external sources of funds differ. Where external long-term finance is important, securities are the main source in the capital market system. In such countries, there is a wide range of capital instruments and of financial institutions, and the latter have an arm's-length relationship with companies. Investors change their holdings through the secondary securities markets, which are large. In credit-based systems, the capital market is smaller, so companies are more reliant on whoever grants credit. This usually means banks, whether under the influence of governments or not. Cable (1985) examined the importance of banks in the German economic system. In this system, investors will find it more difficult to adjust their holdings, so they may be more interested in long-run control of the management.

For the purposes of this article, a development of the Zysman classification is proposed, as in Table 3. For this, the concept of 'insider' and 'outsider' financiers needs to be developed. This idea of insiders and outsiders, which has its roots in the finance literature, has been used before for accounting purposes (e.g., see Nobes, 1988, p. 31), and to discuss contrasting corporate governance systems (e.g., Franks and Mayer, 1992; Kenway, 1994). 'Outsiders' are not members of the board of directors and do not have a privileged relationship with the company (e.g., such

TABLE 3

FINANCING SYSTEMS

	Strong credit	Strong equity
Insiders dominant	I	III
Outsiders dominant	II	IV

166

INTERNATIONAL DIFFERENCES IN FINANCIAL REPORTING

as that enjoyed by a company's banker who is also a major shareholder). They include both private individual shareholders and some institutions. For example, insurance companies and unit trusts normally have widely diversified portfolios, so that any particular holding does not constitute a large proportion of a company's capital. Therefore, such institutions should perhaps be counted as outsiders. By contrast, 'insiders' such as governments, banks, families and other companies are all likely to have close, long-term relationships with their investees. This will involve the private provision of timely and frequent accounting information.

Both of Zysman's credit-based systems fall into category I of Table 3. Category II (a credit-based system with a large amount of listed debt with outsider owners) is plausible but uncommon. A possible example is discussed near the end of this subsection. Category III is an equity-based system where most shares are owned by insiders. In Japan, for example, there are large numbers of listed companies and a large equity market capitalisation, but the shares are extensively owned by banks and other companies (Nobes and Parker, 1995, p. 9 and ch. 13).

Category IV systems involve important equity markets with large numbers of outsider shareholders. In these systems there will be a demand for public disclosure and for external audit because most providers of finance have no involvement in management and no private access to financial information. This is the classic setting of most of the finance literature (e.g., Jensen and Meckling, 1976; Beaver, 1989). More recently, a connection between more disclosure and lower cost of equity capital has been examined in such a context (Botosan, 1997). Pursuing this line, this article suggests that the key issue for financial reporting is the existence or otherwise of such Category IV financing. Ways of measuring this are proposed below.

In a particular country, there may be elements of several of these four systems. For example, small companies are unlikely to be financed by a Category IV system in any country. However, for the moment, let us assume that the economic activity in any country is dominated by one particular financing system. The hypothesis predicting a correlation between the style of corporate financing and the type of accounting system is that the rule-makers for, and the preparers of, financial reports in equity-outsider (Category IV) countries are largely concerned with the outside users. The conceptual frameworks used by the rule-makers of the U.S., the U.K., Australia and the IASC[5] make it clear that this is so. In particular, they state that they are concerned with reporting financial performance and enabling the prediction of future cash flows for relatively sophisticated outside users of financial statements of large companies. By contrast, credit-based countries (mostly Category I) will be more concerned with the protection of creditors and therefore with the prudent calculation of distributable profit. Their financiers (insiders) will not need externally audited, published reports. This difference of purpose will lead to differences in accounting practices. The less common categories (II and III) will be discussed later.

[5]   Statements of Financial Accounting Concepts of the FASB, particularly SFAC 1, *Objectives*; the similar chapter 1 of the ASB's draft *Statement of Principles; Statements of Accounting Concepts* of Australia; and the IASC's *Framework for the Preparation and Presentation of Financial Statements*, para. 15.

TABLE 4

EXAMPLES OF FEATURES OF THE TWO ACCOUNTING CLASSES

Feature	Class A	Class B
Provisions for depreciation and pensions	Accounting practice differs from tax rules	Accounting practice follows tax rules
Long-term contracts	Percentage of completion method	Completed contract method
Unsettled currency gains	Taken to income	Deferred or not recognised
Legal reserves	Not found	Required
Profit and loss format	Expenses recorded by function (e.g., cost of sales)	Expenses recorded by nature (e.g., total wages)
Cash flow statements	Required	Not required, found only sporadically
Earnings per share disclosure	Required by listed companies	Not required, found only sporadically

Empirical researchers would need to establish relevant measures to distinguish the categories (as done, for example, by La Porta *et al.*, 1997). These might include the number of domestic listed companies in a country (or this deflated by size of population), the equity market capitalization (or this deflated by GDP), and the proportion of shares held by 'outsiders'. Although the boundary between the types of financing system may sometimes be unclear (as in many of the classifications in social science, languages, law or, even, biology), the contrast between a strong equity-outsider system and other systems should be clear enough, as the Appendix demonstrates for some countries.

Financial Reporting Systems
It is proposed that financial reporting systems should be divided initially into two classes, for the moment labelled as A and B. Class A corresponds to what some have called Anglo-Saxon accounting and Class B to continental European. To assist researchers in measuring a system, some core features of the two systems are suggested in Table 4. For example, systems of Class A will share all, or a large proportion of, the practices shown for that class. Clear examples of actual systems exhibiting *all* of the features exist.[6]

It is proposed that, for developed countries,[7] the extent that a particular country is associated with Class A or Class B accounting is predictable on the basis of its position with respect to financing systems. If the present accounting system was developed in the past, then reference to the past importance of financing systems

---

[6] For example, Australia, the U.S. and the U.K. exhibit *all* the features of Class A, whereas the dominant systems in France, Germany and Italy exhibit *all* the features of Class B (although a few consolidated statements use a different system and depart from some aspects). Most items in Table 4 are covered by the relevant country chapters of Nobes and Parker (1995) or, for example, see Scheid and Walton (1992) for France, or Gordon and Gray (1994) for the UK.

[7] The idea of 'developed' or 'culturally self-sufficient' is examined further later.

INTERNATIONAL DIFFERENCES IN FINANCIAL REPORTING

will be relevant. Strong equity-outsider markets (Category IV) lead to Class A systems; otherwise Class B systems prevail.

Even if a particular country is traditionally associated with weak equity markets and therefore Class B accounting, the country might change. For example, China has been changing in the direction of a strong equity-outsider market and Class A accounting (Chow *et al.*, 1995). However, the accounting might remain stuck in the past for legal or other reasons of inertia. Nevertheless, in some countries, certain companies might be especially commercially affected. They might adopt Class A accounting by using flexibility in the national rules, by breaking national rules, or by producing two sets of financial statements. Some German examples of these routes can be given. Bayer's consolidated financial statements (for 1994 onwards) have used non-typical German rules, that are different from those used in its parent's statements, in order to comply with International Accounting Standards (IAS). Further, officials of the Ministry of Finance have announced that departure from German rules would be 'tolerated' for such group accounts.[8] In the case of Deutsche Bank (e.g., for 1995), two full sets of financial statements were produced, under German rules and IAS, respectively.

A related issue is that, as noted earlier, there are two aspects of financial reporting which can be separated: measurement and disclosure (e.g., Nair and Frank, 1980). Table 4 contains examples of both aspects. As explained below, the measurement issues seem to be driven by the equity/creditor split, and the disclosure issues by the outsider/insider split. The equity/creditor split leads to different kinds of *objectives* for financial reporting. As suggested earlier, systems serving equity markets are required to provide relevant information on performance and the assessment of future cash flows in order to help with the making of financial decisions. Systems in a creditor environment are required to calculate prudent and reliable distributable (and taxable) profit. By contrast, the outsider/insider split leads to different *amounts* of information: where outsiders are important, there is a demand for more published financial reporting.

It has been assumed here that equity financing systems are normally those which are associated with large numbers of outsiders, so that Class A systems are an amalgam of equity and outsider features. However, if there were countries (Category II of Table 3) with large markets for listed debt but not for listed equities, then one might expect a financial reporting system with the high disclosures of Class A but the measurement rules of Class B. Perhaps the closest example of a system with Class B measurement rules but high disclosures is the German system for listed companies.[9] Germany does indeed have an unusually large market in listed debt.[10]

---

[8] Herr Biener of the German Finance Ministry announced this at the board meeting of the International Accounting Standards Committee in Amsterdam in May 1996. In 1998, German law changed in order specifically to allow this.

[9] This feature of German accounting was highlighted by Nair and Frank (1980), who prepared separate classifications based on measurement and disclosure practices.

[10] For example, in 1993, the number of listed bonds in Germany was 13,309, whereas the number in France was 2,516 and in the U.K. 2,725 (data from *European Stock Exchange Statistics*, Annual Report, 1993).

This way of distinguishing between the forces acting on measurement and those acting on disclosure may help to resolve the difficulties of a cultural explanation as discussed by Baydoun and Willett (1995, pp. 82–8).

Category III (equity-insider) financing would not produce Class A accounting because published financial reporting is unimportant. The main financiers may be interested in performance and cash flows but they have access to private 'management' information.

Colonial Inheritance
Some countries are affected by very strong external cultural influences, perhaps due to their small size or underdeveloped state or former colonial status. Such culturally dominated countries are likely to be using an accounting system based on that of the influential country even if this seems inappropriate to their current commercial needs (Hove, 1986).

Colonial inheritance (Factor 2 in Table 1) is probably the major explanatory factor for the general system of financial reporting in many countries outside Europe (Briston, 1978). It is easy to predict how accounting will work in Gambia (British) compared to neighbouring Senegal (French).[11] The same general point applies to Singapore (Briston and Foo, 1990) or Australia (Miller, 1994). Colonial inheritance extends of course to legal systems and to other background and cultural factors, not just to direct imports of accounting (Parker, 1989). Allied to this are the effects of substantial investment from another country, which may lead to accountants and accounting migrating together with the capital.

Another influence is invasions (Factor 3) which may lead to major influence on accounting, as is the case with Japanese,[12] French,[13] and German[14] accounting. However, when the invader retires, any foreign accounting can be gradually removed if it does not suit the country: Japan closed down its Securities and Exchange Commission when the Americans left, whereas France retained its accounting plan in order to aid reconstruction after World War II (Standish, 1990).

WHY OTHER FACTORS MAY BE LESS USEFUL

If the above conclusions are accepted (i.e., that a general two-class model of financial reporting systems can be built which rests on only the importance of financing systems and colonial inheritance), then most of the seventeen factors listed in Table 1 seem unnecessary as explanatory independent variables, at least for the initial two-class classification. This section explains why, starting with DS's factors.

[11] An unpublished PhD thesis by Charles Elad (University of Glasgow, 1993) shows the colonial influences clearly.

[12] Japan's SEC, its structure of Securities Laws and its stock market owe much to U.S. influence during the occupation following World War II.

[13] The distinguishing feature of French accounting, the *plan comptable*, was first adopted in France while under German occupation (Standish, 1995).

[14] The German accounting plan, though copied in France, was abolished by the occupying Western powers after World War II. A version survived in the communist East Germany until reunification.

INTERNATIONAL DIFFERENCES IN FINANCIAL REPORTING

Tax

Previous writers (e.g., Nobes, 1983) have not been helpful by listing tax as one of the major causes of accounting differences. These writers have, in effect, suggested that Class A accounting systems are not dominated by tax rules whereas Class B systems are; and therefore, that the tax difference is one of the reasons for the difference in accounting systems. However, the disconnection of tax from accounting in Class A systems may be seen as a *result* of the existence of a competing purpose for accounting rather than the major cause of international accounting differences. Lamb *et al.* (1995) look at this in detail, concluding that:

1. Rules for the determination of the taxable profit of businesses will be important in all countries (assuming that taxation of profit is significant).
2. Without some major competing purpose for accounting for which tax rules are unsuitable, tax rules made by governments will therefore tend to dominate accounting, so that tax practices and accounting practices are the same (as in Class B).
3. In some countries (or for some companies), there is the major competing purpose of supplying financial reports to equity-outsider markets (for which tax rules are unsuitable). In this case, for many accounting topics, there will be two sets of accounting rules (and practices): tax rules and financial reporting rules (as in Class A).

Consequently, the tax variable is not needed to explain the difference between Class A and Class B systems. Nevertheless, for those systems where tax and accounting are closely linked (Class B), international differences in tax rules do create international accounting differences. However, these are detailed differences *within* a class of accounting systems which all share the major feature of being dominated by tax rules, which is one of the distinguishing marks of the class.

There is a further important connection here. The equity/credit split in financing, as discussed earlier, coincides with the proposed equity-user/tax-user split: accounting systems designed to serve creditors are systems dominated by tax rules. This is because the calculation of the legally distributable profit (to protect creditors) and the calculation of taxable profit are both issues in which governments are interested. The calculation of legally distributable profit is a different purpose from the calculation of taxable profit but it is not 'competing' in the sense of requiring a different set of rules because both calculations benefit from precision in the rules[15] and from the minimization of the use of judgment,[16] which is not the case for the estimation of cash flows.

---

[15]   For example, in both the U.K. and Germany (typical Class A and Class B countries, respectively), there are large numbers of legal cases on the determination of taxable income and some on the determination of distributable income, but there are few or none on the determination of consolidated accounting profit (i.e., cases where there is no tax motivation).

[16]   In the U.K., and recently in the U.S. with SFAS 115, certain assets are revalued above historical cost; and unsettled profits are taken to income (e.g., on long-term contracts and on foreign currency monetary balances). None of this is possible under German law.

Incidentally, DS follow previous writers and suggest that, 'In many countries, tax laws effectively determine accounting practice' (p. 196). However, they then find that tax is not a useful independent variable in explaining accounting differences. It is argued above that tax is not an independent variable for the main classificatory split. DS failed to find even a correlation, probably because they mis-specified the tax variable by using the marginal rate of corporate income taxes. This measure seems inappropriate for several reasons. First, tax rates change dramatically over time, without any obvious effect on accounting (e.g., the top U.S. rate fell from 46 per cent to 34 per cent in 1987; the main rate in the U.K. rose in 1973 from 40 per cent to 52 per cent, and then fell to 33 per cent in 1991). Second, many systems have more than one marginal rate (e.g., in Germany in 1995, 45 per cent for retained profit but 30 per cent for distributed profit; and, in the U.K., 33 per cent for large companies but 25 per cent for small). Third, the tax burden depends greatly on the definition of taxable income not just on the tax rate. More importantly, in countries with a small connection between tax and accounting (typical of Class A), the tax rate will have little effect on accounting; and in countries with a close connection (typical of Class B), the effect of tax on accounting will be in the same direction and probably almost as strong whether the rate is 30 per cent or 50 per cent. For all these reasons, the level of the marginal rate of tax will not help to predict the financial reporting system.

Level of Education
DS's variable here is the percentage of population with tertiary education. It is hard to see how one could explain the major accounting differences on this basis. Can one explain the large accounting differences between, on the one hand, the U.K., the U.S. and the Netherlands (where Class A dominates) and, on the other hand, France, Germany and Italy (where Class B dominates) on the basis of the rather similar levels of tertiary education? Again, can one explain the remarkable similarities between accounting in Malawi, Nigeria and Zimbabwe (Class A countries) and the U.K. (also Class A) on the basis of the rather different levels of tertiary education? Instead there seems to be a connection with the 'colonial inheritance' point, as discussed earlier and as taken up again in the 'level of economic development' point below. Thus it is not surprising that the education variable did not help DS. Previous suggestions related to this factor (e.g., Radebaugh, 1975) seem, more plausibly, to involve the comparison of developed with less developed countries.

Different levels of professional accounting education might be relevant (Shoenthal, 1989), perhaps especially in developing countries (e.g., Parry and Grove, 1990). However, Nobes (1992) casts doubt upon the relevance of this type of factor for classification. To the extent that this is not another issue related to developed versus developing countries, differences in professional education might be covered by Factor 8 in Table 1 (age and size of accountancy profession) and may be a *result* of accounting differences rather than their cause.

INTERNATIONAL DIFFERENCES IN FINANCIAL REPORTING

Level of Economic Development

It is suggested that the key issue here is not the influence of the stage of economic development on financial reporting (as chosen by DS). Gernon and Wallace (1995, p. 64) agree that there is 'no conclusive evidence' about the relationship. The problem is that, while many African countries with a low level of development have accounting systems rather like the U.K.'s, some have completely different accounting systems rather like that in France. By contrast, the U.K. or the Netherlands have a rather similar level of economic development to that of Germany or Italy but completely different accounting systems.

It would seem plausible to argue that, if accounting systems were indigenously created in all countries, then they would develop differently in developed and undeveloped economies. However, it is suggested that this point is largely overridden by the proposition that developing countries are likely to be using an accounting system invented elsewhere. Perhaps the system has been forced on them, or they have borrowed it. Either way, it is usually possible to predict accounting in such countries by looking at the source of the external influences. Therefore, the level of development is not the key predictor for the split between Class A and Class B. Cooke and Wallace (1990) seem to support the distinction between developed and developing countries when it comes to the influence of various environmental factors on accounting.

Legal Systems

For developed Western countries and for many others (e.g., Japan, South America and most of Africa), it is possible to split countries neatly into codified legal systems and common law systems (David and Brierley, 1985). As DS note, this is of great relevance to the regulatory system for accounting. However, there is a high degree of correlation between equity-outsider financing systems and common law countries, and between credit-insider systems and codified law.[17] On the whole, therefore, the same groupings would result from using a legal system variable rather than from using a financing system variable, as DS find. This again suggests the possibility of double counting. The exception of the Netherlands, which raises further doubts about using the legal variable for accounting classification, is explained below.

For culturally dominated countries, both the legal and accounting systems are likely to have been imported from the same place, so the correlation between these two variables is unsurprising. Both factors can be explained by the colonial influence factor, so the legal factor is not needed. For other countries, there may be aspects of the common law system which predispose a country towards the creation of strong equity-outsider systems (La Porta *et al.*, 1997), but going that far back in the causal chain is not necessary for the present model. For present purposes, it may be more useful to specify the legal variable as the regulatory system for accounting rather than the more general legal system. The variable would be

[17]   This is examined in Nobes and Parker (1995, ch. 1).

measured by locating the source of the most detailed accounting regulations. A 0/1 variable would contrast (i) rules made by professional accountants, company directors, independent bodies, stock exchanges and equity market regulators, and (ii) rules made by tax authorities, government ministries (other than those concerned primarily with listed companies) and legal bureaucrats.

Once more, it could be argued that this version of the legal variable is not independent but is dependent on the financing variable. In strong equity-outsider systems, commercial pressure gives the strongest power over financial reporting to group (i) because, since the financial reporting for the equity/outsiders uses separate rules from tax rules, there is no need for group (ii) to control them. In particular, many of the disclosures (e.g., consolidated financial reports, cash flow statements, segmental reporting, interim reporting) are not relevant for tax or distribution purposes in most jurisdictions. Financial institutions and large companies are sufficiently powerful to persuade group (ii) to allow financial reporting to respond to commercial needs. In common law countries, the importance of group (i) creates no problems of jurisprudence because non-governmental regulation is commonplace. In the rare case of a codified law country with a strong equity market (e.g., the Netherlands), the regulatory system for financial reporting can still give prominence to group (i) although this creates tensions (Zeff *et al.*, 1992). In all systems, group (ii) retains full control over tax rules.

Inflation Levels
Another factor included by DS is the rate of inflation and, once more, previous writers have not been helpful here. For example, although Nobes (1983) did not include inflation as a key variable, Nobes and Parker (1995, p. 19) suggested that 'Without reference to this factor, it would not be possible to explain accounting differences in countries severely affected by it'. However, on reflection, the more important issue is illustrated by other points that they make in the same section:

1. 'accountants in the English-speaking world have proved remarkably immune to inflation when it comes to taking decisive action';
2. 'in several South American countries, the most obvious feature ... is the use of methods of general price-level adjustment';
3. 'the fact that it was *governments* which responded to inflation in France, Spain, Italy and Greece ... is symptomatic of the regulation of accounting in these countries'.

In other words, any accounting system would have to respond at some level of inflation sustained for a certain length of time.[18] The key points are who responds and how they respond. The nature of these responses to inflation is a good indicator of the regulatory system for accounting. In countries where Class A accounting is dominant, professional accountants respond; in countries where Class B accounting is dominant, governments respond within the framework of the tax

[18] From observation of Anglo-Saxon countries, it seems that inflation of above 10 per cent for several years will cause a response (e.g., in the U.K. in the early 1950s or early 1970s), and the same applies to some continental European countries in the 1970s (Tweedie and Whittington, 1984).

INTERNATIONAL DIFFERENCES IN FINANCIAL REPORTING

system.[19] Differential inflation does not cause the difference between Class A and Class B acounting, the regulators typical to the two classes respond differently to it. However, as with some other factors, differential inflation response may lead to differences between the systems *within* Class A or *within* Class B.

Culture

Culture (defined by Hofstede as 'the collective programming of the mind') is clearly a plausible cause of accounting differences as proposed by Gray's (1988) application of Hofstede's (1980) theory. DS's four culture variables (see Table 2) were drawn from Hofstede. However, the attempt to use cultural variables entails large problems (Gernon and Wallace, 1995, pp. 85, 90, 91). Baydoun and Willett (1995, p. 69) also suggest that the mechanisms of the effects are not obvious, and: 'such is the nature of the concepts involved and the state of the available evidence that it is questionable whether Gray's adaptation of Hofstede's theory can in fact be empirically validated in the usual scientific sense' (p. 72).

For the purposes of this article, one can agree with Gray that culture can at least be seen as one of the background factors leading to more direct causes of accounting differences (such as the financing system). Culture may be of more direct help when examining other issues, for example, differences in the behaviour of auditors (Soeters and Schreuder, 1988). It will also be useful later to divide countries into culturally self-sufficient and culturally dominated. As noted in the previous section, the latter countries (e.g., colonies or former colonies) might be expected to adopt practices from other countries. In this sense, culture might indeed overwhelm other factors for certain countries.

Broad Factors

Others of the seventeen factors of Table 1, not proposed by DS but elsewhere in the literature, are too wide to be useful and can be accommodated within more specific factors. On these grounds, history and geography (Factors 11 and 12) can be removed. In a sense, 'history' explains everything, but this is not helpful unless it is known which part of history. For example, colonial history and the history of the corporate financing system are likely to be particularly relevant, so other factors can cover this.

'Geography' is also too broad a factor to be useful. It seems unlikely that the physical nature of a country has a major effect on its dominant class of accounting. For example, the Netherlands and Belgium have very different accounting, although they are similar in physical environment. By contrast, the U.K. and Australia have similar accounting although they are dramatically different in climate, terrain and type of agriculture. A country's location may be relevant for other factors (such as colonial inheritance and invasions) or for certain aspects of its financial history (such as the fact that maritime countries may tend to develop

---

[19] For example, many South American countries respond with compulsory government-controlled systems of general price level adjusted accounting, whereas English-speaking countries responded with rules written by the profession (although there was government involvement) which required some supplementary disclosures (Tweedie and Whittington, 1984).

certain types of trading or markets). However, the relevant aspects of geography should be picked up by other factors. In the meantime, one merely notes that location seems to be overwhelmed by other factors in the sense that New Zealand has rather similar accounting to the distant U.K.; and the Netherlands has very different accounting from its neighbours, Germany and Belgium.

Covariation
Other factors may involve covariation rather than causation. For example, the fact that many English-speaking countries have similar accounting practices is probably not caused by their shared language (Factor 13): the language was inherited with the accounting or with other factors which affect accounting. Language similarities may contribute to the strength of cultural dominance, and language differences may slow down the transfer of accounting technology. However, these points do not make language a key independent variable.

Theory
Theory (Factor 14), in the form of an explicit or implicit underlying framework, is certainly of relevance in some countries.[20] However, there are always competing theories (as examined for accounting by Watts and Zimmerman, 1979). It is suggested here that the degree of acceptance of particular accounting theories within a country *depends upon* other factors, such as the strength of equity markets and the regulatory system.

Results Rather Than Causes
Some factors above have been seen as more results than causes of the major accounting differences. Similarly, the age and size of the accountancy professions (Factor 7) differ substantially around the world,[21] but this is likely to be the *result* of different accounting systems. For example, the comparatively small size of the German auditing profession seems to result from the comparatively small number of audited companies, which in turn results from comparative weakness of equity markets.

Factors More Relevant Outside the Developed World
Certain other factors might not discriminate between developed Western countries, on which most classifications have concentrated. For example, political systems (Factor 15), religion (Factor 16) and stage of economic development (Factor 8) are probably sufficiently homogeneous in these countries that they do not have major explanatory power. They might well be relevant for a broader study, and at levels of classification below the two major classes. For example, religion may have an effect on accounting in some countries (Gambling and Abdel-Karim, 1991; Hamid *et al.*, 1993). Of course, religion and culture may be closely related.

---

[20] For example, the Netherlands is often said to have been influenced by the current value theories of Limperg and the German business economist Schmidt (Zeff *et al.*, 1992; Clarke and Dean, 1990).

[21] For example, see Table 1.1 in Nobes and Parker (1995).

INTERNATIONAL DIFFERENCES IN FINANCIAL REPORTING

Accidents

Close examination of accidents (Factor 17) will generally reveal their causes. However, certainly at the level of detailed accounting practices within a class, 'accident' may be a useful summary explanation. For example, some of the largest differences between U.S. and U.K. accounting (LIFO, deferred tax and goodwill) could be said to have accidental causes.[22] However, it is not necessary to resort to 'accidents' as an explanation of the difference between Class A and Class B accounting. It is suggested that the model which is restated in more detail below is powerful enough without this feature. In the end the validity of this claim is an empirical matter.

Summary on Excluded Factors

Many of the factors which have been examined in this section may be contributory causes to accounting differences or may be *associated* with accounting differences. However, it has been suggested that each can be eliminated as a major reason for the differences identified at the first split of accounting systems into two classes. At lower levels in a classification, many of these factors may be useful explanations of relatively small differences between systems. Further, some of the factors, certainly 'culture', help to explain the different types of capital markets which, according to proposals here, do explain the major groupings.

THE PROPOSED MODEL

The proposed model consists of a number of linked constructs which will be expressed as propositions. Part of the model can be expressed in simplified form as in Figure 2, which amends DS's proposal (summarised in Figure 1). The variables needed have been introduced in the text above, but now need to be marshalled.

The first variable is the type of country culture and the second is the strength of the equity-outsider financing system. This article assumes that some cultures lead to strong equity-outsider markets, and others do not. However, this is an issue for economists and others and is not examined in detail here. The point of departure for the constructs and hypotheses explained below is the second variable: the nature of the equity markets. Suggestions have been made here about how empirical researchers could measure this variable, perhaps leading to a 0/1 (weak or strong equity-outsider market) classification.

A further variable is the type of company. For most companies (insider companies), a controlling stake is in the hands of a small number of owners. For a

FIGURE 2

SIMPLIFIED MODEL OF REASONS FOR INTERNATIONAL ACCOUNTING DIFFERENCES

| External environment | ⟶ | Culture, including institutional structures | ⟶ | Strength of equity-outsider system | ⟶ | Class of accounting |

[22]   This is examined by Nobes (1996), where it is suggested that timing is a key factor. For example, the U.S. requirement to amortize goodwill was introduced earlier than U.K. standard setting on this issue, when goodwill was far less significant.

FIGURE 3

APPLICATION OF FIGURE 2 TO CULTURALLY SUFFICIENT COUNTRIES

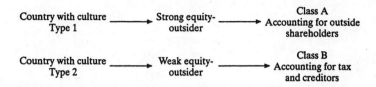

comparatively few companies (outsider companies), control is widely spread amongst a large number of 'outsider' equity-holders. Countries with strong equity-outsider systems generally have a large number of outsider companies which may comprise most of a country's GNP, but other countries may also have a few of these companies.

The fourth variable is the country's degree of cultural self-sufficiency. As discussed earlier, some countries have strong indigenous cultures whereas others have imported cultures which are still dominated or heavily influenced from outside. This dichotomy will be expressed by using the labels CS (for culturally self-sufficient) and CD (for culturally dominated). Researchers might wish to measure this in various ways, for example by the number of decades since a country gained political independence from another. Many developing countries are CD and many developed countries are CS, but there are exceptions. Again, the boundaries between CS and CD are unclear, but researchers should have little difficulty in classifying many countries. Concentration should be placed on aspects of business culture in cases where this may give a different answer from other aspects of culture.

The final variable is the type of financial reporting system (or, in short, 'accounting system') introduced earlier as Class A or Class B. Again, preliminary suggestions have been made about how researchers might measure and classify systems in this way.

The theoretical constructs which link these variables can now be brought together. It is relevant here to repeat the point that more than one accounting system can be used in any particular country at any one time or over time.

The model can be expressed in terms of propositions, which are then explained and illustrated:

P1: The dominant accounting system in a CS country with a strong equity-outsider system is Class A.

P2: The dominant accounting system in a CS country with a weak (or no) equity-outsider system is Class B.

P3: A CD country has an accounting system imported from its dominating country, irrespective of the strength of the CD country's equity-outsider system.

P4: As a country establishes a strong equity-outsider market, its accounting system moves from Class B to Class A.

P5: Outsider companies in countries with weak equity-outsider markets will move to Class A accounting.

INTERNATIONAL DIFFERENCES IN FINANCIAL REPORTING

FIGURE 4

A PROPOSED MODEL OF REASONS FOR INTERNATIONAL
ACCOUNTING DIFFERENCES

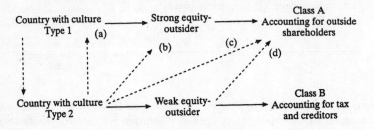

The analysis can begin with culturally self-sufficient (CS) countries (Propositions P1 and P2 above), as illustrated in Figure 3. For these countries, it is suggested that the class of the dominant accounting system will depend upon the strength of the equity-outsider market (or on its strength in the past, if there is inertia). Strong equity-outsider systems will lead to Class A accounting (see Table 4), whereas others will lead to Class B accounting. As explained earlier, the term 'dominant accounting system' is used to refer to the type used by enterprises representing the majority of a country's economic activity. For example, small unlisted enterprises in strong equity market countries might not practise Class A accounting or indeed any financial reporting at all.

Propositions P3 to P5 are now examined. Proposition P3 is that, in culturally dominated (CD) countries, accounting systems are imported. Sometimes a CD country will also have had time to develop the style of equity market associated with the culture. Therein, Propositions P1 or P2 will hold as in CS countries. However, sometimes a CD country may have imported its culture and its accounting system without establishing the related equity market. In this case the accounting system will seem inappropriate for the strength of the equity-outsider financing system. Proposition P4 is that, if either a CS or a CD country with a traditionally weak equity market gradually develops a strong equity-outsider system, a change of accounting towards Class A will follow. Also (P5), in a country with weak equity-outsider markets, there may be *some* 'outsider companies' (as defined earlier). Commercial pressure will lead these companies towards Class A accounting, even if the dominant system in the country is Class B. For such a company, there will be rewards in terms of lower cost of capital[23] from the production of Class A statements, particularly if there is an international market in the company's shares. If legal constraints hinder movement towards Class A accounting, then the company can use extra disclosures or supplementary statements.

Figure 4 shows some aspects of these constructs. The continuous arrows are those from Figure 3. Dotted arrows (a) and (c) concern aspects of Proposition P3.

---

[23] It is argued that equity investors and lenders will be persuaded to provide funds at lower returns to companies using more accepted, familiar and transparent financial reporting (see Botosan, 1997).

Arrow (b) relates to Proposition P4, and Arrow (d) Proposition P5. Some illustrations are:

1 (Arrow a) New Zealand is a CD country with wholesale importation of British culture and institutions (Type 1), including a strong equity-outsider system and Class A accounting. Whether the Class A accounting results from the equity market or from direct cultural pressure is not important to the model; it probably arises from both.

2 (Arrow b) China is a country without a strong equity-outsider tradition but which seems to be moving towards such a system. Class A accounting is following (Davidson *et al.*, 1995).

3 (Arrow c) Malawi is a CD country with very weak equity markets[24] but where the accountancy profession has adopted Class A accounting, consistent with its colonial inheritance from the U.K.

4 (Arrow d) The Deutsche Bank, Bayer and Nestlé are companies from countries with traditionally weak equity markets. These companies are now interested in world equity-outsider markets, so they are adopting[25] Class A accounting for their group accounts.

IMPLICATIONS FOR CLASSIFICATION

Discussions about the reasons for international differences in financial reporting are clearly related to the topic of classification of financial reporting 'systems'. Some implications of the above suggestions for classification researchers are examined here.

Before Darwin, the Linnaean classification was drawn up on the 'intrinsic' basis of observations about the 'essential' differences in the characteristics of species. Later, genetic and inheritance ('extrinsic') issues became the normal basis for classification, but largely came to the same conclusions. In accounting, one may also see both intrinsic and extrinsic classifications (Roberts, 1995), which may lead to similar conclusions. For example, one can extrinsically trace modern U.K. and modern New Zealand accounting back to a common ancestor; and one can intrinsically note many similarities in the accounting systems currently used. However, it is proposed here to discuss the classifications based on intrinsic factors. For this reason, the term 'species', to which Roberts (1995) objected, will be omitted.

It is not proposed here to re-work previous classifications but to suggest implications of the above conclusions for future classification work. Taking the classification by Nobes (1983), some improvements can be suggested, as shown in Figure 5. The two classes are shown, much as in the earlier classification, but the labels are sharper, following Propositions P1 and P2 above. The bottom level of classification is now a 'system' not a country. This accommodates P5 above. In order to make

---

[24] These issues are discussed by Nobes (1996).

[25] For example, Bayer adopted international accounting standards (IASs) for its group accounts for 1994, and Deutsche Bank produce supplementary IAS group accounts for 1995. Nestlé published IAS group accounts.

INTERNATIONAL DIFFERENCES IN FINANCIAL REPORTING

FIGURE 5

EXTRACT FROM PROPOSED SCHEME FOR CLASSIFICATION

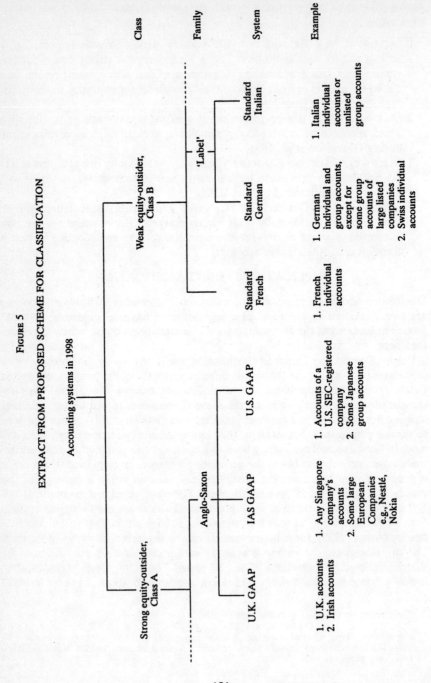

the classification easier to use, the systems could be labelled (e.g., U.S. GAAP). The classification in Figure 5 is by no means complete, for it merely seeks to illustrate the type of amendments proposed for future classifiers.

Below each system, there are examples of users of the system. This accommodates the points made earlier about the meaning of the term 'dominant accounting system'. For instance, U.S. GAAP is used by SEC-registered companies but not by all U.S. companies. Similarly, some Japanese companies are allowed to follow U.S. GAAP for their group accounts for both U.S. and Japanese purposes. As another instance, the 'standard German' system is that used by German companies for individual company accounts and, by most of them, for group accounts. However, several German listed companies are now publishing group accounts in accordance with International Accounting Standards, either by carefully choosing unusual German options (e.g., Bayer for 1994) or by producing two sets of group accounts (e.g., Deutsche Bank for 1995).

Proposition P3 would be relevant for the inclusion of developing countries in a classification. The fourth proposition could be used to predict which countries would move their dominant systems towards Class A in the classification.

POLICY IMPLICATIONS FOR RULE-MAKERS

The import and export of accounting technology (Parker, 1989) seems to be accelerating as a result of globalization and the formation of economic blocs such as the European Economic Area and the North American Free Trade Area. Also, the World Bank has funded advice for China on reforming its accounting; the British Foreign Office for Romania; the European Union for Russia; and so on. This section examines some implications of the article's earlier sections for standard-setters and other rule-makers.

In a CD country, the rule-makers should note that the country's accounting system is likely to have been imported and may not be appropriate for the main purpose of accounting. For example, in a developing country with imported Class A accounting but with few or no listed companies, the paraphernalia of Class A (e.g., extensive disclosure, consolidation, external audit) may be an expensive luxury. Resources might be better spent on establishing a reliable and uniform bookkeeping system, partly for the purpose of improving the collection of tax.

A similar point applies to many former communist countries, where the introduction of Class A accounting for a large proportion of enterprises might be inappropriate. However, for some such countries (perhaps China) where an impression has been created that the population and the government seem keen on moving to an equity-outsider system, the introduction of Class A might be appropriate, at least for large or listed companies.

In CS countries with a credit-insider system, again the rule-makers should think carefully before a generalized introduction of Class A. For example, it is not at all clear that the benefits of Class A would exceed its cost for the bulk of German companies. It is also not clear that there would be much benefit in any improved ability to compare corner grocery shops in Stuttgart with those in Sydney. However,

INTERNATIONAL DIFFERENCES IN FINANCIAL REPORTING

German rule-makers should ask themselves (and are doing so) whether they should assist the large German companies who are being forced by commercial pressures towards Class A. One approach would be exemption from normal German rules for the preparation of consolidated financial statements by such companies.

There is another policy question for governments whose countries do not have equity-outsider financing systems but who wish to encourage them. Would the imposition of a Class A financial reporting system encourage a change in financing system? The thrust of this article is that the financial reporting *follows* from the financing system. This is reminiscent of the debate in the literature about the relationship between double-entry bookkeeping and the rise of capitalism (e.g., Sombart, 1924; Yamey, 1949; Yamey, 1964; Winjum, 1971). The weight of argument seems to rest with those who believe that double entry follows business developments rather than leading them. None of this proves that developments in accounting cannot assist in economic development. However, the *imposition* of Class A might be inappropriate, particularly if done for unlisted companies or within a detailed and slow-moving legal system, given that an important feature of Class A accounting is that it can adapt to commercial circumstances. It might be better to concentrate on making Class A *available* by removing any legal or economic barriers to its usage and by subsidizing education.

In CS countries with equity-outsider financing systems and Class A accounting, the rule-makers should ask whether the full panoply of Class A is necessary for smaller companies or whether a separate financial reporting system should be allowed for them. This issue has largely been resolved in the U.S.A., as discussed earlier, and recent moves in the U.K. have exempted some smaller companies from audit and from the disclosure rules of several standards.[26]

The International Accounting Standards Committee (IASC) does not impose its rules on any enterprises; it merely makes them available to companies or regulators. However, some regulators impose IASs on some or most enterprises in their countries.[27] Also, the World Bank requires its borrowers to use IASs. The IASC should consider whether it could make available some additional 'system' which might be more suitable for financial reporting by unlisted companies.

SUMMARY

This article proposes a general model of the reasons for international differences in accounting practices. Instead of dozens of potential independent variables, it proposes two explanatory factors for the first split of accounting systems into classes. For culturally self-sufficient countries, it is suggested that the class of the predominant accounting system depends on the strength of the equity-outsider market.

---

[26]   In 1994, the audit requirement was removed or reduced for private companies with turnover under £350,000. The Accounting Standards Board published an exposure draft for a Financial Reporting Standard for Smaller Entities in 1996.

[27]   This is approximately the position for Singapore, Hong Kong, and many other Commonwealth countries.

For culturally dominated countries, the class of the accounting system is determined by the cultural influence. However, sometimes an equity-outsider market may gradually develop, or certain companies may be interested in foreign equity markets. This will lead to the development of the appropriate accounting, and it is one of the reasons for the existence of more than one class of accounting in one country.

Many other factors, which had been suggested previously as reasons for accounting differences, result from or are linked to the equity market. Some factors are perhaps reasons for the differences in equity markets, but are too unclear to measure with any precision. A general theory previously proposed by Doupnik and Salter (1995) mixed several of these factors and mis-specified some of them.

Some improvements to the classification of accounting systems have been suggested, incorporating the idea that it is accounting practice systems, not countries, that should be classified. Some implications for rule-makers are suggested, warning against inappropriate transfers of technology.

REFERENCES

Baydoun, N., and R. Willett, 'Cultural Relevance of Western Accounting Systems to Developing Countries', *Abacus*, March 1995.

Beaver, W. H., *Financial Reporting: An Accounting Revolution*, Prentice-Hall, 1989.

Belkaoui, A., *International Accounting*, Quorum, 1995.

Botosan, C. A., 'Disclosure Level and the Cost of Equity Capital', *Accounting Review*, July 1997.

Briston, R. J., 'The Evolution of Accounting in Developing Countries', *International Journal of Accounting*, Fall 1978.

Briston, R. J., and Foo See Liang, 'The Evolution of Corporate Reporting in Singapore', *Research in Third World Accounting*, Vol. 1, 1990.

Cable, J., 'Capital Market Information and Industrial Performance: The Role of West German Banks', *Economic Journal*, March 1985.

Choi, F. D. S., and G. G. Mueller, *International Accounting*, Prentice-Hall, 1992.

Chow, L. M., G. K. Chau and S. J. Gray, 'Accounting Reforms in China: Cultural Constraints on Implementation and Development', *Accounting and Business Research*, Vol. 26, No. 1, 1995.

Clarke, F. L., and G. W. Dean, *Contributions of Limpberg and Schmidt to the Replacement Cost Debate in the 1920s*, Garland, 1990.

Cooke, T. E., and R. S. O. Wallace, 'Financial Regulation and its Environment: A Review and Further Analysis', *Journal of Accounting and Public Policy*, Summer 1990.

Da Costa, R. C., J. C. Bourgeois and W. M. Lawson, 'A Classification of International Financial Accounting Practices', *International Journal of Accounting*, Spring 1978.

David, R., and J. E. C. Brierley, *Major Legal Systems in the World Today*, Stephens, 1985.

Davidson, R. A., A. M. G. Gelardi and F. Li, 'Analysis of the Conceptual Framework of China's New Accounting System', *Accounting Horizons*, March 1995.

Doupnik, T. S., and S. B. Salter, 'External Environment, Culture, and Accounting Practice: A Preliminary Test of a General Model of International Accounting Development', *International Journal of Accounting*, No. 3, 1995.

Federation of European Stock Exchanges, *Share Ownership Structure in Europe*, 1993.

Frank, W. G., 'An Empirical Analysis of International Accounting Principles', *Journal of Accounting Research*, Autumn 1979.

INTERNATIONAL DIFFERENCES IN FINANCIAL REPORTING

Franks, J., and C. Mayer, 'Corporate Control: A Synthesis of the International Evidence', working paper of London Business School and University of Warwick, 1992.

Gambling, T., and R. A. A. Abdel-Karim, *Business and Accounting Ethics in Islam*, Mansell, 1991.

Gernon, H., and R. S. O. Wallace, 'International Accounting Research: A Review of its Ecology, Contending Theories and Methodologies', *Journal of Accounting Literature*, Vol. 14, 1995.

Gonzalo, J. A., and J. L. Gallizo, *European Financial Reporting: Spain*, Routledge, 1992.

Gordon, P. D., and S. J. Gray, *European Financial Reporting: United Kingdom*, Routledge, 1994.

Gray, S. J., 'Towards a Theory of Cultural Influence on the Development of Accounting Systems Internationally', *Abacus*, March 1988.

Hamid, S. R., R. Craig and F. L. Clarke, 'Religion: A Confounding Cultural Element in the International Harmonization of Accounting?', *Abacus*, September 1993.

Harrison, G. L., and J. L. McKinnon, 'Culture and Accounting Change: A New Perspective on Corporate Reporting Regulation and Accounting Policy Formulation', *Accounting, Organizations and Society*, No. 3, 1986.

Hofstede, G., *Culture's Consequences: International Differences in Work-Related Values*, Stage Publications, 1980.

Hove, M. R., 'Accounting Practice in Developing Countries: Colonialism's Legacy of Inappropriate Technologies', *International Journal of Accounting*, Fall 1986.

Jensen, M. C., and W. H. Meckling, 'Theory of the Firm: Managerial Behavior, Agency Costs and Ownership Structure', *Journal of Financial Economics*, October 1976.

Kenway, P., 'The Concentration of Ownership and its Implications for Corporate Governance in the Czech Republic', University of Reading, Discussion Papers in Economics, Series A, No. 288, 1994.

Lamb, M., C. W. Nobes and A. D. Roberts, 'The Influence of Taxation on Accounting: International Variations', Reading University Discussion Papers, 1995.

La Porta, R., F. Lopez-de-Silanes, A. Shleifer and R. W. Vishny, 'Legal Determinants of External Finance', *Journal of Finance*, July 1997.

Meek, G., and S. Saudagaran, 'A Survey of Research on Financial Reporting in a Transnational Context', *Journal of Accounting Literature*, No. 9, 1990.

Miller, M. C., 'Australia', in T. E. Cooke and R. H. Parker (eds), *Financial Reporting in the West Pacific Rim*, Routledge, 1994.

Nair, R. D., and W. G. Frank, 'The Impact of Disclosure and Measurement Practices on International Accounting Classifications', *Accounting Review*, July 1980.

Nobes, C. W., 'An Empirical Analysis of International Accounting Principles: A Comment', *Journal of Accounting Research*, Spring 1981.

——, 'A Judgmental International Classification of Financial Reporting Practices', *Journal of Business Finance and Accounting*, Spring 1983.

——, Ch. 1 in C. W. Nobes and R. H. Parker (eds), *Issues in Multinational Accounting*, Philip Allan, 1988.

——, 'Classification of Accounting Using Competencies as a Discriminating Variable: A Comment', *Journal of Business Finance and Accounting*, January 1992.

——, 'Corporate Financing and its Effect on European Accounting Differences', Reading University Discussion Papers, 1995.

——, *Compliance with International Standards*, UNCTAD, 1996.

Nobes, C. W., and R. H. Parker (eds), *Comparative International Accounting*, Prentice-Hall, 1995.

Parker, R. H., 'Importing and Exporting Accounting: The British Experience', in A. G. Hopwood (ed.), *International Pressures for Accounting Change*, Prentice-Hall, 1989.

Parry, M., and R. Grove, 'Does Training More Accountants Raise the Standards of Accounting in Third World Countries? A Study of Bangladesh', *Research in Third World Accounting*, Vol. 1, 1990.

Radebaugh, L. H., 'Environmental Factors Influencing the Development of Accounting Objectives, Standards and Practices in Peru', *International Journal of Accounting*, Fall 1975.

Radebaugh, L. H., and S. Gray, *International and Multinational Enterprises*, Wiley, 1993.

Rahman, A., H. Perera and S. Ganeshanandam, 'Measurement of Formal Harmonization in Accounting: An Exploratory Study', *Accounting and Business Research*, Autumn 1996.

Roberts, A. D., 'The Very Idea of Classification in International Accounting', *Accounting, Organizations and Society*, Vol. 20, Nos 7/8, 1995.

Scheid, J.-C., and P. Walton, *European Financial Reporting: France*, Routledge, 1992.

Schweikart, J. A., 'Contingency Theory as a Framework for Research in International Accounting', *International Journal of Accounting*, Fall 1985.

Shoenthal, E., 'Classification of Accounting Systems Using Competencies as a Discriminating Variable: A Great Britain–United States Study', *Journal of Business Finance and Accounting*, Autumn 1989.

Soeters, J., and H. Schreuder, 'The Interaction between National and Organizational Cultures in Accounting Firms', *Accounting, Organizations and Society*, Vol. 13, No. 1, 1988.

Sombart, W., *Der Moderne Kapitalismus*, 6th edn, Duncker & Humblot, Vol. 2.1, 1924.

Standish, P. E. M., 'Origins of the *plan comptable général*: A Study in Cultural Intrusion and Reaction', *Accounting and Business Research*, Autumn 1990.

——, 'Financial Reporting in France', Ch. 11 in C. W. Nobes and R. H. Parker (eds), *Comparative International Accounting*, Prentice-Hall, 1995.

Tweedie, D. P., and G. Whittington, *The Debate on Inflation Accounting*, Cambridge University Press, 1984.

Wallace, R. S. O., and H. Gernon, 'Frameworks for International Comparative Financial Accounting', *Journal of Accounting Literature*, Vol. 10, 1991.

Watts, R., and J. Zimmerman, 'The Demand for and Supply of Accounting Theories: The Market for Excuses', *Accounting Review*, April 1979.

Winjum, J. O., 'Accounting and the Rise of Capitalism: An Accountant's View', *Journal of Accounting Research*, Vol. 9, 1971.

Yamey, B. S., 'Scientific Bookkeeping and the Rise of Capitalism', *Economic History Review*, 2nd ser, Vol. 1, 1949.

——, 'Accounting and the Rise of Capitalism: Some Further Notes on a Theme by Sombart', *Journal of Accounting Research*, II, 1964.

Zeff, S. A., F. van der Wel and K. Camfferman, *Company Financial Reporting: A Historical and Comparative Study of the Dutch Regulatory Process*, North-Holland, 1992.

Zysman, J., *Government, Markets and Growth: Financial Systems and the Politics of Industrial Change*, Cornell University Press, 1983.

INTERNATIONAL DIFFERENCES IN FINANCIAL REPORTING

APPENDIX

This appendix contains an example (relating to 1995) of the measures that could be used to distinguish between strong equity markets and others. The data in Table A relate to the eight largest economies in Europe, which are probably all CS countries.

TABLE A

EQUITY MARKET MEASURES

	Domestic equity market capitalization/GDP	Domestic listed companies per million of population
U.K.	1.34	30.2
Netherlands	0.99	14.4
Sweden	0.76	24.4
Belgium	0.50	14.3
France	0.40	12.4
Spain	0.36	9.3
Germany	0.31	8.4
Italy	0.18	4.3

Sources: European Stock Exchange Statistics, Annual Report 1995, Federation of European Stock Exchanges; and *Pocket World in Figures 1995*, The Economist.

In order to identify a Category IV financing system, it would also be necessary to establish that strong equity markets (e.g., U.K. and Netherlands) had a high level of 'outsiders'. This could be done using statistics of ownership of shares (e.g., Federation of European Stock Exchanges, 1993).

PART III

INTERNATIONAL DIFFERENCES AND THEIR EFFECTS

A Review of the Translation Debate

C. W. Nobes

There are many linked but separable matters which might reasonably be included within the problem of currency translation. The concern of this article will be mainly with the translation for consolidation of foreign currency balance sheet items, and the relationship of this to adjustments for specific or general price changes. This leaves the translation of income items and the treatment of foreign currency transactions largely untouched. However, the bulk of controversy and past discussion has been in the area of the translation of balance sheet items and its effects.

I intend here to review critically the premises, arguments and conclusions of academic and professional bodies on both sides of the Atlantic. The literature contains much to mislead the unwary: inconsistent premises, confused argument and straightforward errors of definition. I hope to make it clear how the various issues in the translation debate are connected, and how and why writers differ.

Consolidation and translation

Many of the differences in approach suggested by accountancy bodies and writers stem from differences of view with respect to the purpose of consolidation and translation, and indeed the purpose of financial statements. In some cases, there seems to be little consideration for any underlying principle. Such fundamental confusion has been noted by several writers (e.g. Parker, 1970; Patz, 1977, 1).

In *Accounting Research Study No. 12* (ARS12), Lorensen suggests that translation is a 'measurement conversion process' which should, therefore, preserve the original accounting principles (AICPA, 1972). Many of the criticisms of translation methods are really criticisms of the results of translation, which are imperfect because of the original accounting principles. Further, some arguments in favour of particular methods involve attempts to 'improve' the original principles by taking account of inflation or the *future* effects of a devaluation. For example, one American writer suggests that, when choosing a currency translation method, 'selection ... should be based upon the most probable (economic) impact of a movement in exchange rates' (Smith, 1978). Since most systems of accounting in use, particularly historic cost which was the context of the above quotation, do not intend to reflect economic reality, the suggested selection criterion seems somewhat bizarre.

More generally, much of the argument for and against particular methods, on both sides of the Atlantic, seems to be based on the acceptability of their effects on the consolidated historic cost profits of large companies under the exchange rate and inflation conditions that exist in that particular country at that particular time. Partly for this reason, there are several recent writings in the US (where the temporal method has been in use) against the temporal method (e.g. Smith, 1978; Seidler, 1978).

It should be noted that the next five sections are written in the context of historic cost accounting. Even if this is seen as an unattractive context, it is fairly clearly the one that most multinationals have been and still are in.

Definitions and recent history of methods

One of the problems with the definition of translation methods is that many of them have, in practice, been impure versions of more fundamental methods. However, there might be said to be four underlying translation methods on which variations have been built.

The *closing rate* method translates all balance sheet items at the rate ruling on the balance sheet date (which will be referred to as the 'closing' rate, not the 'current' rate which can be ambiguous). The other three methods involve a mixture of closing and historic rates. The *monetary/non-monetary* (MNM) method uses closing rates for monetary assets and liabilities, and the historic rates relevant to the date the balance was established for other balances. The *current/non-current* (CNC) method uses closing rates for current assets and liabilities, and the relevant historic

Table A

Translation Rates used for Balance Sheet Items Under Historic Cost

	Closing rate	CNC	MNM	Temporal
Fixed assets and long term investments: cost	C	H	H	H
Stocks and short-term investments:				
cost	C	C	H	H
market	C	C	H*	C
Debtors	C	C	C	C
Cash	C	C	C	C
Long-term debt	C	H	C	C
Current liabilities	C	C	C	C

C = closing rate
H = historic rate

*Some variants of MNM translate current items held at NRV using the closing rate

Table B

An Example of Translation

| Foreign HC balances in Picos | Balances | Translated Balances for Consolidation | | | |
		Closing Rate £	CNC £	MNM £	Temporal £
10,000	Fixed Assets	5,000	2,500	2,500	2,500
3,000	Stock (Cost)	1,500	1,500	1,000	1,000
2,000	Stock (NRV)	1,000	1,000	667	1,000
3,000	Debtors	1,500	1,500	1,500	1,500
1,000	Cash	500	500	500	500
19,000	Total Assets	9,500	7,000	6,167	6,500
12,000	Equity	6,000	4,500	2,667	3,000
4,000	Loans	2,000	1,000	2,000	2,000
3,000	Creditors	1,500	1,500	1,500	1,500
19,000	Total Capital	9,500	7,000	6,167	6,500

Historic rate for fixed assets and loans;   4 picos = £1
Historic rate for stocks: 3 picos = £1
Closing rate: 2 picos = £1

rates for others. The *temporal* principle is that translation rates should be determined by the measurement basis. Balances carried at historic cost will be translated using the relevant historic rate; balances carried at present or future values will be translated at the closing rate. The effect of these definitions is summarised and illustrated in Tables A and B.

It can be seen that, under a system of historic cost accounting which did not allow revaluation, the MNM method would be the same as the temporal method, with the exception of such current assets as inventory held at net realisable value

(NRV). In practice, some variants of the MNM method have translated current assets held at NRV at closing rates.

As far as current value (CV) accounting is concerned, the temporal principle would clearly give the same results as the closing rate method. Indeed, if the date on which balances are established under a CV system is taken to be the balance sheet date, the MNM method might also give the same result. The original writings are not entirely clear on this point.

Attempts at understanding the nature and effects of these multitudinous translation methods have not been assisted by the evident confusion even in high places. For example, *Accountancy* (published by the Institute of Chartered Accountants in England and Wales) recently contained an article misleadingly describing the monetary/non-monetary method as the temporal method (Kettel, 1978); whereas *The Accountant's Magazine* (published by the Institute of Chartered Accountants of Scotland) carried an article wrongly describing the current/non-current method as the temporal method (McMonnies and Rankin, 1977). Further, the 1978 *Survey of Published Accounts* (ICAEW, 1979, p. 50) states incorrectly that the temporal method 'is the use of the historical exchange rate ruling at the date when the asset or liability was acquired or the book value established'. This is wrong for liabilities and misleading for assets. Even a distinguished American textbook on accounting theory can quite erroneously report that 'ARB No. 43 also recommends that capital stock, long-term debt and long-term

receivables should likewise be translated in terms of the exchange rates prevailing at the date of the balance sheet' (Hendriksen, 1970). In fact, ARB 43 recommended historic rates.

The recent vacillatory history of translation theory and practice reflects this confusion and the expediency mentioned before. A brief chronology is presented as Table C. As for the dates of origin of the various methods used, the closing rate seems to be the oldest. It was certainly used by British accountants for overseas branches in the nineteenth century (e.g. Plumb, 1891). Long periods of fixed exchange rates remove most of the arguments against the closing rate method. As Table C shows, the CNC method was formally recommended in the United States as early as 1931. However, it was advocated even earlier (Dicksee, 1911). The MNM method can be traced back to 1956. The temporal principle is much more recent and has its first clear expression in 1972.

Table C

History of Statements and Studies

	US	UK	Method
1931	AICPA Bulletin No. 92		CNC
1934	AICPA Bulletin No. 117		CNC
1939	ARB 4		CNC
1953	ARB 43		CNC
1956	S.R. Hepworth		suggests MNM
1960	NAA Research Report No. 36		discusses MNM
1965	APB Opinion 6		MNM
1968		ICAEW, N25	closing or historic rates
1969	APB Statement 3		translate-restate
1970		ICAS, Research Study	closing rate
1972	ARS 12		'temporal'
1972	APB draft Opinion		about losses on long-term liabilities under MNM
1973	FAS 1		about disclosure
1975		ED16	non-committal
1975	FAS 8		'temporal'
1977		ED21	closing rate or 'temporal'
1977	E11		closing rate or 'temporal'
1980		ED27	closing rate (situational)

CNC	= current/non-current
MNM	= monetary/non-monetary
AICPA	= American Institure of Certified Public Accountants
ARB	= Accounting Research Bulletin
APB	= Accounting Principles Board
ARS	= Accounting Research Study
FAS	= Financial Accounting Standard
ICAEW	= Institute of Chartered Accountants in England and Wales
ICAS	= Institute of Chartered Accountants of Scotland
ED	= Exposure draft published by the Accounting Standards Committee
E	= Exposure draft published by the International Accounting Standards Committee

The early use of the closing rate method

The earliest method of translation was the closing rate method. This evolved in the UK and the US when their currencies and those of other developed trading nations were exchanged at fixed rates, and when the currencies of underdeveloped countries were weaker. Therefore, for most important currencies, the problem of choosing an exchange rate did not arise and, for the others, the closing rate was reassuringly conservative. In addition, the closing rate seems obvious at first sight and is simple to use.

However, in a world where exchange rates fluctuate about their fixed parities or, worse, are freely floating, it has been necessary to address the problem of choosing exchange rates. Some of the arguments for using various methods which involve historic rates are looked at in the following sections. Nevertheless, there are still arguments for the closing rate method; but they have to take account of the different world. These latter arguments are also examined later.

Arguments for and against the CNC and MNM methods

The CNC method was common in the inter-war years (see Table C) when exchanged rates were not continually moving in the same direction but were fluctuating reasonably gently. (See Appendix for exchange rate movements.) The argument supporting the CNC method against the closing rate method was that, with fluctuating currencies, the closing rate at any time was unlikely to be the same as the future rate ruling when non-current liabilities had to be repaid. The consequent practical difference from the closing rate method is that gains or losses on non-current items are not recognised (see Table B). This is justified on the ground that any exchange rate movement is quite likely to reverse (several times) in the following months or years.

The effect of the method is also to link fixed assets with related long-term liabilities. Gains and losses on neither of them are reported, unlike the MNM method, below. However, there has been little backing for the CNC method in recent years, not least because exchange rates no longer fluctuate about fixed parities. Consequently, it is unreasonable to hold that exchange rate movements are likely to reverse. The closing exchange rate is probably the best estimate of the future exchange rate for non-current liabilities (Henning *et al.*, 1978). Further, it is reasonably argued that

the definition of current assets and liabilities is a matter of classification, which implies no underlying accounting or economic difference which could be used to determine the appropriate rate of translation (Baxter and Yamey, 1951). These conclusions led to the alternative MNM method as proposed by Hepworth (1956).

As with the CNC method, the MNM method translates non-monetary fixed assets at historic rates and monetary assets at the closing rate. Assets and liabilities are defined as 'monetary' if their amounts are fixed by contract in terms of the currency of the foreign entity. In practice, this tends to include inventories valued at net realisable value (and quoted securities) (Kettel, 1978). This latter exception, which is necessary on the grounds of expediency because of the strange effects of using the historic rate with such assets, suggests that the theory underlying the MNM method is weak. As Lorensen notes (ARS 12, p. 35), inventory cannot be a monetary asset under any reasonable definition, including those used by Hepworth and the National Accounting Association. Inventory is not worth a fixed number of units of the subsidiary's currency.

The difference between the two methods is that MNM exposes long-term liabilities rather than inventories to exchange rate fluctuations. This has been opposed by some, not on theoretical accounting grounds but because of its effect on profits when the parent's currency loses value. In this case, there will be losses shown as a result of long-term liabilities but no gains on fixed assets or inventories. This, it was argued, will be against the real effects of such an exchange rate change, which will actually cause the foreign subsidiary to make larger profits (and dividends) in terms of the parent's currency (Kettel, 1978; APB, 1972; Connor, 1972). However, such a criticism about *future* profits seems hardly relevant under most systems of accounting, let alone historic cost, in the context of which the arguments were made.

It is clear, however, that the practical acceptability of exchange rate methods depended then, as now, mainly on their effects on consolidated profit figures under the economic conditions that happened to be ruling. The above criticisms of the MNM method arose in the US under the novel circumstances of the early 1970s when the dollar was falling against several other currencies (see Appendix). The lack of underlying theory was recognised at this time, and an accounting research study (ARS 12) was commissioned and produced. It was followed by a new financial accounting standard, FAS 8 (FASB, 1975). These documents proposed the temporal principle and incorporated fundamental theoretical reasoning in its favour. Parts of the following discussion can also be used as a justification for the use of historic rates by the MNM method.

Arguments for the temporal principle

ARS 12 and FAS 8 were attempts to provide a logical basis for the choice of rates of exchange for translation, which was not to be restricted to a pure historic cost system of accounting. To start with, at least, economic effects (see later) and the degree to which gains or losses were implied by particular methods were considered less important than a coherent financial accounting theory.

The purpose of consolidation was discussed and concluded to be the presentation of the results of a group as if they were those of a single entity (FAS 8, Appendix D). This leads to the conclusion that the accounting principles of the parent company should be used throughout the group and that the parent's currency should be the single currency used. Under historic cost accounting, the purchase of a foreign subsidiary or the purchase of an asset by a foreign subsidiary should be measured at cost in dollars at the moment of purchase. Each transaction of the foreign subsidiary should have the same effect as if it had been a transaction of the parent. For a US parent, for example, the objective will be to measure and express the assets and liabilities of a foreign subsidiary in dollars and in conformity with US GAAP.

This means that where the parent holds balances at historic cost, for example a machine, then a subsidiary's balances on similar accounts should also be held at historic cost, and translated at historic rates. This will express what it would have cost to buy the asset in the parent's currency on the date of purchase. On the other hand, cash is clearly valued at current value and should therefore be translated at closing rates.

Many balances expressed in money terms imply future amounts of money; for example, debtors, creditors and long-term liabilities. These might be said to require the appropriate *future* rates of exchange. However, fortunately, reality as well as objectivity can be satisfied by using closing rates on the grounds that the present rate of exchange is the best predictor of future rates. This suggestion, that present rates embody expectations, is linked to the efficient market hypothesis (Henning *et al.* 1978). Lorensen in ARS 12 raises other arguments. For example, the loss or gain on exchange

is said to belong to the future period when the exchange rate changes, so the closing rate should be used for present balance sheets. This seems a false argument. If the rate change can be predicted, accountants might be expected to provide now for foreseeable losses. If the rate change cannot be predicted, such provision is impossible rather than inappropriate. Further, Lorensen argues that receivables and payables are stated now at current (rather than future) purchasing power. Under historic cost, this surely tells us little about which exchange rate to use. It is the argument at the start of this paragraph which is convincing, and strong enough by itself.

Various details of the application of the temporal principle can be seen to be consistent with the underlying theory. For example, FAS 8 makes it clear (para. 46) that the 'lower of cost and market' rule for inventory valuation should involve a comparison of historic cost at historic exchange rates with net realisable value at closing exchange rates.

Another consistent detail is the choice of the remittance rate when there are multiple rates. In order to explain this it should be noted that it is the proprietary theory which is dominant behind the temporal method. Foreign subsidiaries are seen as existing in order to provide domestic cash flows by remittance (FAS 8, para. 227). Thus, the remittance rate is appropriate for earnings, for assets measured at market values (which could be sold for remittance) and for assets measured at historic cost because this measures the historic sacrifice in remittances in order to incur the cost of the asset. However, Flower (1976, p. 59) suggests that the investment rate would be more logical for the cost of fixed assets.

There are several supporters of the temporal principle, including Lorensen (in ARS 12), Flower (1976) and Hinton (1978). The arguments, that the translation method should not distort the underlying accounting principles so that consolidation can take place on a consistent basis, and that the method should not be expected to correct for the inadequacies of underlying principles in particular accounting systems, seem sound.

Arguments against the temporal principle are contained in the next section.

Arguments for and against the closing rate method

Acknowledging that we do not now live in a world of fixed exchange rates and that we are prepared to use more respectable criteria than simplicity of operation (and, in the UK, familiarity), do there remain any good arguments for the closing rate method?

It is the objectives of consolidation and translation which are crucial here. Suppose that the aim is 'to represent to decision-makers... foreign investments and operations in a familiar currency framework and... to facilitate comparisons' (AAA, 1975). The arguments against the temporal principle and in favour of the closing rate method follow from this. Perhaps such arguments have been more readily accepted in such countries as the UK and Canada, rather than the US, because of greater familiarity with the concept of foreign parents.

The initial plank of the argument is that foreign subsidiaries do *not* exist mainly in order to make remittances to parents. A foreign subsidiary is a separate entity and it is only its net worth which is at risk, not each individual balance. This 'entity' argument is rehearsed in FAS 8 (para. 140 onwards) and seriously advanced by Parkinson (1972) for 'independent' operations as part of a 'situational' approach, and by Patz (1977, 1, pp. 319–321; and 1977, 2).

In this case, it can be argued that all the balances should be translated at the same rate, which should be the rate ruling at the balance sheet date. It can be further argued that, unless this is done, the original relationships between the various balances and profit items will be upset by using more than one rate. Also, there are fewer problems caused by gains or losses on long-term liabilities because there are similar movements on the assets that were financed by them.

It is argued that the economic and commercial environments of foreign subsidiaries may be quite different from that of the parent. Assets were *not* bought by the parent in its currency, and in many cases could not have been bought at the historic prices translated at historic rates. In this sense, assets do not have an historic cost in terms of the parent's currency. Further, the assets were not bought at the expense of remittance, for the money would otherwise have been used for some other foreign purpose.

At this point, the supporters of the temporal method might reply that if the foreign subsidiary is 'independent' and not for remittances, it should not be consolidated but treated by the *equity* method. In those cases where a subsidiary is centrally controlled and should be consolidated, the temporal arguments about consistency of principles should apply.

It seems clear that there is no precise consensus about the purpose of consolidation. Are consoli-

dated statements intended to amplify parent company statements, to be a more realistic form of parent company statements, to represent the group as if it were a single entity, or to perform some other purpose? The genesis of consolidation and the influence of these competing purposes is very well described by Walker (1978). He points out that it is not at all obvious that full consolidation is the correct approach for subsidiaries, let alone for partially owned foreign subsidiaries. This vagueness of purpose contributes to the confusion of the translation debate.

Returning to the arguments of supporters of the temporal method, they would further hold that a foreign subsidiary's historic cost balances which are translated at closing rates become a meaningless combination which is neither historic cost nor a valuation. The closing rate for historic cost accounting is said to lead to 'conceptual and practical nonsense' (Hinton, 1978). It leads to 'nothing except the product of multiplying two unrelated numbers' (Storey, 1972).

If these dismissals of the theoretical arguments for the closing rate are accepted, there is still further 'economic' argument to hear. For example, Seidler (1972) supports the closing rate method on the basis that, unlike the temporal or MNM methods, it moves profit in the same direction as future earnings streams in the parent's currency. Smith (1978) argues that same point, that subsidiaries in a country with a strong currency show a loss under the temporal method because of long-term liabilities, but actually represent a good investment. However, these are imprecise arguments based on what happens to be expedient under temporary conditions. They are partly criticisms of the underlying historic cost accounting. As Flower (1976, p. 28) says: 'If... the historic rate method... produces unacceptable translated accounts, then the deficiency may well rest with the historic cost based accounts... The underlying problem will not be solved by changing the method of translation to the closing rate method, which... is not theoretically consistent with... accounts based on historic cost'.

It has been noted that the clamour against the temporal method seems to have much to do with the effects on the income statement. A survey has found that 80 per cent of US multinationals were already taking exchange differences to income *before* FAS 8 was introduced (Evans and Folks, 1979). The strength of opposition seems to be related to the fact that, because of the weakness of the dollar, the practice imposed by FAS 8 is now inexpedient.

Recent developments in standard practice

There is currently (June, 1980) no standard practice in the UK. Exposure Draft 21 was much criticised for allowing either closing rates or the temporal principle. The latter was allowed because some UK companies file their financial statements with the SEC, and hence must obey FAS 8 at least for that version of their statements. However, during 1977/78, 94 per cent of the top 300 companies used the closing rate method (ICAEW, 1979, p. 53). The new exposure draft of October 1980 makes its preference for the closing rate method more obvious but allows use of the temporal method under certain circumstances.

In the US, FAS 8 has come under heavy criticism, particularly from practical men rather than from academics. In March 1980 the FASB concluded that the closing rate method had a number of advantages, and announced an intention to prepare a new exposure draft on that basis (issued August 1980).

In Canada, there has been similar uncertainty about the existing proposals for the introduction of the temporal method. However, in Australia, an exposure draft based on the temporal method was issued during 1979. Not surprisingly, the exposure draft of the IASC proposes to allow both the temporal and the closing rate methods. However, it would be unrealistic to expect a standard until the FASB has resolved its difficulties.

Inflation and specific price changes

A somewhat analogous problem to the choice of rates of exchange for foreign currency translation is the choice of 'rates of exchange' for translation of units of a domestic currency over time. Historic cost accounting is a sort of MNM method, and current purchasing power (CPP) accounting might be compared to the closing rate method. Current value accounting, however, is not directly analogous, because it is not the 'rate of exchange' between pounds of different dates which is being adjusted for.

Naturally, when dealing with the financial statements of foreign subsidiaries in periods of changing prices, the above problem is combined (and sometimes confused) with the problem of translation. Many writers on CPP in this context have recommended restatement of the subsidiary's financial statements to CPP using a foreign index, followed by translation at the closing rate of exchange (Zwick and Zenoff, 1969; Parkinson, 1972; Shwayder, 1972; Choi, 1975; AAA, 1975). The restate-translate method is better for resource allocation and performance comparison, it is argued.

However, the sounder arguments from a financial accounting theory point of view appear to be on the other side, and thus for translate-restate (CPP) using a parent country index. (Rosenfield, 1971; Lorensen and Rosenfield, 1974; APB, 1965; Flower, 1976, p. 51). It is argued that restate-translate is wrong because it leads to foreign balances which have been adjusted for foreign inflation being added to domestic balances adjusted for domestic inflation. Since CPP is a historic-cost based system, historic rates should be used to translate the foreign balances. This should be followed by restatement to CPP for consolidation using the price indices of the parent country. Thus, balances which are all expressed in historic units of the domestic currency will all be adjusted for domestic inflation before being added together. Consistency of accounting principles will have been achieved. However, Patz (1977, 1, p. 317) rightly notes that translate-restate is only obviously theoretically correct once a proprietary assumption has been made.

There are criticisms of the *usefulness* of the answers given by translate-restate (CPP). These have not only been made by those who support restate-translate. Perhaps a greater consensus exists when dealing with current value (CV) accounting. There is general support for restate (CV)-translate. (Goudeket, 1960; Parker, 1970; Flower, 1976; IASG, 1976). Here the foreign subsidiary restates its financial statements using some form of current value accounting (perhaps CCA). This is followed by translation using closing rates of exchange. This approach seems less vulnerable to attacks on theoretical or practical grounds.

Purchasing power parities

An alternative approach for dealing simultaneously with translation and inflation uses purchasing power parities (PPPs). The purchasing power parity theory has been developed by economists studying the moments of exchange rates (e.g. Balassa, 1964). It has been adapted by accountants as an alternative to exchange rates, initially particularly for measuring foreign exchange exposure (NAA, 1960; AAA, 1974; Aliber and Stickney, 1975; Patz, 1977, 1, p. 321 ; Patz, 1977, 2). Supporters of PPPs concede that translate-restate (CPP) might be satisfactory if exchange rate movements and relative price level movements cancelled out. However, it is clear that exchange rates are not only affected by relative inflation rates but also by political factors, interest rates, balances of payments, and so on. Considerable stress is placed upon the suggestion that this renders exchange rates 'inaccurate' and unsuitable for translation, for which they were not designed. Some writings are just assertions, which offer no reasoned argument about why it matters what determines exchange rates (AAA, 1974). This question needs to be answered, for we do not reject an historic cost or a current value on the basis of which particular elements of supply or demand have determined a price. It is possible to guess that the above assertions are based on the assumptions of Scott (1975) who sat on the appropriate AAA Committee. If so, the reasoning is based on the idea that the objective of translation is to enable a better prediction of the future. This has already been criticised, particularly in the context of historic cost. Many of Scott's arguments in favour of PPPs and against exchange rates are answered by Clarke (1977), who thinks that neither may be appropriate for many balances.

Fortunately, some arguments in favour of PPPs are more clearly stated. Patz (1977, 1) makes it clear that under proprietary theory of the sort which leads to the temporal method, exchange rates seem sensible. He claims, however, that an entity approach is more suitable and that, in order to preserve the original local meaning of foreign financial statements, PPPs are more appropriate than exchange rates. It is also argued that foreign balances awaiting translation have a 'place significance' which is somewhat similar to the 'time significance' of balances being adjusted for inflation (Patz, 1977, 2, p. 19). The coefficients necessary for translation are based upon ratios of the general purchasing power of the currencies involved. Exchange rates could be used if it can be proved that they approximate to such PPPs. This entity-based theory suggests that a UK parent should be interested in its worldwide command over goods and services not over pounds sterling.

The response to this is that a UK holding company's shareholders *are* interested in command over pounds sterling, and that the local subsidiary's financial statements still remain for other uses (Flower, 1978). However, this does not seem to fit with the idea that consolidation presents the accounts of the *group* rather than amplifying the holding company accounts. As for the 'place significance', Clarke (1978) suggests that domestic goods and foreign goods are just as heterogeneous as domestic money and foreign money,

because of transportation costs and other reasons Therefore, adjusting by PPPs does not provide balances which may sensibly be summed.

There is, no doubt, considerable mileage left in the PPP debate. However, it seems unlikely that Table C will need to be updated on this account in the near future.

Economic effects

It has been noted several times in this paper that some writers have argued for or against particular translation methods at particular times on grounds of the economic effects of resulting profit and asset figures. The late 1970s has seen the development of a considerable literature (mainly American) on the subject of economic and political effects of accounting standards. One of the areas which is often used as an example is currency translation.

Many have argued that accounting standards have considerable effects on profit and asset figures and that, therefore, they have economic effects (Rappaport, 1977; Wyatt, 1977; Solomons, 1978). Zeff (1978, pp. 57–59) has charted the influence of 'economic consequences' on accounting pronouncements in the US since 1941. He says that 'on each of the occasions . . . , outside parties intervened . . . by an appeal to criteria that transcended the traditional questions of accounting measurement and fair presentation'.

The arguments have gone even further, to suggest that accounting rules should be set democratically by politically responsive institutions (Gerboth, 1973; Horngren, 1973; May and Sundem, 1976). There is clearly considerable pressure for such 'democratic' involvement by interested parties. Such pressures hastened the demise of the APB (Zeff, 1978, p. 60). Consequently, the FASB is less dependent on the accounting profession, and has added 'probable economic or social impact' to its conceptual framework (FASB, 1976).

In the case of currency translation, it has been shown that some methods have been criticised because they can cause profits to be smaller or more volatile (Scott, 1975, p. 61; Smith, 1978). The arguments are often not concerned with whether or not this is a better presentation but with any effects on the decision-making of multinationals. However, the arguments against allowing accounting rules to be influenced by political pressures based on probable economic consequences seem very strong. Solomons (1978, p. 69) notes that 'critics of the FASB are asserting that economic behaviour, such as . . . hedging, which would not have been rational under the old accounting rules becomes rational under the new ones. Such an assertion is difficult to defend because the new rules have not changed the underlying cash flows or risks.... Only if significance is attached exclusively to *the bottom line*, rather than to the present value of the enterprise, can the change in behaviour be defended'. Solomons goes on to give several examples where manipulating a measuring device soon gives rise to loss of neutrality, loss of reliability and, then, loss of usefulness. Zeff (1978, p. 63) agrees that 'the FASB would surely preside over its own demise if it were to...make decisions primarily on other than accounting grounds'.

It should not be regretted that different accounting gives rise to different economic decisions. Perhaps some of the decisions made by Rolls Royce and its shareholders in the late 1960s would have been different if SSAP 13 on R & D expenditure had been in operation. To claim that such a standard inhibits R & D expenditure would not prove that the standard should be changed.

Summary

The purpose of this article is to try to clarify the differences in translation methods, and their causes. Some differences are due to different underlying assumptions; others appear to be due to a lack of *consistent* assumptions. The debate has been confused by the use of erroneous definitions and faulty argument. Many translation methods have been advanced in theoretical writings and several have been recommended by professional bodies and used in practice in the UK and the US. A chronology of the development of these methods is provided.

The current/non-current and the monetary/non-monetary methods were attempts to provide a method which was thought to be more suitable than the closing rate method in a world of fluctuating exchange rates. However, the former has attracted particularly heavy criticism on theoretical grounds. The desire to have a consistent underlying financial accounting theory, which would cope with both historic cost accounting and other systems, led to ARS 12 and FAS 8 which introduced the temporal principle. This seems acceptable to many financial accounting theorists on both sides of the Atlantic. However, some practitioners, specialists in business finance and management accountants are opposed to it because of its effects on profits.

Also, alternative accounting assumptions to the proprietary method (on which ARS 12 was based) can be used to favour the closing rate method.

In practice, it might appear that the translation method used in a particular country at a particular time depends little on theories but more on its effects on profits under the ruling exchange rate conditions.

The underlying assumptions about the purpose of financial statements, consolidation and translation affect the way in which adjustments for inflation and specific price changes are linked with a translation method. For CPP, translate-restate seems to fit with the proprietary assumption and the temporal principle. The weight of theoretical arguments appear to be on this side. For CCA, restate-translate is fairly clearly correct.

There is, however, a more fundamental suggestion that exchange rates are not suitable for translation. Some writers propose purchasing power parities, but these have failed to gain general acceptance. There are, also, arguments that suggest that neither exchange rates nor PPPs are suitable for most balances and that, since the proprietary theory is questionable for many multinationals, consolidation is not suitable either.

More recently, the intensity of the debate on the economic consequences of accounting rules about such matters as translation has increased. However, the arguments in favour of 'integrity' and 'neutrality' for accounting standards seem to be the stronger, even if expediency and short-term political matters are beginning to affect more seriously the setting of standards in practice.

References

AICPA, 1972, *ARS 12-Reporting Foreign Operations of US Companies in US Dollars.*
Aliber, R. Z. and Stickney, C. P., 1975, 'Measures of foreign exchange exposure', *Accounting Review*, January.
American Accounting Association, 1974, 'Report of the Committee on International Accounting', *Accounting Review Supplement*, pp. 259–262.
American Accounting Association, 1975, 'Report of the Committee on International Accounting', *Accounting Review Supplement*, pp. 91–95.
APB, 1972. *Proposed Opinion, Translating Foreign Operations.*
Baxter, W. T. and Yamey, B. S., 1951, 'Theory of foreign branch accounts', *Accounting Research*, April.
Balassa, B., 1964, 'The purchasing-power parity doctrine: a reappraisal', *Journal of Political Economy*, December.
Choi, F. D. S., 1975, 'Foreign currency translation', *International Journal of Accounting*, Fall.
Clarke, F. L., 1977, 'A note on exchange rates, purchasing power parities and translation procedures', *Abacus*, June.
Clarke, F. L., 1978, 'Patz on parities, exchange rates and translation', *Accounting and Business Research*, Winter, p. 75.
Connor, J. E., 1972, 'Accounting for the upward float of foreign currencies', *Journal of Accountancy*, June.
Dicksee, L. R., 1911, *Advanced Accounting*, Gee and Co, p. 30.

Evans, T. H. and Folks, W. R., 1979, 'SFAS 8: conforming, coping, complaining, and correcting!', *International Journal of Accounting*, Fall, p. 36.

FASB, 1975, *Accounting for the Translation of Foreign Currency Transactions and Foreign Currency Financial Statements FAS No. 8.*

FASB, 1976, *Conceptual Framework for Financial Accounting and Reporting*—discussion memorandum, para 367.

Flower, J., 1976, *Accounting Treatment of Overseas Currencies*, ICAEW.

Flower, J., 1978, 'A price parity theory of translation: a comment', *Accounting and Business Research*, Winter.

Gerboth, D. L., 1973, 'Research, intuition and politics in accounting enquiry', *Accounting Review*, July.

Goudeket, A., 1960, 'An application of replacement value theory', *Journal of Accountancy*, July.

Hendriksen, E. S., 1970, *Accounting Theory*, Irwin, Homewood, Illinois, p. 232. It should be mentioned, however, that Hendriksen states correctly on another page (233) that the *historical* rate was recommended. References to ABR 43 are omitted in later editions.

Henning, C. N., Piggott, W. and Scott, R. H., 1978, *International Financial Management*, McGraw Hill, New York, pp. 375–377.

Hepworth, S. R., 1956, *Reporting Foreign Operations*, University of Michigan.

Hinton, R. P., 1978, 'Foreign currency transactions', *Accountant*, May 4.

Horngren, C. T., 1973, 'The marketing of accounting standards', *Journal of Accountancy*, October.

IASG (1976) *Guidance Manual on CCA*, London, p. 200.

ICAEW, 1979, *Survey of Published Accounts—1978*, ICAEW, London.

Kettel, B., 1978 'Foreign exchange exposure', *Accountancy*, March, p. 86.

Lorensen, L. and Rosenfield, P., 1974, 'Management information and foreign inflation', *Journal of Accountancy*, December.

May, R. G. and Sundem, G. L., 1976, 'Research for accounting policy: an overview', *Accounting Review*, October.

McMonnies, P. N. and Rankin, B. J., 1977, 'Accounting for foreign currency translation', *Accountant's Magazine*, June, p. 241.

National Accounting Association, *Research Report No. 36*, 1960.

Parker, R. H., 1970, 'Principles and practice in translating foreign currencies', *Abacus*, December.

Parkinson, R. M., 1972, *Translation of Foreign Currencies*, Canadian Institute of Chartered Accountants.

Patz, D. H., 1977 (1), 'The state of the art in translation theory', *Journal of Business Finance and Accounting*, 4, 3.

Patz, D. H., 1977 (2), 'A price parity theory of translation', *Accounting and Business Research*, Winter.

Plumb, H. A., 1891, 'The treatment of fluctuating currencies in the accounts of English companies', *Accountant*, April 4, p. 259.

Rappaport, A., 1977, 'Economic impact of accounting standards—implications for the FASB', *Journal of Accountancy*, May.

Rosenfield, P., 1971, 'General price level accounting and foreign operations', *Journal of Accountancy*, February.

Scott, G. M., 1975, 'Currency exchange rates and accounting translation: a mis-marriage?', *Abacus*, June, p. 59.

Seidler, L. J., 1972, 'An income approach to the translation of foreign currency financial statements', *CPA Journal*, January.

Seidler, L. J., 1978, 'Accounting for foreign currency translation', in *Accounting for Multinational Enterprises*, Eds. D. D. AlHashim and J. W. Robertson, Bobbs-Merrill.

Shwayder, K., 1972, 'Accounting for exchange rate fluctuations', *Accounting Review*, October, p. 749.

Smith, A. F., 1978, 'Temporal method: temporary mode', *Management Accounting (US)*, February, p. 25.

Solomons, D., 1978, 'The politicization of accounting', *Journal of Accountancy*, November.

Storey, R., 1972, Appendix to *ARS* 12.

Walker, R. G., 1978, *Consolidated Statements*, Arno Press, especially ch. 15.

Wyatt, A. R., 1977, 'The economic impact of financial accounting standards', *Journal of Accountancy*, October.

Zeff, S. A., 1978, 'The rise of economic consequences', *Journal of Accountancy*, December.

Zenoff, D. B. and Zwick, J., 1969, *International Financial Management*, Prentice-Hall, p. 500.

Appendix

Selected exchange rates

	US $ to £1	French francs to £1	French francs to $1	German marks to £1	German marks to $1	Brazil cruzeiro to £1	Brazil cruzeiro to $1
1870		25.1	4.98				
Pre-war	4.867	25.22	5.18	20.429	4.198	15	3.080
1914		25.3	5.19				
1915	4.86	25.12	5.24		4.59	17.75	3.17
1916	4.77	28	5.90		5.36	20	4.04
1917	4.76	27.8	5.86		5.53	20	4.27
1918	4.76	27.18	5.72			17.75	3.72
1919	4.76	26	5.47			18.5	3.92
1920	3.7	41	11	340	100.5	13.75	3.72
1921	3.8	54	14	215	57	25.25	6.78
1922	4.2	51.4	12.15	790	186	32	7.87
1923	4.65	62	14	32,000	6890	40	8.60
1924	4.25	84	20	19 billion	4.47 billion	40	9.41
1925	4.74	88	18.57	20	4.22	40	8.44
1926	4.85	129.25	26.59	20.3	4.18	34.25	6.64

Year							
1927	4.85	122	25.10	20.4	4.2	41.75	8.6
1928	4.87	124	25.52	20.45	4.21	40	8.23
1929	4.85	124	25.52	20.4	4.20	40	8.36
1930	4.87	123.9	25.50	20.4	4.20	43.5	8.95
1931	4.87	123.67	25.43	20.4	4.20	53.3	10.97
1932	3.38	86	25.59	14.25	4.24	60	17.86
1933	3.34	86	25.59	14.10	4.2	43.5	12.95
1934	5.0	83	16.6	13.6	2.61	60	16
1935	4.93	74.5	15.31	12.1	2.45	84.9	17.22
1936	4.93	75	15.31	12.25	2.48	86.3	17.33
1937	4.91	105	21.43	12.25	2.48	79.6	16.08
1938	5.0	147	29.4	12.4	2.49	83.5	18.17
1939	4.63	176.5	39.8	11.5	2.49	81.9	19.71
1940	4.03	176.5	43.8		2.5	73.7	19.79
1941	4.03						
1942	4.03					83.6	19.64
1943	4.03					83.6	19.63
1944	4.03					83.6	19.57
1945	4.03	203	49.72			82.8	19.50
1946	4.03	480	119.3			79	18.72
1947	4.03	480	119.3			79	18.72
1948	4.03	864	214.7	13.4	3.33	79	18.72
1949	4.03	1093	350	13.4	3.33	52	18.72
1950	2.80	980	350	11.76	4.2		
1951	2.80	979	349.95	11.76	4.2		
1952	2.79	981	349.95	11.5	4.2		
1953	2.81	982	349.95	11.70	4.2		
1954	2.81	981	349.95	11.73	4.2		
1955	2.79	978	349.95	11.74	4.2		
1956	2.80	982	350	11.71	4.2		
1957	2.79	984	350	11.73	4.2		
1958	2.81	1117	420	11.72	4.2		
1959	2.81	1374	490	11.74	4.18		
1960	2.81	13.74	4.90	11.71	4.17		
1961	2.81	13.7	4.9	11.17	3.99		
1962	2.81	13.7	4.9	11.20	3.99		
1963	2.80	13.7	4.9	11.11	3.97		
1964	2.79	13.7	4.9	11.09	3.97	4400	1610
1965	2.80	13.7	4.9	11.22	4.0	6216	2220
1966	2.79	13.8	4.9	11.09	3.97	6216	2220
1967	2.79	13.8	4.9	11.22	4.01	6130	2200
1968	2.4	11.8	4.9	9.5	3.98	7.6	3.2
1969	2.4	11.8	4.9	9.58	4.01	9.0	3.5
1970	2.4	13.2		8.7		10.4	
1971	2.42	13.3		8.7		11.9	
1972	2.6	13.3		8.3		14.4	
1973	2.4	12.0		7.5		14.6	
1974	2.3	11.2		6.0		14.2	
1975	2.2	9.5		5.4		17.0	
1976	1.8	8.6		4.6		18.3	
1977	1.7	8.5		4.0		21.0	
1978	1.9	9.1		4.1		30.6	
1979	2.0	8.5		3.7		42.5	

Sources: R. L. Bidwell, *Currency Tables*, Rex Collings, London, 1970; CSO, *Financial Statistics* February 1973 and December 1979, HMSO, London, Table 102.

When several rates are quoted in the sources, the rate noted above is the earliest given for the particular year.

[11]

Journal of International Financial Management and Accounting 8:2 1997

Effects of Alternative Goodwill Treatments on Merger Premia: a Comment

Christopher Nobes and Julie Norton*

Lee and Choi (1992) extend their influential paper (Choi and Lee, 1991) on the effects of international accounting differences for goodwill by considering accounting and tax treatments for goodwill in four countries (Germany, Japan, the U.K. and the U.S.). They ask:

> To what extent are merger premia offered by acquirors in our sample countries associated with differing accounting and/or tax treatments for goodwill? This is the question addressed in this paper. (p. 222)

Their conclusion is that:

> the results ... are generally consistent with the expectation that merger premia differences are primarily affected by differential accounting and tax treatments for goodwill in Germany and Japan. (p. 233)

This present "comment" suggests that this conclusion is misleading because the authors misinterpreted the tax rules. The confusion occurs because of a failure to distinguish between goodwill on consolidation and other purchased goodwill. The former arises when a company (or group of companies) acquires another company. Such goodwill therefore arises only in consolidated financial statements. In nearly all countries (certainly including Germany and Japan), such statements are irrelevant for tax purposes because the group is not a taxable entity. For some aspects of tax calculations in some countries, some parts of the group may be aggregated (Lamb, 1995), but even then the consolidated income statement is not directly used (e.g., there are exclusions of one or more of (i) overseas subsidiaries,[1] (ii) joint ventures, (iii) equity-accounted companies, or (iv) subsidiaries in which the holding is less than 75% or 80%,[2] etc.).

Other purchased goodwill (not on consolidation) can arise when a company buys the assets of another company instead of buying the shares

* The authors are, respectively, Coopers & Lybrand Professor of Accounting and Lecturer in Accounting at the University of Reading, England. They are grateful for advice from Etsuo Sawa of the Japanese Institute of Certified Public Accountants.

138   Christopher Nobes and Julie Norton

in the company. Another case of particular relevance in Japan is that non-consolidation goodwill can sometimes arise in the context of legal mergers, which are a common means of achieving a business combination between two Japanese companies. In effect, the non-consolidation goodwill arises in the company about to be merged, as a result of revaluations. This is, of course, not directly relevant for Lee and Choi's paper, because they deal with the acquisition of US companies.

When there is purchased non-consolidation goodwill, since the goodwill arises in a taxable entity, the tax rules in some countries (e.g., Canada, Germany and Japan and, since 1993, the U.S.[3]) allow it to be amortized for tax purposes. By contrast, when a company buys for cash the shares of another company, this does not give rise to goodwill in the purchasing company's balance sheet, and the shares are not depreciated for accounting or tax purposes. In Japan, for example, the words for the two types of goodwill are different: non-consolidation goodwill is called *Eigyoken* or *Noren*, whereas consolidation goodwill is *Renketsu Chosei Kanjyo*.[4]

However, Lee and Choi (1992, p. 222) do not distinguish between the two types of goodwill. Their description of goodwill as tax depreciable in Japan and Germany is only correct for non-consolidation goodwill. Taking the example of Germany, Table 1 contrasts Lee and Choi's description

Table 1. *Accounting and Tax Treatments for Goodwill in Germany*

Accounting	Tax
A. *Choi and Lee*	
1. Write off to reserves, or	Amortize over 15 years
2. amortize, normally over 4 years	
B. *Non-consolidation goodwill*	
1. Expense immediately	Amortize (straight-line)
2. amortize over 4 years,	over exactly 15 years
3. amortize over period expected to benefit, or	
4. in practice, follow the tax rule	
(note: write off to reserves is not allowed)	
C. *Consolidation goodwill*	
1. Write off immediately to reserves	Not relevant for tax purposes
2. amortize over 4 years, or	
3. amortize over useful life	

Source: (A)—Choi and Lee (1992, p. 222)
  (B) and (C)—Ordelheide and Pfaff (1994, pp. 124–127, 190–191) and
    Macharzina and Langer (1995, pp. 275 and 283).

(A) with the position explained in more detail by German authors (B and C). As may be seen, Lee and Choi have recorded the accounting treatment relating to consolidation goodwill, but their tax treatment relates to non-consolidation goodwill. Turning to Japan, the rules relating to non-consolidation and consolidation goodwill are to be found in quite separate sources of authority. The non-consolidation rules (which are relevant for tax deductibility purposes) come from the Commercial Code; whereas consolidation is regulated under the Securities and Exchange Law and the Business Accounting Deliberation Council (Cooke and Kikuya, 1992). The Commercial Code's rules (which are followed by the tax law) do deal with the amortization of goodwill, but no non-consolidation goodwill arises in a Japanese parent company when it buys shares in another company, so there is nothing to depreciate for tax purposes. Table 2 records the position for Japan.

Table 2. *Accounting and Tax Treatments for Goodwill in Japan*

Accounting	Tax
A. *Choi and Lee* Amortize over a reasonable period, normally 5 years	Depreciable
B. *Non-consolidation goodwill* Amortize systematically over a maximum of 5 years; not less than one fifth in any year	Deductible following accounting rules
C. *Consolidation goodwill* Amortize in an amount no less than that computed on a straight-line basis over the appropriate period. Normally amortized over 5 years, although longer periods are allowable if justified. There is also special provision* for some companies registered with the SEC of the USA	Not relevant for tax purposes

Source: (A)—Choi and Lee (1992, p. 222)
(B) and (C)—Cooke and Kikuya (1992, p. 202);
Coopers & Lybrand (1993, p. 25);
Business Accounting Deliberation Council
(1977, Section 4, para. 2 (2)); JICPA
Audit Committee Report, No. 29 of 1978.

Note*: The Ministry of Finance Ordinance which became effective in 1977 allows those Japanese companies which were SEC-registered at the time to continue using US GAAP for Japanese filing purposes. This provision was scheduled to end in 1998, but has been extended for a further three years.

140   *Christopher Nobes and Julie Norton*

It is clear that the rest of Lee and Choi's paper deals with consolidation goodwill, since they are interested to "compare premiums paid by U.S. acquirors with those paid by foreign acquirors of U.S. target companies" (p. 222). Consequently, their hypotheses about the tax effects are wrong, unless managers have been similarly misled on the subject of the tax rules.

Perhaps the most extreme illustration of the confusion is the statement that "goodwill can be amortized against reserves and is also tax deductible in Germany" (p. 225). First, it is misleading to state that goodwill is amortized against reserves. Consolidation goodwill can be written off immediately and fully (not gradually amortized) against reserves; and non-consolidation goodwill cannot be taken to reserves at all. However, the problem which is more relevant here is the suggestion that the former point (using reserves) is an accounting advantage (compared to the U.S. treatment) and the latter point (deductibility) is a tax advantage. The difficulty with this suggestion is that, in a country such as Germany where the tax rules are largely the accounting rules, tax deductibility is only possible if amortization is charged to the income statement (Ordelheide and Pfaff, 1994, p. 80). Therefore, if one used the accounting advantage, there would be no asset left to amortize in order to get the tax advantage. So, the suggestion would not even make sense if consolidation goodwill were tax deductible.

This confusion of tax rules and consequential incorrect analysis of the effects of international tax differences is also to be found elsewhere in the business press (e.g., Pensler, 1988) and the academic press (e.g., Dunne and Rollins, 1992 and 1994; and Dunne and Ndubizu, 1995). It is to be hoped that future papers will disentangle the tax rules relating to consolidation goodwill from those relating to other goodwill.

Notes

1. This is the case in the U.S. (section 1504 (b) (3) of the Internal Revenue Code).
2. 75% applies in the U.K.; and 80% in the U.S.
3. The U.S. treatment for goodwill changed in 1993, when Section 197 of the Internal Revenue Code was changed to allow the straightline amortization of certain intangibles over 15 years.
4. Literally, this means "consolidation adjustment account." Correspondence of October 4, 1995 with Mr. E. Sawa of the Japanese Institute of Certified Public Accountants.

References

Business Accounting Deliberation Council, *Financial Accounting Standards on Consolidated Accounts* (Tokyo: Ministry of Finance, 1977).

Choi, F. D. S. and C. Lee, "Merger Premia and National Differences in Accounting for Goodwill," *Journal of International Financial Management and Accounting*, 3 (1991), No. 3.

Cooke, T. E. and M. Kikuya, *Financial Reporting in Japan* (Oxford: Blackwell, 1992), pp. 209–210.

Coopers & Lybrand, *Accounting Comparisons: UK–Japan* (Gee, 1993).

Doering, J. A., "The Amortization of Intangibles: Before and After Section 197," *Taxes*, (October 1993).

Dunne, K. M. and G. A. Ndubizu, "International acquisition accounting method and corporate multinationalism: evidence from foreign acquisitions," *Journal of International Business Studies* (1995), Vol. 26, No. 2.

Dunne, K. M. and T. P. Rollins, "Accounting for Goodwill: a Case Analysis of US, UK and Japan," *Journal of International Accounting, Auditing and Taxation* (1992), No. 2.

Dunne, K. M. and T. P. Rollins (1994), as Dunne and Rollins (1992) but reprinted in *Readings and Notes on Financial Accounting: Issues and Controversies*, S. A. Zeff and B. G. Dharan eds. (McGraw-Hill, 1994) pp. 339–354.

Lamb, M., "When is a Group a Group? Convergence of Concepts of 'Group' in European Union Corporate Tax," *European Accounting Review*, 4 (1995), No. 1.

Lee, C. and F. D. S. Choi, "Effects of Alternative Goodwill Treatments on Merger Premia: Further Empirical Evidence," *Journal of International Management and Accounting*, 4 (1992), No. 3.

Macharzina, K. and K. Langer, "Financial Reporting in Germany" in *Comparative International Accounting*, C. W. Nobes and R. H. Parker eds. (Prentice Hall, 1995).

Ordelheide, D. and D. Pfaff, *European Financial Reporting: Germany* (Routledge, 1994).

Pensler, S., "Accounting Rules Favor Foreign Bidders," *Wall Street Journal* (24 March 1988).

Journal of Business Finance & Accounting, 25(3) & (4), April/May 1998, 0306-686X

THE USE OF FOREIGN ACCOUNTING DATA IN UK FINANCIAL INSTITUTIONS

SAMANTHA MILES AND CHRISTOPHER NOBES*

INTRODUCTION

The globalisation of securities markets (Smith, 1991; and Scott-Quinn, 1991) has led to an increased use of foreign financial information and to a need for international comparability of financial information. The need for comparability has been recognised by securities regulators (IOSCO, 1995) but the fulfilment of it is some years away. In the meantime, one way of dealing with the problem is for regulators to demand expensive dual reporting or reconciliations.[1] Another way is to pretend that there is no problem, i.e. to negotiate mutual recognition of accounting regulations.

In most markets, the participants use various mechanisms to cope with international accounting differences, such as adjustments of accounting numbers to a benchmark or reliance instead on economic data or comparisons of financial information within a regulatory environment but not from one environment to another. This paper examines the reactions to foreign accounting data of participants in the global equity[2] market who are based in London, which has the world's most international major equity market.[3] The argument proceeds by looking first at previous findings relating to the use of accounting data in a domestic context, then at the few studies in an international context, then at our own survey. In order to interpret the results, it is important to discuss briefly the opposing theories of market efficiency and hence any implications for accounting policy choice which result from international accounting diversity.

USE OF ACCOUNTING DATA IN A DOMESTIC CONTEXT

Some research into UK equity valuation suggests that the annual report is the most important source of information for analysts, although they also use

* The authors are, respectively, Lecturer in Accounting at the University of Bristol and Coopers & Lybrand Professor of Accounting at the University of Reading. They are grateful for the many hours provided by the analysts and fund managers who were interviewed for this research, and to David Ashton, Judy Day, Don Egginton, Alan Roberts and the anonymous referees for comments on earlier drafts of this paper. (Paper received October 1996, revised and accepted August 1997)

Address for correspondence: C.W. Nobes, Coopers and Lybrand Professor of Accounting, Department of Economics, Faculty of Letters & Social Sciences, The University of Reading, P.O. Box 218, Whiteknights, Reading RG6 6AA, UK.

several other sources to build up their picture of a company (Lee and Tweedie, 1981; Arnold and Moizer, 1984; and Day, 1986). Nevertheless, Lee and Tweedie found that analysts had a limited understanding of accounting data; and Day found that few analysts had accounting qualifications, and noted that annual reports are not seen as containing price sensitive information. Arnold and Moizer suggested that analysts may have exaggerated their use of annual reports in order to avoid suspicions of insider dealing. More recent papers (Pike et al., 1993; and Breton and Taffler, 1995) do indeed show an increased reliance on company contacts.

Day reports that analysts make extensive use of ratios (e.g. gearing), and Arnold and Moizer show the use of price/earnings ratios. Pike et al. confirm the importance of price/earnings or price/cash flow ratios, followed by the ratio of net assets per share. They also found only a small usage of technical analysis or of betas. This contrasted with a greater use of technical analysis for domestic purposes in Germany (Darrat, 1987).

Given (i) the heavy reliance on ratios in the UK, and (ii) the lack of accounting sophistication, there would appear to be a temptation for management to engage in various forms of 'creative accounting'. It is widely believed that UK management succumb to the temptation (Griffiths, 1986; Jamieson, 1988; and Smith, 1992 and 1996). This is despite good evidence that major stock markets are efficient, at least in semi-strong form (e.g. Firth, 1976; and Cooper, 1982). Anecdotal evidence (e.g. as discussed by Watts and Zimmerman, 1986, p. 75) concerning the behaviour of managers and the investment community appears to suggest that they may not believe the general empirical evidence supporting market efficiency. It also seems that analysts may be 'functionally fixated' on the 'bottom line' without attending to the details of its calculation (Ashton, 1976; and Abdel-Khalik and Keller, 1979), so that an earnings decreasing accounting change is accompanied by a negative abnormal stock return regardless of the effect of a change in the present value of cash flows.

Running counter to these arguments: (i) it is possible to explain management behaviour in other ways, (ii) anecdotal evidence should be treated carefully, and (iii) belief in inefficiency by market participants does not imply inefficiency. First, some actions of management might be explained via the contracting hypothesis without contravening a belief in market efficiency. Many contracts, such as debt covenants and compensation plans within the firm, rely on accounting numbers. Management may be motivated to select certain accounting procedures because of the implications that they have for such contracts. This has some empirical support, e.g. Zmijewski and Hagerman (1981) and Healy (1985).

Secondly, the anecdotal evidence should be interpreted carefully. It is often considered less informative than more carefully constructed research, although this does not mean that it should be dismissed (Beaver, 1989, p. 142).

Thirdly, belief of inefficiency within the market by individuals does not imply that there actually is market inefficiency. For example, prices may reflect a richer information set than the one accessed by one individual. Certainly, Beaver regards the statement that 'market efficiency implies that fundamental research is useless' as fallacious. This is because analysts competing for information play an important role in the process of generating and disseminating information (including much that is not accounting based) to the investment community. Thus the net effect of their activities need not be valueless but can contribute to market efficiency by producing a richer information system.

Grossman and Stiglitz (1976) suggest that the market can never be fully efficient because there are constantly new shocks to the economy, so that the market can never fully adjust to, and therefore prices can never fully reflect, all the information possessed by informed individuals. The inefficiency may be just enough to provide the revenue required to compensate the informed investors for their analytical activities.

It has also been suggested that the market contains both functionally fixated investors and those who are more sophisticated (Hand, 1990), although this is unproven (Tiniç, 1990). Foster (1988, p. 444) also suggests a myopic hypothesis which states that the capital market has a short term focus on the current year's reported earnings, rather than a focus on a multi-year horizon. This theory helps to explain Hand's hybrid hypothesis. As Tiniç (1990) argues, if both sophisticated and unsophisticated market participants determine stock prices, there must be restrictions on the behaviour of the sophisticated investors which prevent them from exploiting the profit opportunities offered by mispriced securities. De Long et al. (1990) suggest that such restrictions may be a limited time horizon (as proposed by Foster), risk aversion or lack of wealth. For this theory to stand, unsophisticated investors must also be unable to learn that there are profit opportunities from mispriced securities.

In terms of particular accounting choices used to test market efficiency, the cases of LIFO in the US and of goodwill in the UK are instructive. The former is a real accounting choice with economic consequences via the tax advantage of adopting LIFO, and the latter is a cosmetic accounting example. Despite a large amount of empirical work on LIFO adoption (e.g. Biddle, 1980; Ricks, 1982; Abdel-Khalik and McKeown, 1978; Biddle and Ricks, 1988; and Jennings, Mest and Thompson, 1992), it is still not clear whether the market can see through a change in accounting policy, although a large number of factors (rather than just the reaction of the market to the 'bottom line') has been suggested to explain why management might forgo the tax advantages of LIFO. Examples include Fellingham's (1988) signalling theory, Beaver's (1989, p. 41) contracting perspective and Morse and Richardson (1983) who suggested firm size.

The fear of an unsophisticated market reaction to the effects of goodwill rules on profit seems to have been an important driving force in standard setting discussions in the UK (Holland, 1990; Waller, 1990; and Nobes,

1992). Empirical research does suggest that UK companies pay more for subsidiaries than US companies do because of the different goodwill rules (Choi and Lee, 1992). This may be partly due to lack of information (Duvall et al., 1992), or to the existence of different corporate governance systems resulting in different constraints being placed on management.

Breton and Taffler (1995) show that, in practice, UK analysts are not good at correcting for creative accounting when calculating ratios. The UK's Accounting Standards Board has attempted to reduce the scope for creative accounting in certain areas (e.g. by including all exceptional and extraordinary items within earnings).[4] Ironically, this has led analysts to create the concept of 'headline earnings' (IIMR, 1993) which excludes extraordinary and certain exceptional items, thereby preserving and expanding the scope for creative interpretation of these words. In Germany, the analysts' association (DVFA) has a definition of earnings which is designed to exclude several discretionary and tax-based items (Busse von Colbe et al., 1991). Some research (e.g. Rees et al., 1992; and Harris et al., 1994) suggests that DVFA adjusted information is more value-relevant than the original German annual reports.

In a domestic context, it is therefore at best unproven that the market is efficient in deciphering accounting numbers, given the empirical evidence supporting efficient markets, functional fixation and Hand's hybrid system, and anecdotal evidence of the proliferation of creative accounting. When adding an international dimension, further issues arise, as examined below.

CROSS-BORDER ANALYSIS

Choi and Levich (1991) interviewed users of cross-border data in 52 organisations in five major financial centres. They found that over half the users reported an effect on their market decisions due to accounting diversity. The others adopted local perspectives or relied on economic data. Those reporting an effect mostly tried to re-state foreign financial statements to a more familiar accounting basis. Some, however, avoided certain countries because of accounting differences.

Choi et al. (1983) looked at the interpretation of financial ratios from overseas. They suggested that there needs to be adjustment for institutional and other issues, as well as for accounting differences, before there can be successful international comparisons. Aron (1991) showed the difference in average price/earnings ratios between certain stock markets. There are also several studies concerned with differential degrees of conservatism across countries in the measurement of earnings (e.g. Weetman and Gray, 1991; Emenyonu and Gray, 1992; and Norton, 1995). These studies use reports published by foreign companies listed on the New York Stock Exchange which reconcile domestic accounting to US rules.

We have drawn on this cross-border research in order to establish areas of investigation about the behaviour of analysts with respect to foreign accounting data. It also seems reasonable to extrapolate from the research summarised above relating to domestic analysis. For example, it seems likely that analysts are at least as unsure about comparative international accounting practices as they are about domestic ones. The following propositions are suggested in the context of the assessment of foreign companies by London-based analysts and fund managers:

1. Analysts and fund managers are not qualified accountants.
2. Accounting differences affect[5] the work of users.
3. Users rely more heavily on non-accounting data than on accounting data.
4. Users restate accounts before analysis.
5. Users restrict investment to countries or sectors with more familiar accounting.
6. Users are not knowledgeable about the major international accounting differences.

INTERVIEWS

Some of the above propositions might be susceptible to market-based research. For example, Choi and Lee's (1992) work might be extended to examine aspects of restatement of accounting data. However, the above propositions examine behavioural issues and would generally seem to require questionnaire or interview methodology which does not allow elaborate statistical analysis.

A questionnaire approach has been used elsewhere (Weaver, 1996). This paper, which can be seen as a series of case studies, reports on interviews with 17 London-based international analysts and fund managers. Interviews have the advantage over questionnaires of the ability to collect a richer series of answers by reducing ambiguity and investigating interesting lines of enquiry. There are disadvantages, such as a limited sample size and the likelihood of interviewer bias. Attempts can be made to reduce the bias (e.g. Clarkson, 1967; and Day, 1986), and in the case of this research, there were always two interviewers present, who made simultaneous notes and compared them soon after each interview. The interviews were semi-structured, using a template of questions in the same order, but allowing extra questions where they seemed relevant, for example following up interesting lines of enquiry.

The 17 interviewees worked for six large institutions (one ultimately controlled in the UK, one from the US, and four from continental Europe). The institutions were self-selecting in the sense that they agreed to take part in the interview process. This may introduce a bias if this means that certain types of institution were excluded, e.g. those which were uncomfortable with their lack of international accounting expertise or those opposed to assisting outside research. The number of interviewees compares with those used in previous research: 18 individuals by Day (1986); 12 London-based firms by Choi and Levich (1991) and participants from five firms by Breton and Taffler (1995). Nevertheless, our findings can only be regarded as indicative, and may not accurately represent the whole population of UK analysts who use foreign accounting data in their work.

A pilot interview was conducted in March 1994 with four fund managers from a continental European based institution. The pilot was instructive, particularly in identifying the need to establish the organisational structure of the firm, e.g. whether analysts/fund managers concentrated on certain geographical areas or on sectors, international accounting diversity being potentially more important to the latter because inter-country comparisons must be made. It also became clear that some interviewees would be nervous about their lack of accounting knowledge, and would be more forthcoming if the interviews were not tape-recorded. It was therefore decided to use two interviewers for each interview, without tape-recording.

The 17 interviewees (nine analysts, five fund managers, and three analyst managers) were seen individually between April 1994 and March 1995, the interviews lasting about 45 minutes. The data which follows is based on the survey excluding the pilot. The Appendix summarises some biographical data relating to the interviewees, which has been used to cross reference the results.

In general, the analysts provided reports for external fund managers. As will be seen, the fund managers assume that the analysts make accounting adjustments for international diversity. The former are, therefore, less likely to see accounting diversity as a problem. Where useful, the findings below distinguish between analysts and fund managers. Another possibly relevant distinction for the *analysts*, which is brought out below, is between those specialising in particular sectors and those specialising in particular countries. By contrast, all the fund managers were basically geographically specialised.

FINDINGS

Our findings are explained here in the order of the six propositions outlined above.

Accounting Expertise

As may be seen from the Appendix, only two of the 17 interviewees had accounting qualifications (and none of the four pilot interviewees had). This is consistent with a similar finding by Day (1986) relating to domestic analysts.

Are Users Affected by International Differences?

Table 1 shows findings relating to whether the interviewees perceived international accounting differences to affect investment decisions. This was explained as whether there were difficulties in understanding foreign financial statements or problems with the comparability of accounts which caused the users to alter their investment criteria. The interviewees were nearly equally split on this subject, with no evidence that greater experience leads to more effect. However, if the subjects are grouped into 'sector' and 'country' experts, a strong association can be seen between sector expertise and a tendency to perceive an effect on investment decisions: seven out of eight sector experts reported an effect, whereas only two out of nine country experts did. This is not driven by the analyst/manager classification because the fund managers were equally split between 'yes' and 'no'; nor is it due to any greater experience of sector specialists (they had average experience of 5.2 years, against country specialists' 8.6 years).

Those nine interviewees who reported an effect were asked follow-up questions on the nature of the effect on their behaviour. Assessment of foreign companies was said to be affected in the following ways:

(i) reluctance to rely on accounting information (1 out of 9);
(ii) necessity to restate to some degree which was considered time-consuming (3 out of 9);
(iii) avoidance/reduction of investment due to a lack of understanding foreign accounting (3 out of 9); and
(iv) problems experienced in understanding accounting but not insurmountable ones (2 out of 9), e.g. requiring a more detailed analysis of the notes to the accounts than usual.

Those eight interviewees who saw no problem with accounting diversity fell into the following categories:

(i) reliance on reports of brokers (3 out of 8);
(ii) lack of use of accounting information (1 out of 8);
(iii) lack of perception of accounting diversity (1 out of 8);
(iv) markets viewed from domestic perspective because price setters are domestic (1 out of 8); and
(v) international comparisons not undertaken due to being a country specialist (2 out of 8).

Thus, these case studies suggest that investment decisions are generally affected by accounting diversity for sector experts but not for country experts.

Coping Techniques

Macro-economic data was used by 14 out of 17 interviewees, for purposes including:

Table 1

Do Accounting Differences Affect Capital Market Decisions? (No. of Interviewees)

Profession	Yes	No	Total
Analyst-sector	6	1	7
Analyst/manager-sector	1	–	1
Analyst-country	–	2	2
Fund manager (– basically country specialists)	2	2	4
Analyst/manager-country	–	3	3
Total	9	8	17

- to identify growth areas in an economy,
- to check that a company's forecasts were plausible,
- to identify cyclical factors, such as inflation and interest rates.

Two interviewees did not use macroeconomic data because they were fund managers who relied on analysts, and one analyst adopted a 'bottom-up' approach which focused on individual companies without looking at the macro-economy.

All interviewees (including the fund managers) reported the use of trend analysis and ratio analysis. About half the interviewees looked at companies over five to ten years in order to cover at least one business cycle. The others used two to four years, partly because the lack of availability of data was a problem (e.g. in emerging countries) and partly because comparability was made difficult after accounting changes (e.g. as a result of the implementation of EU Directives).

Ratio analysis ranged from the comprehensive by some analysts to a check for anomalies by three fund managers. Standard spreadsheets were in common use, with between six and nine ratios being normal. Six out of 17 interviewees preferred cash flow ratios (i.e. ratios based on an adjusted profit figure) but price/earnings ratios were seen as the most important by the other 11.

In conclusion, although non-accounting data is generally used, it does not supplant the use of accounting data.

Restatement

Restatement of foreign accounting data to a benchmark before analysis is not common. Only one interviewee (an analyst) undertook substantial, but not full, restatement (to a UK basis). Two more analysts made a few adjustments, particularly by adding back goodwill amortisation. Two analysts and one fund manager said that, where available, they used a company's reconciliation data to US or International Accounting Standards (IASs), and another used DVFA[6] figures.

On further investigation, it was clear that these analysts were unaware that, at least up until 1995, IASs were sufficiently flexible that almost any US or UK practice was acceptable. This flexibility meant that it was also quite possible for most continental European companies to choose national options in order to comply with IASs while retaining practices very different from either UK or US accounting.

The remaining eleven interviewees (i.e. 7 out of 8 fund managers and all the manager/analysts) did not adjust or use available reconciliation data. Further questioning revealed that the reasons for this included:

(i) 7 out of 8 fund managers assumed that analysts had already made the necessary adjustments (7 out of the 11 interviewees who did not adjust/ reconcile);

(ii) accounting data is not sufficiently important to use resources to adjust it (2 out of 11);

(iii) cultural differences are more important than accounting differences and cannot be adjusted for by restatement (1 out of 11); and

(iv) domestic figures should be used for single-country portfolios, and even for international portfolios because price-setting is done by investors using domestic data (1 out of 11).

Some comment seems appropriate on the implications of these responses. Reason (i) above is especially interesting, as the fund managers' assumption is wrong (based on our study). Reasons (ii) and (iii) are unimpressive, given that all interviewees used accounting data for ratio analysis, at least to some extent. Although ratio analysis may overcome some of the problems for country analysts, extensive use of provisions for income smoothing in some countries[7] may make apparent trends misleading. For cross-country sectoral analysis, the use of ratios will not solve problems in cases where numerator and denominator are affected in opposite directions.[8] Reason (iv) may not be true for the large listed companies which our interviewees were generally concerned with. Even for single-country portfolios, accounting differences are important for analysis: otherwise how would one know, for example, that it is important to adjust for the highly varied goodwill treatments in France (see below)?

It is now possible to summarise our findings with respect to restatement. Full restatement was not undertaken by any interviewee. Six interviewees (five of them analysts, i.e. a slight majority of the nine analysts) made some adjustments or used available reconciliations. One fund manager did this, but most of them incorrectly assumed that analysts made full-scale restatement.

318   MILES AND NOBES

Avoidance of Countries/Sectors

On the matter of avoiding particular countries, most interviewees (9 out of 17) were not in a position to do this because they had been allocated one country or a small range of countries. However, three interviewees (all of them fund managers or manager analysts) did avoid certain countries, particularly those with low regulation and lack of disclosure rather than those with incomprehensible accounting. China, Turkey and Vietnam were mentioned in this context, but there was also concern over Austria, Greece, India and Portugal. The treatment of provisions in Germany and Switzerland was seen as suspect. One fund manager who had a free rein for continental Europe avoided Austria, Italy and Germany because of a perception of poor accounting despite the strength and importance of the economies.

Three of the country specialists (3 out of 9) who did have a choice of sectors avoided certain of them because of accounting difficulties. In particular, this applied to financial services, including insurance companies.

In summary, there is some evidence to show that users avoid countries (3 out of 8) and sectors (3 out of 9) but most interviewees had little choice for at least one of the two dimensions.

Awareness of International Differences

Interviewees were asked whether they could rank countries in terms of conservatism of the measurement of earnings (for example, as in Radebaugh and Gray, 1993). Most interviewees (12 out of 17) made suggestions which were consistent with that literature. For example, UK accounting was universally thought to be less conservative than US accounting, which in turn was seen as less conservative than Japanese. Several interviewees were alert to the relevance, for these comparisons, of inflation, exchange rate movements and stage of the business cycle.

Interviewees were asked about awareness of international differences in certain major areas of accounting: goodwill, inventory costing and deferred tax. Although the range of countries covered was large, the interviews focused on differences between France, Germany, Japan, the UK and the USA.

In the case of goodwill, all sector analysts correctly identified UK practice, but most other interviewees did not, as Table 2 shows. This finding is consistent with those above concerning the greater use of adjustments by sector analysts. Table 3 shows that a similar overall picture emerges for recognition of US practices, but that there is decreasing knowledge for Germany, then France and Japan. Again, for these four countries, the greatest proportion of correct answers was given by the sector analysts, but this detail is not shown in order to avoid a proliferation of similar tables. As usual, the fund managers relied on analysts' reports to have corrected for the goodwill differences, but some analysts did not know the goodwill treatments (as noted

Table 2

Recognition of UK Goodwill Practices (interviewees by category)

	Correct Treatment Identified	Incorrect Treatment Identified	Not Important/ Don't Know	Country Not Relevant[1]	Total
Analyst-sector	6	–	–	1	7
Analyst-country	–	–	2	–	2
Fund manager	2	–	2	–	4
Analyst/manager-sector	–	–	1	–	1
Analyst/manager-country	1	–	2	–	3
Total	9 (53%)	– (–%)	7 (41%)	1 (6%)	17 (100%)

Note:
[1] Accounting knowledge relating to a country is not relevant because that country is not focused upon for investment.

Table 3

Recognition of Goodwill Practices (no. of interviewees)

	Correct Treatment	Incorrect Treatment	Not Important/ Don't Know	Country Not Relevant	Total
UK	9 (53%)	–	7 (41%)	1 (6%)	17 (100%)
US	8 (47%)	–	6 (35%)	3 (18%)	17 (100%)
Germany	2 (12%)	1 (6%)	4 (23%)	10 (59%)	17 (100%)
France	1 (6%)	–	7 (41%)	9 (53%)	17 (100%)
Japan	–	–	6 (35%)	11 (65%)	17 (100%)

above) and only one analyst adjusted for goodwill differences. However, some analysts stripped goodwill and its amortisation out of the accounts for analysis for any country.

Several country analysts tended to think that goodwill was either unimportant or uniformly treated within a country, but neither of these ideas is likely to be the case for the group reports of listed companies.[9] As examples of the importance of goodwill:

- Daimler-Benz' Form 20-F reconciliation for 1993 showed adjustments of DM287m (47% of earnings) and DM2284m (13% of net assets) from German to US rules.

- The French group, Total, would show earnings 20% higher for 1995 if they had adopted the UK practice of writing goodwill off against reserves.

- On average,[10] for the 42 UK companies listed on the New York Stock Exchange in 1993/4, the US reconciliation adjustment for goodwill

Table 4

Recognition of Inventory Flow Assumptions (no. of interviewees)

	FIFO*	LIFO Also Allowed and Common*	Not Important/ Don't Know	Country Not Relevant	Total
UK	3 (18%)	–	13 (76%)	1 (6%)	17 (100%)
US	–	3 (18%)	11 (65%)	3 (18%)	17 (100%)
Germany	–	–	7 (41%)	10 (59%)	17 (100%)
France	–	–	8 (47%)	9 (53%)	17 (100%)
Japan	–	–	6 (35%)	11 (65%)	17 (100%)

Note:
* Shaded areas represent correct recognition.

amounted to a decrease in earnings of 33% and an increase in net assets of 76%.

Turning to inventory valuation, the interviews covered the flow assumptions for the determination of cost (e.g. FIFO/LIFO). As Table 4 shows, there was very little knowledge on this subject, although a few recognised that LIFO is not acceptable in the UK but is in the US and in some other countries. All interviewees thought that inventory valuation was an unimportant area, and none adjusted for it. The fund managers relied on analysts. Upon further investigation as to why the analysts thought the issue unimportant, the following reasons were raised:

(i) low inflation, therefore little difference between FIFO, LIFO, etc. (5 out of 17),
(ii) the effects of different methods cancel out over time (4 out of 17),
(iii) stock levels are low in the sector dealt with (e.g. capital goods) (4 out of 17),
(iv) high stock turnover (1 out of 17).

These are unconvincing reasons because:

(i) The use of LIFO accumulates an 'error' in the balance sheet valuation, so that inflation of 20 years ago may be relevant. It is true that lack of price movements reduce the current earnings effect, except that, when stocks are physically reduced, earnings *rise* because old stocks are deemed to be used up.
(ii) Most accounting differences cancel out over time, but analysis concentrates on yearly earnings figures and values shown at a particular date. As noted in (i), a LIFO error will accumulate in the balance sheet.
(iii) Stock levels are unlikely to be so low as to make this factor irrelevant in most sectors.

(iv) High stock turnover has no effect on LIFO valuation,[11] and would actually *increase* the difference between LIFO and FIFO.

As examples of the effects of LIFO even in a period of low inflation, the US companies, General Motors (1992) and Caterpillar (1994), respectively report LIFO undervaluation 'errors' in the balance sheet amounting to 43% and 70% of net assets. General Motors also report an 11% 'error' in the calculation of earnings for 1992.[12]

The third area investigated was deferred tax. As an example of how important this topic can be, research elsewhere (Weetman and Gray, 1991) has shown that it contributes a major difference for UK companies reconciling to US rules; on average an increase of 4.9% to earnings in 1988. For Germany, France and Japan, the timing/temporary differences which cause deferred tax are often unimportant at the level of individual companies, but can become substantial in group financial statements, especially for France (Scheid and Walton, 1992, ch. 13).

As Table 5 shows, the lack of knowledge in this area was almost total, with only one interviewee correctly identifying partial allocation as the UK practice, but four of them incorrectly suggesting that deferred tax is generally larger in UK than in US financial statements. Two interviewees recognised that the causes of deferred tax were unlikely to be significant in Germany. Three interviewees thought that deferred tax was the amount provided (and soon to be paid) relating to the year's profit. A few analysts ($^3/_{17}$), suggested that they sometimes removed deferred tax balances from liabilities before analysis. Even Scandinavian analysts were not alert to the large deferred tax balances now being generated, for example, by application in Sweden of US-style principles to the treatment of untaxed reserves in consolidated balance sheets.[13]

In some cases, interviews extended to discussion of such issues as pension costs and the capitalisation of leases. Most interviewees were unaware of

Table 5

Recognition of Deferred Tax Practices (no. of interviewees)

	Full Allocation*	Partial Allocation*	Generally Does Not Arise*	Not Important/ Don't Know	Country Not Relevant	Total
UK	4 (23%)	1 (6%)	–	11 (64%)	1 (6%)	17 (100%)
US	–	3 (18%)	–	11 (64%)	3 (18%)	17 (100%)
Germany	–	–	2 (12%)	5 (29%)	10 (59%)	17 (100%)
France	–	–	–	8 (47%)	9 (53%)	17 (100%)
Japan	–	–	–	6 (35%)	11 (65%)	17 (100%)

Note:
* Shaded areas represent correct recognition.

international differences and there was a consensus that these issues were not adjusted for by analysts in their reports.

Summarising the discussion above concerning Tables 3 to 5, it is clear that there was a lack of knowledge of international differences. Of the three major areas investigated, even knowledge of UK practices was largely restricted to the area of goodwill and particularly to sector analysts.

The somewhat greater expertise and concern of sector analysts with international differences is presumably, in some measure, due to their being forced to address financial statements from several countries. The existence of accounting differences then becomes unavoidably plain, whereas a country analyst may be misled by a mask of national uniformity of presentation which may cover important sectoral accounting differences and may also encourage the analyst to ignore differences between the base country and the target country.

IMPLICATIONS FOR MARKET EFFICIENCY

Evidence has been presented here indicating a strong reliance on accounting numbers, principally through ratio analysis, when undertaking international investment appraisal. Restatement of these accounting numbers back to a common benchmark was not undertaken nor was published reconciliation data generally utilised. An interesting finding was the assumption made by fund managers that analysts undertake full restatement when compiling reports, thus fund managers believed that these reports contained comparable ratios. If an analyst/manager is not aware of accounting differences which influence accounting numbers, as evidenced in this study, the resulting analysis is likely to be misleading and may result in inefficient distributions of resources.

Even if an analyst/manager invests in only one foreign country, then ignorance of the foreign accounting practices may lead to incorrect decisions even if there is no bias in the expectation of values or returns. This is because variations in practices between companies within a country (e.g. with respect to goodwill amortisation lives or to income smoothing using provision movements) may distort the interpretation of the comparative prospects of those companies.

Where there is a choice of countries, the ratios of foreign companies may differ from an analyst's domestic norms without reflecting an increase or decrease in financial risk or rewards. As noted earlier, German and Japanese companies traditionally (and on average) measure profit more conservatively than US or UK companies; and Japanese companies have had lower liquidity ratios for a long period. When inserted into ratio analysis without adjustment, such figures may lead to long-run under-investment into such countries because their companies look noticeably worse than UK or US companies for most ratios. Even *after* restatement, international ratio analysis can be misleading due to underlying cultural, economic and legal differences (e.g. McLeay, 1995).

An extreme form of this problem is country-avoidance due to (i) lack of familiarity with accounting, (ii) accounting which discloses too little information, (iii) foreign exchange risk, or (iv) repatriation or expropriation risks. These are, of course, different issues. The first is related to potential inefficiency. Country-avoidance due to this first issue is clearly significant when it relates to economically important countries such as Germany and, to a lesser extent, Austria and Italy. It suggests that their corporate cost of capital will be higher than it needs to be, and it may explain the increasing use of US rules or international standards in Germany and Switzerland.[14]

The evidence presented here which provides *prima facie* support for the functional fixation hypothesis does not in itself dispute market efficiency within national stock exchanges, as domestic share prices tend to be determined principally by domestic investors. Furthermore, it is still unclear exactly how international stock markets assimilate information because research in this area is inconclusive.

Our findings are behavioural and anecdotal, and should therefore be treated with care, as noted earlier. Nevertheless, there is no reason to believe that our sample was atypical, except to the extent that the interviewees may have been *better* informed than the world's average analyst/fund manager because they were volunteers and because they worked for offices of very large international institutions in the world's most 'international' market.

SUMMARY AND CONCLUSIONS

Previous research on the UK investment community has related to domestic analysis. Much of it was carried out before the extensive globalisation of markets from the middle of the 1980s. The only earlier analogous paper dealing with cross-border issues (Choi and Levich, 1991) did not concentrate on one financial centre nor on financial institutions. It covered only some of the issues examined here, and in less detail. The present research reports on the behaviour of members of the London investment community with respect to foreign accounting data. Interviews were conducted with 17 users of such data in six institutions. The results may not be representative of the whole population of users of foreign accounting data, but there is no reason to believe that the population is more sophisticated on average than our sample.

The findings can be summarised under six propositions:

1. Most interviewees had no accounting qualification.
2. Most sector experts saw accounting differences as having an effect on investment decisions but most country experts did not.

3. Most interviewees used macro-economic data but not instead of trend
    and ratio analysis using accounting data.
4. A large majority of the analyst interviewees (and all the fund
    managers) did not restate accounting data to a benchmark, and most
    did not use available reconciliation data. However, the fund managers
    assumed that analysts do restate.
5. There is some evidence that, where there is scope to do so, users avoid
    some countries or sectors because of accounting problems.
6. A large majority of interviewees were not aware of accounting
    differences in major topic areas, and only the sector analysts were, in
    some cases, aware of UK or US practices.

Previous research (either domestic or cross-border) did not deal with the
differences between analysts and fund managers, which are seen as major here.
Nor had the difference between sector analysts and country analysts been
pointed out. Also, although not surprising in the light of domestic research,
the degree of ignorance on international differences has not been documented
before.

Previous research is not conclusive as to how stock markets assimilate
information and set prices, some of the evidence suggesting that there is scope
for successful window dressing in the domestic UK market. In an international
context, it would appear that there may be even greater scope if all
participants use accounting data (point 3 above), but they do not restate it
(point 4), perhaps partly because they are inexpert (point 1) and unaware of
the international differences (point 6). Country experts are probably wrong to
be blasé about the differences (point 2) because in many countries (with the
clear exception of the US) disclosure is worse than in the UK and the rules
allow even more flexibility for the manipulation of earnings figures. This all
suggests that incorrect investment advice and decisions are likely. To the
extent that companies in certain countries or sectors are avoided (point 5),
their cost of capital will rise due to the perception of poor accounting.

There would seem to be scope for better accounting training for users of
international information and advantages from continuing harmonisation of
accounting rules and practices.

APPENDIX

The Interviewees

Countries/Sectors Covered	Length of Experience in International Investment (Years)	Fund Manager or Analyst	Accounting Qualification
Japan	10	Fund Manager	No
Continental Europe	3.5	Fund Manager	No
Asia	25	Fund Manager	Partial
South East Asia	6.5	Fund Manager	No
UK (US in the past) Consumer goods, Beverages, Media, Pharmaceutical	12	Fund Manager	Yes
Far East: Mining, Tobacco, Food & Beverages	4	Analyst	No
USA and Canada	12	Both	No
Europe: Chemicals, Oil, Pharmaceuticals, Paper	4	Both	No
Capital Goods: UK, US, France, Germany, Sweden, Switzerland, Italy, Luxembourg	5	Both	No
European Chemicals	6	Analyst	No
Transport & Aviation: Europe, US, Japan	14	Analyst	No
France	4	Analyst	No
Switzerland & Belgium: Food, Oil & Gas in UK	2	Analyst	No
Sweden, Germany, France: Capital goods	0.5	Analyst	Yes
Turkey	4	Analyst	No
Scandinavian Banks	3	Analyst	No
Central Europe and Mediterranean	7	Analyst	No

NOTES

1 As, for example, demanded by the SEC for foreign registrants who wish to be listed on the New York Stock Exchange.
2 The analysts and fund managers in this survey dealt only with equities. Foreign bond markets are covered by other personnel. This suggests that the information costs of dealing in foreign markets are, to some extent, duplicated. This is a research issue to be pursued elsewhere.
3 For example, Cochrane (1994) shows that foreign equity turnover in 1992 was 43.2% for London, 6.8% for New York, 1.5% for Germany, 8.5% for Zurich and 0.3% for Tokyo.

4 Previously, large numbers of debit items were shown as extraordinary in order to escape from *SSAP 3*'s original definition of earnings. However, *FRS 3* defines 'ordinary' so widely that there will seldom be any items that are extraordinary. Furthermore, *FRS 3* amends the definition of earnings to include extraordinary items.

5 That is, affect decision-making due to difficulties of understanding, comparability, etc.

6 *Deutsche Vereinigung für Finanzanalyse und Anglageberatung*, the German analysts association (see Busse von Colbe et al., 1991).

7 See, for example, the corrections for German provisioning in the US GAAP reconciliations in the Annual Reports of Daimler-Benz AG for 1993 or 1994.

8 For example, UK goodwill practice makes income higher and net assets lower, compared to US, French or Japanese practice.

9 Goodwill is often important in such reports, particularly in its effects on earnings. Even listed Japanese companies may have bought many overseas subsidiaries. Practices vary dramatically within France, Germany and Japan (e.g. Nobes and Parker, 1995, chs. 11 to 13).

10 This is a simple average. The figures collate the data shown in Ernst & Young (1994).

11 High stock turnover would bring more up-to-date costs into a LIFO calculation of cost of sales but would still deem the oldest stock ever bought to be left in the balance sheet.

12 The 1992 Annual Report (p.24) shows a $294.7m increase in earnings due to the effect of LIFO in the context of falling inventory quantities. The post-tax loss (before effects of accounting changes) was $2,620.6m.

13 Arguably these would be treated as reserves under UK practices. The effect can be very important. For example, the shareholders' funds of Telia AB for 1994 are shown as SEK 19,842m, but would be 9.4% higher if deferred tax had been treated as reserves.

14 For example, from 1994, Bayer and Schering have used international standards for their group accounts. The same applies to Adidas, Deutsche Bank and Hoechst from 1995. Nestlé and many other Swiss companies do the same.

15 So far, two of the five institutions that we used for the research have asked for training courses on these issues, partly as a result of this research. See a similar point in Breton and Taffler (1995).

REFERENCES

Abdel-Khalik, A.R. and T.F. Keller (1979), *Earnings or Cash Flows: An Experiment on Functional Fixation and Valuation of the Firm* (American Accounting Association).

———— and J.C. McKeown (1978), 'Understanding Accounting Changes in an Efficient Market: Evidence of Differential Reaction', *Accounting Review* (October).

Arnold, J. and P. Moizer (1984), 'A Survey of the Methods Used by UK Investment Analysts to Appraise Investments in Ordinary Shares', *Accounting and Business Research* (Summer).

Aron, P. (1991), 'Japanese P/E Ratios in an Environment of Increasing Uncertainty', ch. 8 in Choi (1991).

Ashton, R.H. (1976), 'Cognitive Changes Induced by Accounting Changes: Experimental Evidence on the FFH', *Journal of Accounting Research*, Vol. 14, Supplement.

Beaver, W.H. (1989), *Financial Reporting: An Accounting Revolution* (2nd ed., Prentice Hall, Englewood Cliffs, New Jersey).

Biddle, G.C. (1980), 'Accounting Methods and Management Decisions: The Case of Inventory Costing and Inventory Policy', supplement to *Journal of Accounting Research*, Vol. 18.

———— and W.E. Ricks (1988), 'Analyst Forecast Errors and Stock Price Behaviour near the Earning Announcement Dates of LIFO Adopters', *Journal of Accounting Research*, Vol. 26 (Autumn).

Breton, G. and R. Taffler (1995), 'Creative Accounting and Investment Analyst Response', *Accounting and Business Research* (Spring).

Busse von Colbe, W., K. Geiger, H. Haase, H. Reinhard and G. Schmitt (1991), *Ergebnis nach DVFA/SG* (Schäffer Verlag, Stuttgart).

Choi, F.D.S. (1991), *Handbook of International Accounting* (Wiley, New York).

———— and C. Lee (1992), 'Effects of Alternative Goodwill Treatments on Merger Premia:

Further Empirical Evidence', *Journal of International Financial Management and Accounting*, Vol. 4.

Choi, F.D.S., H. Hino, S.K. Min, S.O. Nam, J. Ujiie and A. Stonehill (1983), 'Analyzing Foreign Financial Statements: The Use and Misuse of International Ratio Analysis', *Journal of International Business Studies* (Spring/Summer).

―――― and R.M. Levich (1991), 'Behavioral Effects of International Accounting Diversity', *Accounting Horizons* (June).

Clarkson, G.E.P. (1967), *Portfolio Selection: A Simulation of Trust Investment*, The Ford Foundation doctoral dissertation series (Prentice Hall, Englewood Cliffs, New Jersey).

Cochrane, J.L. (1994), *Are US Regulatory Requirements for Foreign Firms Appropriate?* (NYSE Inc. Publication).

Cooper, J.C.B. (1982), 'World Stock Markets: Some Random Walk Tests', *Applied Economics*, No. 5 (October).

Darrat, A.F. (1987), 'Money and Stock Prices in West Germany and the UK: Is the Stock Market Efficient?', *Quarterly Journal of Business Economics* (Winter).

Day, J. (1986), 'The Use of Annual Reports by UK Investment Analysts', *Accounting and Business Research* (Autumn).

De Long, J.B., A. Schleifer, L.H. Summers and R.J. Walderman (1990), 'Noise Trader Risk in Financial Markets', *Journal of Political Economy*, Vol. 98, No. 4.

Duvall, L., R. Jennings, J. Robinson and R.B. Thompson II (1992), 'Can Investors Unravel the Effects of Goodwill Accounting?', *Accounting Horizons* (June).

Emenyonu, E.N. and S.J. Gray (1992), 'European Community Accounting Harmonisation: An Empirical Study of Measurement Practices in France, Germany and the United Kingdom', *Accounting and Business Research* (Winter).

Ernst & Young (1994), *UK/US GAAP Comparison* (Kogan Page, ch. 6).

Fellingham, J. (1988), 'Discussion of the LIFO/FIFO Choice: An Asymmetric Information Approach', *Journal of Accounting Research*, Vol. 26, supplement.

Firth, M. (1976), 'The Impact of Earnings Announcements on the Share Price Behaviour of Similar Type Firms', *Economic Journal* (June) 1976.

Foster, G. (1988), *Financial Statement Analysis* (2nd ed., Prentice Hall, Englewood Cliffs, New Jersey).

Griffiths, I. (1986), *Creative Accounting: How to Make Profits What You Want Them to Be* (Sidgwick and Jackson, London).

Grossman, S.J. and J.E. Stiglitz (1976), 'Information Competitive Price Systems', *American Economic Review*, Vol.66, Papers and Proceedings.

Hand, J.R.M. (1990), 'A Test of the Extended Functional Fixation Hypothesis', *Accounting Review*, Vol. 65, No. 4 (October).

Harris, T.S., M. Lang and H.P. Möller (1994), 'The Value Relevance of German Accounting Measures: An Empirical Analysis', *Journal of Accounting Research* (Autumn).

Healy, P. (1985) 'The Impact of Bonus Schemes on the Selection of Accounting Principles', *Journal of Accounting and Economics*, 7 (April).

Holland, A. (1990), *Accounting for Goodwill: The UK Stock Market Implications of the Proposed New Rules* (Yamaichi International (Europe) Limited, January).

Institute of Investment Management and Research (IIMR) (1993), *The Definition of Earnings* (IIMR, Kent).

IOSCO (1995), 'IASC and IOSCO Reach Agreement', Press Release by IOSCO and IASC (11 July).

Jamieson, M. (1988), *A Practical Guide to Creative Accounting* (Kogan Page), London.

Jennings, R., D.P. Mest and R.B. Thompson II (1992), 'Investor Reaction to Disclosures of 1974–5 LIFO Adoption Decisions', *Accounting Review*, Vol. 67, No. 2 (April).

Lee, T.A. and D.P. Tweedie (1981), *The Institutional Investor and Financial Information* (ICAEW, London).

McLeay, S. (1995), 'International Financial Analysis', in C. Nobes and R. Parker (eds.), *Comparative International Accounting* (Prentice Hall, ch. 5).

Morse, D. and G. Richardson (1983), 'The LIFO/FIFO Decision', *Journal of Accounting Research*, Vol. 21, No. 1 (Spring).

Nobes, C.W. (1992), 'A Political History of Goodwill in Britain: An Illustration of Cyclical Standard Setting', *Abacus* (September).

Norton, J. (1995), 'The Impact of Financial Accounting Practices on the Measurement of Profit and Equity: Australia Versus the United States', *Abacus* (September).

Pike, R., J. Meerjanssen and L. Chadwick (1993), 'The Appraisal of Ordinary Shares by Investment Analysts in the UK and Germany', *Accounting and Business Research* (Autumn).

Radebaugh, L.H. and S.J. Gray (1993), *International Accounting and Multinational Enterprises* (Wiley, New York), p. 390.

Rees, W.P., P.F. Pope and C.M. Graham (1992), 'The Information Content of German Analysts' Adjustments to Published Earnings', Working paper 92/040 (University of Strathclyde).

Ricks, W.E. (1982), 'The Market's Response to the 1974 LIFO Adoptions', *Journal of Accounting Research*, Vol. 20, No. 1 (Autumn).

Scheid, J-C. and P. Walton (1992), *European Financial Reporting: France* (Routledge, London).

Scott-Quinn, B. (1991), *Investment Banking: Theory and Practice* (Euromoney, London).

Smith, R.C. (1991), 'Integration of the World's Financial Markets: Past, Present and Future', ch. 2 in Choi (1991).

Smith, T. (1992), *Accounting for Growth: Stripping the Camouflage from Company Accounts* (Century Business, London).

———— (1996), *Accounting for Growth* (2nd ed., Blackwell).

Tiniç, S.M. (1990), 'A Perspective on the Stock Market's Fixation on Accounting Numbers', *Accounting Review*, Vol. 65, No. 4 (October).

Waller, D. (1990), 'If Balance Sheets Don't Balance: On Blue Arrow's Widely Differing US and UK Figures', *Financial Times* (30 January).

Watts, R. and J.L. Zimmerman (1986), *Positive Accounting Theory* (Prentice Hall).

Weaver, S. (1996), 'International Financial Statement Analysis: The Reaction of the UK Investment Community to International Accounting Differences', Unpublished Ph.D. Thesis (University of Reading).

Weetman, P. and S.J. Gray (1991), 'A Comparative International Analysis of the Impact of Accounting Principles on Profits: The USA versus the UK, Sweden, and The Netherlands', *Accounting and Business Research* (Autumn).

Zmijewski, M. and R. Hagerman (1981), 'An Income Strategy Approach to the Positive Theory of Accounting Standard Setting/Choice', *Journal of Accounting and Economics*, Vol. 3 (August), pp.129–49.

PART IV

EUROPEAN HARMONIZATION

The Evolution of the Harmonising Provisions of the 1980 and 1981 Companies Acts*

C. W. Nobes

The 1980 and 1981 Companies Acts of the United Kingdom are substantial pieces of legislation. They dramatically affect financial reporting, in ways which may not be anticipated by a study of the Companies Acts 1948, 1967 and 1976 (which are added to, rather than repealed by, the above Acts). This is because the origins of the new legislation lie outside the Anglo-Saxon accounting tradition;[1] these Acts are part of a process of harmonisation of laws within the European Communities (EC).[2] In this case, particularly for the 1981 Act, the pattern which was originally chosen as a basis for harmonisation was German, as will be shown.

It is fairly well established that, if one organised the countries of the developed Western world into a small number of groups by their accounting practices, the United Kingdom and West Germany would be in different groups (Mueller, 1967; Nair and Frank, 1980; Nobes and Parker, 1981). The United Kingdom presents a good example of 'accounting as an independent discipline'; of pragmatic accounting; of accounting based on the judgement of 'fairness'. West German accounting, on the other hand, is held up as an example of detailed prescription (by company and tax laws) of formats, measurement rules and disclosure; of accounting which seeks correctness and legality. Thus, it is not surprising that the new UK legislation, being based on German law, introduces many changes, some of which are revolutionary.

This paper is concerned with those substantial parts of the 1980 and 1981 Acts which result from

Directives[3] of the EC. Topic by topic, the origins of the new British legislation will be traced to earlier continental law. It should be stressed that the object of this paper is not directly to examine EC harmonisation or the changes to accounting in any other country.

Evolution of the 1980 Act

Those provisions of the 1980 Companies Act which are analysed here result from the second Directive. This section examines how they fit in with existing continental European practice, which is clearly the origin of the second Directive, both drafts of which were published before the UK acceded to the EC (see Figure 1).

1. Company Names

In most Member States of the EC it has long been possible to tell whether a company is public or private by looking at its name.[4] The split in Germany goes well back into the last century. In France, the 'private company' (*Sàrl*)[4] form dates from 1925, after the absorption into France of the former German territories of Alsace and Lorraine following the post-war Treaty of Versailles. At that point many *GmbH*[4] companies suddenly became French; the form was legalised and it spread rapidly. In the Netherlands, the *BV*[4] was invented in 1971 following the first draft of the second Directive.

The second Directive demands such separation. For the UK, the 1980 Companies Act achieved this by leaving private companies' names unchanged, and causing public companies (which are fewer and

---

*I gratefully acknowledge the useful comments of D. A. R. Forrester, R. H. Parker, I. C. Stewart and an anonymous referee on earlier drafts of this paper.

[1]The 'Anglo-Saxon accounting tradition' is used throughout this paper to refer to the broad consensus, of British origin, which exists on accounting matters throughout most of the English-speaking world. This is perhaps typified by 'fairness' and 'substance over form'.

[2]In 1983, these are ten: Belgium, Denmark, France, Greece, Luxembourg, Ireland, Italy, Netherlands, United Kingdom and West Germany. The word 'communities' refers to the European Economic Community (Common Market), the European Coal and Steel Community and Euratom.

[3]Directives are pieces of 'secondary legislation'. They are drafted by the EC Commission, approved by the Council of Ministers, and sent to the governments of Member States for enactment as national laws.

[4]The private company forms in West Germany, France and the Netherlands are *Gesellschaft mit beschränkter Haftung (GmbH)*, *Société à responsibilité limitée (Sàrl)* and *Besloten Vennootschap (BV)*, respectively. These are not the exact equivalents of the UK private company. Instead, they have some elements of partnerships, particularly in the way in which capital is held.

Figure 1
EC Directives of Especial Relevance to Accounting

Directives on Company Law	Dates of Drafts	Date Approved in Brussels	UK Law
Second	1970, 1972	1976	1980
Fourth	1971, 1974	1978	1981
Seventh	1976, 1978	1983	

more easily visible) to change their names to include 'public limited company' or 'p.l.c.' (S2). The use of the expression, 'proprietary company,' which is found in several Commonwealth countries, was proposed for small private companies in the Green Paper (DOT, 1979) which preceded the 1981 Act. However, this proposal was not enacted.

The legal distinction remains that only a public company's shares may be offered to the public. Thus a listed company must be public. However, there is little point in stressing this distinction unless other differences also follow. Both the 1980 and the 1981 Acts do introduce further differences.

2. *Minimum Capital Requirements*

It has been normal in continental Europe for there to be minimum capital requirements for companies. (For examples, see footnote 5.) The second Directive imposes such a requirement for public companies. The UK has now inherited these continental provisions in that the 1980 Act introduced a minimum requirement of £50,000 issued share capital for UK public companies (S85). No such requirement has been introduced in the UK for private companies.

3. *Number of Members*

The minimum number of members of a public company is reduced from 7 to 2 (S2). This does not seem to be predictable from the continental European practice ruling before the second Directive (see footnote 6). However, there is now harmonisation on a minimum of 2 for all types of companies throughout the EC.

4. *Distributable Income*

Until 1980, the definition of legally distributable income was not to be found in British statute law, but in a miscellany of cases dating back to the last century; for example, *Lee v. Neuchatel Asphalte*

Co. (1889) and *Verner v. General and Commercial Investment Trust Ltd.* (1894). These cases were sometimes difficult to apply, and appeared contradictory.

In Germany, there has been no similar problem. The strict and uniform application of detailed historic cost rules has been designed to lead to a conservative and reliable figure for distributable profit to protect creditors. The same figure is used for accounting profit and for taxable profit. Such a coincidence is attempted in the definition of distributable profit of a company in the second Directive and the UK's 1980 Companies Act (S39): 'its accumulated realised profits . . . less its accumulated realised losses'. However, since it is clear that UK law does not impose uniform rules for the measurement of accounting profit, the Act lays down that, irrespective of the accounting methods used by a company, the legally distributable profit must be based on strict historic cost rules. For example, if any fixed assets have been revalued and depreciation has been based on the revalued amounts, then an adjustment must be made to 'correct' the depreciation charge for the purposes of calculating distributable profits. However, such a calculation, or its result, need not be disclosed in the published accounts. Familiarity with the strict application of the principle of 'purchase price or production cost' in German accounting as determined by the 1965 *Aktiengesetz* (share law or public company law) would render these rules unsurprising. The Directive and the 1980 Act go further by adding more restrictions relating only to public companies.[7]

It is one of the ironies of the legal system of Britain and parts of the Commonwealth that the archaic British case law on distributable profits now applies in several countries (e.g. Australia and New Zealand) but not in the UK.

Evolution of the 1981 Act

In the case of the fourth Directive, the EC Commission entrusted the task of preparing the *avant projet* (the unpublished preliminary draft) to a working party chaired by a German, Professor Elmendorff. It is not surprising, then, that the first draft of the Directive, published in 1971, bears resemblances to the German *Aktiengesetz (AktG)* of 1965. The Directive applies to public and private

---

[5] Before the enactment of the second Directive, the West German minimum capital requirements were: DM 20,000 (*GmbH*), DM 100,000 (unlisted *AG*), and DM 500,000 (listed *AG*). The French figures were the same in francs. Other EC countries also had such requirements.

[6] The pre-Directive numbers, for private and public companies respectively, were: West Germany (2 and 5); France (2 and 7); Netherlands (2 and 2); Italy (1 and 2); UK (2 and 7).

[7] S40 states that a distribution must not be made by a public company if it would reduce net assets below the aggregate of capital and undistributable reserves. The latter are defined at length, and include share premium and capital redemption reserve fund. This requirement will only be more restrictive than S39 where there is an unrealised deficit on revaluation. A connected new requirement in the 1980 Act (S34) is that, where the net assets of a *public* company fall to half or less of the called-up share capital, an extraordinary general meeting shall be called.

companies (except for banking, insurance and shipping companies) of all Member States. It deals with statutory annual balance sheets, profit and loss accounts and notes, but not with supplementary statements like current cost accounts or funds flow statements.

One curious feature of the 1981 Act is that it contains no instructions[8] about consolidation, and that in various places (like the standard formats) adjustments have to be made for this. Given that statutory accounts for groups of companies in the UK are usually consolidated accounts, this omission might seem hard to understand. However, although the *AktG* required consolidation of domestic subsidiaries by German public companies, consolidation is rare in much of continental Europe (Parker, 1981a) and was rarer still in the days of the early drafts of the fourth Directive. This may explain its absence from the fourth Directive and thus from the 1981 Companies Act. The accession of the UK, Ireland and Denmark to the EC in 1973 was followed by the drafting of the seventh Directive (see Figure 1) which deals with consolidation. This is a substantially Anglo-Saxon document.

The evolution of the accounting provisions of the 1981 Act will be analysed under four headings. In each case, the concentration will be on locating the source of the provisions. In most cases, this will involve tracing provisions from the 1965 *AktG*, through the various drafts of the fourth Directive, to the 1981 Act.

It is not intended here to discuss whether the changes brought from German legislation into British legislation are 'good' or 'bad'. There has been much prior argument about, for example, whether the imposition of uniformity in accounting would be useful. This might now be regarded as a case for empirical investigation rather than further speculation.

1. *Formats*

Compared with traditional Anglo-Saxon accounting, perhaps the most obvious feature of the *AktG*, the fourth Directive, and the 1981 Companies Act is the prescription of uniform formats. In the UK, formats have not been compulsorily imposed by statute before, except for special companies, like those in life assurance or public utilities. Also, there have never even been format rules in accounting standards.[9] This revolutionary change

---

[8]There are references to group accounts in the 1981 Act, but only to make clear that the Act applies to them.

[9]SSAP 10 (published by the UK accountancy bodies in 1975) gives formats for funds flow statements in an appendix, but clearly states that they are merely suggestions. SSAP 16 (CCA, 1980) also provides suggested formats, and SSAP 6 (1974) suggests a presentation for extraordinary items.

is not only the most obvious of the changes imposed by the 1981 Act, but also one which will be very difficult to avoid. As will be shown later, although the letter of the law also introduces some fundamental changes of principle and detail in the areas of valuation and measurement, it will probably be possible for many companies to avoid important changes to their practices in these areas in the short run.

When tracing the history of formats back into the last century one does come across an optional format for balance sheets in the British Companies Act of 1856 and the consolidating Act of 1862, which remained in force until 1908 (Edey, 1979; Parker, 1981b). Nevertheless, the evolution of the 1981 Act must be traced through previous German law not previous British law.

Perhaps because of the importance of banks and creditors, and the lack of importance of individual shareholders, German accounting has concentrated on the protection of creditors and on cost and management accounting, not on financial statements for shareholders. It was for internal, management accounting purposes that uniform formats were first developed. It appears that the first comprehensive chart of accounts was published in Germany by J. F. Schaer in 1911 (Scherpf, 1955). Such charts were used by industry in the first World War. In 1927, Schmalenbach published *Der Kontenrahmen*, which was followed by the publication of model charts for different industries (Forrester, 1977). Under the National Socialists, the ascendant ideology of controlling the economy led naturally to the compulsory adoption of charts of accounts, particularly as the price mechanism was not operating due to controls on prices and money, and thus some alternative allocation mechanism was needed (Singer, 1943). The Germans also used a system of uniform cost accounting in France in the early 1940s.

As for uniform published financial statements, these were developed in Germany, France and other continental countries. The Germans introduced compulsory formats in the law of 1931 (Barth, 1953). The French first issued a national accounting plan *(plan comptable général)* in 1947 (revised 1957 and 1979). This included both a chart of accounts and formats for published accounts (Most, 1971).

The *AktG* of 1965 lays down formats in its sections 151 and 157 (Mueller and Galbraith, 1966). The *AktG* offered no choice between formats, nor any substantial flexibility within a format. As might have been expected, there was considerable difficulty in arriving at agreed formats for the first draft of the fourth Directive (EC Commission, 1971), even among the six Member States belonging to the EC in 1971 (Niehus, 1971). This shows itself in the inclusion in the Directive of two balance sheet formats and four profit and

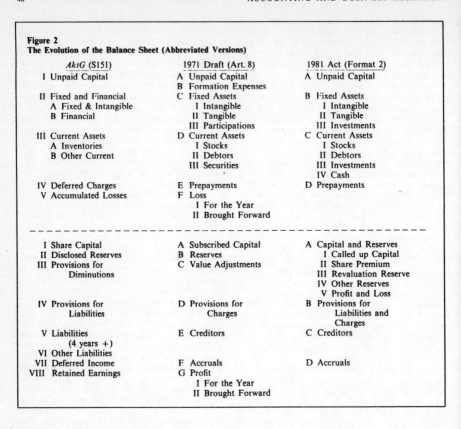

Figure 2
The Evolution of the Balance Sheet (Abbreviated Versions)

AktG (S151)	1971 Draft (Art. 8)	1981 Act (Format 2)
I Unpaid Capital	A Unpaid Capital	A Unpaid Capital
	B Formation Expenses	
II Fixed and Financial	C Fixed Assets	B Fixed Assets
A Fixed & Intangible	I Intangible	I Intangible
B Financial	II Tangible	II Tangible
	III Participations	III Investments
III Current Assets	D Current Assets	C Current Assets
A Inventories	I Stocks	I Stocks
B Other Current	II Debtors	II Debtors
	III Securities	III Investments
		IV Cash
IV Deferred Charges	E Prepayments	D Prepayments
V Accumulated Losses	F Loss	
	I For the Year	
	II Brought Forward	

I Share Capital	A Subscribed Capital	A Capital and Reserves
II Disclosed Reserves	B Reserves	I Called up Capital
III Provisions for	C Value Adjustments	II Share Premium
Diminutions		III Revaluation Reserve
		IV Other Reserves
		V Profit and Loss
IV Provisions for	D Provisions for	B Provisions for
Liabilities	Charges	Liabilities and
		Charges
V Liabilities	E Creditors	C Creditors
(4 years +)		
VI Other Liabilities		
VII Deferred Income	F Accruals	D Accruals
VIII Retained Earnings	G Profit	
	I For the Year	
	II Brought Forward	

loss account formats. These remained largely unaltered in the second draft (EC Commission, 1974) and the final Directive (EC Commission, 1978).

Looking first at the balance sheet, *AktG* S151 was reproduced with slight amendment as Article 8 of the 1971 draft of the fourth Directive (see Figure 2). This is a two-sided (or horizontal) balance sheet, with assets on the left. The only significant change between the 1971 draft and those of 1974 and 1978 is in the classification of reserves. The *AktG* and the 1971 draft Directive show profits as the last item on the *credit* side of the balance sheet, and losses as the last item on the *debit* side. Such a treatment of profits fits better with a creditors' or entity view rather than a proprietors' view: 'it contains no implications that ... the proprietors possess any particular lien' (Edwards, 1981, p. 17). This had been the presentation shown in the British 1856 Act, and was common in Britain before the Second World War. Edwards (1981, p. 17) notes that perhaps 'it

reflects the mechanical approach to accounts construction then prevailing'.

However, in the final Directive, a more Anglo-Saxon approach to reserves is allowed. Format 2 of the 1981 Act (see Figure 2) follows the Directive, except for permitted deletions like formation expenses, which was a necessary heading for practice in some countries. Figure 2 illustrates the gradual and slight changes in the formats over the sixteen year period. It shows only the first two levels of headings. A third level (of sub-sub-headings) is omitted from Figure 2, but in each case does exist and is preceded by Arabic numbers.

However, it should not be supposed that UK balance sheets will in future look like the expanded version of this Format 2 of the 1981 Act. There are several reasons why this will probably not be the case. First, the Directive contains another format.[10]

---

[10] Article 9 of the 1971 and 1974 drafts, which became Article 10 in the 1978 version.

Figure 3
Balance Sheet Format 1 from the 1981 Companies Act

A. *Called up share capital not paid*
B. Fixed assets
   I Intangible assets
     1. Development costs
     2. Concessions, patents, licences, trade marks and similar rights and assets.
     3. Goodwill
     4. *Payments on account*
   II Tangible assets
     1. Land and buildings
     2. Plant and machinery
     3. Fixtures, fittings, tools and equipment
     4. *Payments on account and assets in course of construction*
   III Investments
     1. *Shares in group companies*
     2. *Loans to group companies*
     3. *Shares in related companies*
     4. *Loans to related companies*
     5. Other investments other than loans
     6. Other loans
     7. *Own shares*
C. Current assets
   I Stocks
     1. Raw materials and consumables
     2. Work in progress
     3. Finished goods and goods for resale
     4. *Payments on account*
   II Debtors
     1. Trade debtors
     2. *Amounts owed by group companies*
     3. *Amounts owed by related companies*
     4. Other debtors
     5. Called up share capital not paid
     6. Prepayments and accrued income
   III Investments
     1. *Shares in group companies*
     2. *Own shares*
     3. Other investments
   IV Cash at bank and in hand

D. *Prepayments and accrued income*
E. Creditors: amounts falling due within one year
     1. Debenture loans
     2. Bank loans and overdrafts
     3. Payments received on account
     4. Trade creditors
     5. Bills of exchange payable
     6. *Amounts owed to group companies*
     7. *Amounts owed to related companies*
     8. Other creditors including taxation and social security
     9. Accruals and deferred income
F. Net current assets (liabilities)
G. Total assets less current liabilities
H. Creditors: amounts falling due after more than one year
     1. Debenture loans
     2. Bank loans and overdrafts
     3. Payments received on account
     4. Trade creditors
     5. Bills of exchange payable
     6. *Amounts owed to group companies*
     7. *Amounts owed to related companies*
     8. Other creditors including taxation and social security
     9. Accruals and deferred income
I. Provisions for liabilities and charges
     1. Pensions and similar obligations
     2. Taxation, including deferred taxation
     3. Other provisions
J. *Accruals and deferred income*
K. Capital and reserves
   I Called up share capital
   II Share premium account
   III Revaluation reserve
   IV Other reserves
     1. Capital redemption reserve
     2. Reserve for own shares
     3. Reserves provided for by the articles of association
     4. Other reserves
   V Profit and loss account

This is shown in Figure 3, and is a vertical or statement form of the format in Figure 2. Member States are allowed to adopt one format or to permit companies to make the choice, as long as they are consistent. The 1981 Act does the latter, and presents the vertical form as 'Format 1', presumably on the grounds that it corresponds much more closely with previous UK practice for published accounts (at least those of large companies) (ICAEW, 1980). Format 1 contains broadly the same headings, sub-headings and sub-sub-headings as Format 2, except that current liabilities are shown separately and positioned so as to enable a calculation of net current assets and then assets net of current liabilities.

Secondly, there are several ways in which flexibility is allowed. The *AktG* in S151 permits (i) different classifications for particular trades, (ii) extra detail to be added, and (iii) empty headings to be omitted. The Directive contains these provisions, and also allows Arabic number headings to be combined where the amounts are separately immaterial or where this would lead to greater clarity.[11] The 1981 Act includes these provisions, and also notes that the letters and numerals preceding the headings need not be shown. This

---

[11]In this latter case, the information must be shown by note (Article 4).

accords with continental practice, but is not actually stated in the *AktG* or the Directive.

Thirdly, extra flexibility exists within the Directive's and hence the Act's formats, which was not present in the *AktG*. This takes the form of several alternative presentations of particular items,[12] in addition to the deletions mentioned above (e.g. formation expenses). This compromising of the original inflexible German format leads to uneasy results. For example, if the option is taken to show all accruals under J (a Germanic position) within Figure 3 (the British-style format), the size of 'net current assets' can be artificially increased by the amount of the short-term accruals.

All these provisions and the formats themselves are contained in Part I of Schedule 1 of the 1981 Act. Rather confusingly, this Schedule, which also contains accounting principles and disclosure rules, became Schedule 8 of the 1948 Companies Act. Taking all the most Anglo-Saxon options, and assuming that certain items will be immaterial or may be removed to notes, might mean that the italicised items in Figure 3 will not appear in many British balance sheets. Naturally, the letters and numerals will also be omitted. Also, given that one is concerned with a consolidated balance sheet, further items have been italicised; but a heading would need to be inserted for 'minority interests'. The lack of references to, or suitable headings for, consolidation in the 1981 Act has already been mentioned.

Another feature which may require explanation for Anglo-Saxon accountants is the omission of proposed dividends (as current liabilities in the balance sheet, and as appropriations 'below the line' in the profit and loss account). Again, the explanation lies in the predominant, 'legalistic' continental view of proposed dividends as amounts not established at the balance sheet date because they require the later approval of the shareholders. The 1981 Companies Act specifically (in Part I, Sch. 1) requires companies to adjust the profit and loss account for this. There is no instruction to adjust the balance sheet. Thus, proposed dividends may be shown separately under creditors or may be included under some other heading.

Turning now to the profit and loss account, there is one format only in the *AktG* (S157), but four in each of the versions of the Directive and in the 1981 Act. The format in the *AktG* contains 32 headings, whereas the nearest to it in the Directive and the 1981 Act[13] contains about 20 headings. These are statement formats, which combine together expenses and revenues by their financial accounting nature; for example, all salaries to-

gether and all depreciation together (see Figure 4). This Germanic format might also be said to be production-oriented; it compares input with output (not sales with cost of sales), which is perhaps more the view of a business economist than of an accountant. Thus, the turnover is adjusted for changes in stocks and for use in the construction of fixed assets. The effect is reminiscent of a value added statement, and might seem attractive to some users as a compromise between that and a traditional profit and loss account.

The alternative in the Directive which will probably be most popular in the UK is presented in the 1981 Act as Format 1 (see Figure 5). This is also a vertical statement format and is identical to Format 2 from line 7, but it is sales-oriented and it combines expenses by stage of production. This format involves the disclosure of cost of sales and gross profit, whereas Format 2 does not, because of lack of information about how much wages, depreciation, etc to include in cost of sales. Some UK companies thus prefer Format 2.

The remaining two formats in the Directive and the Act are two-sided versions of Format 1 and Format 2, with charges (i.e. *debits*) on the left and income (i.e. *credits*) on the right.

The provisions relating to flexibility are the same as for the balance sheet, and one might note that all the headings in Figure 4 are preceded by Arabic numbers. The Act requires the inclusion of items for dividends, movements on reserves and pre-tax profit. Other items, like 'minority's share of profit' may be added.

Overall, profit and loss accounts in the UK have become much more detailed, with the disclosure of more information about expenses. Such details have been normal in German accounts.

These provisions relating to formats apply for *all* companies to the statutory annual accounts as drawn up for shareholders and audited. Although the Directive allowed some exemptions here, there are no exemptions in the UK's 1981 Act from the requirements to send full audited accounts to shareholders. However, there are some exemptions from *publication* for smaller *private* companies, as will now be discussed.

2. Publication

A further innovation in British law is that the 1981 Act introduces reduced *publication* requirements by size of company. This only applies to private companies. All public companies and large private companies must send to the Registrar of Companies, who gives access to the public, the full accounts as drawn up and audited.

Differential publication requirements were a feature of British Acts until 1947.[14] For example, the

---

[12]For example, in Figure 3, unpaid capital (A) and prepayments (D) may be (and, in the UK, presumably will be) shown under debtors (C, II, 5 and 6).

[13]Article 20 in 1971 and 1974; Article 21 in 1978, and Format 2 of the 1981 Act.

[14]To a large extent the 1948 Act removed the differentiation between private and public companies. However, a special class of 'exempt private companies' survived until the 1967 Act.

Figure 4
Profit and Loss Account Format 2 (1981 Companies Act)

1. Turnover
2. Change in stocks of finished goods and work in progress
3. Own work capitalised
4. Other operating income
5. (a) Raw materials and consumables
   (b) Other external charges
6. Staff costs:
   (a) wages and salaries
   (b) social security costs
   (c) other pension costs
7. (a) Depreciation and other amounts written off tangible and intangible fixed assets
   (b) Exceptional amounts written off current assets
8. Other operating charges
9. Income from shares in group companies
10. Income from shares in related companies
11. Income from other fixed asset investments
12. Other interest receivable and similar income
13. Amounts written off investments
14. Interest payable and similar charges
15. Tax on profit or loss on ordinary activities
16. Profit or loss on ordinary activities after taxation
17. Extraordinary income
18. Extraordinary charges
19. Extraordinary profit or loss
20. Tax on extraordinary profit or loss
21. Other taxes not shown under the above items
22. Profit or loss for the financial year

1907 Act required disclosure of balance sheet information by public companies but not private companies; the 1928 Act required companies to circulate profit and loss accounts to shareholders

Figure 5
Profit and Loss Account Format 1
(1981 Companies Act)

1. Turnover
2. Cost of sales
3. Gross profit or loss
4. Distribution costs
5. Administrative expenses
6. Other operating income
7. Income from shares in group companies
8. Income from shares in related companies
9. Income from other fixed asset investments
10. Other interest receivable and similar income
11. Amounts written off investments
12. Interest payable and similar charges
13. Tax on profit or loss on ordinary activities
14. Profit or loss on ordinary activities after taxation
15. Extraordinary income
16. Extraordinary charges
17. Extraordinary profit or loss
18. Tax on extraordinary profit or loss
19. Other taxes not shown under the above items
20. Profit or loss for the financial year

but not to the Registrar (Edwards, 1981, part II). Nevertheless, the 1981 Act cannot sensibly be traced to these precedents, which are too distant and do not concern exemptions by *size* of company. However, publication requirements dependent upon size are commonplace in continental Europe. They are found in the *AktG* (S157), which exempts an unlisted company from showing the details making up gross profit in the profit and loss account, if the company's balance sheet total does not exceed DM 3m (or it is a family company not exceeding DM 10m). Also, such provisions are found in a later German law, the Publicity Law *(Publizitätsgesetz)* of 1969, which requires all legal entities to publish audited accounts, irrespective of their business form, if they are above two of three size criteria for two years (see Figure 6).

There are somewhat similar rules in the Netherlands, where *BV*s are exempted from the need to publish profit and loss accounts where they fall below the limits shown in Figure 6. Also, in France, listed companies with assets in excess of FF 10m have been obliged to publish annual and interim figures in the *Bulletin des annonces légales et obligatoires.*

The Directive allows various exemptions which may be traced to the above precedents.[15] The 1981

---

[15]Articles 11, 12, 27, 44 and 47 of the 1978 Directive.

Figure 6
Publication Requirement Size Criteria

	Germany–1969 Publizitäts-gesetz*	Netherlands BVs	UK 1981 Act* Small	Medium
Balance Sheet Total	DM.125m	Fl.8m	£0.7m	£2.8
Turnover	DM.250m		£1.4m	£5.75
No. of Employees	5000	100	50	250

*A company must fall below two out of the three limits.

Act does not take full advantage of these exemptions (SS5–11), but does allow small private companies (see Figure 6) not to publish profit and loss accounts and most notes, and to abridge the balance sheet by omitting the headings and amounts preceded by Arabic numbers. This is reminiscent of the rules for *BV*s in the Netherlands. Medium-sized private companies are allowed to combine the gross profit items in their *published* profit and loss accounts. This is reminiscent of S157 of the *AktG*.

3. Accounting 'Principles'

In the area of accounting 'principles' there are also major changes for British accounting in the 1981 Companies Act. There are three levels of 'principles' (the word used in the Act). The first, and 'vaguest', level consists of a strengthened re-affirmation of the requirement for accounts to present a true and fair view. The paramount nature of the principle is made much clearer in S1 of the 1981 Act, which revises S149 of the 1948 Act:

> Subsection (2) above [the true and fair view] overrides the requirements of Schedule 8 to this Act and all other requirements of the Companies Acts 1948 to 1981 . . . .
> (b) if, owing to special circumstances . . . , compliance with any . . . requirement . . . would prevent . . . complying with that subsection . . . , the directors . . . shall depart from that requirement . . .

This principle was not contained in German Law, nor in the first draft of the fourth Directive. However, presumably as a result of pressure from the governments of the UK, Ireland and the Netherlands, the principle was inserted in the 1974 draft and became predominant in the final Directive. This process is illustrated in Figure 7. It should be noted that the UK parliament did not define the 'special circumstances' in S1 of the 1981 Act, as the Directive would have allowed. It will become clear below that the British accountancy profession intends to claim exemption from some detailed provisions on this ground.

The second level of principles has again been substantially affected by Anglo-Saxon accounting.

Four accounting conventions of a British accounting standard, SSAP 2 (ASC, 1971), are enshrined in Article 31 of the Directive and in Part II of Schedule 1 of the 1981 Act. The conventions are: going concern, consistency, prudence and accruals. The first and the last were missing from the first draft of the Directive. However, a fifth principle has been taken from German law, i.e. that assets and liabilities should be valued separately (for example, using the lower of cost and net realisable value) before being added together. More importantly, it is of course a fundamental change of philosophy to find fairly detailed accounting concepts imposed by statute in the UK. This change clearly results from the *AktG*, which enacted accounting principles, including three of the five in the 1981 Act.

The third level of principles is more detailed and involves the encroachment of statute into territory previously regarded as that of the profession. Here, the influence of the *AktG* on the new British legislation is again clear. In order to enable comparisons within and between industries, to perform sensible aggregations of companies' accounting figures, and to control the economy, it has seemed appropriate in several continental countries not just to establish uniform formats but to ensure that the items within them are uniformly valued and measured.

The following rules are found in the *AktG*, the Directive and the 1981 Companies Act (Schedule 1); the sources are noted in that order in brackets after each item:

(i) Fixed assets shall be carried at purchase price or construction cost (S153; Art32; para. 18).

(ii) Intangibles may only be shown as assets if acquired for valuable consideration (S153; Arts 9 and 10; para. 8, notes 2 and 3).

(iii) Fixed assets with limited useful lives must be depreciated (S154; Art35; para. 18).

(iv) The basic rule for valuing current assets is 'lower of cost or net realisable value' (S155; Art39; para. 23).

(v) Current asset valuation may use FIFO, LIFO, or similar method (S155; Art40; para. 27).

Figure 7
'True and Fair' in the Fourth Directive

1965 *Aktiengesetz* (S149): 1. The annual financial statements shall conform to proper bookkeeping principles. They shall be clear and well set out and give as sure a view of the company's financial position and its operating results as is possible pursuant to the valuation provisions.

1971 Draft (Art2): 1. The annual accounts shall comprise the balance sheet, the profit and loss account and the notes on the accounts. These documents shall constitute a composite whole.
2. The annual accounts shall conform to the principles of regular and proper accounting.
3. They shall be drawn up clearly and, in the context of the provisions regarding the valuation of assets and liabilities and the lay-out of accounts, shall reflect as accurately as possible the company's assets, liabilities, financial position and results.

1974 Draft (Art2): 1. (as 1971 Draft).
2. The annual accounts shall give a true and fair view of the company's assets, liabilities, financial position and results.
3. They shall be drawn up clearly and in conformity with the provisions of this Directive.

1978 Final (Art2): 1. (as 1971 Draft).
2. They shall be drawn up clearly and in accordance with the provisions of this Directive.
3. The annual accounts shall give a true and fair view of the company's assets, liabilities, financial position and profit or loss.
4. Where the application of the provisions of this Directive would not be sufficient to give a true and fair view within the meaning of paragraph 3, additional information must be given.
5. Where in exceptional cases the application of a provision of this Directive is incompatible with the obligation laid down in paragraph 3, that provision must be departed from in order to give a true and fair view within the meaning of paragraph 3. Any such departure must be disclosed in the notes on the accounts together with an explanation of the reasons for it and a statement of its effect on the assets, liabilities, financial position and profit or loss. The Member States may define the exceptional cases in question and lay down the relevant special rules.

Further rules, which are consistent with German practice, are:
(vi) Research costs, preliminary expenses and expenses on issue of securities must not be capitalised (para. 3).
(vii) Purchased goodwill (where capitalised) must be written off over its useful life (para. 21). This does not apply to goodwill on consolidation.

The above are merely examples of the detail to which the 1981 Act specifies valuation rules. The *content* of the rules is not out of character for British accounting, but their statutory nature is a fundamental change. However, there follow four examples of the way in which the character of traditional British accounting will probably overcome the new rules in particular cases:

(a) In order to avoid writing off purchased goodwill through the profit and loss ac-

count [see (iii) and (vii) above], British companies will probably write off existing goodwill against reserves before preparing their first balance sheet under the Act. In future, they may ensure that goodwill is never capitalised and thus needs no depreciation. Incidentally, although goodwill on consolidation is not covered by the 1981 Act, the requirements to be introduced as a result of the seventh Directive will be similar.

(b) The Act defines prudence as the inclusion only of 'profits realised' (Sch. 1, para. 12). This in itself seems more restrictive than the Directive, which refers to 'profits made' (Art31). However, after representations from the accountancy bodies, the Act included a note that 'realised' should be taken in the context of 'principles generally accepted' (Sch. 1, para. 90). Thus, for example, it will be acceptable to take a proportion of profit on long-term contracts as they proceed (SSAP 9, ASC, 1975).

(c) In direct contravention of (iii) above, it will still be possible for companies not to depreciate investment properties. Again an appeal to the overriding principle of 'true and fair' will be made, backed up by reference to SSAP 19, the standard which allows this (ASC, 1981). This standard was issued after the 1981 Act, and the ASC made specific reference to this.[16]

(d) In the UK before the 1981 Act, LIFO was normally unacceptable for both financial accounting and taxation purposes (ASC, 1975, App. I, para. 12). The enactment of the provision which specifically allows LIFO will not necessarily alter this. The accounting standard remains in force, and the Accounting Standards Committee might reasonably hold that the Act is 'minimum' legislation which by no means stops the profession from narrowing down from what is legally available to what gives a true and fair view. (Tweedie, 1983; Hoffman and Arden, 1983.)

Nevertheless, the imposition of valuation rules by statute is not just important as a philosophical change; it will be very significant in practice in some areas. For example, the following practices, some of which were certainly found in the UK particularly among smaller companies, are made illegal:

(a) capitalisation of certain costs, as in (vi) above;

(b) failure to depreciate goodwill (when capitalised) or most buildings (in the latter case, some companies have previously put up with audit qualifications as a price of this) (Sch. 1, paras 18 and 21);

(c) failure to use 'lower of cost and net realisable value' for stocks or (more frequently) current asset investments.

Another main area where the strictness of the *AktG* has been watered down concerns historical cost. Although the 1981 Act, like the 1980 Act, is written in the context of historical cost, there are provisions in the Directive (Art33) and the 1981 Act (Sch. 1, paras 29–34) which allow alternative rules to a strict Germanic interpretation of this. Departures from historical cost are allowed, ranging from *ad hoc* revaluations of fixed assets to full scale current cost accounting (CCA) as statutory accounts. Even the first draft of the Directive (before British entry to the EC) allowed for such departures, which would have been necessary to allow for the practice of many Dutch companies

(Arts 30 and 31). However, the effect is clearly to destroy the attempt to establish uniform accounting measurement rules.

Nevertheless, there is a fundamental change from the previous UK position, in which a company could present statutory CCA accounts without historical cost information. As part of the price for adopting (or having previously adopted) an alternative to 'Germanic Accounting' for any item, many disclosures are required by Schedule 1 of the 1981 Act.[17] In effect, these would allow the reconstruction of historical cost accounts, which does represent a measure of harmonisation (as opposed to standardisation).

Disclosure

The fourth major area of accounting provisions in the 1981 Act is a series of disclosure requirements[18] which are additional to those of the Companies Act 1948 to 1980. Many of them may be traced to the *AktG*.

Conclusion

During the twentieth century, until the 1980 Companies Act, British legislation relating to financial reporting has been fairly sparse and has moved forward in an evolutionary way, often *following* 'best practice'. The advent of the 1980 and 1981 Companies Acts brings about several changes. Some of these changes are revolutionary because their inspiration comes from outside the Anglo-Saxon world; the most obvious single source being the German *Aktiengesetz* of 1965. For example, introduction of a distinct label and minimum capital requirements for public companies, of compulsory formats and detailed measurement rules for financial reports, and of reduced publication requirements for smaller companies may be better understood by tracing their ancestry. There are some cases where the British accounting tradition may manage to side-step the detailed requirements of the new legislation, but even here the changed letter of the law may have an important influence in the longer run.

---

[16]Paras. 9–13 of the supplementary statement to SSAP 19.

[17]The disclosures include: (i) the valuation basis used (para. 33), (ii) the comparable historical cost amount or the difference therefrom (para. 33), (iii) the comparable accumulated depreciation under historical cost or the difference (para. 33), (iv) the revaluation reserve relating to all departures (para. 34), (v) a note of valuation revisions due to adoption of alternative methods in the year (para. 42), (vi) the year of valuation (para. 43), (vii) for assets revalued in the year, the names or qualifications of the valuers (para. 43).

[18]These are to be found in part III of Schedule 1 of the 1981 Act, which replaced Schedule 8 of the 1948 Act. Article 32 of the Directive contains many of them. There is one repeal, in that S16 of the 1981 Act removes the requirement of S20 of the 1967 Act to disclose exports.

References

ASC, *Accounting for Investment Properties, SSAP 19*, Accountancy Bodies, London 1981.

ASC, *Stocks and Work in Progress, SSAP 9*, Accountancy Bodies, London 1975.

Barth, K., *Die Entwicklung des deutschen Bilanzrechts*, Band I Handelsrechtlich, Stuttgart 1953, pp. 291–3.

DOT, *Company Accounting and Disclosure*, Cmnd. 7654, HMSO, 1979.

EC Commission, 'Proposal for a Fourth Directive', *Bulletin of the European Communities*, November 1971.

EC Commission, *Industrial Policy and the European Community*, Brussels, November 1972, p. 5.

EC Commission, 'Amended Proposal for a Fourth Directive', *Bulletin of the European Communities*, Supplement 6, 1974.

EC Commission, 'Fourth Directive on Company Law, 78/660', *Official Journal*, 1978, L 222/11, or *Trade and Industry*, 11 August 1978.

Edey, H. C., 'Company Accounting in the Nineteenth and Twentieth Centuries' in T. A. Lee and R. H. Parker, *The Evolution of Corporate Financial Reporting*, Nelson, London 1979.

Edwards, J. R., *Company Legislation and Changing Patterns of Disclosure in British Company Accounts 1900–1940*, Institute of Chartered Accountants in England and Wales, London 1981.

Forrester, D. A. R., *Schmalenbach and After*, Strathclyde Convergencies, Glasgow 1977.

Hoffman, L. and M. H. Arden, 'Legal Opinion on True and Fair View', *Accountancy*, November 1983.

ICAEW, *Survey of Published Accounts*, Institute of Chartered Accountants in England and Wales, London 1980, p. 182.

Most, K. S., 'The French Accounting Experiment', *International Journal of Accounting*, Fall 1971.

Mueller, G. G., *International Accounting*, Macmillan, New York 1967, Part I.

Mueller, R. and E. G. Galbraith, *The German Stock Corporation Law*, Knapp, Frankfurt 1976.

Nair, R. D. and W. G. Frank, 'The Impact of Disclosure and Measurement Practices on International Accounting Classifications', *Accounting Review*, July 1980.

Neihus, R., 'Harmonized EEC Accounting—A German View of the Draft Directive for Uniform Accounting Rules', *International Journal of Accounting*, Spring 1972, p. 102.

Nobes, C. W. and R. H. Parker, *Comparative International Accounting*, Philip Allan, Oxford 1981, chs. 3, 5 and 7.

Parker, R. H. (a), 'Consolidation Accounting' in Nobes and Parker (1981).

Parker, R. H. (b), 'The Want of Uniformity in Accounts: A Nineteeth Century Debate', in D. M. Emanuel and I. C. Stewart, *Essays in Honour of Trevor R. Johnston*, University of Auckland 1981.

Scherpf, P., cited in Niehus [1972] as *Der Kontenrahmen*, Max Verlag, Munich 1955, p. 8.

Singer, H. W., *Standardized Accountancy in Germany*, Cambridge University Press 1943.

Tweedie, D., 'The ASC in Chains: Whither Self-Regulation Now?', *Accountancy*, March 1983; and 'True and Fair Rules', *Accountants' Magazine*, November 1983.

14

The European Accounting Review 1996, **5:2**, 361–373

Some mysteries relating to the prudence principle in the Fourth Directive and in German and British law

Lisa Evans and Christopher Nobes
Napier University, and University of Reading, UK

ABSTRACT

Article 31 of the Fourth Directive, which specifies the general valuation principles to be applied in the preparation of financial statements, shows a difference in emphasis between the different language versions. Except for the English version of the Directive, all others emphasize prudence, as opposed to the other valuation principles required by the article. The earlier drafts of the Directive are examined in an attempt to trace the development of this difference between the English and the other language versions. It seems that the particular wording of Article 31 with its relatively greater weight on prudence probably results from UK influence, more specifically from SSAP 2. A possible solution is then suggested as to why this particular emphasis on prudence was not retained in the English version of the Directive. Further, it is noted that German law did not explicitly make prudence an overriding concept before the Fourth Directive and nor does the German implementation of Article 31.

INTRODUCTION

One of the key differences in accounting practices in Europe relates to differential degrees of conservatism.[1] German accounting, and to a certain extent that of most other continental member states of the European Union, tends to emphasize the principle of prudence relatively more than the other valuation principles listed in the Fourth Directive on Company Law.[2] The UK might be taken as an exemplar of the opposite view. For example, Gray (1980) proposed a conservatism index, and saw Germany as noticeably more conservative than the UK. Instances of greater German conservatism may be found in the opposition in that country to (1) the percentage-of-

---

Address for correspondence
Lisa Evans, Department of Accounting and Finance, Napier University, Sighthill Court, Edinburgh EH11 4BN, UK.

0963–8180

completion method for long-term contracts (e.g. Ordelheide, 1993), and (2) the taking of gains on unsettled foreign currency monetary items.

The reasons for these differing approaches have been discussed in detail elsewhere,[3] and include the closeness of German accounting to German tax rules and the importance of creditor protection. The EC Forum spent considerable effort in 1994 and 1995 looking at 'prudence v. matching' (e.g. FEE, 1994). However, none of the publications on this subject have pointed out the following mysteries or tried to solve them:

1 Prudence was not explicitly mentioned in the first draft of the Fourth Directive or in the preceding German law.
2 The idea of explicit reference in the Fourth Directive to prudence (and an emphasis on it) seem to come from a British accounting standard.
3 Despite this, the English version of the Directive is the only one not to emphasize prudence.
4 The implementation of the Directive in German law does not carry forward the emphasis on prudence in the German version of the Directive.

THE FOURTH DIRECTIVE

The importance of prudence in German accounting is supported by the German wording of Article 31 of the Directive (see Appendix A) which, while introducing the other valuation principles with phrases which would translate, for example, as 'going concern is to be presumed'; '... consistency shall apply', etc., appears to place special emphasis[4] on prudence by stating that 'Der Grundsatz der Vorsicht muss *in jedem Fall* beachtet werden'. (Article 31 (1)(c) – emphasis added) – ('The principle of prudence must be observed *in any event*'. A more literal translation may stress this emphasis even more: 'The principle of prudence must be observed *in every case*'.)

Strangely, the English version of the Directive does not emphasize prudence. Article 31 (1)(c) reads: 'valuation must be made on a prudent basis' (see Appendix A). This may have been what led Rutteman (1984: 11) to state: 'The prudence concept they [the EEC Commission] deem to take precedence over the accruals concept, although the Directive nowhere says so.' As noted, the German version of the Directive does in fact say so. Furthermore, an examination of the other language versions shows that it is the English version of the Directive, rather than the German one, which is the exception. For example, the French version states: 'le principe de prudence doit *en tout cas* être observé ...' (emphasis added). The same stress is found in the Italian, Spanish, Portuguese and Danish versions. The Dutch version reads: 'het voorzichtigheidsbeginsel moet *steeds* in acht worden genomen ...' (emphasis added), i.e. 'the principle of prudence must always be observed ...'.

ORIGIN OF THE EMPHASIS

This raises the question of where this emphasis on prudence in the directive originates. If it had been a German influence, one might have expected to find the emphasis in the *Aktiengesetz* (*AktG*) of 1965 which formed the basis for the Fourth Directive (Nobes, 1983). However, there is no explicit mention of prudence in the *AktG*, which refers to the more detailed requirements of the Handelsgesetzbuch (*HGB*). However, although prudence is consequently referred to in the legal commentaries on the Act,[5] there is no specific emphasis on it. Furthermore, as noted in the introduction, the first draft of the Fourth Directive (1971, Article 28), which was published by the Commission before the UK, Ireland and Denmark joined the EU in 1973, does not mention prudence at all. Nevertheless, prudence is implied in the other general (valuation) principles, which deal with realization and accounting for contingencies (Article 28 (1)(b)), deficiencies becoming apparent after the balance sheet date (Article 28 (1)(c)) and a requirement to account for depreciation whether the accounts show a profit or a loss (Article 28 (1)(d)). The other valuation principles of Article 28 are consistency, separate valuation of asset and liability items, and the requirement for one year's closing balance sheet to correspond to the following year's opening balance sheet.

The situation changed by the time of the second draft (1974). The going concern and the accruals principles were introduced, and the idea of prudence was made explicit. The former subparagraphs (b) to (d) of Article 28 (as listed above) now became integrated within the new paragraph dealing with prudence (28 (c)), effectively making the realization principle a 'sub-principle of the prudence principle' (Ordelheide, 1993: 83). Also, the German version of the 1974 draft contains the explicit emphasis on prudence mentioned above, as do all the other language versions, *except for the English version.*

Incidentally, the term used in the English version of the 1974 draft was 'conservatism' (as in US documents, see *Accountancy*, 1971), rather than 'prudence', the latter only appearing in the final form of the Directive. Table 1 (see words in italics) shows how the two terms were used in various documents in English in the 1970s. There seems to be little systematic difference between the two terms, except that 'prudence' might be used to avoid the connotations of secret reserves and other practices once associated with the older word 'conservatism'. A shift such as that from 'conservatism' to 'prudence' in the wording of the drafts of the English version of the directive (between 1974 and 1978) could be achieved[6] by negotiation with the secretariat of the Council of Ministers.

Table 1 Chronology of events and publications

1961	AICPA Accounting Research Study 1: rejects *conservatism*
1965	AICPA Accounting Research Study 7: includes *conservatism*
December 1969	Accounting Standards Steering Committee formed
October 1970	APB Statement 4: *conservatism* as a 'modifying convention', not as a 'pervasive principle'
Februrary 1971	ED 2: *prudence* as overriding
November 1971	Fourth Directive first draft: no explicit reference to the concept
November 1971	SSAP 2: *prudence* as overriding
January 1973	UK joins EC (but previously observer status on Groupe d'Etudes)
July 1973	IASC formed
October 1973	Trueblood Committee reports
Februrary 1974	Fourth Directive second draft: *conservatism* emphasized
1974	UEC Recommendation No. 1 (lists four concepts, but no emphasis)
April 1974	IASC Exposure Draft E1: *prudence* as a selection criterion
January 1975	IAS 1: *prudence* as a selection criterion
July 1978	Fourth Directive: *prudence* emphasized

A further English language nuance (Rutteman, 1984: 6) is that Article 28 (in 1971 and 1974) requires that 'Only the profits *earned* at the date of the balance sheet may be included' (emphasis added), whereas Article 31 of the directive refers to 'profits made', and the British law[7] has 'profits realised' (see Appendices A and B). This change seems to be an attempt to broaden the scope of the phrase to make it less conservative. In the case of 'realised', this word was chosen[8] to be consistent with the UK's implementation in 1980 of the Second Directive's definition of distributable profits, which rests on the word 'realised'.

There were no other significant changes concerning prudence between the 1974 draft and the final Directive in any of the other language versions.[9] Article 28 of the drafts becomes Article 31 in the Directive.

If we cannot look to German precedent for the explicit inclusion of and emphasis on prudence in the 1974 draft and the final Directive, reference must be made to the main event that led to other changes from the 1971 to the 1974 version of the directive: the accession of the UK, Ireland and Denmark. It is clear that the arrival of these three countries was the cause of the insertion of the 'true and fair view' requirement in the 1974 draft (Nobes, 1993), so the above changes in the lower level accounting principles may also have resulted from this.

By 1974, the UK and Ireland had recently[10] seen the publication of the first accounting standards and, with particular relevance to the above, of SSAP 2, which lists four 'fundamental accounting concepts': going concern, accruals, consistency and prudence – with particular emphasis on prudence:

'...; provided that where the accruals concept is inconsistent with the "prudence" concept the latter prevails' (para. 14 (b)).

The influence of SSAP 2 seems to have operated through the Groupe d'Etudes, which advised the Commission on accounting matters:

> The Groupe D'Etudes has discussed this directive at considerable length and has issued two reports, the first in June last year and the second in April of this year. From the British viewpoint, we can, I feel, be satisfied with the Groupe's work, since its main recommendations include the following points:
> 1. The fundamental purposes of annual accounts should be to show a true and fair view. ...
>
> ...
>
> 3. The section on valuation rules should commence in its first article by stating that there are four basic accounting concepts – those of going concern, consistency, matching or accruals and prudence. Again *the English terms were included in the official French text of the Groupe's second report.* (Bartholomew, 1973: 424–9, emphasis added)

In the light of the above there seems little doubt that the changes proposed were UK influenced (for further evidence see, for example, the interview by Lafferty (1974) with John Grenside, one of the UK representatives in the negotiations surrounding the Fourth Directive). This may lead to the suggestion that the emphasis on prudence in relation to the other principles also originated in the UK. Another reference to the report by the Groupe d'Etudes seems relevant in this context:

> In dealing with Article 28, concerning certain general principles of valuation, the Study Group observes that the general principles include four basic concepts:
>
> 1 The going concern concept
> 2 The concept of consistency
> 3 The matching or accruals concept
> 4 The concept of prudence
>
> The application of the third concept is not prescribed as such in the provisions. ...
> The Study Group proposes that this concept should be incorporated in Article 28. *It states, however, that it is necessary to place these concepts in order of importance. As the concept of prudence is of primordial [sic] importance, its relationship to the concept of accruals and matching must be stated.* (Accountancy, 1973a: 4 – emphasis added)

A FURTHER MYSTERY

Given the apparent UK influence which seems to have led to the provisions of SSAP 2 being incorporated into the Fourth Directive, it is particularly strange that the English versions of the 1974 draft and of the final Directive are the only ones which do not retain the supremacy of prudence.

The potential explanations for the special wording in the English version seem to be:

1 a wording which was openly agreed in Council negotiations;
2 a wording lobbied for by the UK and agreed privately by the Council secretariat;
3 a wording arranged by the Council secretariat in order to make the drafting more acceptable to the UK, but not discussed with any delegation; or
4 a linguistic accident.

It is clear that (1) and (2) were not the case. None of the articles of the time, and none of the papers or the recollections[11] of the negotiators fit this explanation. If either (3) or (4) was the case, presumably the UK delegation would have objected to the wording if it had not suited them. Here, it seems useful to note that there was a change in the prevailing ethos in the UK from an emphasis on prudence to an emphasis on accruals within a relatively short time: between 1971 (the publication of SSAP 2) and 1974 (the second draft of the Fourth Directive).

A chronology of potentially relevant events is shown as Table 1. In the USA, Accounting Research Study (ARS) No. 7 of the AICPA[12] listed ten 'basic concepts', among them those which became the four of SSAP 2. By 1970, the Accounting Principles Board had downgraded conservatism to a 'modifying convention' (APB, 1970). Conservatism had also been criticized in ARS No. 1 (Moonitz, 1961) and by Sterling (1967: 131) who rejects it as 'deliberate understatement' and as a concept which 'has lost favour in accounting circles, that is not applied in practice as much as it once was' (110). This was part of a move from stewardship accounting and the protection of creditors towards the provision of information intended for financial decisions by investors. A landmark along this way was the 1973 US report of the Trueblood Committee on the objectives of financial statements.

It is clear that this trend, and increasing inflation, were already affecting the UK (Hinton, 1972: 58):

> The concept of conservatism, suitable perhaps in an era when only creditors and private owners had an interest in financial statements, is inconsistent with another basic concept, vigorously proclaimed by accountants, that accounting must be fair and free from bias. Conservatism and fairness are inconsistent concepts, since conservatism serves some users of financial statements to the detriment of others. Conservatism is basically biased; it seeks to protect the purchaser and the lender, but disregards the interests of the seller and the borrower.

Similarly, Buckley (1973) points out that the objectives of financial statements depend on the user group and change with time; in this context, he also criticizes the use of historical cost (1973: 64):

> Developed in an age when there was little or no divorce of ownership and control, stewardship accounts served the then prevailing business environment perfectly well. But now financial reporting objectives have changed; the users of financial statements want more than reports on stewardship. In addition the balance sheet of

an enterprise reflects, under generally accepted accounting principles, historic cost rather than the true value of economic resources locked up in the entity.

In 1973 the IASC was formed. In 1974 it issued its first Exposure Draft, which appears to cover much the same ground as SSAP 2. This is hardly surprising if one considers the way the IASC worked:

> It is the committee's intention to make a collection of the standards of the written work in the nine [founder] nations, and sift it to the basics. The resulting material, free from any unnecessary sophistication, will then be made into an exposure draft, and on further refinement will be published as a definite document. (*Accountancy*, 1973b: 4)

However, the resulting IAS 1 shows a move away from SSAP 2's emphasis on prudence, by not recognizing it as a fundamental assumption but only as one of three[13] considerations which 'should govern the selection and application by management of the appropriate accounting policies ...' (para. 9). This reflects the US view discussed above, which seems already to have been affecting the UK. No doubt, the involvement of US and UK representatives in the IAS 1 discussions speeded up this effect, which then fed into negotiations in Brussels from 1973. This possibility is confirmed by one of the UK negotiators of the time.[14]

Incidentally, by the stage of the negotiations in the Council of Ministers leading up to the final Directive in 1978, relatively subtle points and language differences would not have been dwelt on. National negotiators were mainly interested in achieving drafts in their own languages which could be 'lived with'.[15]

IMPLEMENTATION OF THE DIRECTIVE

The next part of the mystery is that the Directive's emphasis on prudence did not appear (at least, not directly in the words used) in the resulting laws of Germany or the UK (see Appendix B). Of course, in the case of the UK this may not be surprising because the emphasis is missing from the English version of the Directive, but how does one explain the continuing absence of the emphasis in German law, as amended by the 1985 *Bilanzrichtliniengesetz*?

Ordelheide and Pfaff (1994: 133) refer to the amended German Commercial Code, (*HGB*), §252 (1) in claiming that:

> The essential principle is the prudence principle (HGB §252 (1), No. 4). It is made concrete through the acquisition cost principle, the principle of lower of cost and market value and the realization principle, among others. In addition the following *complementary and supporting* principles should be noted:
>
> 1 The principle of balance sheet continuity (HGB §252 (1), No.1).
> 2 The 'going concern' principle (HGB §252 (1), No.2).
> 3 The principle of item-by-item valuation (HGB §252 (1), No.3).

4 The accruals principle (HGB §252 (1), No.5).
5 The consistency principle (HGB §252 (1), No.6). (emphasis added)

However, the emphasis on prudence is not obvious from a scrutiny of the German law itself (see Appendix B). *HGB* §252 does not stress the prudence principle in comparison with the other principles. It does not state that the prudence principle is the 'essential principle', nor does it define the other principles as 'complementary and supporting'. It merely requires prudence in a list of six principles all of which have to be complied with.

One can only assume that the Directive's emphasis on prudence was not explicitly included in *HGB* §252 because it was taken for granted, or could be presumed because of the more detailed valuation rules of the *HGB*, which implement the more 'prudent' options of the Fourth Directive, and because of the provisions of *Grundsätze ordnungsmässiger Buchführung* (*GoB*), which also favour a prudent approach to accounting. The context is that interpretation of a law in the Roman legal system takes more account of implicit principles than would apply in the English legal system.

The following reference to a legal commentary on the *HGB* (Baumbach *et al.*, 1989) may serve as an illustration of the preference for prudence. The *HGB* §252 (2)[16] allows departure from the detailed principles of §252 (1) in justified exceptional cases, but the legal commentary suggests that exceptions are possible from all principles except prudence:

> **Ausnahmen:** II ist hier ohne praktische Bedeutung; Ausnahmen sind idR nicht 'begründet' oder entsprechen nicht den GoB.
> **(Exceptions:** II is here without practical significance; exceptions are, as a rule, not 'justified' or do not correspond to GoB.)

SUMMARY

The supremacy of prudence over the other principles is codified in all language versions of the Fourth Directive except for the English version. This is surprising, since an examination of the development of the Directive suggests that it was particularly the British SSAP 2 which influenced Article 31 of the Fourth Directive with respect to the following:

1 the introduction of prudence as an explicit principle,
2 the supremacy of the prudence principle.

A possible reason for the omission of the emphasis on prudence in the English version of the Directive (and therefore in the Companies Act 1981) has been suggested.

A further curiosity is that German law, which otherwise places greater emphasis on prudence than does UK law, has not implemented the emphasis on it in the relevant passage of the *HGB*. This appears to be due to German *GoB* and to the detailed valuation rules of the *HGB*, in which greater emphasis on prudence as compared to the accruals principle is implicit and which implements the more prudent options of the directive.

NOTES

The authors are grateful for comments on an earlier draft to John Dyson and David Young (Napier University), Dieter Ordelheide (Goethe Universität, Frankfurt am Main), Bob Parker (University of Exeter) and Alan Roberts (University of Reading), and for advice from Sir John Grenside CBE, Frank Jenkins (of the Department of Trade and Industry), Michael Renshall CBE and Tom Watts CBE who were involved on behalf of the UK in governmental and Groupe d'Etudes negotiations of the Fourth Directive in the 1970s.

1   The words 'conservatism' and 'prudence' are used in this paper. Both can be found in official documents. There seems to be little difference in the meanings of the words.
2   See for example Ordelheide (1993: 83); Ordelheide and Pfaff (1994: 133–6); Nobes and Parker (1995: 45–7).
3   See for example Busse von Colbe (1984: 125–6); Choi and Mueller (1992: 40–3); Haller (1992); Macharzina and Langer (1995: 269); Nobes (1992: 7–23); Perera (1989).
4. Of course, it would have been possible to emphasize prudence even more by placing it as the first of the principles, or by specifically making accruals subordinate to prudence. We are grateful to Frank Jenkins for pointing this out.
5   A legal commentary on para. 39 of the *HGB* from before the implementation of the Fourth Directive (Baumbach *et al.*, 1985: 144) discusses the section of German law which influenced the content of Article 28. Paragraph 39 refers to the duty to draw up a balance sheet (*Bilanz*). The legal commentary lists, with reference to other laws and *GoB*, the following principles to be applied in doing so: clarity, truth, completeness, continuity, prudence.
6   Frank Jenkins, who was one of the representatives of the UK in these negotiations, confirms this (letter of 23 February 1995).
7   Now in Schedule 4, para. 12a to the Companies Act 1985. The word 'realised' is further defined in para. 91, in a way which refers to 'principles generally accepted'.
8   As footnote 6.
9   The German word for prudence (*Vorsicht*) did not change.
10 ED 2 (the exposure draft for SSAP 2) was published in February 1971 and the SSAP itself in November of the same year. The stress on prudence was moved from the Explanatory Note part of the ED, to the Definition of Terms part of the SSAP.
11 Sir John Grenside, Frank Jenkins, Michael Renshall and Tom Watts (see references in other footnotes) have no papers or recollections which suggest that the UK delegation was aware of or pushed for the difference in the emphasis of prudence in the English version. However, they suggest that they would have approved of the absence of emphasis.
12 American Institute of Certified Public Accountants; see Grady (1965).
13 The other two being substance over form and materiality.
14 For example, by Michael Renshall (who was involved in the negotiations at the Groupe d'Etudes and at governmental level) in a letter of 22 February 1995. However, Sir John Grenside (also closely involved) suggests that there was no

direct influence of IASC discussions (minuted telephone conversation of 28 February 1995).
15 This is recorded, in a letter of 22 February 1995 by Tom Watts, who was an honorary UK civil servant for the purposes of the Council of Ministers negotiations.
16 This implements Article 31 (2) of the Directive.
17 Amended by the 1989 Companies Act to read as follows: 11. Accounting policies shall be applied consistently within the same accounts as from one financial year to the next.

REFERENCES

Accountancy (1971) 'Accounting standards go forward', February, 54–5.
Accountancy (1973a) 'Study Group steps forward on harmonisation', May.
Accountancy (1973b) 'International accountancy: a beginning', August.
Accounting Principles Board (1970) *Statement of the Accounting Principles Board 4. Basic Concepts and Accounting Principles Underlying Financial Statements of Business Enterprises. New York: American Institute of Certified Public Accountants.*
Bartholomew, E. G. (1973) 'The EEC, company law and accountants', *The Accountant's Magazine*, August, 424–9
Baumbach, A., Duden, K. and Hopt, K. (1985) *Handelsgesetzbuch*, 26 Auflage, Munich: C. H. Beck
Baumbach, A., Duden, K. and Hopt, K. (1989) *Handelsgesetzbuch*, 28 Auflage, Munich: C. H. Beck
Buckley, A. (1973) 'The financial statement ... ', *Accountancy*, August.
Busse von Colbe, W. (1984) 'A true and fair view: a German perspective', in Gray, S. J. and Coenenberg A. G. (eds) *EEC Accounting Harmonisation: Implementation and Impact of the Fourth Directive*, North Holland: Elsevier, pp. 121–128.
Choi, F. D. S. and Mueller, G. G. (1992) *International Accounting*, New Jersey: Prentice-Hall.
FEE (1994) *Discussion Paper on the Application of Prudence and Matching in Selected European Countries.*
Grady, P. (1965) *Research Study No. 7. Inventory of Generally Accepted Accounting Principles for Business Enterprises.* New York: American Institute of Certified Public Accountants.
Gray, S. J. (1980) 'The impact of international differences from a security-analysis perspective: some European evidence', *Journal of Accounting Research*, Spring.
Haller, A. (1992) 'The relationship of financial and tax accounting in Germany: a major reason for accounting disharmony in Europe', *International Journal of Accounting*, 27: 310–23.
Hinton, P. R. (1972) 'Objectives of financial statements', *Accountancy*, November.
Lafferty, M. (1974) 'Fourth Directive .... what's in it for us?' *Accountancy*, July: 30–2.
Marcharzina, K. and Langer, K. (1995), 'Financial reporting in Germany' in Nobes and Parker (1995).
Moonitz, M. (1961) *Research Study No.1. The Basic Postulates of Accounting.* New York: American Institute of Certified Public Accountants.
Nobes, C. W. (1983), 'The evolution of the harmonising provisions of the 1980 and 1981 Companies Acts', *Accounting and Business Research*, Winter: 43–53.
Nobes, C. W. (1992) *Accounting Harmonisation in Europe: Process, Progress and Prospects*, London: Financial Times Business Information.

Nobes, C. W. (1993) 'The true and fair view requirement: impact on and of the Fourth Directive', *Accounting and Business Research*, Winter.

Nobes C. W. and Parker, R. H. (1995) *Comparative International Accounting*. Hemel Hempstead: Prentice Hall.

Ordelheide, D. (1993), 'True and fair view: a European and a German perspective', *European Accounting Review*, 1, 81–90.

Ordelheide, D. and Pfaff, D. (1994) *European Financial Reporting. Germany*, London: Routledge.

Perera, M. H. B. (1989) 'Towards a framework to analyse the impact of culture on accounting', *International Journal of Accounting*, 24, 42–56.

Rutteman, P. (1984) *The EEC Accounting Directives and their Effects*, University College Cardiff Press.

Sterling, R. R. (1967) 'Conservatism: the fundamental principle of valuation in traditional accounting', *Abacus*, 3 (2): 109–32.

APPENDIX A: ARTICLE 31, FOURTH DIRECTIVE (1978)

German Version

Artikel 31

(1) Die Mitgliedstaaten stellen sicher, daß für die Bewertung der Posten im Jahresabschluß folgende allgemeine Grundsätze gelten:

a)   Eine Fortsetzung der Unternehmenstätigkeit wird unterstellt.

b)   In der Anwendung der Bewertungsmethoden soll Stetigkeit bestehen.

c)   Der Grundsatz der Vorsicht muß *in jedem Fall* beachtet werden. Das bedeutet insbesondere:

   aa) Nur die am Bilanzstichtag realisierten Gewinne werden ausgewiesen.

   bb) Es müssen alle voraussehbaren Risiken und zu vermutenden Verluste berücksichtigt werden, die in dem Geschäftsjahr oder einem früheren Geschäftsjahr entstanden sind, selbst wenn diese Risiken oder Verluste erst zwischen dem Bilanzstichtag und dem Tag der Aufstellung der Bilanz bekanntgeworden sind.

   cc) Wertminderungen sind unabhängig davon zu berücksichtigen, ob das Geschäftsjahr mit einem Gewinn oder einem Verlust abschließt.

d)   Aufwendungen und Erträge für das Geschäftsjahr, auf das sich der Jahresabschluß bezieht, müssen berücksichtigt werden, ohne Rücksicht auf den Zeitpunkt der Ausgabe oder Einnahme dieser Aufwendung oder Erträge.

e)   Die in den Aktiv und Passivposten enthaltenen Vermögensgegenstände sind einzeln zu bewerten.

f)   Die Eröffnungsbilanz eines Geschäftsjahres muß mit der Schlußbilanz des vorhergehenden Geschäftsjahres übereinstimmen.

(emphasis added)

English Version

Article 31

1. The Member States shall ensure that the items shown in the annual accounts are valued in accordance with the following general principles:

(a) the company must be presumed to be carrying on its business as a going concern;

(b) the methods of valuation must be applied consistently from one financial year to another;

(c) valuation must be made on a prudent basis, and in particular:

  (aa) only profits made at the balance sheet date may be included,

  (bb) account must be taken of all foreseeable liabilities and potential losses arising in the course of the financial year concerned or of a previous one, even if such liabilities or losses become apparent only between the date of the balance sheet and the date on which it is drawn up,

  (cc) account must be taken of all depreciation, whether the result of the financial year is a loss or a profit;

(d) account must be taken of income and charges relating to the financial year, irrespective of the date of receipt or payment of such income or charges;

(e) the components of asset and liability items must be valued separately;

(f) the opening balance sheet for each financial year must correspond to the closing balance sheet for the preceding financial year.

APPENDIX B: IMPLEMENTATION OF ARTICLE 31 INTO NATIONAL LAW

Handelsgesetzbuch Paragraph 252

Allgemeine Bewertungsgrundsätze

(1) Bei der Bewertung der im Jahresabschluß ausgewiesenen Vermögensgegenstände und Schulden gilt insbesondere folgendes:

1. Die Wertansätze in der Eröffnungsbilanz des Geschäftsjahrs müssen mit denen der Schlußbilanz des vorhergehenden Geschäftsjahrs übereinstimmen.

2. Bei der Bewertung ist von der Fortführung der Unternehmenstätigkeit auszugehen, sofern dem nicht tatsächliche oder rechtliche Gegebenheiten entgegenstehen.

3. Die Vermögensgegenstände und Schulden sind zum Abschlußstichtag einzeln zu bewerten.

4. Es ist vorsichtig zu bewerten, namentlich sind alle vorhersehbaren Risiken und Verluste, die bis zum Abschlußstichtag entstanden sind, zu berücksichtigen, selbst wenn diese erst zwischen dem Abschlußstichtag und dem Tag der Aufstellung des Jahresabschlusses bekanntgeworden sind; Gewinne sind nur zu berücksichtigen, wenn sie am Abschlußstichtag realisiert sind.

5. Aufwendungen und Erträge des Geschäftsjahrs sind unabhängig von den Zeitpunkten der entsprechenden Zahlungen im Jahresabschluß zu berücksichtigen.
6. Die auf den vorhergehenden Jahresabschlußstichtag angewandten Bewertungsmethoden sollen beibehalten werden.

Companies Act 1985, Schedule 4, Section A Accounting principles

10. The company shall be presumed to be carrying on business as a going concern.
11. Accounting policies shall be applied consistently as from one financial year to the next[17]
12. The amount of any item shall be determined on a prudent basis, and in particular—

    (a) only profits realised at the balance sheet date shall be included in the profit and loss account; and
    (b) all liabilities and losses which have arisen or are likely to arise in respect of the financial year to which the accounts relate or a previous financial year shall be taken into account, including those which only become apparent between the balance sheet date and the date on which it is signed on behalf of the board of directors in pursuance of [section 233] of this Act.

13. All income and charges relating to the financial year to which the accounts relate shall be taken into account, without regard to the date of receipt or payment.
14. In determining the aggregate amount of any item the amount of each individual asset or liability that falls to be taken into account shall be determined separately.

15

Accounting and Business Research, Vol. 24, No. 93, pp. 35–48, 1993 35

The True and Fair View Requirement: Impact on and of the Fourth Directive

Christopher Nobes*

Abstract—The overriding British legal requirement for financial reporting of giving 'a true and fair view' (TFV) has been exported to continental Europe via the European Community's (EC) Fourth Directive on Company Law. This paper considers accounting rules in continental Europe before this process, and traces the gradual acceptance of the predominance of TFV in the drafting of the Directive after UK accession to the EC. The signifiers used in different European languages in the various drafts of the Directive are examined. It is noted that all (eight) other versions contain only one adjective (generally equivalent to 'faithful') rather than true *and* fair. The origins of the Dutch *getrouw*, the French *fidèle*, etc. are looked into. As the Directive evolved, and particularly as it was implemented in the twelve EC states, greater linguistic variety emerged, such that five countries changed the wording from the original Directive and two others qualified the wording. Whether this affects what TFV signifies is investigated. Countries can also be divided into several groups with respect to the effects of having the TFV in law. The extremes appear to be the UK and Germany.

This paper traces the development of the true and fair view (TFV) requirement in the Fourth Directive, and then the relevant effects of this element of the Directive on the laws and practices in EC member states.

In the context of the UK, Walton (1991) suggests that we should follow Saussure (1919) and distinguish between the signifier and the signified when examining the TFV. The signifiers are the words 'give a true and fair view', whereas the signified is the underlying idea. What is signified by a particular signifier can change. For example, in order to give a TFV it might, over time, become necessary (i) to disclose transfers from reserves, or (ii) to present consolidated accounts of a holding company, or (iii) to capitalise certain leases, or (iv) to include current value information.

It is suggested here that, when studying the TFV, a third dimension is necessary: the effects. There are particularly two types of effect: (i) any adjustments (designed to promote a TFV) to detailed accounting rules at the stage of national implementation of the EC Directives (called here 'direct effects'), and (ii) any continuing effects of the existence of the legal requirement for TFV on directors, auditors and rule-makers (called here 'indirect effects').

This paper examines the signifier in English; in all the other language versions of the EC Fourth Directive; and in the legal implementations in the twelve EC member states. Then there are preliminary observations concerning the signified and the effects throughout the EC.

Source of True and Fair

It will be suggested below that the origins of the concept of the predominance of the 'true and fair view' (TFV) are British, although the signifiers used in other European languages are, in general, not literal translations of this. The TFV wording (see Table 1) appeared first in British law in the Companies Act 1947 and was then consolidated into the 1948 Act (Parker, 1989, pp. 20–1). The previous British legal requirement (e.g. Companies Act 1900, S. 23) was that 'a true and correct view' should be given but this was changed after advice from the accountancy profession that 'correct' was too precise a word to reflect the practice of accounting and auditing (Walker, 1984; Rutherford, 1985). Other combinations of 'full', 'fair', 'true' and 'correct' had been used in nineteenth century laws. The change of signifier in 1947 may have had no effect on what was signified.

*The author is Coopers & Lybrand Professor of Accounting, University of Reading. He is grateful for advice on earlier drafts from David Alexander (University of Hull), John Bowen-Walsh (Institute of Chartered Accountants in Ireland), Walther Busse von Colbe (Ruhr Universität-Bochum), Octavio Gastambide Fernandes (Câmara dos Revisores Oficias de Contas, Lisbon), Maria Leonor Fernandes Ferreira (Technical University of Lisbon), Steve Goldberg (Purdue University), John Hegarty and Saskia Slomp (FEE, Brussels), Karel Van Hulle (EC Commission), Horst Kaminski (Institut der Wirtschaftsprüfer, Düsseldorf), P. Lepidas (SOL, Athens), Dieter Ordelheide (Goethe Universität, Frankfurt), Bob Parker (University of Exeter), Alan Roberts (University of Reading), Fulvia Rocchi (Università degli Studi di Venezia), Brian Rutherford (University of Kent), Jean-Claude Scheid (INTEC, Paris), Antonio Socías Salvá (Universitat de les Illes Balears), George Tridimas (University of Reading), Peter van der Zanden (Ernst & Young, Eindhoven), Peter Walton (LSE), Geoff Whittington (University of Cambridge), Stefano Zambon (Università degli Studi di Padova), Steve Zeff (Rice University), and two anonymous referees.

Table 1
General Purpose Requirements in UK law, German law and the Fourth Directive

1948 Companies Act (S. 149)	1. Every balance sheet of a company shall give a true and fair view of the state of affairs of the company ... and every profit and loss account [etc.].
	3. ... the [detailed] requirements of [the 8th Schedule] shall be without prejudice. ... to the general requirements of subsection (1) ...
1965 *Aktiengesetz* (§ 149)	1. The annual financial statements shall conform to proper bookkeeping principles. They shall be clear and well set out and give the surest possible insight of the company's financial position and its operating results pursuant to the valuation provisions.
1971 Draft (Art. 2)	1. The annual accounts shall comprise the balance sheet, the profit and loss account and the notes on the accounts. These documents shall constitute a composite whole.
	2. The annual accounts shall conform to the principles of regular and proper accounting.
	3. They shall be drawn up clearly and, in the context of the provisions regarding the valuation of assets and liabilities and the lay-out of accounts, shall reflect as accurately as possible the company's assets, liabilities, financial position and results.
1974 Draft (Art. 2)	1. (as 1971 Draft)
	2. The annual accounts shall give a true and fair view of the company's assets, liabilities, financial position and results.
	3. They shall be drawn up clearly and in conformity with the provisions of this Directive.
1978 Final (Art. 2)	1. (as 1971 Draft)
	2. They shall be drawn up clearly and in conformity with the provisions of this Directive.
	3. The annual accounts shall give a true and fair view of the company' assets, liabilities, financial position and profit or loss.
	4. Where the application of the provisions of this Directive would not be sufficient to give a true and fair view within the meaning of paragraph 3, additional information must be given.
	5. Where in exceptional cases the application of a provision of this Directive is incompatible with the obligation laid down in paragraph 3, that provision must be departed from in order to give a true and fair view within the meaning of paragraph 3. Any such departure must be disclosed in the notes on the accounts together with an explanation of the reasons for it and a statement of its effect on the assets, liabilities, financial position and profit or loss. The Member States may define the exceptional cases in question and lay down the relevant special rules.

The meaning of TFV (what is signified by it) has been discussed elsewhere from several points of view (e.g. Chastney, 1975; Flint, 1982; Rutherford, 1985; Harris, 1987; Lyas, 1992). What is signified by TFV has been acknowledged by lawyers in the UK as changeable because it is related to prevailing accepted accounting practices (Hoffman and Arden, 1983; Arden, 1993). As for effects, it was the absence of rules rather than the presence of the TFV that was traditionally important in the UK. Hopwood (1990) suggests that the TFV became particularly important to Britain only when seen as a means of countering legalism in the 1971 draft of the Fourth Directive. Parker and Nobes (1991) make the related point that the TFV seems to have been increasingly useful to the British profession as accounting rules became more codified in standards (from 1970) and in law (from 1981). The signified and the effects of TFV for British directors and auditors are noted later.

Incidentally, that the same signifier (and similar signifieds) can have different indirect effects (i.e. those not written into the detail of the law) may be illustrated by comparing the UK and Australia. What is signified by TFV in the UK and Australia is probably very similar in terms of how things should be valued and measured and what things should be disclosed (e.g. Parker, 1991a). However, the legal imposition of TFV in Britain is an overriding one (see Table 1), but in Australia TFV overrides neither law nor standards. The Australian Corporations Act 1989 (amended 1991) provides only that the directors shall 'add such information and explanation as will give a true and fair view' (S. 299 (1))

(Miller, 1993; Parker, 1994). In the US, a different signifier is used, but here the indirect effect is also clearly different from that in the UK: US financial statements are required to 'present fairly *in conformity with* generally accepted accounting principles'.[1]

In summary, in terms of indirect effects, the TFV may be used by standard setters, directors or auditors in the UK, Australia and the US. However, only in the UK can it also be used to override the law or standards.

For the present purpose, the distinguishing features of TFV in EC Directives are taken as being (i) the implication of an underlying reality, the portrayal of which is more important than any particular rules of practice, and, therefore, (ii) the requirement for the rules to be broken if this is necessary in order to portray the reality.

Impact on the Directive

The work on the *avant projet* for the Fourth Directive began in 1965 under the chairmanship of Dr. Elmendorff.[2] Elmendorff's committee, which first met in 1966, comprised professional accounting experts from the six countries that were then members of the EC. It was to be expected that a German would chair such a project, because the Germans had the most developed company law on accounting in the EC, in particular their public companies Act, the *Aktiengesetz* (AktG) of 1965.

German law, in common with the rules of most continental countries had no explicit or implicit requirement for TFV. The relevant section of the AktG (§ 149) is reprinted in Table 1. It requires that the surest possible insight (*einen möglichst sicheren Einblick*) is to be achieved but only as far as is possible in accordance with the valuation provisions of the Act. This implies that overvaluation is not acceptable but that undervaluation is.[3] Clarity is also mentioned but truth and fairness are not. In France, the requirement was *regularité et sincerité*;[4]

in Italy, *chiarezza e precisione* and *evidenza e verità*[5] (see Ferrero, 1991 for more details). The main purpose[6] of these words seems not to signify 'fair' in its sense of 'not misleading', and the rules certainly did not require departures from the detail of the regulations on this basis.

The Elmendorff Committee delivered a draft of the Fourth Directive to the EC Commission in 1968 (and a draft of the Seventh in 1969). The Committee last met in 1970. The first draft of the Fourth Directive was published by the Commission in 1971. The general purpose clause (Article 2, paragraphs 2 and 3) bore a strong resemblance to that in the AktG, as Table 1 shows. Here, again, fairness did not feature, and 'accuracy' was to be subject to the provisions of the Directive. The requirement to use 'principles of regular and proper accounting' would have been familiar to German lawyers or auditors but not to those of all other EC countries.

January 1973 saw the arrival of the UK, Ireland and Denmark in the Community. Denmark had little accounting law; it had accepted Anglo-American influences since World War II but had no TFV or similar requirement (Christiansen, 1992, p. 104). The UK and Ireland also had little law on how to do accounting, but they did have the legal predominance of 'true and fair'. Negotiation led to many changes in the Directive, some of which are discussed by Nobes (1983). In particular, as Table 1 shows, the TFV requirement was to be found in the second published draft (1974) of the Directive. It has been confirmed[7] by the secretary to the Elmendorff Committee and by the EC Commission that it was the UK's accession to the EC that began this process. The requirement to use principles of regular and proper accounting was changed to a requirement to conform to the provisions of the Directive.

The only continental EC country which was an exception to the lack of TFV was the Netherlands, where the Annual Accounts of Enterprises Act 1970 contained the overriding requirement that accounts should enable a sound insight and should be shown faithfully and systematically (see Table 2 and Appendix 1). It has been suggested elsewhere that Dutch accounting should be seen as having more in common with Anglo-Saxon than with continental accounting (e.g. Parker, 1991b). The word for 'faithful' (*getrouw*) may also mean fair, as discussed below. It seems that the prior lack of such a provision in Dutch accounting law was due more to the sparseness of law than to any point of

---

[1]Emphasis added. See Zeff (1992) for an analysis of this case. David Alexander has pointed out that perhaps unpromulgated GAAP could override promulgated GAAP, but it seems unlikely that the SEC would accept this since the SEC gives 'substantial authoritative support' to the FASB in Accounting Series Release 150 of 1973. Also Statement on Auditing Standards 69 puts fairness into the framework of GAAP. This is despite the AICPA Code of Professional Conduct (Rule 203, Interpretation 203–1) which warns against allowing a literal interpretation of a rule to result in misleading financial statements.

[2]Dr. Elmendorff was trained as a business economist and then a Wirtschaftsprüfer. He was founder of one of the larger German accountancy firms, now Wollert-Elmendorff Deutsche Industrietreuhand GmbH.

[3]That is, in addition to the general international requirement for prudence and the unusually strong German version of this (e.g. Gray, 1980), the AktG requires not the most accurate or the most fair but the most sure/safe insight.

[4]In accordance with the rules and in good faith.

[5]Clarity and preciseness; obviousness and truth (Civil Code, Arts. 2423 and 2217).

[6]The Tribunale di Milano (23.12.1968) held that it meant mainly giving information to all interested parties.

[7]Conversation with Horst Kaminski (1.3.1993), and letter from Karel Van Hulle, Head of Company Law Section of the EC Commission (11.1.1993).

Table 2
The Origins and Spread of True and Fair (for translations see Appendix I)

1	2	3	4	5
Country	Words in Law before Directive (first appearance)	Words in Directive	Implementation of Directive	Words in Law if Different from Directive
UK	a true and fair view (1947)	a true and fair view	1981	—
Ireland	a true and fair view (1963)	a true and fair view	1986	—
Netherlands	1. geeft een zodanig inzicht dat een verantwoord oordeel kan worden gevormd... 2. geeft getrouw en stelselmatig (1970)	een getrouw beeld	1983	1. (as in 1970) 2. geeft getrouw, duidelijk en stelselmatig
Denmark	—	et pålideligt billede	1981	et retvisende billede
France Luxembourg Belgium	—	une image fidèle (een getrouw beeld in Flemish)	1983 1984 1985	— — —
Germany	—	ein den tatsächlichen Verhältnissen entsprechendes Bild	1985	Unter Beachtung der Grundsätze ordnungsmässiger Buchführung (then, as Directive)
Greece	—	ten pragmatiki ikona	1986	—
Spain	—	una imagen fiel	1989	la imagen fiel ... de conformidad con las disposiciones legales
Portugal	—	uma imagem fiel	1989	uma imagem verdadeira e apropriada (1989 plan)
Italy	—	un quadro fedele	1991	rappresentare in modo veritiero e corretto

philosophy or practice. Although Dutch *accounting* law had no TFV requirement before 1970, the Registeraccountants Act (Auditing Law) of 1962 required the auditor to testify to faithfulness (*getrouwheid*). In accounting and auditing practice, '*getrouw*' also has a long history, as explained in the following section.

The influence of the *Groupe d'Etudes* should be mentioned here. This committee of EC accountancy bodies had been formed at the request of the EC Commission in order to advise on matters such as Directives.[8] The Elmendorff Committee was a predecessor. Representatives from the UK, Ireland and Denmark joined fully when their countries acceded to the EC in 1973. However, before this, the *Groupe d'Etudes* had already come to the view[9] that the TFV was the right accounting philosophy. This may seem curious, but the UK already had observer status at the *Groupe d'Etudes*. Also, although it has been sometimes impossible to persuade, for example, the German government to agree with certain Anglo-Saxon accounting ideas, it has been easier to achieve consensus with the German accountancy profession, often represented by partners from German offices of multinational accounting firms.[10] The Economic and Social

---

[8]At the beginning of 1987, a new body, the *Fédération des Experts Comptables Européens* (FEE), took over this role and that of the *Union Européenne des Experts Comptables, Economiques et Financiers* (UEC).

[9]Published opinion in June 1972.
[10]The author uses first hand accounts or personal experience of over a decade's membership of *Groupe* and *FEE* committees. His memory is confirmed by the *FEE* Secretary General (letter from John Hegarty, 19.11.1992), and by Karel Van Hulle of the EC Commission (letter of 11.1.1993).

Committee (ECOSOC) of the EC is required to give opinions on draft Directives. In February 1973, it suggested that 'faithful picture' should replace 'accuracy' in Article 2.3 of the 1970 draft. However, the *Groupe d'Etudes* and the ECOSOC did not propose the predominance of TFV over rules.

The 1974 draft of the Directive contained requirements both to give a TFV and to comply with the provisions of the Directive. However, the draft did not deal with cases where the two requirements might conflict. One interpretation of this is that use of the provisions would automatically lead to a TFV, so that the specific TFV requirement related to matters on which there were no provisions or to cases where there was a need to give extra information. As will be explained, this is the German view, and by implication, it is also now the view in the US and Australia, as already noted. This interpretation was not acceptable to the profession in countries like the UK, where it is argued that the TFV is the ultimate objective, which implies the need in certain circumstances to override other legal provisions (e.g. Tweedie, 1983). For example, from this standpoint, the practice in some continental countries of writing off assets for accounting purposes in order to take advantage of generous tax depreciation might be legally sanctioned but should not be permitted in accounts because it would not give a true and fair view.

This full-blooded version of the significance of TFV (discussed further later) triumphed in the 1978 adopted version of the Directive, as shown in Table 1. At the formal level, this could be seen as a victory for Anglo-Saxon accounting philosophy. Its effects on practice are more complex, as will be seen later.

Language in the Directive

Rutherford (1983) sets out the signifiers analogous to TFV in the versions of the Directive in six languages. Table 2 (column 3) in this paper shows the signifiers in all the languages as prepared by the EC Commission in the 1978 adopted Directive (and subsequently for Greece, Spain and Portugal). It seems possible to classify these as in Figure 1, using literal translations of the adjectives involved. On this basis, eight[11] languages have a unitary wording and only English has a dual wording (i.e. true *and* fair).

Whether the English 'true and fair' signifies a dual concept or a portmanteau is investigated elsewhere by Walker (1984), Nobes and Parker (1991a) and Parker and Nobes (1991). These last two papers conclude that UK financial directors of large companies see TFV as unitary. However,

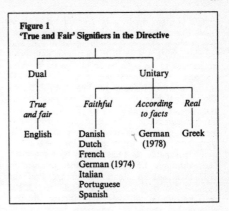

Figure 1
'True and Fair' Signifiers in the Directive

	Dual		Unitary	
	True and fair	*Faithful*	*According to facts*	*Real*
	English	Danish	German	Greek
		Dutch	(1978)	
		French		
		German (1974)		
		Italian		
		Portuguese		
		Spanish		

their auditors see it as dual: approximately, 'truth' is taken to mean that the accounts are in accordance with facts, and 'fairness' that they are not misleading.

What is the origin of the unitary signifier? Column 2 of Table 2 shows any analogous wording in laws before the Fourth Directive. It has been suggested above that only the UK, Ireland and the Netherlands had 'true and fair' or its analogue. Given that all the other versions use a unitary signifier, can it be maintained that English is the source? As shown in the next paragraph, it seems that Britain is the main source of the idea that there is an underlying TFV, the presentation of which should override rules. However, we need to look elsewhere for the source of the predominant type of signifier.

Given (i) that, even in the Netherlands, earlier law did not actually refer to the *'getrouw beeld'* of the Directive, (ii) that the draft Fourth Directive had no TFV requirement until *after* the UK and Ireland had joined the EC, and (iii) the confirmation from the Elmendorff Committee, the case for British origins seems certain. Parker (1989) certainly regards the TFV as a British export to the Commonwealth and then the EC. The Spanish also acknowledge a British origin (Socías, 1991, p. 38), as do the Germans (Busse von Colbe, 1984, p. 121) and the French (CNCC, 1984). Further, as will be noted later, the Italian Ministerial Commentary on their 1991 law specifically refers to the British version as the original. Nevertheless, Ordelheide (1993) points out that the exact formulation of the Fourth Directive was an EC matter, and that the resulting TFV sections in all EC laws sweep away previous provisions, including the British. In particular, all official language versions are formally equal, and none is to be seen as the original.

Given the clear British origins of the overriding nature of the TFV, the source of the majority

---

[11]Van Hulle (1993, p. 100) is wrong to state that Portuguese has a dual signifier in the Directive. This is so for the Portuguese law but not for the Portuguese versions of the Directives.

unitary signifier needs to be investigated in more detail. The Dutch word *'getrouw'* had been evident outside the law before the auditing Act of 1962 and the accounting Act of 1970. Its origins have been traced back to the audit report of Cooper Brothers Co. and Price, Waterhouse & Co. in the 1932 annual report of Unilever (Zeff *et al.*, 1992, p. 99). The original English version of the audit report said 'true and correct view'; the Dutch translation was *'getrouw beeld'*, which it remained even when the British Companies Act 1947 caused the English version to change to 'true and fair view'. This seems reasonable, as it has already been suggested that, although the English signifier changed in 1947, there was no intention to change what was signified. Not only was *'getrouw beeld'* seen as the best translation of the two different English phrases, but also of the American 'present fairly' (Zeff *et al.*, 1992, p. 101). However, as noted earlier, the US 'present fairly' has a noticeably different significance from the British 'give a true and fair view', and Zeff (1990) argues elsewhere that the best English signifier for the Dutch *'getrouw beeld'* is given by the British phrase not the American.

The French signifier *'image fidèle'*, which has a clear echo in the later Italian *'quadro fedele'* or Spanish *'imagen fiel'*, can be traced back in the accounting literature to 1920 (Chaveneau, 1920). It seems that a draft French law of 1921 would have required balance sheets to give *'une image aussi fidèle que possible'* (Pasqualini, 1992, p. 37). The word *'fidèle'* in this context can be traced back further to a law in Berne of 1860 and the Swiss Commercial Code of 1863 (Pasqualini, 1992, p. 37).[12] It seems that this French expression was 'the leading one' in the commission.[13] The unitary wording *'fidèle'*, like any other adjective, has layers of meaning. At one level, it could imply 'faithful' as in 'faithful representation' (e.g. IASC's Conceptual Framework, para. 33). At another level, it could signify preparation of the accounts 'in good faith'. However, the French governmental body in charge of the *plan comptable* suggested that *'image fidèle'* was a bad translation of TFV, without offering an alternative (CNCC, 1984).

The German signifier in the 1974 draft of the Directive fitted neatly with all these continental equivalents (i.e. *einen getreuen Einblick*). *'Einblick'* had been the word in the 1965 AktG. However, the final version of the Directive moves away from both adjective and noun to *'ein den tatsächlichen Verhaltnissen entsprechendes Bild'* (see Appendix 1 for translation). Incidentally, in all other languages the

Directive's signifiers for TFV in 1978 are the same as those in 1974.

It is clear that the use of a unitary signifier tells us little about what is signified. This will be examined further in the later section on language in the EC laws.

A Note on Language in the Seventh Directive

The Seventh Directive concerns consolidated accounts. As noted above, an early draft was prepared by the Elmendorff Committee in 1969, but a draft was not published by the Commission until 1976 nor adopted by the Council until 1983. The Seventh Directive applies many of the provisions of the Fourth to group accounts and specifically demands that:

> Consolidated accounts shall give a true and fair view of the assets, liabilities, financial position and profit or loss of the undertakings included therein taken as a whole. (Article 16(3))

The rest of Article 16 contains the overriding TFV provisions as in Article 2 of the Fourth Directive (see Table 1).

The Seventh Directive uses the same signifiers in all languages for TFV as the Fourth Directive had done. For example, despite the fact that Denmark had before 1983 already implemented signifiers different from the Danish version of the Fourth Directive (see next section, and Table 2), the Danish version of the Seventh Directive uses the same signifiers as the Fourth. One interesting point is that the 1976 German draft of the Seventh Directive used the *'einen getreuen Einblick'* wording (as in the 1974 draft of the Fourth Directive), whereas the 1978 draft and the 1983 final versions used the longer wording of the 1978 final version of the Fourth Directive (see Table 2).

Impact of the Directive

The Fourth Directive took many years to implement, as Table 2 (column 4) shows. Some countries anticipated the content and then made subsequent legal adjustments (such as Belgium); others were quick off the mark (such as the relative newcomers, Denmark and the UK); some were slow (such as founder EC member, Italy) or had joined the EC after the adoption of the Directive (Greece, Spain and Portugal). The laws come into force on dates after those shown in Table 2. In the case of the last country, Italy, this means usually implementation for 31.12.1993 year ends. The more general effects of the Fourth Directive are examined elsewhere (e.g. Gray and Coenenberg, 1984). This section examines the TFV specifically.

The implementation of the TFV requirement shows the ability of countries to impose their own culture on what, to some of them, was an alien

---

[12]I am particularly grateful to Alan Roberts for the historical references in this paragraph.
[13]Letter from K. Van Hulle of 11.1.1993, and conversation with H. Kaminski of 1.3.1993.

concept. This expresses itself in the signifiers, the signified and the effects.

Signifiers and the Signified

When it comes to implementations of the laws in the member states, several further linguistic complications are added to those of the previous section, as column 5 of Table 2 shows. In seven cases (for the five exceptions, see below), the national laws implementing the Directive follow the words in the Directive as prepared in Brussels. The Belgian law implements both the French and the Dutch signifiers from the Directive. The Luxembourg law implements the French. The lengthy wording in the German law follows from the Directive as adopted in Brussels rather than being a subsequent invention of the German parliament. However, as discussed later, even in the German case (and the Spanish) important words were *added*.

The five departures from the Directive's signifiers will now be examined. The Dutch revised earlier legal wordings rather than exactly following the Directive. The 1970 Law was amended by adding the word *'duidelijk'* (clearly) from Art. 2.2 of the Directive. Other national implementations also contain the clarity requirement. The Dutch also retained the fundamental requirement of giving a sound insight, and it is this requirement which is the overriding one. The Danes substituted *'retvisende'* for the Directive's *'pålideligt'*, moving from 'faithful' towards 'right-looking' or 'not misleading', which seems close to 'fair'.

In the case of Italian, the Directive used the word *'fedele'* (consistent with the Dutch/French), but this was rejected by the drafters of the Italian law. The train of linguistic events is somewhat complex. The 1942 Civil Code allows departure from the legal valuation rules for *speciali ragioni* (special reasons).[14] This ambiguous provision did not lead in practice to major departures, even for inflation accounting in the 1970s. However, in the revaluation law of 1983 (so-called Visentini-bis; 72/1983, Art. 9), *speciali ragioni* were defined as those where departure from legal rules was necessary in order to give *un quadro fedele*. As mentioned earlier, these Italian words had first appeared in published form in Article 2 of the draft EC Directive in 1974.

When it came to the drafting of the Italian law to implement the Fourth Directive (Decreto Legislativo n. 127/1991), the words *'quadro fedele'* were deliberately not used, perhaps because they already had the above particular usage in Italian law. In the *Relazione Ministeriale* (Ministerial

Commentary) to the new law, it was stated that *'rappresentare in modo veritiero e corretto'* had been adopted because *'sembra costituire la più esatta traduzione dell'espressione* true and fair view *dalla quale trae origine la norma della Direttiva'*.[15]

Despite this attempt to match the English, *'veritiero e corretto'* seems nearer to the abandoned British phrase 'true and correct' (although it has already been noted that the Dutch translation of 'true and fair' was the same as that for 'true and correct'). The word *'corretto'*, in a law in a Roman law country, appears to mean[16] 'in accordance with legal rules'. The Ministerial Commentary states that *'veritiero'* requires that the preparers of the accounts *'operino correttamente le stime'* (make correct valuation estimates); so *'veritiero'* rests partially on *'corretto'*. In combination, *'veritiero e corretto'* does not seem intended to signify what is understood in the UK by 'true and fair'.

The Spanish moved from 'a faithful picture' to 'the faithful picture' as discussed below. The *Plan General de Contabilidad*[17] notes that *la imagen fiel* deals with the double concept of lack of bias and objectivity, and there is also a reference to truth.[18] The Portuguese have the Directive's *'imagem fiel'* in the Commercial Code but departed from this in the *Plano Oficial de Contabilidade* in an attempt to translate the English original. The resulting *'verdadeira e apropriada'* seems the most literal of all the versions.

In terms of a classification of the signifiers in laws, four out of twelve countries have a dual expression, as shown in Figure 2. However, this superficial classification disguises the fact that:

(i) a dual signifier can have a more unitary meaning (e.g. in Italy, *'veritiero'* is defined partly in terms of *'correttamente'*), and by contrast

(ii) a single adjective (e.g. *fidèle* or *fiel*) can have layers of meaning.

There is a further linguistic point. In most translations, the indefinite article is used, leading to the conclusion (e.g. Flint, 1982; *Mémento Pratique Lefebvre*, 1992, 355, 3, 3) that a number of different financial statements could give *a* true and fair view of any particular state of affairs or profit or loss.

---

[14] *'Se speciali ragioni richiedono una deroga alle norme di questo articolo, gli ammistratori e il collegio sindacale devono indicare e giustificare le singole deroghe nelle loro relazioni all'assemblea'* (Art. 2425).

[15] 'It seems to represent the most exact translation of the phrase *true and fair view* from which the original rule in the Directive derives'.

[16] I am grateful to several Italian colleagues for help in this area. For an earlier reference confirming this, see Colombo (1977) who says that the correct valuation will follow only if and when there is conformity with the rules of the law (p. 19).

[17] General accounting plan of 1990, parts 1, 4 and 5 of which are obligatory for Spanish companies. *La imagen fiel* is dealt with in part 1.

[18] *'la doble noción de imparcialidad y objetividad'* and *'un tercero podría formarse sobre "la verdadera"'* (para. 10).

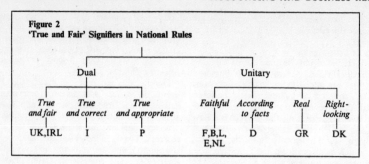

The exceptions are:

(i) *Italian Law.* Although the Italian Directive had '*un quadro fedele*', the law rephrases the requirement in such a way that no article is used.

(ii) *Spanish Law.* Although the Spanish Directive had '*una imagen fiel*', the Spanish Law substitutes '*la imagen fiel*', which is also followed in audit reports.[19] It has been suggested that this is an attempt to imply precision in the law.[20]

(iii) *Dutch Law.* As Table 2 shows, the law departs from the Directive in a way that avoids using an article.

(iv) *Greek Directive and Law.* In Greek, *the* real picture is to be presented. This may have appeared to the Greek draftsmen to make linguistic sense because, although there could be several reasonable/faithful pictures, it might have been thought that there can only be one *real* picture (however philosophically unsound that might be).

Conclusion on What is Signified

The section immediately above has to some extent considered what is signified by TFV. It seems clear that, although changes in rules and practice effect TFV, it must be intended to have an existence independent of rules or general practice. Otherwise, the Fourth Directive's requirements in Article 2.4 and 2.5 for extra information or departure from rules would not make sense. A further example is Article 14 of the Seventh Directive, which requires exclusion of dissimilar subsidiaries from consolidation when inclusion would not give a TFV.

Ordelheide (1993) suggests that, in cases of conflict, the ultimate meaning of TFV in any (or all) EC jurisdictions can now only be decided by the

European Court, which may construe a meaning quite different from that intended by the inventors of the source phrase. One can certainly agree with Ordelheide that the UK meaning may not be legally relevant elsewhere. However, given that what is signified by TFV is related to practice (i.e. to what the readers of accounts expect to see), and given that practice is clearly different in different EC countries, it is hard to see that a Court could arrive at the view that TFV meant the same thing in each EC country. Bird (1984) concurs that different signifieds are likely to arise, as does Van Hulle (1993). Ordelheide has suggested[21] that, in practice, the Court would set out a broad enough meaning that different countries could fit their different interpretations into it. Van Hulle (1993) also provides a gloss on this by suggesting that, even though accounts may give a TFV in their state of origin:

in order to be true and fair for readers in another Member State, some further explanations are no doubt required. This is the reason why the Accounting Directives require in many instances further information in the notes to the Accounts.

However, it seems implausible that a Danish company could be taken to task for not making disclosures that might specifically help a Greek reader. Presumably, also, Van Hulle did not intend the apparent implication that this was the only or the main reason for further disclosures.

Effects

As noted earlier, it seems possible to distinguish between (i) any direct effects on detailed accounting rules that may have accompanied the implementation of the TFV, and (ii) the continuing indirect effects of the legal imposition of the TFV requirement. With respect to the overriding nature of the TFV, the idea that departure from a specific provision of the law should rest upon the opinion of standard setters, directors or auditors is hard

---

[19]E.g. the audit report of Arthur Andersen on CEPSA's 1991 accounts. Interestingly, the company's English translation of the report refers to '*a true and fair view*'.

[20]F. Grau, Company Secretary of CEPSA in Brussels on December 3, 1992.

[21]Notes from discussion with Dieter Ordelheide at EIASM Conference in Edinburgh, 18 June 1993.

to accept, even for English lawyers (Tweedie and Kellas, 1987), let alone for those in a civil law framework. The national stances towards the implementation of the Directive may be classified into three main types:

(i) Continued dominance of TFV. In the UK and Ireland, the continued primacy of the TFV has been used both by standard setters and by directors and auditors to enable commercial circumstances of various sorts to prevail over specific legal considerations (Parker and Nobes, 1991). The primacy of TFV has been used by the standard setters to override the details of the law in several cases. For example:

(a) SSAP 9 (Stocks and Work in Progress, para. 39 and Appendix 3, para. 12) suggests that LIFO should not normally be used because it will not give a true and fair view, whereas the Fourth Directive (Art. 40) and the British law specifically allow it (Companies Act 1985, Schedule 4).

(b) SSAP 19 (Investment Properties) requires investment buildings not to be depreciated whereas the Fourth Directive and, therefore, the British law require all fixed assets with limited useful lives to be depreciated (Companies Act 1985, Schedule 4).

(c) Other cases where 'true and fair' has been used may not override the detail of the law but address conflicts in it. For example, SSAP 20 (Foreign Currency Translation) requires the taking to income of gains on unsettled long-term foreign currency loans. This is not 'prudent', which is a mandatory principle in the Directive, and therefore the gains are not distributable. However, the Directive (Article 31.2) and the British law do allow departures from the basic principles for accounting. SSAP 20 claims that, in this case, the accruals convention (also a mandatory principle in the Directive) should override prudence in order to give a TFV.

The EC Contact Committee has concluded that the TFV override can only be used in cases relating to individual companies rather than to general circumstances (EC, 1990). This would be a problem for the UK at least for point (b) above.[22] However, the conclusions of the Contact Committee have no direct authority, and Alexander (1993) suggests that the Committee's conclusion is clearly invalid in terms of the Fourth Directive, given that Article 2.5 allows member states to define the exceptional circumstances and lay down the relevant special rules. This seems correct, despite Van Hulle's (1993) suggestion that Article 2.5 was designed to

restrict flexibility not to increase it. To take the UK as illustration, according to the British Companies Act 1985 (as amended in 1989), the Accounting Standards Board can be interpreted as being delegated with the setting of accounting standards on behalf of the member state, so a standard could define departures (though only for exceptional cases).

A further aspect of the indirect effects of TFV concerns whether departure from legal provisions is to be seen as a last resort to be used only when even extra information is insufficient. This seems to be the view of the Contact Committee (EC, 1990). However, it is not the view of UK standard setters (e.g. Tweedie and Kellas, 1987, p. 93). The Companies Act 1989 amended the TFV section to move the law more towards the standard setters' view.[23]

Cases where UK directors have not complied with law in the name of TFV include, for example, non-consolidation of subsidiaries or departure from formats of financial statements. Cases of non-compliance with standards include the base stock method of inventory valuation and non-revaluation of investment properties (Parker and Nobes, 1991, p. 355).

In the Netherlands, the primacy of 'sound insight' and 'faithful' also continues (see Table 2). These concepts are used by the *Raad voor de Jaarverslaggeving* (RJ, Council for Annual Reporting; see Parker, 1991b or Zeff *et al.*, 1992) when producing *Richtlijnen* (Guidelines), and by directors and auditors when interpreting the law and Guidelines or in areas where there is no such guidance. However, since the Netherlands has a Civil Code system, the RJ would not feel able to set Guidelines which override law. Countries other than the UK and Ireland interpret the 'special circumstances' of Article 2.5 of the Directive (see Table 1) in a way that would not allow general departures to be formulated.

(ii) Enthusiastic change. In some countries, the implementation of the Fourth Directive was used as a means of changing accounting in an implicitly Anglo-Saxon direction. Governments (including stock market regulators) may have already been moving in this direction as capital markets expanded and international capital flows grew. Denmark, for example, was first to implement the Directive, included many options and seems closer in line with the UK and the Netherlands now than before the Directive. In the case of France, it has been suggested that the *image fidèle* requirement had the direct effect of undermining the strength of tax-based rules (Pham, 1984), though the relationship between tax and accounting is complex

---

[22] It may not be a problem for point (a) because SSAP 9 is merely narrowing down options allowed by the Directive, nor for point (c) where there is a conflict in the Directive.

[23] 'If in special circumstances [in the case of any company,] compliance with any of those provisions is inconsistent with the requirements to give a true and fair view [even if additional information were provided in accordance with sub-section (4)], the directors shall depart from that provision . . .' S. 226 of the 1985 Act as amended; bracketed parts deleted in 1989.

(Standish, 1991). The undermining is only obvious in the regulations relating to consolidated accounts (where tax is not relevant) which result from the implementation of the Seventh Directive. Moves in the direction of Anglo-Saxon accounting had already been made by many large French groups, and such a process suited the Stock Exchange regulatory body, the Commission des Opérations de Bourse. Article 29 of the Seventh Directive is relevant here. It allows that:

> ... a member state may require or permit the use in the consolidated accounts of other methods of valuation [than the parent's] in accordance with the [Fourth Directive]. (Article 29.2).
> Where assets to be included in consolidated accounts have been the subject of exceptional value adjustments solely for tax purposes, they shall be incorporated in the consolidated accounts only after those adjustments have been eliminated. A member state may, however, require or permit [no] elimination, ... provided [disclosure]. (Article 29.5).

No member states have *required* the 'other methods' of Article 29.2, but all except Portugal and Greece have allowed them. In no member state is there a requirement not to permit the eliminations of Article 29.5. The result of this combination of provisions is that companies in most member states have greater room for manoeuvre in group accounts than in individual accounts.

In the case of France, group accounts can move, and for many groups have moved, away from former tax-based rules towards several 'substance over form' and accruals accounting features, such as the capitalisation of leases, the recognition of deferred taxation, and the recognition of unsettled gains on currency amounts (Scheid and Walton, 1992).

The authoritative *Mémento Pratique Francis Lefebvre* (1992) suggests that the effects in France of the legal requirement to give *une image fidèle* should be in those areas where the rules do not exist or where they are not sufficiently detailed. A further point is that the French implementation of the Directive's Article 2.4 (see Table 1) requires the extra information to be given '*dans l'annexe*' (in the Notes), whereas the Directive and, for example, the UK law do not specify where, allowing for the financial statements themselves to contain the extra information.

To some extent, the moves away from tax-based and legal form accounting are reflected in Spain. Indeed, it has been suggested that the arrival of the TFV led to a 'thorough accounting transformation' (Casanovas, 1992). One specific example is that substance over form has been addressed in the area of leasing. The 1989 law implementing the Fourth Directive requires finance leases to be capitalised.

However, because this might appear to be 'untrue' in law even if 'fair' in substance, the 1990 *Plan General de Contabilidad* requires the leases capitalised to be shown as intangible assets (i.e. the *rights* to use the assets), whereas in other capitalising countries they would be included as tangible assets.

Despite some changes, Spain has nevertheless put *imagen fiel* firmly into the context of legal provisions. The Commercial Code (Book 1, ch. III, section 2, Art. 34,2) states:

> The annual accounts must be drafted with clarity and show the true and fair view of the net assets, financial situation and net profit or loss of the business, in conformity with the legal provisions.

The last five words are not in the Directive, nor in the laws of most member states[24] (see the further German exception below). The 1990 *Plan General de Contabilidad* also states (Part 1, Accounting Principles, para. 1) that:

> The application of the accounting principles included in the following sections should mean that annual accounts, drafted with clarity, will show the true and fair view of the net assets, financial situation and net profit or loss of the business.

This makes it even clearer in Spain than in France that, although the TFV seems to have affected specific rules, this does not imply that individual companies and auditors have much freedom to apply it.

In Portugal, too, the implementation of the Fourth Directive saw the official *Comissão de Normalização Contabilística* using words in the plan (see Table 2) that were designed[25] to establish a legal basis to allow movement away from tax rules in certain cases. The plan also requires substance over form (Principle 4f). The combination of these requirements has led to uncertainty in Portugal, for example about the need and legality of revaluations in times of price instability (Fernandes Ferreira, 1992).

The FEE Survey (FEE, 1991) of published accounts shows (from a fairly small sample)[26] the following on the subject of departures from legal provisions in order to give a true and fair view:

> In 10 instances departures from provisions of the national legislation for that reason are reported: in Belgium, Denmark (three), France (two), Ireland, Luxembourg (two) and the United Kingdom. In seven of those 10 cases

---

[24]The Luxembourg law of 1984 does not include these words, but the official guidance on audit reports from the Institut des Réviseurs d'Entreprises does.
[25]Letter of 9.2.1993 from Sen. Fernandes of the Câmara dos Revisores Oficias de Contas.
[26]341 Companies from nine EC countries.

the reason for the departure was explained in the accounts (p. 27).

FEE (1992) examines this in more detail, showing that the UK and Irish departures were caused by compliance with standards, and three of the other five were departures from formats. It should be noted that a German example does not appear. For Spain, Italy and Portugal, the Directive was not in force for the accounts surveyed.

(iii) Specific rules continue to override general rules. In Germany, which seems to be an extreme example of this case, it is assumed that compliance with the legal provisions will normally ensure that a TFV is given.[27] In particular, the *Bilanzrichtlinien-Gesetz* of 1985, which implemented the Fourth, Seventh and Eighth Directives, is the only EC implementation which does not specifically require the true and fair view to override legal provisions in exceptional cases (i.e. it does not implement Article 2.5; see Table 1). The German law uses the words from the Directive but, like the Spanish, precedes them with words which might be translated approximately as 'in compliance with accepted accounting principles' (see Table 2). This helps to rob the TFV of its significance. There are some legal requirements which have been seen as inimical to TFV (von Wysocki, 1984). There are even legal views (cited by Ordelheide, 1990, p. 8) that the TFV refers only to the notes to the accounts, and has no effect in interpreting the detailed rules or for filling gaps in rules relating to the financial statements. Certainly, as in France, the German rules require the extra information called for by Article 2.4 of the Directive to be presented in the notes (*im Anhang*).

It is suggested that German tradition would have had to have been overturned in order to allow TFV to override specific rules (Otte, 1990). Unlike France, there have been few direct effects caused by the legislators making changes designed to reflect commercial substance. This is not, of course, intended to be a criticism of Germany: like the UK, Germany has found its own way of continuing with its traditions despite the Directive. Ordelheide (1990) suggests that national accounting rules tend to resist attempts at harmonisation.

One feature of German accounting that may be seen as a counter-example is the option (§308, HGB) to depart from certain tax-based rules in the preparation of group accounts. A minority of large German groups take advantage of this (Treuarbeit, 1990).

Italy seems to be a further example within this third category of country. Firstly, unlike the cases of France and Spain, no amendments were made

to legal accounting principles specifically in order to allow 'substance' to override 'form', apart from the compulsory content of the Directives themselves. Certainly, the drafters of *principi contabili*[28] would not expect to be able to override the law. Indeed, the implementation of the Directives may cause accounting practices of some large listed groups to move *away* from a number of 'substance-based' practices, in that previously the accounts of listed companies followed *principi contabili* and IASC standards, which are close to UK/US rules. Secondly, the Ministerial Commentary on the 1991 Law notes that, although it is not possible to specify the exceptional circumstances which would require the rules to be departed from, these would be '*casi veramente eccezionali*'. This suggests extreme rarity or, in practice, that '*veritiero e corretto*' is the same as being in conformity with the rules. Thirdly, the auditors of listed companies were previously required by Presidential Decree to check that accounts followed correct accounting principles[29] but these words were removed in 1991.

Nevertheless, the legal amendments of 1991 do require far more information than most Italian companies were giving. Also, it is possible that some reduction in the influence of tax law will arise as a result of the testing of '*veritiero e corretto*' in the courts.

Continuum of Effects of TFV

From the above discussion it seems possible to suggest that EC countries can be seen as on a continuum with respect to the effects of the TFV. Starting from the most strong, five different positions may be identified (example of countries are given):

Case I	TFV is used by directors/auditors in interpreting the law and standards or where there is no law or standard, and sometimes to override the law or standards. TFV can also be used by standard-setters to make rules that override details of the law. (UK, Ireland).
Case II	TFV (and 'insight') is used by directors/auditors as the basic principle in interpreting the law and (non-governmental) guidelines. It can be used by them to override guidelines and, potentially, in exceptional cases, the law. It is also used by guideline-setters to make rules but not to override the law. (The Netherlands).

---

[27]A minute of the EC Council states that this may normally be taken to be the case (Council R 1961/78 [ES93] 18.7.1978, No. 2).

[28] 'Accounting principles' as published by a joint committee of the Italian professional bodies: Dottori Commercialisti and Ragionieri.

[29]Decreto Presidente della Repubblica No. 136, 31.3.1975: '*secondo corretti principi contabili*'.

Table 3
Summary of Some Relationships between TFV Signifier, Signified and Effects

1. Same signified but different signifiers (e.g. probably little change in 1947 to what the British law signified despite the wording change from 'true and correct' to 'true and fair').

2. Apparently similar signifiers with different signifieds (e.g. the different signifieds of the apparently similar signifiers in the UK and Portugal or in the Netherlands and Spain).

3. Same signifier but changing signified (e.g. changing signified of TFV in the UK, as lease capitalisation became standard practice).

4. Same signifier and similar signified but different indirect effects of having TFV in law (e.g. same words in UK and Australia with similar meaning in terms of acceptable or necessary accounting practices for most transactions, but quite different legal status).

5. Same signifier but changing effect of having TFV in law (e.g. the increasing practical importance of having TFV in British law from 1970 to date).

6. Signifiers intended to be the same by the EC Commission but with different effects (e.g. continuum of decreasing significance of TFV in UK, France, Germany).

7. Same non-English signifier to translate three different English signifiers (e.g. the use by the Dutch of *getrouw beeld* to translate 'true and correct view', 'true and fair view' and 'present fairly').

8. Same English signifier represented at different times by more than one signifier in another language (e.g. German signifiers of 1974 and 1978; and changing Danish, Portuguese and Italian signifiers from Directive to national rules).

Case III The arrival of TFV was used by lawmakers to allow some change towards 'substance' rather than 'form'. It may be used by directors/auditors when there are no governmental requirements, or to interpret requirements and, in principle, to override them in exceptional cases. (France, Spain).

Case IV TFV may be used by directors/auditors to interpret government requirements or in cases where there are no requirements. In very exceptional cases, which in practice will probably not arise, it could be used to depart from the law. (Italy).

Case V It is unresolved whether TFV relates only to notes or whether it might be usable by directors/auditors to interpret government requirements or in cases where there are no requirements. It is clear, however, that TFV cannot be used to depart from the law. (Germany).

Summary and conclusion

The legal requirement for annual accounts to give a true and fair view uses different signifiers, implies different signifieds and has different effects from time to time and from place to place. A summary of the diversity of the relationships between signifier, signified and effects is shown in Table 3, in each case with examples drawn from this paper.

The non-English signifiers at TFV's first official EC appearance in the 1974 versions of the Directive (or later versions for Greek, Spanish and Portuguese) all involve one adjective only (generally corresponding to 'faithful'). The French and Dutch signifiers have decades of history in the context of accounting. By the time the Directive had been implemented into laws, six out of ten non-English-speaking countries had departed from the Directive's original words, apparently in some cases in an attempt to get closer to the English. Further diversity is likely as the Fourth Directive spreads to the European Economic Area and to Eastern Europe, giving rise to signifiers in Swedish, Finnish, Polish,[30] etc.

The reason why the signified changes over time, and presumably from place to place, is because the TFV is connected to practice, although intended to be an independent concept.

In the UK there was little effect in having TFV in law while there were no detailed laws or even standards. However, as regulation increased from the 1970s, so directors and auditors found TFV useful for special cases. At a similar time, the perceived UK need to counter EC-based regulation of accounting, which also involved rules alien to

[30] A Polish ministerial decree of 15.1.1991 requires a true and fair view in the context of the regulations. The words used are '*rzetelny i jasny obraz*', which seem to be literally translated from English. However, an Act, which has higher authority, was passed in October 1991 requiring correctness and honesty (*prawidlowosc* and *rzetelnosc*), which seems to be drawn from interwar Polish legislation. I am grateful to Marek Schroeder of Birmingham University for this information.

UK practices, gave prominence to the TFV as an argument to be used by the UK profession and by the UK government in Brussels.

Except in Ireland and the Netherlands, there was no analogy to the overriding British TFV requirements elsewhere in Europe. This position has been maintained in practice by Germany, at least for the content of the financial statements themselves. Other EC countries fall between these two extremes, in some cases with the arrival of the TFV being accompanied by significant changes in the accounting rules in the direction of Anglo-Saxon practices. In particular, in some countries (e.g. France and Spain) it seems to have been used by regulators as a philosophy to accompany reform of the rules. However, although the detailed rules have changed, the continuing indirect effects for directors, auditors and rule-makers of the fact that there is a TFV legal requirement is small in these countries.

In some countries, then, the TFV legal requirement has moved from non-existence to existence without effects; in others from non-existence to existence with small direct effects on rules and marginal indirect effects. Paradoxically, in terms of the usefulness of the TFV legal provision to directors, auditors and non-governmental rule-makers, perhaps the greatest *change* in effects from 1970 to date has been in the UK.

References

Accountancy (1990), 'Doubts about UK Practice', November, p. 11.

Alexander, D. (1993), 'A European True and Fair View?', *European Accounting Review*, Vol. 2, No. 1.

Alexander, D. and S. Archer (1992), *The European Accounting Guide*, Academic Press.

Bird, P. (1984), 'What is "A True and Fair View"?', *Journal of Business Law*, November.

Busse von Colbe, W. (1984), 'A True and Fair View: A German Perspective', in Gray and Coenenberg (1984).

Casanovas, I. (1992), 'Spain and the Process of Harmonization with EC Accounting Regulations', in J. A. Gonzalo, *Accounting in Spain*, Asociación Española de Contabilidad y Administración de Empresas, p. 169.

Chastney, J. G. (1975), *True and Fair View—History, Meaning and the Impact of the Fourth Directive*, Institute of Chartered Accountants in England and Wales.

Chaveneau, J. (1920), 'Les bilans—Etablissement et verifications aux points de vue commercial, industriel et fiscal', *Librairie Arthur Rousseau*, cited in G. Haddou, 'Fiscalité et Comptabilité; Evolution Législative depuis 1920', *Revue Francaise de la Comptabilité*, July-August 1991.

Christiansen, M. (1992), 'Denmark' in Alexander and Archer (1992).

CNCC (1984), cited in Rutherford (1989) as *Assises Nationales du Commissariat aux Comptes, Documents du Travail*, Compagnie Nationale des Commissaires aux Comptes.

Colombo, G. E. (1977), 'La Disciplina Italiana della Revisione', *Rivista dei Dottori Commercialisti*, January-February.

EC (1990), *Accounting Harmonisation in the EC. Problems of Applying the Fourth Directive*, Commission; commented on in *Accountancy* (1990).

FEE (1991), *European Survey of Published Accounts*, Routledge.

FEE (1992), *Analysis of European Accounting and Disclosure Practices*, Routledge.

Fernandes Ferreira, R. (1992), 'Free Valuations of Tangible Fixed Assets', paper presented at the EAA Conference, Madrid.

Ferrero, G. (1991), *I Complementari principi della 'Chiarezza', della 'Verita' e della 'Correttezza' nella Redazione del Bilancio d'Esercizio*, Giuffrè Editore.

Flint, D. (1982), *A True and Fair View in Company Accounts*, Institute of Chartered Accountants of Scotland.

Gray, S. J. (1980), 'The Impact of International Accounting Differences from a Security-Analysis Perspective: Some European Evidence', *Journal of Accounting Research*, Spring.

Gray, S. J. and A. G. Coenenberg (1984), *EEC Accounting Harmonization*, North Holland.

Harris, N. G. E. (1987), 'Fairness in Financial Reporting', *Journal of Applied Philosophy*, Vol. 4, No. 1.

Hoffman, L. and M. Arden (1983), 'Counsel's Opinion on True and Fair', *Accountancy*, November 1983.

Hopwood, A. G. (1990), 'Ambiguity, Knowledge and Territorial Claims: Some Observations on the Doctrine of Substance over Form: A Review Essay', *British Accounting Review*, March, p. 84.

Lyas, C. (1992), 'Accounting and Language', in M. Mumford and K. V. Peasnell (eds.), *Philosophical Perspectives on Accounting*, Routledge.

Miller, M. C. (1993), 'Financial Reporting in Australia', in T. E. Cooke and R. H. Parker (eds.), *Financial Reporting in the West Pacific Rim*, Routledge.

Nobes, C. W. (1983), 'The Origins of the Harmonising Provisions of the 1980 and 1981 Companies Acts', *Accounting and Business Research*, Winter.

Nobes, C. W. (1989), *Interpreting European Financial Statements*, Butterworths.

Nobes, C. W. and R. H. Parker (1991a), 'True and Fair: a Survey of UK Financial Directors', *Journal of Business Finance and Accounting*, Spring.

Nobes, C. W. and R. H. Parker (1991b), *Comparative International Accounting*, Prentice Hall.

Nobes, C. W. and S. Zambon (1991), 'Piano, Piano: Italy Implements the Directives', *Accountancy*, July.

Ordelheide, D. (1990), 'Soft-Transformations of Accounting Rules of the Fourth Directive in Germany', *Les Cahiers internationaux de la Comptabilité*, Editions Comptables Malesherbes.

Ordelheide, D. (1993), 'True and Fair View—A European and a German Perspective', *European Accounting Review*, Vol. 2, No. 1.

Otte, H-H. (1990), 'Harmonisierte Europäische Rechnungs-legung', *Zeitschrift für Betriebswirtschaft*, No. 42.

Parker, R. H. (1989), 'Importing and Exporting Accounting: the British Experience' in A. G. Hopwood (ed.), *International Pressures for Accounting Change*, Prentice Hall.

Parker, R. H. (1991a), 'Financial Reporting in the UK and Australia', ch. 7 in Nobes and Parker (1991b).

Parker, R. H. (1991b), 'Financial Reporting in the Netherlands', ch. 10 in Nobes and Parker (1991b).

Parker, R. H. (1994), 'Debating True and Fair in Australia: An Exercise in Deharmonisation?', *Journal of Accounting, Auditing and Taxation*, forthcoming.

Parker, R. H. and C. W. Nobes (1991), 'Auditors' View of True and Fair', *Accounting and Business Research*, Autumn.

Pasqualini, F. (1992), *Le Principe de l'Image Fidèle en Droit Comptable*, Litec.

Pham, D. (1984), 'France' in Gray and Coenenberg (1984).

Rutherford, B. A. (1983), 'Spoilt Beauty: The True and Fair View Doctrine in Translation', *AUTA Review*, Spring.

Rutherford, B. A. (1985), 'The True and Fair View Doctrine: A Search for Explication', *Journal of Business Finance and Accounting*, Vol. 12, No. 4.

Rutherford, B. A. (1989), 'The True and Fair Doctrine: Some Recent Developments', in G. Macdonald and B. A. Rutherford, *Accounts, Accounting and Accountability*, Van Nostrand.

Saussure, F. de (1919), *Cours de Linguistique Génèrale*, Payot: Lausanne, translated as *Course in General Linguistics*, Philosophical Library: New York, 1959.

Scheid, J.-C. and P. Walton (1992), 'France' in Alexander and Archer (1992).

Socias, A. (1991), *La Normalización Contable en el Reino Unido, Francia, Alemania y España*, Asociación Española de Contabilidad y Administración de Empresas.

Standish, P. E. M. (1991), 'Financial Reporting in France', ch. 8 in Nobes and Parker (1991b).

Treuarbeit (1990), *Konzernabschlüsse '89*, IDW-Verlag.

Tweedie, D. P. (1983), 'True and Fair Rules', *Accountant's Magazine*, November.

Tweedie, D. P. and J. Kellas (1987), 'Off-Balance Sheet Financing', *Accountancy*, April.

Van Hulle, K. (1983), 'Truth and Untruth about True and Fair', *European Accounting Review*, Vol. 2, No. 1.

Von Wysocki, K. (1984), 'Germany' in Gray and Coenenberg (1984).

Walker, R. G. (1984), *A True and Fair View and the Reporting Obligations of Directors and Auditors*, National Companies and Securities Commission, Melbourne.

Walton, P. (1991), *The True and Fair View: A Shifting Concept*, Occasional Research Paper No. 7, Chartered Association of Certified Accountants.

Zeff, S. A. (1990), 'The English Language Equivalent of Geeft een Getrouw Beeld', *De Accountant*, October 1990, p. 83.

Zeff, S. A. (1992), 'Arthur Andersen & Co. and the Two-part Opinion in the Auditor's Report: 1946–1962', *Contemporary Accounting Research*.

Zeff, S. A., F. van der Wel and K. Camfferman (1992), *Company Financial Reporting: A Historical and Comparative Study of the Dutch Regulatory Process*, North Holland.

Appendix I

Translations of Words in Table 2 and Elsewhere

Netherlands	geeft een zodanig inzicht dat een verantwoord oordeel kan worden gevormd	presents an insight such that a well-founded opinion can be formed
	geeft getrouw, duidelijk en stelselmatig	presents faithfully, clearly and consistently (over time)
	een getrouw beeld geven	present a faithful picture
Denmark	et pålideligt billede	a faithful picture
	et retvisende billede	a right-looking picture
Germany	(unter Beachtung der Grundsätze ordnungsmässiger Buchführung) ein den tatsächlichen Verhältnissen entsprechendes Bild	(in compliance with accepted accounting principles) a picture in accordance with the facts
France	une image fidèle	a faithful picture
Greece	ten pragmatiki ikona	the real picture
Spain	una (la) imagen fiel ... (de conformidad con las disposiciones legales)	a (the) faithful picture ... (in conformity with the legal provisions)
Portugal	uma imagem fiel	a loyal view
	uma imagem verdadeira e apropriada	a true and appropriate view
Italy	un quadro fedele	a faithful picture
	rappresentare in modo veritiero e corretto	presents in a true and correct way

[16]

Accounting and Business Research, Vol. 24. No. 96, pp. 319–333. 1994

European Rule-making in Accounting: The Seventh Directive as a Case Study

Graham Diggle and Christopher Nobes*

Abstract—This paper analyses EC rule-making, using the Seventh Directive as a case study. Three stages of a Directive's life are identified, with different key players taking the lead. The paper analyses the evolution of the Seventh Directive up to its adoption in 1983, looking at 19 key features. The adopted Directive is close to previous UK consolidation practices, but investigation shows that, from its origins in the late 1960s to the published drafts of the late 1970s, it showed clear German parentage. The coalition of forces leading to the major changes from German to UK practices is examined.

Introduction

The Seventh Directive on company law, concerning consolidated accounts, was adopted by the EC[1] Council in 1983, after many preceding drafts (see Table 1 for detailed references). The purpose of this paper is to propose a framework for understanding the setting of Directives, to analyse the evolution of the Seventh Directive and to suggest why, in this case, particular national influences seem to have dominated. The paper does not in general follow the Directive into subsequent member state laws. This is a large and different task, which has been carried out in detail by the Fédération des Experts Comptables Européens (FEE) (1993).

The background to the Seventh Directive is that the Fourth Directive (on annual accounts of individual companies) had been adopted in 1978. Nobes (1983) traces its development, noting particularly the influences from the German Public Companies Act (*Aktiengesetz*) of 1965. The Elmendorff Committee, which had completed the *avant projet* for the Fourth Directive in 1968,

*The authors are, respectively, senior lecturer in accounting at Oxford Brookes University and Coopers & Lybrand Professor of Accounting at the University of Reading. They are grateful, for comments on earlier drafts, to Adolf Coenenberg (Universität Augsburg), Dieter Ordelheide (Goethe Universität, Frankfurt), Bob Parker (University of Exeter), Alan Roberts (University of Reading), Peter Wessel (Moret Ernst & Young, Eindhoven) and two referees. Correspondence should be addressed to Professor C. Nobes, Department of Economics, Faculty of Letters and Social Sciences, University of Reading, P.O. Box 218, Whiteknights, Reading RG6 2AA.

[1]EC is used in this paper to mean 'European Communities'. Despite the fact that the EC became a constituent part of the European Union in 1993, the programme of Directives and such organs as the Commission remain EC not pan-EU matters.
[2]This was confirmed to the authors on 1.3.1993 by Herr Horst Kaminski of the Institut der Wirtschaftsprüfer, who had been secretary to the Elmendorff Committee. For more details on the Committee, see Nobes (1993).

delivered[2] a memorandum on group accounting to the EC Commission in 1970. Just as the *Aktiengesetz* (AktG) stamped much of the Fourth Directive with its character, one would expect to see substantial influence of German legislation in the Seventh Directive: Dr. Elmendorff came from Germany, which had the EC's most developed company law at the time; and the UK was not then a member of the EC. However, a reading of the eventual Seventh Directive does not give the impression of German origins. One would rather have the impression of Anglo-Saxon[3] sources for most of its provisions.

This paper first examines rule-making in accounting, considering EC Directives in particular. The evolution of the Seventh Directive is then used as a case study. Finally, conclusions are offered about the nature and effects of the forces operating on the rule-making system.

Rule-making in accounting

A number of papers have examined the process of national standard-setting. For example, Watts and Zimmerman (1978) examine lobbying behaviour in a US context (and that paper prompts many reactions); Mumford (1979) notes a cycle in the degree of interest in and the solutions proposed for inflation accounting in the UK; Hope and Briggs (1982) and Hope and Gray (1982) examine UK policy-making in two controversial areas; Laughlin and Puxty (1983) explore the politics of

[3]'Anglo-Saxon' is used here as a label for countries where accounting has traditionally been seen as a professional (not a governmental) field, where fairness is the objective, where tax rules are less influential, where conservatism is constrained by matching, where the pressures for disclosure overcome secrecy, where consolidation has a long history. Approximately, this means English-speaking countries, with a few others, such as the Netherlands and Denmark. The expression 'continental' is used here to denote the alternative system.

Table 1
Chronology

1965	Aktiengesetz
1968	Elmendorff *avant projet* of the Fourth Directive
1969	Publizitätsgesetz
1970/71	Elmendorff memorandum on consolidated accounts as draft of additions to Fourth Directive (XIV/533/71)
1971	First draft of the Fourth Directive
1973	UK, Ireland and Denmark join the EC
1973	Commission's note on consolidation (XI/669/73)
1974	Second draft of Fourth Directive
1974	Groupe d'Etudes comment on Commission's 1973 note (GEEC-6DSA-17774)
1976	First draft of Seventh Directive[a]
1977	Comments by Economic and Social Committee on draft Seventh Directive[b]
1978	European Parliament comments on draft Seventh Directive[c]
1978	Fourth Directive adopted
1978	Second draft of Seventh Directive[d] (issued in January 1979)
1983	Seventh Directive adopted[e]

References
[a] *Bulletin of the European Communities*, Supplement 9/76.
[b] *Official Journal of the European Communites*, 75, 26.3.1977.
[c] *Official Journal of the European Communities*, 163, 10.7.1978
[d] COM (78) 703 final.
[e] *Official Journal of the European Communities*, 18 July 1983 (DJ, 1983, L193).

standard-setting; Nobes (1992) examines the political forces in the case of the UK goodwill debate. There has also been some analysis of the process of *international* standard-setting (e.g. Wallace, 1990). However, little seems to have been written about the forces at work in accounting rule-making at the European Community level.

Laughlin and Puxty (1983) note that some writers believe that accounting rule-making is or should be a technical activity and others believe that it is or should be a political activity. In the context of the EC's harmonisation programme, it is particularly obvious that political pressures are at work, given that the final negotiations on Directives are conducted by representatives of the governments of member states. Furthermore, there has never been any pretence that a coherent conceptual framework should be used in this context or that one is even implicit. Nevertheless, particularly in the drafting stages, lawyers and accountants are heavily involved, and the Directives have technical as well as political input.

Hope and Gray (1982) examine the literature relating to the modelling of the political decision-making process. They suggest that one might begin with Dahl's (1961) pluralist approach in which 'an attempt is made to study specific outcomes in order to determine who ... prevails in decision-making' (Polsby, 1963, p. 113). They note that Lukes (1974) criticises this as one-dimensional in that it leaves out the ways in which power can be used to ensure that the potential issues are not decided or not even considered. However, Hope and Gray (p. 536) conclude that, for analysis of an accounting issue that has been settled after observable conflicts on

key issues, the one-dimensional pluralist approach is the most suitable. Following these ideas, the interested parties, the key issues and the eventual decisions are identified in order to illuminate the rule-making process in the case of the Seventh Directive.

The various stages of the Seventh Directive's progress can be charted:

Stage 1: Avant Projet
As has been mentioned, a memorandum on the subject of EC rules on consolidation was prepared in 1970 by a committee of professional accountants, chaired by a German. At that date, there were only six members of the EC (see the dates in Table 2). A version of this memorandum was issued by the Commission in 1971 in the context of the recently published first draft of the Fourth Directive (see Table 1 for chronology and references). The memorandum was presented in terms of new draft Articles 50 to 57 to be added to the Fourth Directive to cover group accounting. This had several German features (to be explained further later):

(i) definition of the group based on central control;
(ii) requirement to comply with the provisions of the law but no requirement to give a true and fair view;
(iii) uniform formats;
(iv) the group accounts should maintain the valuation bases of the constituent individual accounts;

Table 2
Members of the EC, with Dates of Joining

Anglo-Saxon* accounting	*Continental* accounting*
Netherlands (1957)	France (1957)
UK (1973)	W. Germany (1957)
Ireland (1973)	Italy (1957)
Denmark (1973)	Belgium (1957)
	Luxembourg (1957)
	Greece (1980)
	Spain (1986)
	Portugal (1986)

*see footnote 3

(v) no goodwill to be recognised;
(vi) no consolidation of associates or joint ventures.

Following this, in 1973, the Commission produced a note on the co-ordination of laws on consolidation, proposing a Directive on the subject. The Groupe d'Etudes (a body representing EC professional accountants, which had its origins in the Elmendorff Committee) commented on this in 1974 (again, see Table 1 for references). By this time, the EC had been enlarged by the accession of the UK, Ireland and Denmark.

Given that EC countries might be seen as divided into two quite different groups (see Table 2) with respect to accounting (e.g. Nair and Frank, 1980; Nobes, 1992), one might expect the consensus of professional accountants in the EC to have changed from 1970 to 1974 as a result of the influx of 'Anglo-Saxon' countries in 1973. Indeed, the Group d'Etudes in its 1974 comments made several Anglo-Saxon suggestions:

(i) the Directive should be as general as possible and only lay down basic rules, leaving the details for national and international accounting organisations (one notes that the International Accounting Standards Committee had been formed in 1973);
(ii) the objective of the consolidated accounts should be to give a true and fair view;
(iii) consolidation should be based on ownership of more than 50% of voting rights;
(iv) the possibility of excluding dissimilar subsidiaries;
(v) uniform group accounting policies;
(vi) goodwill should be recognised;
(vii) permission to use the equity method for associated companies and proportional consolidation for joint ventures.

This remarkable change in the consensus professional view needs further explanation, which is attempted in the concluding section of this paper.

Stage II: Published Drafts of the Directive
The second main element of the process is the published drafts of a Directive. In the case of the

Seventh Directive, there were drafts in 1976 and 1978. The drafting is controlled by Commission staff, predominantly lawyers from codified law countries.[4] This would lead one to expect a sympathy with the approach of German law, which was so evident in the Fourth Directive (Nobes, 1983). As the paper will show, the 1976 and 1978 drafts were indeed close to the consolidation provisions of the *Aktiengesetz* and largely ignored the Anglo-Saxon suggestions of the 1974 Groupe d'Etudes paper.

Stage III: Government Negotiations
The final stage in the evolution of a Directive is the negotiation in the committees of the Council of Ministers. Here full rein can be given to political pressures. One would expect to see the effects of nationalism, lobbying by preparers of accounts, concerns by governments over tax revenues and competitiveness, etc. As will be shown, in the case of the Seventh Directive, the really major changes from German practices occurred at this stage (i.e. after 1978). To some extent, as usual, the addition of options enabled international agreement, but there was also a coalition of forces in favour of movement towards Anglo-Saxon accounting.

Plan of the Argument Below
Before drawing conclusions on the political processes at work, this paper examines the evolution of the Directive in 19 major areas (see Appendix 1) under five main headings:

- Scope of consolidation
- Preparation of consolidated accounts
- Consolidation methods
- Goodwill
- Size exemptions

In general, from now on, three documents are considered: the AktG of 1965, the First Draft of 1976 and the adopted Directive of 1983. Another

---

[4]For most of this period, Hermann Niessen was in charge of company law. More recently, Gisbert Wolff has succeeded him. Both are German lawyers. Their subordinate, Karel van Hulle (now head of accounting), is a Belgian lawyer.

document of some relevance is the amended pro-posal of 1978, which was prepared by the Commis-sion after the content of the Fourth Directive was settled and after consideration of the First Draft of the Seventh Directive by the Economic and Social Committee and the European Parliament (for de-tails, see Vangermeersch, 1985). The 1978 amend-ments (see Appendix 2) are referred to below where appropriate. Table 1's chronology also covers these documents.

Scope of consolidation

The AktG had required consolidated accounts to be prepared, but the scope of group accounting was very different from that envisaged by the EC legislation. Under the AktG (§329), only groups with AGs and KGaAs as parent companies had to prepare consolidated accounts; foreign subsidiaries could be excluded from consolidation; and no reference was made to associated companies (with the implication from §153 AktG that these were to be carried in the group accounts at historical cost). The first of these issues (i.e. who must prepare consolidated accounts) saw an expansion in the Implementation Act for the AktG[5] by the inclusion of GmbH companies with AG or KGaA sub-sidiaries. Also, the *Publizitätsgesetz* (PublG) of 1969 extended the requirements of the AktG to all groups, independent of legal form, that were above certain size criteria.[6]

The first eight Articles of the First Draft (Sup-plement 9/76 Group Accounts: Proposal for a Seventh Directive) announce a still broader scope. Consolidated accounts, according to this First Draft, are to be prepared wherever a group *con-tains* a GmbH, an AG or a KGaA (or equivalent companies, e.g. UK public or private limited com-panies) whether as a parent or a subsidiary, and all group undertakings are to be consolidated regard-less of their domicile (First Draft, Article 6 (1) (a) and (b)). Anti-avoidance is one of the motivations at work here: it would be all too easy to circumvent the purpose of the Directive by placing an unincor-porated enterprise at the head of the group (Supplement 9/76, p. 23). Eventually there is an option to narrow this scope to groups with parents of the relevant legal form—as will be made clear below.

Definitions of Parent
The definitions of parent and subsidiary company that had been used in member states appeared to fall into two types. The Explanatory

Memorandum (Supplement 9/76, p. 20) accompa-nying the First Draft divides them into:

(i) A very general definition that rests on the idea of a group of legally independent units which operate as a single economic unit. (It is significant that this type is described as pertaining in one member state, which is not named.)
(ii) A much more concrete and precise kind of definition, e.g. ownership of the majority of shares or control of a majority of the voting rights.

The first of the two cases is illustrated by the AktG, under which the evidence of uniform direc-tion (*'einheitliche Leitung'*) was the criterion for whether consolidated accounts were prepared or not:

If the combine [*sic*] enterprises of a combine are under the uniform direction of a stock corporation ... the board of management of the head association ... shall prepare ... a consolidated balance sheet and a consoli-dated profit and loss statement ... (AktG §329, translation: Mueller and Galbraith, 1976).

The AktG (§§16–18) contains several criteria for determining the existence of uniform direction, including (a) the existence of a control contract, (b) integration of one company into the other,[7] or (c) (rebuttably) majority ownership of the shares (not the voting rights).

In the Explanatory Memorandum quoted above, the EC authors make it plain that a choice has to be made between the two types of group definition: the former (i.e. (i) above) has the advan-tage of greater flexibility and it reaches to the heart of the idea of the group. It is selected for the First Draft.

Therefore the Commission developed, in these early stages, a general and comprehensive defi-nition of the group. It did so by stating what a subsidiary is (one which may be subject to the controlling influence of another—Art. (2)(1)), and that this relationship may be presumed in certain circumstances (ownership of the majority of sub-scribed capital, control of the majority of voting rights, or the power to appoint the majority of the board of directors). However, as in the AktG, the touchstone of the definition of the group is 'uni-form direction'. The exercise of uniform direction over two or more undertakings defines them as a group. A parent-subsidiary relationship as de-scribed above allows us to presume uniform direc-tion, but uniform direction may exist even where there is no evidence of the criteria for a parent-sub-sidiary relationship.

---

[5]§28 of the *Einführungsgesetz zum AktG*.
[6]Undertakings coming above two of the three criteria: bal-ance sheet total of DM 125 m, sales of DM 250 m and over 5,000 employees.

[7]The AktG §18(1) says *'eingegliedert ist'*.

The wording '*einheitliche Leitung*' also appears in the German version of Articles 3 and 4 of the First Draft and is used in the commentary to the draft (Supplement 9/76, p. 21). As noted, it is its flexibility that commends this definition to the EC legislators; a single test which excludes majority shareholdings where no control is intended, but includes minority shareholdings where actual control is exercised. By contrast, a legalistic definition of all specific circumstances under which a group would be held to exist would also have the disadvantage of requiring precise circumstances for exceptions, which can lead to abuse as the authors of the First Draft point out (Supplement 9/76, p. 21).

In the final version of the Seventh Directive (hereafter called 'the Directive'), the Commission seems to have made an about-face on this issue, notwithstanding their earlier defence of the general and flexible clause. Article 1 of the final version gives a series of definitions of the narrow, legalistic type rejected earlier; a majority of voting rights (Art. 1(1)(a)); the right to appoint or remove the majority of the board (Art. 1(1)(b)); and control of a company through a contractual agreement (Art. 1(1)(c)). This necessitates the allowing of a number of exceptions (Art. 13; see later). In addition, 'and pending subsequent co-ordination', actual exercise of a dominant influence or the management of two or more companies on a unified basis may be grounds for requiring consolidated accounts if member states so wish (Art. 1(2)(b)). Far from setting the tenor of this aspect of the law, the German concept of the group has been relegated to an option that is subject to future revision.

Legal Form of Parent

On the issue of the legal form of the parent, the Directive (Art. 4(2)) allows a member state to choose whether to require consolidation if (i) the parent is a limited company (AG, KGaA or GmbH, in the case of Germany) or (ii) the group *contains* such a company. The former was (and is) the British position. The latter had been the German and the First Draft's position (Art. 6(1)(a)).

No Parent

A further case is where there is no parent undertaking at all: two or more formally unconnected undertakings may be managed on a unified basis as a result of legal arrangements or overlapping management. The AktG (§329) refers to group undertakings under unified management. However, according to the AktG (§18(2)), *einheitliche Leitung* could exist without a parent. The resulting group would be called a '*Gleichordnungskonzern*'.

Similarly, the First Draft (Arts. 4(1) and 7(1)) requires the preparation of group accounts by any limited company in such a case: undertakings that do not stand in a parent-subsidiary relationship to one another also form a group if they are under unified management. This case of the 'horizontal group' is specifically mentioned in the commentary (Explanatory Memorandum, p. 22). The Directive (Art. 12) *allows* a member state to require this 'horizontal' consolidation, presumably for the protection of lenders or employees in the 'group'.

Sub-group Consolidation

Another topic where German origins may be detected is 'sub-group consolidation'. The AktG (§330(1)) requires AG and KGaA parents to produce group accounts even if they are themselves subsidiaries. However, there is an exemption for those sub-groups included in a higher consolidation using German law (even if the higher consolidation is performed by an ultimate parent outside Germany).[8] In effect, this meant that sub-group consolidation was not common because few AGs or KGaAs were subsidiaries of parents falling outside of the AktG or PublG.[9] Likewise, the First Draft (Art. 6(2)(a)) requires all companies of the relevant legal form[10] which are parents to prepare accounts for their sub-group. Article 6(2)(b) also requires partial consolidation where the ultimate parent company has its domicile outside the EC, and relates to all EC-domiciled parents at the top of their 'family trees' within the EC.

The First Draft would have had an effect dramatically wider than that of the AktG. This is because the First Draft has no sub-group exemptions and because it extends the consolidation requirement to all sub-groups headed by all types of limited company (e.g. in the German context, to GmbHs which are the vast majority[11] of limited companies).

There seems to be no German or British precedent for this. The EC Commission justified these demands as being necessary for the protection of all interest groups connected with the subsidiary companies:

> Why, in other cases, is the drawing up of consolidated accounts for a sub-group still thought necessary when consolidated accounts are already available for the group as a whole? The Commission considers that sub-group accounts play a useful part in

---

[8]Any such foreign group accounts must be published in the *Bundesanzeiger* and audited by a Wirtschaftsprüfer (§330(2)).

[9]There were only about 2,000 AGs and very few KGaAs in 1983. Very large GmbHs came under the rules of the *Publizitätsgesetz* of 1969, which approximately applied AktG rules. There was a large incentive for subsidiaries to avoid audit and publication rules by being GmbHs.

[10]The Article also requires other (non limited-company) parents to prepare sub-group accounts if the group includes a limited company, but only if the sub-group is not included in a higher consolidation.

[11]There were about 260,000 GmbHs in 1983.

supplementing the information already given in the group accounts and add to the protection of the various parties having an interest in dependent group companies required to draw up such accounts. The shareholders and the creditors obtain a better view of their company's position ... This information cannot be evaluated without these other two documents. The situation might arise, for example, where the sub-group accounts showed a profit while the group accounts showed a loss. Both sets of information are important for shareholders in dependent group companies (Supplement 9/76, pp. 23, 24).

The rationale is extended to the protection of other interest groups (including regional or state interests in the case of some important subsidiary groups) and the importance of the principle is underlined to the extent that no exceptions to this rule are envisaged. One could also detect a mistrust of preparers in the comment:

There is some danger of group accounts, and in particular those of large groups with a large number of operations in different countries, becoming a jumble in which a great deal of important information is lost (Supplement 9/76, p. 24).

In the final version of the Directive, the scope clause (Article 1) continues to include all EC-domiciled parent companies—a definition that would include parents which are themselves subsidiaries of other companies. However, the full force of this began to be diluted in the 1978 amended proposal by adding exemptions (see Appendix 2). In the final Directive, exemptions from the preparation of group accounts must in general[12] be made available to subsidiary companies that are wholly or 90% owned by parents domiciled in the EC (Article 7). For other subsidiary companies, sub-group accounts can be dispensed with so long as these are not requested by the shareholders (Article 8). As a member state option, subsidiaries of non-EC parents may also be exempted, provided these prepare accounts in conformity with the provisions of the Seventh Directive or are equivalent to such accounts (Seventh Directive, Article 11), whatever 'equivalent' may eventually be held to mean (FEE, 1993, ch. 4). This last provision was originally introduced in the 1978 revised draft, although in that draft an EC auditor had to verify the compliance or equivalence. In effect, sub-group consolidation has been eliminated in the adopted Directive, except where it is required as a protection of the interests of the minority shareholders or

[12]Under certain conditions, e.g. that the sub-group is included in a higher consolidation.

in certain cases where the ultimate parent is outside the EC.

Legal Form of Subsidiaries

It should be noted that, although a member state may choose to require only parent *companies* to prepare group accounts, the required scope of consolidation clearly goes beyond subsidiary companies to cover all *undertakings* (i.e. including unlimited companies and unincorporated entities). This was clear from the AktG §329 (as quoted above). It may also be found in the First Draft (Art. 1, etc.) and in the Directive (Art. 1, etc.). This is different from previous British legal precedent (Companies Act 1948) or accounting standard (SSAP 14) which are drafted in terms of subsidiary *companies*. An explanatory point here is that unlimited entities are of greater economic significance in Germany than in the UK (Macharzina and Langer, 1991).

Foreign Subsidiaries

The AktG §329(2) allows foreign subsidiaries to be excluded from consolidation, which would have relieved the group from the difficulties of non-uniform accounting policies and of currency translation. However, even from the 1970 Elmendorff proposals, this permissive exclusion is abandoned in the context of international rules. Foreign subsidiaries are specifically to be included according to the First Draft (Art. 6) and the Directive (Art. 3).

Dissimilar Activities

The issue of exclusion of undertakings on the grounds of different activities was similarly reviewed and revised. In the First Draft, no such exclusion was to be possible:

A diversity of activities within a group is not in itself a valid reason for permitting undertakings to be excluded from consolidation. An individual company may also undertake different activities and will not be prevented from drawing up annual accounts. Some of the difficulties which might arise in such cases with regard to consolidation may be avoided by inserting special headings in the accounts with appropriate entries in the notes to the accounts, or by effecting a consolidation in terms of the different kinds of activity (Supplement 9/76, p. 26).

No exact version of such an exclusion existed in the AktG either, although §329(2) required the exclusion of a subsidiary from consolidation if it would impair the value of the disclosures in the consolidated financial statements. The 1978 revised draft *permits* the exclusion of subsidiaries that have very different activities from the rest of the group (Art. 10A). Article 14 of the Directive instead *requires* exclusion of subsidiaries from the consolidated accounts if, because of their different activities, their inclusion would impair the true and fair view given by the group accounts.

This is clearly a version of the then prevailing Anglo-Saxon idea whereby particularly financial subsidiaries were routinely treated by the equity method in group accounts. This practice was overturned by SFAS 94 in the US (1987) and the subsequent IAS 27. This change of mind occurred *after* the Directive was adopted. It is ironic, therefore, that the UK standard setters have had to try to circumvent the implementation in the Companies Act 1989 of Article 14 of the Directive by stating (in FRS 2, para. 25 of 1992) that this exclusion of subsidiaries on the grounds of 'true and fair' is exceptional.

Excludable Subsidiaries

Other *permitted* exclusions change across the documents. The AktG (§329(2)) allows immaterial subsidiaries to be excluded, as does the First Draft (Art. 10). The Directive (Art. 13) allows exclusions where the subsidiary is immaterial; where there are severe long-term restrictions on management; where the information necessary would involve disproportionate expense or undue delay; or where the shares are held exclusively with a view to resale. This extensive list goes beyond German precedent but is very similar to the permitted exclusions of the British Companies Act 1948 or the required exclusions of the British SSAP 14 (see Appendix 1).

Preparation of consolidated accounts

Other changes from the First Draft revise positions that otherwise would have given the Directive a German flavour.

Accounting Date

AktG (§331(3)) requires group companies to have the same accounting date or to prepare, and have audited, special accounting statements covering the period of the consolidated accounts (i.e. not just interim statements). This strict requirement is carried through to Article 14 (1)(e) of the First Draft, including the requirement to have any special accounts audited. The insistence on a common accounting date and accounting policies is justified by the EC legislators by the fact that a company with dominant influence over others would be in a position to insist on these matters (Supplement 9/76, p. 29). In the final Directive, Article 27(3) permits a group company to have a balance sheet date up to three months before that of the consolidated accounts. A greater difference in time would necessitate only interim accounts for the intervening period to be drawn up, and there is no mention of audit in this context. This is more

in line with Anglo-Saxon practice of the period (e.g. SSAP 14, para. 18).

Accounting Policies

The AktG, the 1971 draft of the Fourth Directive and the *avant projet* for the Seventh Directive do not contain a 'true and fair view' requirement. However, this changes by the 1974 version of the Fourth Directive and by the First Draft of the Seventh Directive (Art. 9). In these two documents, the true and fair view requirement has a status equal with the requirement to comply with the provisions of the Directive. However, by 1978, in the adopted version of the Fourth Directive and in the European Parliament amended version of the Seventh Directive, the true and fair view is required to override[13] other provisions, although not the scope of the group.[14] This is obviously a move in the UK direction.

As to uniform group accounting policies, the AktG §331(1) requires consolidated accounts to take up the values as they appear in the single entity accounts, except when they are not in accordance with German principles[15] (§336 (3)). The First Draft's Article 15 also requires the same values to be consolidated as they appear in the single entity accounts. This is presumably a measure to prevent manipulation and also aids readers of both the single entity accounts and consolidated statements to gauge the impact of the former on the latter. However, in order to ensure a coherent view of the results and financial position of the group, as if from the standpoint of a single economic entity, the First Draft includes the additional provision that all group companies use the same valuation methods (Art. 15(b) and (c)). That is, the German emphasis on transparency has been supplemented by the need to show a true and fair view of the group. The Explanatory Memorandum makes this explicit: 'The group accounts can only give the desired true and fair view ('*getreuen Einblick*')[16] where the items contained therein are valued on an identical or at least comparable basis' (Supplement 9/76, p. 29).

In the final version of the Directive, Article 29(2) requires the consolidating company to use the same valuation methods in the group accounts as in its own accounts (although member states may

---

[13] For a detailed examination of the wordings and strengths of the true and fair requirement in EC countries, see Nobes (1993).

[14] The true and fair requirement in the Seventh Directive relates to the undertakings included in the group accounts not to which undertakings shall be included.

[15] The values must be in accordance with *Grundsätze ordnungsmässiger Buchführung*, which are not fully codified.

[16] The 1976 draft of the Seventh Directive, like the 1974 draft of the Fourth Directive, contains the words '*einen getreuen Einblick*'. These words are replaced in the final versions of both Directives (1978 and 1983, respectively) by the longer wording now familiar in German law (see Nobes, 1993 for more detail).

prescribe or allow the use of different valuation methods, provided these are disclosed). Assets and liabilities of group companies using different rules must be revalued according to group valuation methods. The elimination of inter-company profit can, according to Article 26 of the Seventh Directive, be limited to the group's share of those profits rather than the total. This is not the case in the AktG (§331(2)) or in the First Draft (Art. 14). There seems to be neither German nor British (nor US)[17] precedent for this.

Consolidation methods

Acquisitions and Mergers

In the AktG, only full consolidation is dealt with. By contrast, the First Draft, in Articles 12 and 18, describes full and proportional consolidation. The Seventh Directive describes three methods in Articles 19, 20 and 32, having added the pooling of interests method. This takes account of the range of European practice.

The method of full consolidation described in the First Draft (Art. 12) is Anglo-Saxon. The Explanatory Memorandum (p. 27) discusses the choice that had to be made in this respect:

> In one Member State, consolidation is normally carried out on the basis of the net assets of the undertaking to be consolidated as it stands at the end of each financial year. Under this method, the reserves formed by the undertaking to be consolidated during its group membership will disappear into the consolidation differences and will not be shown under the group reserves in the group accounts. The consolidation differences will therefore change every year according to the movement of the reserves held in the undertaking to be consolidated.

This describes the predominant practice[18] in Germany on the basis of AktG 1965 (§331) (Beeny, 1975, p. 29), and is contrasted with the Anglo-Saxon method, leading as the latter does to a fuller presentation of movements on group reserves instead of hiding transfers to and from reserves in the 'difference on consolidation'. Since the results before and after acquisition are thereby strongly differentiated, the clarity of the picture of the group's financial position and the results of its activity is enhanced. Article 19 of the Seventh

Directive retains this method. The treatment of goodwill resulting from this calculation is considered in the next subsection.

Merger accounting for situations in which the acquiring company has issued shares as consideration for its controlling participation in another company is not described as a separate technique in the AktG. Beeny (1975, p. 30), however, points out that the then normal German acquisition method of consolidation approximates to what in the UK would be called the merger method: shares issued as consideration were recorded at their nominal value as were the shares transferred to the 'acquiring' company, the assets and liabilities were transferred at their book values rather than fair values and there was no distinction between pre- and post-acquisition profits in calculating the difference on consolidation. Despite (or perhaps because of) this similarity, there was no separate mention of merger accounting in the AktG.

In the First Draft, there is also no mention of merger accounting. This is not surprising, given this German background, the lack of use of the method in most of continental Europe and the fact that it was of uncertain legality in the UK and Ireland in 1976.[19] However, the method was made legal in the Companies Act 1981 in the UK, although it has not been made legal in Ireland. After the 1981 Act, the UK's Accounting Standards Committee issued ED 31 on the subject of merger accounting in 1982. The UK put pressure on the EC to include merger accounting as an option in the Directive, and this resulted in Article 20, which is a member state option.

Associates and Joint Ventures

As mentioned earlier, the AktG did not recognise a particular treatment for associates or joint ventures, which were therefore to be treated as investments. However, in the First Draft (Art. 17) and the Directive (Art. 33), the equity method is demanded for associates and allowed for joint ventures. Proportional consolidation is the member state optional alternative for joint ventures. This is consistent with UK practice of the time, and that of several other member states. The definition of an associate (in the Directive and the First Draft) is broadly in line with the UK's (i.e. based on significant influence, generally holdings of between 20% and 50%). Previous French precedent was holdings of $33\frac{1}{3}$% to 50%; Dutch precedent, 25% to 50%. In the 1970s, most other EC countries did not have rules on group accounting or did not allow the equity method.

---

[17]ARB 51 requires complete elimination.

[18]We are grateful to Dieter Ordelheide for pointing out that one interpretation of the capital consolidation method was that the initial consolidation difference was not subsequently changed, but reserves were adjusted. This was called the *'modifizierte anglo-amerikanische Methode'* (see Busse von Colbe and Ordelheide, 1976, pp. 98 ff.).

[19]The illegality concerns the issue of shares at par, without the creation of a share premium account. This was suspected to be illegal, but was not clearly so until the 1980 tax case of Shearer v. Bercain.

Goodwill

Calculation

The precise calculation of goodwill is also an issue where the evolution can be followed. On this subject, the AktG referred only to individual accounts. Goodwill could not be recognised as a specific asset, but individual assets acquired when acquiring an enterprise could be held at inflated values:

If ... the consideration paid for the acquisition of an enterprise exceeds the values of the individual assets of the enterprise at the date of the acquisition, then the difference may be included in the captions of fixed and financial assets. The amount must be shown separately and amortised by depreciations of at least one fifth in each subsequent fiscal year. (AktG §153 (5); translation: Mueller and Galbraith, 1976.)

Such increased values would be taken through to group accounts. However, the prohibition on recognising goodwill as a separate asset was not removed for the group accounts. Consequently, where the parent had bought the shares of a company for more than the book value of its net assets, a consolidation difference was shown in the group balance sheet, as discussed earlier.

By contrast, Article 12 of the First Draft states that, up to a point, the consolidation difference at the date of acquisition must be allocated to the related asset and liability captions:

Differences arising from compensation shall be entered directly against the relevant items in the group consolidated balance sheet. Any balance not so attributable shall be shown as a separate item with an appropriate heading.

One could read from this that 'fair values' of assets were generally to be the end result, with goodwill as the excess.

However, this mixture of the German feature of starting with book values and the Anglo-Saxon features of acquisition date and fair values was abandoned. Consequently, in Article 19(1) of the final Directive, there is an option between: (a) initial use of book values at the date of first consolidation followed by allocation to items whose 'value' is above or below their book values, and (b) initial use of (fair) 'values' of identifiable assets and liabilities at the date of acquisition.

Subsequent Treatment

Article 16 of the First Draft envisaged that any residual difference on consolidation should be posted to a special caption (goodwill) and written off over a period not exceeding five years. Although not specifically stated, depreciation through the profit and loss account is presumed to be the requirement. The amortisation period is the same as that for the revalued assets in §153(5) AktG, quoted above. The revised 1978 version of the draft is more flexible (see Appendix 2), and Article 30(1) of the final Directive provides for goodwill to be amortised over a period of up to five years or longer up to its useful economic life (as according to Article 37 of the Fourth Directive). In addition, Article 30(2) allows direct deduction from reserves. Each of these changes is a move away from the AktG.

Size exemptions

The AktG, which applied to AGs and KGaAs, did not contain exemptions from its rules based on size criteria. However, the *Publizitätsgesetz* of 1969 had applied many of the rules of the AktG to other types of company (principally GmbHs)[20] above certain size criteria.[21] This idea of exempting smaller companies from certain provisions was absorbed into the Fourth and Seventh Directives, based on the same type of criteria (i.e. balance sheet total, net turnover and average number of employees), though at much lower size levels.

In the Directives there are two such sets of thresholds[22] and therefore three size categories of company or group (small, medium and large). The Seventh Directive refers to the appropriate Articles in the Fourth Directive to establish the exact size criteria. The exemptions in the First Draft of the Seventh Directive are as follows:

Small groups: exempt from audit (Art. 23); abbreviated format for balance sheet publication (Art. 24).
Medium and small groups: abbreviated format for profit and loss account publication (Art. 11).

These are somewhat extended in the 1978 amended proposal (see Appendix 2). In the final Directive, none of the exemptions appears specifically. Instead, there is a member state option to exempt small and medium groups from the preparation (and, therefore, obviously from audit) of group accounts (Art. 6). This is a very broad exemption, of which *all* member states have taken some advantage (FEE, 1993). Clearly, the German idea of reducing burdens for smaller companies was retained in the Directive (and indeed has been exported to the UK).

---

[20] However, those GmbHs with AG or KGaA subsidiaries would already have been covered.
[21] See footnote 6.
[22] The two-of-three rule is kept. The size criteria in the 1974 draft are, for small companies: balance sheet total of Ecu 100,000; sales of Ecu 200,000; and 20 employees. For medium companies: Ecu 1m; Ecu 2m; and 100 employees. By the final Directive of 1978, the criteria for small companies are Ecu 1m; Ecu 2m; and 50 employees. For medium companies: Ecu 4m; Ecu 8m and 250 employees.

Conclusions

The Start Point and the Direction of Movement

It is clear from the analysis above that the German 1965 *Aktiengesetz* was an important model for the first published draft of the Seventh Directive. It is also clear that there are increasing differences from the AktG as one moves to the First Draft, then to the 1978 amended proposal, and then to the final Directive.

This prompts the question of whether a particular direction of movement can be discerned. In the period of evolution of the Directive (late 1960s to 1983), the countries in the EC with the most detailed rules on group accounting, apart from Germany, were the UK and Ireland.[23] The British Companies Act 1947 (consolidated as the 1948 Act) contained instructions to prepare group accounts and a number of detailed provisions. SSAP 1 of 1971 regulated accounting for associates; SSAP 14 of 1978 contained basic rules for the preparation of group accounts; ED 3 of 1971 and ED 31 of 1982 had dealt with acquisition accounting and merger accounting; and ED 30 of 1982 proposed rules on goodwill. All the while, very extensive 'generally accepted practice' was in operation.

The first three columns of Appendix 1 show, for 19 main features of the Directive, how most of the provisions gradually moved away from the AktG. It can be seen that, in the following 14 cases, the final Directive was closer to UK rules or practice (column 4 of Appendix 1) than to the AktG. Mostly, this results from substituting UK rules for German rules, but in a few cases by adding a UK option to German rules. In all these instances, the Directive led to changes to German law. The 14 cases (using the numbering of Appendix 1) are:

1. Definition of parent.
2. Legal form of parent company.
3. Groups with no parent company
6. Foreign subsidiaries included.
7. Dissimilar subsidiaries excluded.
8. Permitted exclusions.
10. True and fair view override.
11. Uniform policies required.
13. Merger accounting allowed.
14. Equity method required for associates.
15. Joint ventures to be equity accounted or proportionally consolidated.
16. Date of goodwill calculation.
17. Use of fair values.
18. Choice of goodwill treatment.

An International Coalition

The remarkably broad front over which the changes in the Directive took place, mainly from 1979, suggest a substantial coalition in the EC in favour of the Anglo-Saxon methods.[24] It was noted in the early part of this paper that in Stage I of the process (the *avant projet*) a similar change to professional consensus had occurred much earlier, by 1974. An explanation for this shift is proposed now.

In the 1970s, the countries with experience of group accounting for most groups over many decades were the UK, Ireland and the Netherlands.[25] Denmark had introduced consolidation requirements in 1973 (Christiansen, 1992). All these countries were heavily influenced by multi-national companies, multinational accounting firms and US practice. France, through the efforts of the Commission des Opérations de Bourse (founded in 1967), was encouraging the development of consolidation in the 1970s and was also influenced by the practices of New York and London (Standish, 1991; Scheid and Walton, 1992). It is suggested that professional accountants from at least the five countries referred to in this paragraph were sufficiently persuasive by the time of the Groupe d'Etudes' memorandum of 1974 to overcome the earlier German-based consensus of the original six countries. Further clues to this move are that:

(i) For most EC countries, a typical professional representative on the Groupe d'Etudes and other similar bodies is a partner in a large accountancy firm, with strong Anglo-American influences.

(ii) German and other civil law country representatives were comparatively relaxed about changes away from the AktG in the field of consolidation because such changes have no effect on either taxation or distributable profit, which are the key issues in German accounting. Further, there was no long tradition to defend, since German consolidation practices dated only from after 1965 when the AktG came into force.

From 1974 onwards the coalition built further, as will be explained, so that by Stage III (governmental negotiations) it was very powerful. The International Accounting Standards Committee

---

[23]Similar Irish laws followed the British Companies Act 1948. Standard-setting was carried out jointly for the UK and Ireland from 1970 to 1990 by the Accounting Standards Committee and its predecessor.

[24]'Anglo-Saxon' is defined in footnote 3. 'Anglo-Saxon methods' refer here to the broad consensus that the fair view demands the production of consolidated accounts and that these should include foreign subsidiaries, equity accounted associates, fair valued assets of subsidiaries, etc.

[25]The UK and Ireland have already been discussed. Reference for extensive consolidation practice in the Netherlands includes Zeff et al. (1992).

containing four EC states[26] as permanent board members had, in 1976, issued its consolidation standard (IAS 3) which was consistent with UK practice. In its 1977 opinion[27] on the First Draft, the EC's Economic and Social Committee noted the publication of IAS 3 and encouraged the Commission to establish maximum conformity between international and European rules. The Italian governmental regulatory body for listed companies (CONSOB) had also called for the use of international accounting standards for group accounts in 1981. The Groupe d'Etudes had also issued several documents[28] in favour of the moves shown in Appendix 1. By contrast, Greece, Spain and Portugal, where consolidation was rare or non-existent in the 1970s, did not join the EC until 1980, 1986 and 1986, respectively. By the end of the 1970s, the scene was set for a major move towards UK group accounting.

Changes Stage by Stage
A suggested explanation for the change to professional consensus in Stage I has been given above. In Stage II, the Commission largely ignored this change and drafted a Directive clearly based on the AktG. Again, it has already been suggested that this is not surprising given the control by lawyers from a civil law tradition, who were basically supplementing the Fourth Directive, which had a clear German feel. Some changes were made in the second (1978) draft of the Directive; the major ones (those in Appendix 2, except for the first one) being consequential on the amendments agreed in the adopted version of the Fourth Directive of the same year. However, most of the major changes occur after 1978, once the Directive entered Stage III (negotiations in the Council of Ministers). Incidentally, the 1971 memorandum proposed eight Articles; the First Draft contained 21 Articles; the 1978 draft added eight further Articles;[29] and the adopted Directive contained 51 Articles. The increase after 1978 was largely due to extra options, exemptions and transitional provisions.
As suggested above, the international context of Stage III (the period from 1979 to 1983) would have supported a move from German to Anglo-Saxon consolidation techniques. Further, the German governmental negotiators would have been less concerned with changes required by the

Seventh Directive than with the Fourth for the same reasons as suggested for professionals as in (ii) above: the lack of relevance of group accounts for the calculations of tax and distribution of profit, and the lack of a long tradition of group accounting in Germany. Indeed, the subsequent German implementation of the Seventh Directive chose to take several of the Directive's Anglo-Saxon options into law.[30] Incidentally, the final Council of Ministers negotiations were carried out in the first half of 1983 when Germany held the presidency of the Council.
By contrast, the prevailing UK opinion was that the really important financial statements were the group accounts. One continental European governmental negotiator has commented that generally the UK negotiators adopted 'a rather uncompromising manner as though no other text than that of the British Companies Act could ever qualify for inclusion in the Directive'.[31] It was also possible to use the conclusions of IAS 3 (agreed by a committee with a large EC presence, as noted earlier) as persuasive argument for change from the published drafts of the Directive.

Political Players
Three main players have been identified as being particularly associated with the three stages: respectively, professional accountants at the *avant projet* stage, Commission lawyers at the published draft stage, and governmental negotiators leading up to the adoption of the Directive. However, each group was involved in more than its own stage. For example: (i) it was the Commission that requested the initial professional memoranda and set their terms of reference; (ii) the profession commented on the published drafts in Stage II and on many private drafts in Stage III; (iii) certain members of the profession were involved in Stage III as governmental advisers or even delegates;[32] (iv) governmental pressures would have been brought to bear on the Commission at all stages; and (v) the Commission would have defended its ideas in Stage III.
The fundamental objectives of these main players may be as follows. The professional accountants would be keen to ensure that the Directive

---

[26]France, West Germany, Netherlands, UK-and-Ireland. The UK and Ireland were jointly represented on the board of the IASC by nominees of the Consultative Committee of Accountancy Bodies.
[27]*Official Journal* of the EC, C75/1977, p.6.
[28]See, for example, a remark on this in the Commission's Explanatory Memorandum preceding the 1978 amended proposal.
[29]The 1978 draft retained the numbering of 1976, so new Articles were inserted as '17A', etc.

[30]For example, the German 1985 *Bilanzrichtliniengesetz* changes German law by not requiring horizontal consolidation and by exempting groups not headed by a limited company. There are also options to use the Anglo-Saxon version of fair value accounting and to depart from the parent's valuation rules in the group accounts (see FEE, 1993).
[31]Peter Wessel, one of the Dutch negotiators on the Fourth and Seventh Directives, suggests this in a letter of 1 November 1993.
[32]For example, Paul Rutteman of Arthur Young (as it was then) extensively advised the UK governmental negotiators; and Peter Wessel of Moret Limperg was appointed as a temporary special governmental delegate.

would continue to allow their own preferred national practices, and they might have an evangelical wish to see such practices spread throughout Europe. The Commission staff aim for, and are largely judged on, the successful adoption of Directives and the subsequent co-ordination of laws. They will favour legalistic solutions and have little interest in economic conceptual frameworks. Governmental negotiators will be alert to policy considerations such as taxation and international competitiveness, though the former may be of little significance in this particular case. Governments will also respond to strong lobby groups, e.g. the accountancy profession in the UK or industrialists in Germany. These groups will be aiming to preserve the status quo, to maintain flexibility, to minimise costs, and so forth. One powerful example of the influence of corporate lobbyists is the inclusion of special Articles in the Seventh Directive that enable the unique consolidation practices of Unilever and Royal Dutch Shell to continue (Articles 12 and 15). Other lobbyists who

might work through the Economic and Social Council, among other routes, would include unions and analysts who would be interested in better quality information and more disclosures.

In summary, what became the Seventh Directive was first drafted in the late 1960s by a committee chaired by a German (with no UK member). Throughout the whole period until 1983, the Commission employee responsible for the Directive was a German lawyer. The final Council of Ministers' negotiations in the first half of 1983 were conducted while Germany was presiding. Nevertheless, although the earliest memoranda and the First Draft were close to the AktG, the Directive itself was far removed; most of the change having occurred in the Council stage from 1979. This is connected with the building of a coalition of opinion in favour of change, which had formed in professional groups by 1974 and more generally by 1979. This paper has proposed a model of EC rule-making and has examined the evolution of the Seventh Directive in detail for the first time.

Appendix 1: Evolution of consolidation rules

AktG	First Draft	Seventh Directive	UK practice (before 1983)
Scope			
1. Definition of Parent: Uniform direction (§329), evidenced by controlling influence, control contract, complete integration, or (rebuttably) majority ownership of equity (§§16–18).	Uniform direction (Arts. 3 and 4). Controlling influence may be exercised (Art. 2(1)). Presumed where: Majority of voting rights (Art. 2(2)(a)). Right to appoint majority of board (Art. 2(2)(b)). Actual exercise of control (Art. 2(2)(c)).	Majority of votes (Art. 1(1)(a)), or right to appoint majority of board (Art. 1(1)(b)), or right to exercise dominant influence over board (Art. 1(1)(c)), OR* has exercised dominant influence over board (Art. 1(1)(d)(aa)), or control agreement (Art. 1(d)(bb)), OR* actual exercise of dominant influence (Art. 1(2)(a)), OR* uniform direction (Art. 1(2)(b)).	Majority of the equity (1948 Act, S. 154), or controls the composition of the board (1948 Act, S. 154), *but* exclusion if not controlled (SSAP 14, para. 21).
2. Groups with AGs and KGaAs as parents (§329). Also, groups containing such companies (EG AktG, §28), and other large groups (PublG).	Groups containing AGs, KGaAs, or GmbHs (Art. 6(1)(a)).	Parent undertaking is an AG, KGaA or GmbH OR* where group contains such a company (Art. 4(1) and (2)).	Parent is limited company (1948 Act, S. 150(1))

3. Uniform direction requires horizontal consolidation (§§18(2) and 329).	Unified management requires horizontal consolidation (Art. 4(1)).	Horizontal consolidation is a member state option (Art. 12).	No consolidation if no parent.
4. Sub-group consolidation only where ultimate parent does not produce group accounts per AktG (§330).	All limited company parents must produce group accounts even if consolidated themselves (Art. 6(2)(b)).†	Not required unless requested by shareholders (Art. 8) OR* in certain cases if ultimate parent is outside EC (Art. 11).	Not required if the company is a wholly owned subsidiary of another British company (1948 Act, S. 150(2)(a)).
5. Subsidiary undertakings (§330).	Subsidiary undertakings (Art. 2).	Subsidiary undertakings (Art. 1).	Subsidiary companies (1948 Act, S. 154).
6. Foreign subsidiaries could be excluded (§329).	Domestic and foreign subsidiaries to be consolidated (Art. 6(1)(b)).	Domestic and foreign subsidiaries to be consolidated (Art. 3(1)).	Domestic and foreign subsidiary companies to be consolidated (1948 Act, S. 150(1)).
7. Exclusion required if value of disclosures impaired (§329).	No exclusion.†	Exclusion required if subsidiaries are so different as to impair the true and fair view (Art. 14).	Exclusion required if subsidiaries are so dissimilar as to be misleading (SSAP 14, para. 21).
8. Exclusion permitted where immaterial (§329).	Exclusion permitted where immaterial (Art. 10).†	Exclusion permitted where immaterial, severe long-term restrictions, expense or delay, shares held for resale (Art. 13).	Exclusion permitted where impractical, immaterial, expense or delay, misleading or harmful, very different (1948 Act, S. 150(2)(b). Exclusion required where so dissimilar to be misleading, not controlled, severe restrictions, temporary control (SSAP 14, para. 21).

Preparation of consolidated accounts

9. Same date for group companies, or special accounts to group date (§331(3)).	Same date for group companies, or special accounts to group date *and* audit (Art. 14(1)(e)).	Same date for group companies OR* date within 3 months prior to group date, or interim accounts (Art. 27(3)).	Same date unless good reasons then make adjustments and disclose (1948 Act, S. 153(1)).

Accounting values/policies

10. Proper principles. As sure a view as possible according to the valuation rules (§149).	True and fair view (Art. 9(2)).†	True and fair view overrides (Art. 16).	True and fair view overrides (1948 Act, S. 149).

(continued on next page)

11. Same values as in single entity accounts, but not uniform policies (§331(1)).	Same values as in single entity accounts and uniform policies (Art. 15).	Uniform policies, therefore revaluations where necessary (Art. 29).	Uniform policies (therefore adjustment where necessary) or, in exceptional cases, disclosure and numerical reconciliation (SSAP 14, para. 16).
12. Elimination of 100% of intra-group profit (§331(2)).	As AktG (Art. 14).	As Draft, OR* elimination of only group's share (Art. 26).	No rule, but general practice to eliminate fully.

Consolidation methods

13. Full consolidation (§331).	Acquisition method (Art. 12).	Acquisition method (Art. 19) OR* merger accounting (Art. 20).	Acquisition method or merger accounting (general practice, e.g. ED 31).
14. Associates at cost (§153).	Equity method (Art. 17).	Equity method (Art. 33).	Equity method (SSAP 1).
15. Joint ventures at cost (§153).	Equity method OR* proportional consolidation (Art. 18).	As Draft (Art. 32).	Equity method or proportional consolidation (SSAP 1, para. 10).

Goodwill

16. Difference on consolidation calculated each year (§331).	Goodwill calculated at time of acquisition (Art. 12).	Goodwill calculated at time of first consolidation or at acquisition (Art. 19).	Goodwill calculated at acquisition (general practice, e.g. ED 30).
17. Difference calculated using book values (§331(1)).	Goodwill calculated using book values then allocated to individual net assets as far as possible (Art. 12).	Goodwill calculated starting with book values at first consolidation OR* using fair values at acquisition. (Art. 19).	Goodwill calculated using fair values (general practice, e.g. ED 30).
18. Difference not amortised.	Goodwill amortised over up to 5 years (Art. 16.).†	Goodwill amortised against profit over up to 5 years or longer, OR* immediately written off against reserves (Art. 30).	Goodwill immediately written off against reserves or amortised over useful life (general practice; e.g. ED 30).

Size exemptions

19. AktG extended by Publizitätsgesetz but only to large undertakings.	Size exemptions for audit and formats (Arts. 11, 23, 24).†	Size exemptions a member state option for the preparation of group accounts (Art. 6).	No size exemptions.

*OR denotes a member state option.
†A change from the 1976 position first appears in the 1978 version.

Appendix 2

Important Changes in the 1978 Amended Proposal for the Seventh Directive (same Article numbers as 1976 Draft)

Art. 6(2). Sub-group consolidated accounts may be dispensed with provided a parent at a higher level has produced consolidated accounts in conformity with the Seventh Directive. Any minority shareholders must approve.

Art. 9(4 and 5). Where application of the rules would not lead to a true and fair view, additional information must be provided or, in exceptional cases, the rules must be departed from.

Art. 16. Member states may authorise a write-off period for goodwill on acquisition of greater length than the five years of the First Draft, provided the expected useful life of this asset is not exceeded.

Art. 24. Small groups to be exempted from publishing a profit and loss account and directors' report. Medium groups can publish an abbreviated balance sheet and notes.

References

Beeny, J. H. (1975), *European Financial Reporting—Germany* (London: ICAEW).

Busse von Colbe, W. and Ordelheide, D. (1976), *Konzernabschlüsse*, 2nd ed. (Wiesbaden: Gabler).

Christiansen, M. (1992), 'Denmark' in Alexander, D. and Archer, S., *The European Accounting Guide* (London: Academic Press).

Dahl, R. A. (1961), *Who Governs? Democracy and Power in an American City* (Yale University Press).

FEE (1993), *Seventh Directive Options and their Implementation* (London: Routledge).

Hope, T. and Briggs J. (1982), 'Accounting Policy Making—Some Lessons from the Deferred Taxation Debate', *Accounting and Business Research*, Spring.

Hope, T. and Gray, R. (1982), 'Power and Policy Making: The Development of an R & D Standard', *Journal of Business Finance and Accounting*, Winter.

Laughlin, R. C. and Puxty, A. G. (1983), 'Accounting Regulation: An Alternative Perspective', *Journal of Business Finance and Accounting*, Autumn.

Lukes, S. (1974), *Power: A Radical View* (Macmillan).

Macharzina, K. and Langer, K. (1991), 'Financial Reporting in Germany', Ch. 9 in Nobes, C. W. and Parker, R. H., *Comparative International Accounting* (Hemel Hempstead: Prentice Hall).

Mueller, R. and Galbraith, E. G. (1976), *The German Stock Corporation Law* (Frankfurt: Knapp).

Mumford, M. (1979), 'The End of a Familiar Inflation Accounting Cycle', *Accounting and Business Research*, Spring.

Nair, R. D. and Frank, W. G. (1980), 'The Impact of Disclosure and Measurement Practices on International Accounting Classifications', *Accounting Review*, July.

Nobes, C. W. (1983), 'The Origins of the Accounting Provisions of the 1980 and 1981 Companies Acts', *Accounting and Business Research*, Winter.

Nobes, C. W. (1992), 'A Political History of Goodwill in the UK: An Ilustration of Cyclical Standard Setting', *Abacus*, Vol. 28, No. 2.

Nobes, C. W. (1993), 'The True and Fair View: Impact on and of the Fourth Directive', *Accounting and Business Research*, Winter.

Polsby, N. W. (1963), *Community Power and Politcal Theory* (New Haven: Yale University Press).

Scheid, J.-C. and Walton, P. (1992), 'France' in Alexander, D. and Archer S., *The European Accounting Guide* (London: Academic Press).

Standish, P. E. M. (1991), 'Financial Reporting in France' in Nobes, C. W. and Parker, R. H., *Comparative International Accounting* (Hemel Hempstead: Prentice Hall).

Vangermeersch, R. (1985), 'The Route of the Seventh Directive of the EEC on Consolidated Accounts—Slow, Steady, Studied and Successful', *International Journal of Accounting*, Spring.

Wallace, R. S. O. (1990), 'Survival Strategies of a Global Organization: The Case of the International Accounting Standards Committee', *Accounting Horizons*, June.

Watts, R. and Zimmerman, J. (1978), 'Towards a Positive Theory of the Determination of Accounting Standards', *Accounting Review*, January.

Zeff, S. A., van der Wel, F. and Camfferman, K. (1992), *Company Financial Reporting* (Amsterdam: North Holland), Ch. 2.

17

The European Accounting Review 1995, 4:2, 249–254

International accounting harmonization
A commentary

Christopher Nobes
University of Reading

Christian Hoarau's paper in this issue*of the journal is stimulating, and provides us with much to react to. I take up several issues here, attempting to be equally stimulating. Naturally, I will not dwell on those matters on which I agree with him. I start with some details and lead up to the major points.

GLOBALIZATION

Hoarau suggests that 'Although the internationalization of economies is an old phenomenon, the international harmonization of accounting is only a recent preoccupation' (p. 217). The contrast of 'internationalization *phenomenon*' with 'harmonization *preoccupation*' is false. One could equally claim that the phenomenon of internationalization of accounting is old (see, for example, Parker, 1989) whereas explicit preoccupation with harmonization of economies is relatively recent.

COMPARABILITY PROJECT

There are many references in Hoarau's paper (e.g. p. 219) to the IASC's E 32 project as though it were not concluded. However, it came to a conclusion in November 1993. Incidentally, it is of relevance to some points below that several of the resultant changes to international accounting standards (IASs) do not slavishly follow US practice but are inconsistent with it.[1]

QUALITY OF US STANDARDS

Hoarau detects (p. 221) that the Americans are implying that SEC acceptance of another country's rules or of IASs instead of US GAAP would

Address for correspondence
Department of Economics, PO Box 218, Whiteknights, Reading RG6 6AA, UK.

0963–8180

* For details, see references list in the Introduction to this book.

involve a loss of quality. Surely this is self-evident. Hoarau himself agrees that IASs 'cover a narrower spectrum of subjects, are less specific about principles, less detailed in methodology and even less complete in terms of disclosure requirements' (p. 221).

Consequently, is it not equally self-evident that the SEC must at present demand restatement or reconciliation to US GAAP in order to provide a level playing field for US investors and preparers? Do not the dramatic changes to income measurement and disclosures by Daimler-Benz and many other companies when subjected to SEC disciplines prove the point beyond a peradventure?

SCOPE OF HARMONIZATION

Hoarau states (p. 226) that the 'influence of international harmonization is limited in France to consolidated financial statements'. Presumably we are to interpret this as referring to the influence of IASC rather than EU harmonization, because major changes to French *individual* accounts did occur as a result of harmonization in the early 1980s with the implementation of the Fourth Directive. Even limiting the meaning of international harmonization to non-EU influence, it would still not be fair to say that international harmonization was limited to group accounting, because some of these early 1980s' changes to French individual accounts can be traced back, via the Fourth Directive, to the 'same underlying idea of accounting' (p. 221) which is said to support 'international' US/UK/IASC practices; for example, (1) the great expansion of disclosure caused by the addition of the *annexe*; and (2) the rearrangement of the French balance sheet to show the year's result as part of shareholders' funds.

OPTIONS IN GROUP ACCOUNTS

Hoarau regrets the introduction into France of options for group accounts to include certain 'international' practices, including forms of inflation accounting, use of LIFO, capitalization of interest, recognition of translation gains and use of different formats. This has 'broken down the homogeneity of the French accounting model' (p. 226). What does Hoarau mean by 'international' practices? He cannot mean those recommended by the IASC because there were no IASC *requirements* to do any of the above five options and some of them were not addressed at all by IASC standards. Similarly he cannot mean the USA, because: (1) the optional balance sheet format allowed for French groups is totally unlike any US format,[2] although it is used by British and Dutch companies; (2) the optional use of current purchasing power or replacement cost is completely inconsistent with US GAAP, and again owes more to British and Dutch precedent; (3) even the option to use LIFO is an unclear case since LIFO is a minority US practice (AICPA, 1992) and is certainly not *required* in the USA; indeed the US delegation at the IASC voted to delete the LIFO option as part of the comparability project.

NEEDS OF CREDITORS AND EMPLOYEES

Before agreeing with Hoarau's implication that continental European accounting provides better information for creditors and employees, one would first need to be convinced that these users need different information *instead* of that provided for shareholders. If, alternatively, they need *extra* information, we would have to be clear what it was and then it could be provided separately. Hoarau does not attempt to settle these points.

Hoarau suggests that US-style methods for accounts reduce 'their usefulness to the needs of stock exchange investors alone' (p. 228). Is the US-style information provided by Daimler-Benz' Form 20-F *less* useful for creditors and employees than the information in Daimler-Benz' statutory German accounts? I do not believe so.

In particular, Hoarau claims that the option to use the Anglo-Saxon *par fonction* format for the consolidated income statement is to be deplored because it gives less useful information to employee representatives than the traditional *par nature* format. However, it seems disingenuous for Hoarau to claim that the traditional French group information has been better for employees, given that the great majority of French companies (even some listed ones) did not produce consolidated accounts *at all* until they were recently introduced (Scheid and Walton, 1992) in response to the sort of Anglo-Saxon influences regretted by Hoarau.

Furthermore, Hoarau claims (p. 228) that the *par nature* format permits 'the direct calculation of added value and gross trading margin'. However, according to another French commentator, Richard (1988, pp. 22, 23), difficulties in the approach of the *plan comptable* lead to 'the impossibility of a precise calculation of value added' whereas the Anglo-Saxon income statement *par fonction* 'allows a correct calculation of value added'. As for the 'gross trading margin' claim, this is only true for retail businesses. For manufacturing businesses, it is the Anglo-Saxon *par fonction* format which calculates gross trading margin (gross profit). The *par nature* format allows the calculation of *excedent brut d'exploitation* (i.e. gross operating margin).

BENCHMARKS, ETC.

Hoarau's paper's subheading is 'American hegemony or mutual recognition with benchmarks'. Hoarau's preferred route to harmonization is mutual recognition accompanied by reconciliations to international benchmarks established by an international committee of standard setters. I think that there are several problems with this. First, an international committee of standard setters would presumably have to include representatives from governmental bodies for such countries as France, Germany and Japan where the government is in charge of accounting rules. Judging by the slow progress of the EC Contact Committee and the EC Forum, such a committee would find it even more difficult than the IASC does to achieve Hoarau's desired 'international accounting rules which contain no options and prescribe a single accounting treatment for each issue covered' (p. 231).

Secondly, there is no guarantee that such a committee would not also be biased towards US practices, since the US is 'ahead' on most issues, as Hoarau admits. For example, to the extent that the IASC seems to come up with American solutions, it does so despite the fact that the US is at present only one out of fourteen voting members on the IASC and that the US vote is not cast by the FASB or the SEC but by the AICPA[3] which has no direct involvement in US rule-making. Further, IASC working parties on particular issues frequently come up with US-style proposals even when they have no US or other Anglo-Saxon members.

The third problem with Hoarau's proposal is that, since companies would have to reconcile from national practice to the benchmark for each of many issues, the resulting notes would be complex. Fourthly, this would not, in substance, be mutual recognition.[4]

In summary, Hoarau's proposal would be cumbersome even if it were feasible; and his subheading seems to contain a false dichotomy and a misleading description of the proposal.

AMERICAN IMPERIALISM

Behind Hoarau's paper seems to lie that anti-Americanism which we Europeans so easily feel. Little unites us so well as *Schadenfreude* at the failure of Euro Disney or *Angst* at the thought that one day there may be a McDonalds 'restaurant' in Piazza San Marco. The French have been perhaps the most honest in identifying *le défi americain* (Servan-Schreiber, 1967); witness the activities of the language police at the Académie Française and the French attitude to US films at the 1993 GATT negotiations. However, these feelings may lead to ill-focused attacks (see above).

Hoarau's major issue is that 'international harmonization ... comes into conflict with ... the economic, social and cultural contexts of different accounting systems' (p. 220). To some extent, this issue has already been examined. However, the main point is that the regretted changes brought about in France from the late 1980s have *not* resulted directly from the influence of the IASC or of the USA. They have resulted from the *choices* made by the French when implementing the Seventh Directive. Indeed, of the fifteen EU member states, France uniquely has introduced a substantially separate regime for groups compared to that for individual companies.

Hoarau complains that harmonization copies the Anglo-Saxon system in concentrating on providing information for the investor. This, of course, is inevitable for the sort of harmonization which, as Hoarau notes, 'is mainly sought by actors in the international capital markets' (p. 218). Of course such harmonization (particularly of group accounts) disregards various features of accounting systems designed to collect national tax, or to help control a national economy, or to be a neat exercise in double entry. The point is that no country is forced to join in with IASC harmonization or to mimic US accounting. From the 1960s, France had various possibilities related to accounting, including: (1) to ignore US influences or IASC requirements, or (2) to change its economy towards an internationalized market system[5] and then to adopt certain features of Anglo-Saxon accounting that fit such a system; or (3) to maintain traditional French accounting but to allow a different set of rules for those accounts of interest to the international market (e.g. group accounts of some listed companies). In fact, France has exhibited elements of all these three. Far from being in opposition to 'the diversity of accounting models and the needs to which these models are meant to respond' (p. 231), the voluntary adoption in France of certain Anglo-Saxon accounting features for certain purposes seems to be a *response* to these diverse needs.

NOTES

The author is Coopers & Lybrand Professor of Accounting at the University of Reading, England. He is grateful to the editors for commissioning this comment and to R. H. Parker and A. D. Roberts for suggestions on an earlier draft.

1   For example, IAS 9 *requires* development expenditure to be capitalized under certain conditions (this is not allowed under US GAAP); and IAS 22 limits the amortization period for goodwill to twenty years (whereas US GAAP specifies a maximum of forty years).

2   It is a financial position (*en liste*) format, which is very rare in the US (AICPA, 1992), and has an increasing order of liquidity, which is opposite to the US order.

3   The acronyms in this list refer to the Financial Accounting Standards Board (which issues standards), the Securities and Exchange Commission (which enforces standards and can over-rule the FASB), and the American Institute of Certified Public Accountants.

4   Mutual recognition generally means the mutual acceptance of existing accounting practices, not detailed reconciliations (e.g. FEE, 1993).

5   Note the formation of the Commission des opérations de bourse in 1967 and its encouragement of stock markets, consolidated accounting, disclosures, etc.

REFERENCES

AICPA (1992) *Accounting Trends and Techniques*. AICPA.

FEE (1993) *Seventh Directive Options and their Implementation*. Routledge, ch. 4.

Parker, R. H. (1989) 'Importing and exporting accounting: the British experience'. In Hopwood, A. G. *International Pressures for Accounting Change*. Prentice Hall, 7–29.

Richard, J. (1988) 'Compte de résultat: classement par nature ou classement par fonctions', *Revue Fiduciare Comptable*, 132, 20–34.

Scheid, J.-C. and Walton, P. (1992) 'France'. In Alexander, D. and Archer, S. *European Accounting Guide*. Academic Press.

Servan-Schreiber, J.-J. (1967) *Le défi americain*. Editions Denoël.

18

The European Accounting Review 1998, **7:1**, 125–148

Accounting in Europe

Harmonization of the structure of audit firms: incorporation in the UK and Germany

Lisa Evans and Christopher Nobes
Napier University and University of Reading, UK

ABSTRACT

The Eighth EU Council Directive addresses the harmonization of the conditions for the approval of auditors. This paper deals specifically with the approval of incorporated audit firms, which is regulated by Article 2 of the Directive, and with the extent to which the Eighth Directive has improved *de jure* harmonization of the rules for incorporated audit firms between UK and German law. The development of Article 2 from the proposal to the final version of the Directive is studied, as is the implementation of Article 2 into UK and German law and the reasoning behind the choices made by both Member States in this process. Although considerable changes were made to the laws of both countries, little greater *de jure* harmony was achieved.

INTRODUCTION

The Eighth EU Council Directive addresses the harmonization of the conditions for the approval of auditors. A working party had prepared an *avant projet* of a Directive to deal with the minimum qualification of auditors as early as May 1972, but the official Proposal (hereafter 1978 Draft) for the Directive was not published until 1978; the Amended Proposal (hereafter 1979 Draft) in 1979; and the final version in 1984. A chronology of the development of the Eighth Directive is given in Table 1.

This paper deals specifically with the rules relating to incorporated audit firms, which are found in Article 2 of the Directive. Van Hulle (1992) argues that this is one of the areas not satisfactorily resolved by the Eighth Directive because considerable national differences remain. He suggests that further initiatives by the Commission may be necessary. Similarly, Nordemann

Address for correspondence
Lisa Evans, Department of Accounting and Finance, Napier University, Sighthill Court, Edinburgh EH11 4BN, UK.

0963–8180

Table 1 Chronology of the development of the Eighth Directive

(Unpublished) draft prepared by working party of Commission	30.05.72
Proposal for Eighth Directive (No. C 112/6)	13.05.78
Amendments proposed by European Parliament (No. C 140/154)	05.06.79
Opinion of the Economic and Social Committee (No. C 171/30)	09.07.79
Amended Proposal for Eighth Directive (No. C 317/6)	18.12.79
Council of Ministers/Working Party: revised (unpublished) drafts	1980–84
Eighth Council Directive (No. L 126/20)	10.04.84

(The items in bold print are publications in the *Official Journal of the European Communities*. For the Proposal and the Amended Proposal the actual issue dates were somewhat earlier, i.e. the Proposal dates from 24.4.1978 and the Amended Proposal from 5.12.1979.)

(1989) implicitly suggests that the Directive did not help harmonization of the authorization of firms.

The aim of this paper is to establish the extent to which the Eighth Directive has improved *de jure* harmony of the rules for incorporated audit firms between UK and German law. It examines the development of Article 2 from the draft to the adopted version of the Directive, examines UK and German views voiced during this process and, as far as possible, identifies probable influences of these two Member States. It further examines the implementation of Article 2 into UK and German law and the reasoning behind the choices made in this process.

UK and German law were chosen as case studies for this paper for a number of connected reasons. The two countries represent opposing accounting traditions, as has been suggested by the classifications carried out, for example, by Mueller (1967, 1968), Nair and Frank (1980), Nobes (1983, 1984/1992), or through studies based on Hofstede's (1984) identification of cultural patterns such as Gray (1988), Perera (1989) and Perera and Mathews (1990).

The two countries are often quoted as representatives of the Anglo-Saxon (or Anglo-American) and the continental European accounting traditions (see Perera, 1989 – who in turn refers to Mueller, 1967, and to Nobes, 1983, 1984/1992); or as representatives of the micro- and the macro-uniform-based systems (Nobes, 1983). Further they are often referred to as examples of different degrees of influence by the accounting professions on accounting regulation, different degrees of the professions' self-regulation versus state regulation, and of differing emphases on 'professionalism' (see, for example, Perera, 1989). This is related to a further important difference, i.e. that the UK has a common law-based legal system, while that of Germany is based on codified Roman law (David and Brierley, 1978). This legal difference has, *inter alia*, a significant influence on each country's interpretation of the 'true and fair view' principle. Further, there are differences in sources of finance for enterprises and, related to this, the importance of capital markets. While in Germany finance has traditionally been provided by banks (both as equity owners and as lenders), in the UK large companies have placed more reliance on finance through 'external' shareholders.[1] This latter difference in particular has also led to a greater emphasis on audit and publication requirements in the UK (Nobes and Parker, 1995).

However, Vieten (1995) challenges, in particular, the distinction between statutory control in Germany on the one hand, and a strong profession in the UK on the other. He points out that the traditionally claimed dichotomy between the UK and German accounting systems may no longer hold true for the professional frameworks in that, due to European company law harmonization, a near convergence has been achieved mainly because 'By increasing the scope for government intervention Britain is moving closer to the German system . . .' (Vieten, 1995: 495). However, apart from the apparent trend towards a stronger influence by the state in the UK, Vieten highlights more differences than similarities, thereby indicating that the old categorizations are still at least partly valid. Vieten himself points out that '. . . the audit objective under German law is to test for accordance with the relevant legislation' (*ibid.*: 500), rather than mainly to give an opinion on the true and fair view. This appears to be one of the essential differences between UK and German auditing, and may well lie at the heart of or be symptomatic of the old distinctions.

Categorization attempts are, almost by definition, simplifications, and Vieten does succeed in making the reader aware that the categorization may be subject to change, that the boundaries of the dichotomy may well be shifting and that the classifications are not always clear-cut. However, similar issues with respect to recent changes and their effect on the 'classification by regulation' were raised by Nobes (1984/1992).[2]

REGULATION BEFORE IMPLEMENTATION OF ARTICLE 2 OF THE DIRECTIVE

UK

According to the Companies Act (CA) 1985 s.389(6), audit firms were not allowed to incorporate in the UK. This restriction dated from the 1928 Act and had been instigated by the Institute of Chartered Accountants in England and Wales (ICAEW):

> . . . on the grounds that only individual auditors were in a position to express a personal audit opinion and take full responsibility for that opinion. This in turn reflected the generally accepted view of the time that the partnership structure was the appropriate form of business organisation for professional men.
>
> (Department of Trade and Industry – DTI, 1986: 61)

Germany

Section 5 (paragraphs 27 to 36) of the *Wirtschaftsprüferordnung* (WPO – Regulation for Auditors) deals with firms of *Wirtschaftsprüfer* (WP – auditors). Paragraph 27 specified, and still specifies, what legal forms are allowed for firms of WP: *Aktiengesellschaft* (AG – approximately equivalent to a public limited company), *Kommanditgesellschaft auf Aktien* (KGaA – a public company with at least one personally liable member), *Gesellschaft mit beschränkter Haftung* (GmbH – private limited company), *offene Handelsgesellschaft* (OHG – a form of partnership) or *Kommanditgesellschaft* (KG – limited partnership).[3,4]

Before the implementation of the Eighth Directive, paragraph 28 of the WPO specified (*inter alia*) that:

- the members of the supervisory board and of the management and the personally liable *Gesellschafter*[5] must be WP;
- under certain conditions *vereidigte Buchprüfer* (vBP – 'sworn-in' auditors[6]), *Steuerberater* (StB – qualified tax advisors) or experts from other areas who are not WP may be permitted to become members of the supervisory board, of the management, or personally liable *Gesellschafter*; although the number of these persons may not exceed the number of WP in the above positions;
- for the AG and KGaA the shares must be registered and may be transferred only with the agreement of the firm; the latter also applies to the transfer of shares in a GmbH.[7]

There was no reference to share ownership or voting rights.

Paragraph 34 dealt (and still deals) with the withdrawal of the authorization of firms of auditors, where the conditions for approval are no longer met. In some circumstances (para. 34 (1)(2)) authorization may not be withdrawn if the firm meets the required conditions within a specified time span.

ARTICLE 2 AND ITS DEVELOPMENT

Article 2 of the Directive (see Appendix) outlines the rules for approval of persons or firms. Only approved persons shall carry out statutory audits. Natural persons, as well as firms, may be authorized by the authorities of the Member States. Natural persons would have to fulfil the detailed requirements of the Directive about the qualification of auditors. Firms would have to fulfil the following conditions:

- the natural persons carrying out audits on behalf of the firms would have to meet the requirements of the Directive about the qualification of auditors;
- natural persons or firms meeting these requirements must hold the majority of the firm's voting rights; and
- natural persons or firms meeting these requirements must make up the majority of the firm's administrative or management body (unless there are only two such members, in which case it is sufficient for one of the two to meet the requirements).

The Directive offers an exemption to the second of these conditions (extract from Art. 2 (1)(b)(ii)):

> However, those Member States which do not impose such majority at the time of the adoption of this Directive need not impose it provided that all the shares in a firm of auditors are registered and can be transferred only with the agreement of the firm of auditors and/or, where the Member State so provides, with the approval of the competent authority.

The Directive also provides that the Member States may allow the authoritative bodies governing auditing to be professional associations.

The 1978 Draft had been less comprehensive than this (see Appendix). It did not require that the majority of members of management and administrative bodies be made up of persons qualifying as auditors under the conditions of the Directive. The 1979 Draft dropped a clause which had qualified the majority ownership requirement by restricting it to companies formed after implementation of the Directive. However, an idea similar to this exemption, but going even further, was reintroduced in the final Directive (see quotation above).

There are provisions concerning the non-interference by persons who are not themselves qualified as auditors. However, these became far less detailed between the Drafts (see Article 2 (2)(a)) and the final version, and they were moved to Article 27 (in the section: 'Professional integrity and independence'). A provision dealing with confidentiality was also relaxed in the 1979 Draft to the effect that audit reports and documents were no longer required to be withheld from the knowledge of non-qualified persons in the firm; this provision was dropped in the final version. In addition, the final version (Article 2 (1)(b)(iii)) introduced the requirement for the management and administrative bodies of firms to consist of a majority of qualified auditors or firms. At the same time it introduced the escape clause quoted above concerning the firm's ownership.

It appears, therefore, from Article 2 in the final version that ownership, but not administration and management, may be in the hands of a majority of persons or firms not qualifying under the provisions of the Directive. However, this concession concerning ownership only applies to Member States which had not imposed this requirement regarding majority previously; in other Member States, ownership too would have to be in the hands of a majority of persons or firms meeting the requirements of the Directive.

POSSIBLE INFLUENCES ON THE DIRECTIVE

It is clear that the idea of incorporation of audit firms has continental rather than British antecedents, but that both German and UK views were, to some extent, accommodated by the re-drafting.

British views

The 1978 Draft's Article 2 proposed to offer the Member State option to allow audit firms to incorporate. There does not appear to have been any resistance to this from the UK government, presumably because it would have been desirable from a UK point of view to have as many options as possible. However, the option represented a major change for UK legislation, and it caused a mixed reaction from the profession. Bartholomew (1978: 334) sees the following difficulties with the Draft's requirement that Member States shall approve only 'natural persons who satisfy at least the conditions specified in the following Articles' to carry out statutory audits and which denies others not so qualified access to all documents relating to the audit:

- This might require the exclusion of partners in accounting firms who would not be auditors under the Directive's rules, but whose specialism (e.g. taxation) might be required for the completion of the audit. As can be seen from Table 2, this requirement was substantially weakened in the 1979 Draft and dropped in the final version.
- It might cause problems for (a) quality control reviews of international firms, if these reviews were carried out by personnel not qualified under the provisions of the Directive, and (b) audits of multinational companies involving such personnel.

Similar points (with reference to Article 2) were made in a letter and a memorandum by the Consultative Committee of Accounting Bodies (CCAB) to the Department of Trade (*Accountancy*, 1981).

German views

German legislation before the Directive allowed audit firms to be incorporated and would have met the requirements of Article 2 (albeit by taking advantage of the exemption clause with respect to voting rights) except for two points:

- The Directive required the majority of the members of administrative or management bodies to be qualified auditors under its rules, while the German law merely required that non-WP should *not exceed* the number of WP on the supervisory board, the management, or as personally liable *Gesellschafter*.
- Following from this, German law did not have (and did not require) any exemption for cases where the relevant bodies were made up of only two persons.

Niessen (1984) claims that, due to the differences in the Member States' legislation, the provisions concerning firms of auditors were very much contested during the negotiations. This led to a weakening of the provision concerning the majority of voting rights for the benefit of those Member

States for whom this rule would have been new. Niessen claims that, without this compromise, the finalization of the Directive would not have been possible.

Bartholomew (1978: 334) suggests that this exemption was introduced for the benefit of Germany, in order to prevent legal difficulties. Due to their historical development, the large German audit firms were often owned by banks or the State. Had Article 2 been implemented without the exemption, these owners would have been barred, which would have violated the German constitution and could have given cause to legal proceedings against the State. In the most bizarre case, the State (as majority owner of Treuarbeit AG) would have to have dispossessed itself.[8]

This suggested cause of the exemption is also supported by the following quote from Strobel (1984), which further highlights the German concern:

> The principle of the liberal profession in auditing is an obstacle for firms of auditors. If those circles which wanted to limit the Directive to a strictly liberal profession basis had succeeded, this would have meant the end of our large firms of auditors and thereby also of the concentration of audit firms. *Meanwhile,* inter alia *the German side of negotiations has achieved a solution* which leaves our concentration of audit firms untouched and *thereby also secures the existence of Treuarbeit AG, which is owned by the Federation and the Länder, as well as that of similar firms.*[9]
>
> (Strobel, 1984: 954 translation – emphases added)

It appears, however, that the latter part of Strobel's argument, i.e. the continued existence of state-owned firms (or others with a majority of outsider participation) is the more valid one. For example, English[10] experience has shown that the ban on firms being legal entities is no obstacle to a concentration of the firms.

The 'price' of the Directive's exemption clause in Article 2 (1)(b)(ii) (as discussed above, i.e. that the majority of voting rights need not be held by auditors fulfilling the Directive's conditions if '. . . all the shares in a firm of auditors are registered and can be transferred only with the agreement of the firm of auditors . . .') was no problem from a German point of view since this provision already existed.

Other German concerns included the following:

- A desire for a tightening of the provisions of Article 2 is apparent in the suggestions made by a body representing German accounting academics (von Wysocki, 1979). With respect to Article 2 (2)(a) of the draft (see Appendix), they recommended further regulation to ensure independent and unbiased audit work by firms in which outsiders have an interest. To achieve this, they suggest a strengthening of the technical/professional position of the supervisory board or the management.
- Lück (1979), also commenting on the Proposal, welcomed the provision preventing non-auditors from owning a majority of the share capital of firms of WP. However, he thought that the provisions did not go far

enough, since they did not appear sufficiently able to prevent inter-connections between firms of auditors and outsiders, even audit clients. He suggested that the Commission should reconsider the question of whether outsiders should be excluded from participation altogether.

- Another point of criticism is the wording of Article 2 (2)(a) (see Lück, 1979; and Wirtschaftsprüferkammer und Institut der Wirtschaftsprüfer in Deutschland e.V. (WPK and IdW – the Chamber of Auditors and the Institute of Auditors in Germany), 1979). With reference to the provisions concerning the assignment of audit staff, confidentiality and access to audit documents, Lück points out that there is a paradox in the regulations because the Directive allows management participation of non-auditors, but effectively prevents this through detailed rules which tie their hands. The WPK and IdW argue that, for specific issues, the auditor may need to rely on the expertise of non-auditors (who may belong to the audit firm's management). They therefore suggest a wording according to which the audit documents would not be withheld from non-auditors as long as these work for the firm of auditors and are subject to the same secrecy rules as the auditors.
- The body representing German accounting academics would have preferred ownership of new firms to be exclusively in the hands of auditors, although they acknowledge that the constitutional implications would have to be considered for existing firms (Sieben and von Wysocki, 1979).

Similar concerns were voiced in the UK with respect to the original restrictive wording of Article 2 (a), especially sub-paragraphs (1) and (3). The problems were addressed in the 1979 Draft and the provisions were considerably watered down in the final version (as discussed in the previous section). Although some German commentators suggested a tightening of the rules on participation of outsiders, the main German influence appears to have been the introduction of the exemption clause with respect to majority of ownership/voting rights (see above – e.g. Bartholomew, 1978; Strobel, 1984).

IMPLEMENTATION IN THE UK

Department of Trade and Industry (DTI) consultation

In 1986 the DTI published a consultative document inviting comments on both the implementation of the Eighth Directive and other issues which the necessary review of the legislation would give an opportunity to address. While it was felt that to comply with the minimum requirements of the Directive would require little change to legislation, the DTI also sought correspondents' views on such matters (partly related to the implementation of the Directive) as the incorporation of audit firms or the legislation on auditors' qualifications.

As mentioned above, according to the CA 1985, corporate entities could not be appointed as auditors. However, the DTI document suggests that, to some extent, the arguments made against incorporation had in recent years lost relevance. The DTI summarized the main arguments in favour of incorporation as follows:

- Incorporation would better enable audit firms to adopt management structures corresponding to their size and business diversity.
- Firms could more easily compete with companies in other industries in attracting specialist staff (e.g. by offering perks such as share ownership and by avoiding the conflict inherent in the requirement for all partners of accounting firms to be accountants – although the latter is, of course, an issue not necessarily linked to incorporation).
- Incorporation would have certain financial advantages, in particular with reference to raising capital.
- Incorporation would place firms on a similar footing to incorporated firms in other European countries. There might thus be advantages with respect to competition and rules on mutual recognition.
- Other financial services companies might be able to be authorized to audit if the companies met the legislation's minimum requirements. (This argument would of course not be congenial to accountants, since it would be against their interests to see the market or audit services opened to non-accountants.)
- There might be certain advantages with respect to limiting auditors' liability (in that, by forming a limited liability company, individuals would be protected against personal bankruptcy in cases of litigation).

The following arguments were made against incorporation:

- The partnership structure places responsibility on the individual partners and is therefore the most appropriate business form for accountants.
- Lack of personal liability, and the possibility of non-auditors as part-owners, would represent a risk to independence and integrity.
- Directors or employees of audit firms would have less incentive for 'adopting the highest professional standards' (DTI, 1986: 67) (presumably because they would not necessarily be the (only) owners of the business). The quality of service provided might be reduced.
- Outside ownership might negatively affect partners' commitment to the audit firm.

The document further sought views on any additional safeguards beyond the requirements of the Directive that might be adopted if incorporation was to be allowed. This could, in particular, address:

- the requirements of the Directive's Article 2 (presumably with reference to the provision that the majority of shareholders or members of the administrative or management bodies should be auditors[11]);
- any rules on integrity and independence over and above those applying to partnerships and sole practitioners (e.g. with respect to outside shareholders; for example, it was suggested that such shareholders should not be allowed to be audit clients or companies related to them);
- the requirement for indemnity insurance.

Response from firms

KPMG Peat Marwick McLintock (1987) was one of the UK audit firms expressing their views on incorporation. They did not object in principle to incorporation and did not perceive this to have a negative effect on the public interest, but objected to the idea of outside shareholders. Their objection was not based on concerns about auditor competence and the resulting quality of the audit, but rather on concerns about auditor independence and confidentiality. The most obvious problem, i.e. the audit client holding shares in the audit firm, had been addressed by the DTI. KPMG felt that the same person should not be allowed to hold a directorship with the auditor *and* his client.[12] They were further concerned about:

> situations where the outside interest in the corporate auditor also has a financial interest in a company being audited by the corporate auditor. These interests are not restricted to share interests but also include loans to that other company. We ... suggest that an interest as a commercial competitor, or as a potential predator, should also be regarded as an interest which could affect independence [*ibid.*: 4].

It was further felt that outside interests would raise public concern about confidentiality, even if this were addressed by rules on the security of confidential information.

As a further argument against outside interests, reference was made to developments in Germany (cf. 'Implementation in Germany', below):

> Germany, by contrast, is a leading international business country which has allowed audits to be carried out by corporate auditors, and previously with no restriction on the extent of outside interests ... in 1985 the German Government introduced a law which requires all new corporate auditors to be wholly owned by persons working in the business of the corporate auditor and with a majority of voting shares being held by qualifying interests. Further, for existing corporate auditors the law effectively requires that all further issues of shares, or sales of shares by outside interests, are to be qualifying interests or other internal interests.
> ...
> At a time when there is no indication of any relaxation of the independence environment in the international business world, and when a leading member of the Community, Germany, is taking steps to strengthen independence, we think it

Table 2 Views of large accounting firms on five incorporation issues (Source: *Accountancy Age*, 1988: 5)

Firm	1	2	3	4	5
Arthur Andersen	0%	49%	total ban	yes	yes
BDO Binder Hamlyn	49.9%	49.9%	49.9%	no	no
Clark Whitehill	25%	19.9%	total ban	yes	yes
Ernst & Whinney	49.9%	25%	25%	no	no
Hodgson Impey	25%	25%	25%	no	·no
Moores & Rowland	25%	49%	total ban	no	no
Neville Russell	49.9%	25%	total ban	no	yes
Peat Marwick McLintock	49.9%	25%	total ban	no	no
Robson Rhodes	49.9%	25%	allowed: no limit specified	no	no

1: Limit on voting shares for non-auditors in firm
2: Limit on percentage of shares allowed to outsiders
3: Limit on outsiders' voting rights
4: Ban on outsider-shareholder directors
5: Ban on outsider-shareholders influencing appointment of director

would be astonishing if the UK were to introduce legislation which could lead to a weakening of the independence environment [*ibid.*: 6].

However, KPMG's views,[13] in particular with respect to outside shareholders, were not totally shared by all the other large firms. Table 2 shows a summary of the views of a number of large firms.

The Law

The UK implemented the Eighth Directive through the Companies Act 1989. This resulted in few practical changes: its main impact appears to have been that more rules were laid down in legislation, instead of being left to the accounting profession. One of the more important changes was the removal of the prohibition for auditors to incorporate (with effect from 1 October 1991). Section 25 of the 1989 Act states that:

(1) a person is eligible for appointment as company auditor only if he –

  (a) is a member of a recognized supervisory body,[14] and
  (b) is eligible for the appointment under the rules of that body.

(2) An individual or a firm may be appointed as company auditor.
   . . .

'Firm' can refer to a partnership or to a body corporate. This effectively removes the old prohibition of CA 1985 s.389(6).

Part II of the Act's Schedule 11 lays down the following minimum rule for Recognized Supervisory Bodies (RSBs):

4. – (1) The body must have rules to the effect that a person is not eligible for appointment as company auditor unless –

 (a) in the case of an individual, he holds an appropriate qualification;
 (b) in the case of a firm –
   (i) the individuals responsible for company audit work on behalf of the firm hold an appropriate qualification, and
   (ii) the firm is controlled by qualified persons (. . .).

The profession's implementation

In May 1989 the Independence and Incorporation Committee of the three Chartered Institutes published a report summarizing the responses (by auditors, users and preparers of accounts) to a Consultative Document which they had issued (ICAEW, ICAS, ICAI, 1988b).[15] They recommended that:

- At least 75% of shareholders' voting rights in an incorporated audit firm should be held by auditors.
- At least 75% of the voting rights on the board of directors of an incorporated audit firm should be held by auditors.
- Restrictions imposed on the ownership and management of incorporated firms of auditors should also apply, with appropriate adjustments, to partnerships.
- Other restrictions imposed by professional guidance in order to safeguard independence should apply equally to partners in audit firms and to shareholders and directors of incorporated firms of auditors.

(ICAEW, 1989: 1)

The Institutes' report addresses the importance of independence, in particular in the UK's environment, which involves the exercise of professional judgement and the overriding importance of the true and fair view, rather than the '. . . mechanical compliance with detailed rules . . .' (ICAEW, ICAS, ICAI, 1989: 8). In this context it was pointed out that independence and integrity are mental attitudes which should be protected and developed by the ethos of the firms, and which cannot be assured through detailed rules or procedures relating to any one particular audit.

The independence and integrity of audit firms would be endangered, according to the Institutes, if ownership or control were in the hands of outsiders – this might lead to a greater emphasis on profit-orientation as opposed to independence and integrity. On the other hand, it was suggested that, for example, a 51% majority of ownership or management rights in the hands of auditors would not necessarily guarantee control. It was suggested that 5% or 10% outside ownership would be no threat. However, 30% would give a certain amount of influence to outsiders. This led the Institutes to suggest that a minimum of a 75% majority of voting rights should be owned,[16] and, on the board of directors, 75% of the voting rights should be held by auditors. No other restrictions on the holding of the minority interests were deemed necessary. The Institutes would not require the remaining 25% of shares or voting rights to be held by non-auditor *insiders* (i.e. persons working for the firm). The requirement relating to shares should relate to voting rights as well as to all share capital in aggregate. Further, restrictions should be imposed on group structures, in order to avoid dilution of control.

It was further suggested that outsiders and non-auditor insiders should be made subject to the rules of the Institutes. The Institutes would, in this respect, monitor and impose sanctions on the firms, which should satisfy the criterion of being 'fit and proper persons'.[17] The Institutes further suggested that '... the transfer of shares in an audit firm should be subject to approval by the Board'. This would require consideration of the rules for 'fit and proper persons' and thus prevent shares from being freely traded (*ibid.*: 11–12).[18]

Richards (1990) points out that the DTI considered the above suggestions to be going too far and to be detrimental to competition.[19] Similar concerns were voiced by Sir Gordon Borrie, the then Director General of Fair Trading, in a report addressed to the DTI (*CA Magazine*, 1991a). However, 'The profession's initial reaction to Sir Gordon's report has been one of slight bewilderment: the prospect of auditing firms being run by unqualified operators is not likely to silence critics of the present system' (*ibid.*: 60). The Institutes subsequently defended their position (and criticized that of the Director General) in a letter to the Corporate Affairs Minister in which the need for prevalence of auditor independence over competition considerations was stressed (*CA Magazine*, 1991b). However:

> After discussions with the DTI, the Institutes made modifications to peripheral ownership rules but these still did not persuade OFT director general Sir Gordon Borrie to change his mind. Corporate Affairs Minister John Redwood then used his powers under the 1989 Companies Act to overrule his objections.
>
> (*Accountancy*, 1991: 10)

It appears that, possibly due to the profession's self-imposed restrictions, there was no immediate interest in incorporation, in particular not from the large firms (*Accountancy*, 1989). A survey commissioned by Arthur Young showed a lack of interest in accounting firms by investors. This was partly blamed on accounting firms' traditional lack of disclosure (*Accountant's Magazine*, 1988: 5).

Summary for the UK

In summary, UK legislation implements only the minimum requirement of Article 2, which is that a firm of auditors must be controlled by qualified persons (where this is defined mainly with respect to voting rights). However, the Institutes felt that it would not be sufficient to safeguard auditor independence if control meant only a mere majority of voting rights. In their capacity as Recognized Supervisory Bodies they therefore implemented a requirement that at least 75% of voting rights should be held by qualified auditors. This also applies to voting rights on the management body. The

Association of Chartered Certified Accountants (ACCA) and the Association of Authorised Public Accountants (AAPA) only require the majority of voting rights to be held by qualified auditors; qualified auditors also need to hold only a majority of the voting rights on the management body.

IMPLEMENTATION IN GERMANY

The changes to paragraphs 28 and 34[20] of the WPO which were necessary to implement Article 2 of the Directive were introduced in the *Bilanzricht-liniengesetz* (BiRiLiG – Accounting Directives Law) of 1985. Paragraph 28 was changed as follows: the word 'exceed' was substituted with 'reach' (*erreichen*), i.e. it was established that WP must form at least a majority of the supervisory or management board members or personally liable *Gesellschafter*. Further, the following phrase was introduced: 'if the firm has only two supervisory board members, managers or personally liable *Gesellschafter*, then one of them must be a *Wirtschaftsprüfer*'.

A new sub-paragraph 4 was introduced into Paragraph 28, listing (*inter alia*) the following further conditions for the authorization of firms of auditors:

- only WP, firms of WP meeting the conditions of the sub-paragraph, or, provided they are employed by the firm, vBP, StB, *Steuerbevollmächt-igte* (StBv – a lower qualification of tax advisor), lawyers or other persons whose position as member of the supervisory or management bodies or as personally liable *Gesellschafter* has been specially authorized may be *Gesellschafter*;
- the shares in the firm may not be held on behalf of third parties;
- WP or firms of WP must hold the majority of the shares and the voting rights in the firm (this also applies to the capital/shareholding of the limited partners in a KG);
- the articles of association (or, respectively, the partnership contracts) must specify that only those *Gesellschafter* may exercise their specific rights (*Gesellschafterrechte*) who are WP.

For existing firms, the new rules would only apply in cases of sale or succession.

A report by three members of the *Bundestag* who were members of the drafting committee explains the reasoning behind the changes as follows:

A *Kapitalbindung* (a form of capital/financial tie) is introduced for firms of WP and vBP. The Legal Committee is of the opinion that the participation of outsiders in the profession can only be reconciled with the practising of a liberal profession with great difficulty. Even the authorisation of corporations to carry out these activities is questionable, because a legal person is placed between the auditor and his client. Thereby the responsibilities may become obscured and numerous dependencies may be established.[21]

(BD 10/4268: 93 translation)

The report further points out that, since 1931, when the profession began to be regulated, outsiders, in particular credit institutions, had been giving up their stakes in firms of WP. This was apparently due to the fact that outside ownership was not customary internationally, and also to growing doubts in Germany about auditor independence where firms were partly owned by outsiders.

On the other hand, a trend apparently began to emerge for medium-sized firms of WP to be founded by non-auditors, in particular by members of consulting professions who would like to be able to offer their clients the additional service of an audit. It appears that their motivation was two-fold: they would be able to influence the audit, and they would not lose the consultation fees to an audit firm providing both services. It was felt, therefore, that the legislator would have to take steps to prevent auditors from being gradually restricted to being employees of corporations partly owned by non-auditors, instead of continuing the independent tradition of the liberal professions.

This new legislation was felt to have far-reaching consequences. In particular, after 31 December 1987 it would be impossible for existing firms not fulfilling the new requirements to participate in the foundation of new firms (IdW, 1986).

In summary, Germany implemented changes going much further than Article 2 of the Eighth Directive and further than the UK implementation.

SUMMARY AND CONCLUSIONS

The above discussion has highlighted a number of issues symptomatic of the differing accounting and legal traditions in the UK and in Germany. In accordance with prior classifications (see 'Introduction', above), in the UK a self-regulating accounting and auditing profession and a common law legal system are apparent. These issues are linked to an emphasis on professional judgement and the principle of the true and fair view. In Germany, a more state-controlled, 'weaker' profession is apparent, as is a civil law-based legal system with greater emphasis on compliance with detailed rules, which also reflects on the audit (see above).

The review of the legislative changes brought about by the implementation of the Eighth Directive supports this distinction, in that the UK government effectively delegated the authority over the approval of auditors to the profession. Even at the level of the legislative changes, which implement only the minimum requirements of Article 2, the UK profession was heavily involved in the consultation process. Even more typical however is the fact that it *was* just the minimum requirements which were made law, while the profession laid down the more detailed and stricter rules, which went beyond the requirements of the Directive. The profession's desire to lay down stricter rules was linked to the importance placed on independence especially in an environment involving the exercise of professional judgement.

In Germany, however, in spite of some consultation of other parties, the legislative process, and thus the rule-making for auditors, was very much in the hands of the government. The stricter rules, going beyond the requirements of the Directive, were laid down in statute.

The second main issue illustrated here relates to the content of the detailed rules. The above discussion outlined the reversal of the attitudes and legal provisions concerning the incorporation of audit firms in the UK and in Germany. The attitude in the UK before the implementation of the Eighth Directive appeared to be that '... the partnership structure was the appropriate form of business organisation for professional men' (DTI, 1986: 61) and the idea of outside interests in an audit firm was met with concern. By contrast, in Germany, the majority of audit firms had chosen to organize themselves as corporate entities, and outside interests were allowed and fairly common. With the implementation of the Eighth Directive, the UK dropped the prohibition of incorporation and allowed outside interests – though after considerable debate and discussion of concerns voiced by the profession. German legislation, on the other hand, now prohibits shareholdings by outsiders in new firms. Although it could be argued that some degree of harmonization has been achieved in that both countries now permit incorporation, the legal situation regarding ownership of audit firms reflects a reversal of the original position.

Havermann (1993), with reference to the pre-Eighth Directive situation, comments on the astonishment of UK accountants when they were told that WP were allowed to organize themselves in corporations, in which outsiders were allowed to hold shares. He points out that, since then, the situation has started to turn into the reverse, i.e. while German law does not permit outsider-shareholdings in new firms of WP, UK law now allows both incorporation of audit firms and outsider-shareholdings. This raises the question of whether this shift implies a changing perception of auditors and audit in both countries, i.e. perhaps greater emphasis on commercialism in the UK, and greater emphasis on independence and 'professionalism' in Germany. It further raises the question of the extent to which the organizational culture of the international Big Six firms affects such changes.

Considering the reversal of the original position in the UK and Germany, Nordemann (1989) points out that it is questionable whether the Eighth Directive improved the situation in the way intended by the Commission.

This may be due to the fact that harmonization as proposed by the European Commission deals with convergence of detailed rules, but not with the underlying issues. While there are differing cultures and traditions with respect to the financing of companies, and thus also with respect to ownership structures, accountability and the role of the audit, it is not surprising that harmonization of the detailed rules will remain superficial.

In summary, if the UK and Germany had taken advantage of certain options allowed by Article 2, very little change would have been required to their rules on authorization of audit firms. However, triggered by the requirement to implement the Eighth Directive, both countries made choices in their implementations which, to an extent, reversed their original positions.

ACKNOWLEDGEMENTS

The authors are grateful for comments on earlier versions from John Dyson and Nicholas Grier (Napier University), Liesel Knorr (IASC), Brenda Porter (Cranfield University), and David Hatherly (University of Edinburgh). We are also grateful for helpful comments from two anonymous referees.

NOTES

1   Other symptoms of this difference are that there is a lower number of listed companies in Germany, that share capital is less distributed in Germany and that small investors are 'less important'. Because of these differences the German system tends to emphasize creditor protection while the UK system emphasizes shareholder protection. These differences in turn explain the relative importance given to the prudence principle on the one hand, and the true and fair view principle on the other hand.

2   Nobes (1992) also makes the point that apparent similarities may be either homologues (i.e. things derived from the same origin, but possibly different in appearance) or analogues (i.e. things often similar in appearance and serving similar purposes, but of different origins). He refers to David and Brierley (1978), who point out that for the classification of legal systems it is important not to be misled by superficial similarities. Nobes therefore suggests that one needs to look for homologues when classifying accounting systems.

3   Since 1995 it is also possible for WP to organize themselves in a different form of partnership, the *Partnerschaftsgesellschaft*.

4   Another research project currently undertaken by the authors suggests that determinants for the choice of legal form of audit firms in Germany are mainly organizational and legal considerations, taxation, liability considerations and publication requirements, but also historical factors (see also, for example, Havermann, 1993; Schruff, 1992; Markus, 1996).

5   The term '*Gesellschafter*' has not been translated because of its ambiguity: it can mean 'partner', e.g. a partner in a KG, or 'shareholder', as e.g. in a GmbH or AG. Here it refers to a partner in a KG. The equivalent English term would be 'member', but this would be confusing in this context.

6   A lower qualification than that of WP with lower entry requirements; entry to this branch of the profession had been closed since 1961 but it was revived with the implementation of the *Bilanzrichtliniengesetz* (BiRiLiG – Accounting Directives Law).

7   Teckemeyer (1986) suggests that, due to these provisions, further regulation about share-ownership in firms of WP had been considered unnecessary until the passing of the BiRiLiG.

8   We are grateful to Professor Dr Lothar Schruff (University of Göttingen) for pointing this out.
9   'Das prüferische Freiberuflerprinzip steht Prüfungsgesellschaften im Wege. Hätten jene Kreise obsiegt, die die Prüferrichtlinie auf eine strenge Freiberuflerschaft festlegen wollten, so hätte dies das Ende unserer großen Prüfungsgesellschaften und damit auch der Prüfungskonzentration bedeutet. *Indessen hat u.a. die deutsche Verhandlungsseite eine Lösung erziehlt*, die unsere Prüfungskonzentration unangetastet läßt und *dabei auch die Existenz der im Bundes- und Länderbesitz stehenden Treuarbeit AG sowie ähnlicher Gesellschaften sichert'* (emphases added). Vieten (1995: 508) defines 'liberal professions' (*freie Berufe*) as follows: ' "Free" occupation is a technical term in the German context, denoting a specifically state-sponsored profession, whose function is not to be regarded as a commercial activity.'
10   As opposed to Scottish law, under which partnerships are legal entities.
11   For example, the DTI intended to restrict the period (Art. 2 (1)) allowed for incorporated audit firms which ceased to comply with the requirements of Article 2 to correct the situation from the Directive's two years to three months.
12   'Nevertheless, we note, and welcome, the Department's proposal to introduce legislation prohibiting a corporate auditor from auditing a company in which it holds shares or which conversely, has an interest in the shares of the corporate auditor. We note the proposal that the prohibition might be extended to cases where the corporate auditor and a potential client have a common director, and in our view this would be essential' (KPMG-Peat Marwick McLintock, 1987: 3) The Government's proposals were *inter alia* published in *The Accountant's Magazine*, Feb. 1988: 16–17. It was clearly intended that a blanket prohibition as outlined above should be included in the legislation implementing the Eighth Directive. This would presumably have taken the form of a Statutory Instrument under section 27(2) of the Companies Act 1989. However, to date, no such Statutory Instrument appears to have been passed, and the above situations remain regulated under the professional bodies' Ethical Guides, which, as rules of the RSBs, have gained quasi-legal status.
13   KPMG's reported views in Table 2 appear to have been modified slightly since its 1987 publication. For a more detailed discussion of the firms' views on these and related issues see *Accountancy Age*, 1988: 5.
14   Recognized Supervisory Body is defined in the CA 1989 as

> . . . a body established in the United Kingdom (. . .) which maintains and enforces rules as to –
>
> (a) the eligibility of persons to seek appointment as company auditors, and
> (b) the conduct of company audit work,
>
> which are binding on seeking appointment or acting as company auditors either because they are members of that body or because they are otherwise subject to its control.

The four professional bodies whose members had been authorized to audit previously under the CA 1985, namely the ICAEW, the Institute of Chartered Accountants of Scotland (ICAS), the Institute of Chartered Accountants in Ireland (ICAI) and the Association of Chartered Certified Accountants (ACCA), gained recognition as RSBs, and were later joined by a fifth body, the Association of Authorised Public Accountants (AAPA).

15   This was preceded by an earlier report of the three Institutes' Working Party on Independence and Incorporation (ICAEW, ICAS, ICAI, 1988a), which had recommended, *inter alia*, that non-auditors employed by the firm should be allowed to hold up to 49% of shares while 'outsiders' should be allowed to hold only non-voting shares, and no more than 25% of all shares, and that they should not be allowed to appoint or influence the appointment of the firm's management. The recommendations of this publication were apparently a compromise, in particular with respect to outside shareholdings, which the English Institute would have preferred to outlaw (see *Accountancy*, 1988).

16   '75% control is also relevant to UK company law requirements on special and extraordinary resolutions, which are necessary for (i) alteration of the company's objects, (ii) alteration of the company's articles, (iii) reduction of the company's capital, and (iv) certain measures relating to a members' voluntary winding up of the company' (ICAEW, ICAS, ICAI, 1989: 10).

17   This implements the requirement of the Directive's Article 3 that auditors must be persons of 'good repute'.

18   The Institutes further supported the following suggestions:

● to apply the rules relating to incorporated businesses also to partnerships (this would in effect mean that up to 25% of the partners in a partnership could be outsiders);

● to apply the rules and percentages suggested to all firms; no exemptions would be permitted on grounds of size (with no use of the exemption permitted by the Directive's Article 2(1) (iii)); and

● to require additional disclosure for the register of auditors and firms: beneficial shareholders should be disclosed; a distinction should be made on the register between non-auditors and outsiders; and the shareholding held by each representative of these groups should be disclosed.

19   See also a further consultative document published by the DTI in December 1989, which addresses specifically this issue.

20   There was only a very small change to paragraph 34, concerning the time span allowed to correct certain situations in which the conditions for approval were no longer met.

21   'Es wird eine Kapitalbindung für Wirtschaftsprüfungs- und Buchprüfungs-gesellschaften eingeführt. Der Rechtsausschuß ist der Auffassung, daß die Beteiligung Berufsfremder an solchen Gesellschaften mit der Ausübung eines freien Berufs nur schwer vereinbar ist. Bereits die Zulassung von Kapital-gesellschaften für die Ausübung dieser Tätigkeiten ist bedenklich, weil eine juristische Person zwischen den Prüfer und seinen Mandanten gestellt wird. Die Verantwortlichkeiten können dadurch verwischt und zahlreiche Abhängigkeiten begründet werden.'

REFERENCES

Accountancy (1981) 'CCAB demands changes to Eighth Directive on auditors', February: 6.

Accountancy (1988) 'Compromise reached, debate goes on', March: 5.

Accountancy (1989) 'Few takers for "important freedoms"?', September: 9.

Accountancy (1991) 'RSBs at the ready', September: 10.

Accountancy Age (1988) '. . . still divided over incorporation', 20 October: 5.

The Accountant's Magazine (1988) 'Safeguarding auditors' independence', March: 5.

Bartholomew, E. G. (1978) 'The EEC and auditors' qualifications', *Accountant's Magazine*, August: 333-5.

CA Magazine (1991a) 'Auditing rules attacked by Borrie', May: 60.

CA Magazine (1991b) 'Audit regulations report challenged', July: 59–60.

Clayton, M. (1984) 'Eighth Directive: the UK's successful bargain', *Accountancy*, April: 16–17.

Council of the European Communities (1978) 'Proposal for an Eighth Directive . . .', *Official Journal of the European Communities* No. C 112, 13.5.1978: 6–10.

Council of the European Communities (1979) 'Amended Proposal for an Eighth Directive . . .', *Official Journal of the European Communities* No. C 317, 18.12.1979: 6–15.

Council of the European Communities (1984) 'Eighth Council Directive', 84/253/EEC, *Official Journal of the European Communities* No. L 126, 12.5.1984: 20–6.

David, R. and Brierley, J. E. C. (1978) *Major Legal Systems in the World Today*. London: Stevens.

Department of Trade and Industry (1986) *Regulation of Auditors. Implementation of the EC Eighth Company Law Directive. A Consultative Document.*

Department of Trade and Industry (1989) *Ownership and Control of Firms of Auditors under the Companies Act 1989. A Consultative Document by the Department of Trade and Industry.*

Deutscher Bundestag (1985a) *Bundestags-Drucksache BD 10/3440*. Bonn: Verlag Dr. Hans Heger.

Deutscher Bundestag (1985b) *Bundestags-Drucksache BD 10/4268*. Bonn: Verlag Dr. Hans Heger.

Gray, S. J. (1988) 'Towards a theory of cultural influence on the development of accounting systems internationally', *Abacus*, 24(1): 1–15.

Havermann, H. (1993) 'Die Wirtschaftsprüfungsgesellschaft – Struktur und Strategie eines modernen Dienstleistungsunternehmens', in Baetge, J. (ed.) *Rechnungslegung und Prüfung – Perspektiven für die neunziger Jahre*. Düsseldorf: IdW-Verlag, pp. 41–59.

Hofstede, G. (1984) *Culture's Consequences, International Differences in Work-related Values*, abridged edition. Beverly Hills: Sage Publications.

Institut der Wirtschaftsprüfer e.V. (1986) *Wirtschaftsprüferhandbuch*. Düsseldorf: IdW-Verlag.

Institute of Chartered Accountants in England and Wales (1989) *The Companies Bill: Part II*. News Release.

Institute of Chartered Accountants in England and Wales, Institute of Chartered Accountants of Scotland, Institute of Chartered Accountants in Ireland (1988a) *Report of the Working Party on Independence and Incorporation*. February.

Institute of Chartered Accountants in England and Wales, Institute of Chartered Accountants of Scotland, Institute of Chartered Accountants in Ireland (1988b) *Independence and Incorporation. A Consultative Document*. October.

Institute of Chartered Accountants in England and Wales, Institute of Chartered Accountants of Scotland, Institute of Chartered Accountants in Ireland (1989) *Report of the Independence and Incorporation Committee*. May.

KPMG Peat Marwick McLintock (1987) *Independence and Incorporation of Auditors. Submission by Peat Marwick McLintock*. October 1987.

Lück, W. (1979) 'Zur Harmonisierung nationaler Rechtsvorschriften bei der Zulassung als Abschlußprüfer in der EG. Analyse des Vorschlags einer 8. EG-Richtlinie', *Der Betrieb*, 7: 317–24.

Markus, H. B. (1996) *Der Wirtschaftsprüfer. Entstehung und Entwicklung des Berufes im nationalen und internationalen Bereich.* München: Verlag C. H. Beck.

Mueller, G. G. (1967) *International Accounting.* New York: Macmillan.

Mueller, G. G. (1968) 'Accounting principles generally accepted in the United States versus those generally accepted elsewhere', *International Journal of Accounting Education and Research*, 3(2): 91–103.

Nair, R. D. and Frank, W. G. (1980) 'The impact of disclosure and measurement practices on international accounting classifications', *Accounting Review*, LV(3): 426–50.

Niessen, H. (1984) 'Die Regelung der Europäischen Gemeinschaft über die Zulassung der Abschlußprüfer als Teil der Koordinierung des Gesellschaftsrechts', *Die Wirtschaftsprüfung*, 15/16: 408–12.

Nobes, C. (1983) 'A judgemental international classification of financial reporting practices', *Journal of Business Finance and Accounting*, 10(1): 1–19.

Nobes, C. (1984/1992) *International Classification of Financial Reporting*, first and second editions. London: Routledge.

Nobes, C. and Parker, R. (1995) *Comparative International Accounting*, fourth edition. Hemel Hempstead: Prentice-Hall.

Nordemann, H. H. J. (1989) 'Der Europäische Wirtschaftsprüfer – Mythos oder Realität?', *Die Wirtschaftsprüfung*, 23/24: 671–9.

Perera, M. H. B. (1989) 'Towards a framework to analyse the impact of culture on accounting', *International Journal of Accounting*, 24: 42–56.

Perera, M. H. B. and Mathews, M. R. (1990) 'The cultural relativity of accounting and international patterns of social accounting', *Advances in International Accounting*, 3: 215–51.

Richards, H. (1990) 'Auditors and supervision', *Accountant's Magazine*, April: 40–1.

Schruff, L. (1992) 'Wirtschaftsprüfer, Formen der Berufsausübung', in Coenenberg, A. G. and Wysocki, K. (eds) *Handwörterbuch der Revision.* Stuttgart: C. E. Poeschel Verlag, pp. 2190–9.

Sieben, G. and von Wysocki, K. (1979) 'Empfehlungen zum Vorschlag einer 8. EG-Richtlinie der Kommission Rechnungswesen im Verband der Hochschullehrer für Betriebswirtschaft e.V.', *Betriebswirtschaftliche Forschung und Praxis*, 5: 423–33.

Strobel, W. (1984) 'Die neue EG-Prüferrichtlinie und ihre berufsständische Bedeutung', *Der Betriebs-Berater*, 15: 951–61.

Teckemeyer, H. (1986) 'Wirtschaftsprüfer-Examen, vereidigte Buchprüfer-Examen, Anerkennung von Wirtschaftsprüfungsgesellschaften – gestern und heute', *Die Wirtschaftsprüfung*, 23: 650–9.

Van Hulle, K. (1992) 'Wirtschaftsprüfung, EG', in *Handwörterbuch der Revision*, second edition. Stuttgart: C. E. Poeschel Verlag, columns 2225–34.

Vieten, H. (1995) 'Auditing in Britain and Germany compared: professions, knowledge and the state', *European Accounting Review*, 4(3): 485–511.

von Wysocki, K. (1979) 'Zur endgültigen Fassung der 7. und 8. EG-Richtlinie. Vorschläge der Kommission Rechnungswesen im Verband der Hochschullehrer für Betriebswirtschaft e.V.', *Der Betrieb*, 31: 1472–3.

Wirtschaftsprüferkammer (ed.) (1994) *Gesetz über eine Berufsordnung der Wirtschaftsprüfer (Wirtschaftsprüferordnung)*. Düsseldorf: IdW-Verlag.

Wirtschaftsprüferkammer und Institut der Wirtschaftsprüfer in Deutschland e.V. (1979) 'Zum Vorschlag einer 8. EG-Richtlinie über die Zulassung der mit der Pflichtprüfung des Jahresabschlusses von Kapitalgesellschaften beauftragten Personen. Stellungnahme der Wirtschaftsprüferkammer und des Instituts der Wirtschaftsprüfer in Deutschland e.V.', *Der Betrieb*, 29: 1378–82.

APPENDIX: ARTICLE 2, EIGHTH DIRECTIVE

Art.	1978 Draft	1979 Draft	Art.	Final Version
	Member States shall approve to carry out statutory audits of the annual accounts of the companies referred to in Article 1 only:	unchanged	1	Statutory audits of the documents referred to in Article 1 (1) shall be carried out only by approved persons. The authorities of the Member States may approve only:
1	natural persons who satisfy at least the conditions specified in the following Articles;	unchanged	1(a)	natural persons who satisfy at least the conditions laid down in Articles 3 to 19;
2	legal persons or other types of professional companies or associations which satisfy the following conditions:	unchanged	1(b)	firms of auditors which satisfy at least the following conditions:
2(a)	The partners, members, persons responsible for the management, administration, direction or supervision of such professional companies or associations who do not personally fulfil the conditions laid down in this Directive shall exercise no influence over the statutory audits carried out under the auspices of such approved professional companies or associations.	unchanged	27	Member States shall ensure that at least the members and shareholders of approved firms of auditors and the members of the administrative, management and supervisory bodies of such firms who do not personally satisfy the conditions laid down in Articles 3 to 19 in a particular Member State do not intervene in the execution of audits in any way which jeopardizes the independence of the natural persons auditing the documents referred to in Article 1 (1) on behalf of such firms of auditors.

Art.	1978 Draft	1979 Draft	Art.	Final Version
	The law shall, in particular, ensure:	The law shall, in particular, ensure:		
-	that the abovementioned persons may not participate in the appointment or removal of auditors and that they may not issue to the latter any instruction regarding the carrying out of audits;	that the above-mentioned persons may not intervene in the choice of natural persons acting as auditors on behalf of the company or association and that they may not issue to the latter any instruction regarding the carrying out of audits;		
-	that such persons shall not hold a majority of the capital of such professional companies or associations constituted after the entry into force of measures implementing this Directive and that they may not thereafter increase their holding so as to obtain a majority of the capital of existing professional companies or associations;	that such persons do not hold a majority of the capital or voting rights of such professional companies or associations;	1(b) (ii)	a majority of the voting rights must be held by natural persons or firms of auditors who satisfy at least the conditions imposed in Articles 3 to 19 with the exception of Article 11 (1) (b); the Member States may provide that such natural persons or firms of auditors must also be approved. However, those Member States which do not impose such majority at the time of the adoption of this Directive need not impose it provided that all the shares in a firm of auditors are registered and can be transferred only with the agreement of the firm of auditors and/or, where the Member State so provides, with the approval of the competent authority;
	[no equivalent]	[no equivalent]	1(b) (iii)	a majority of the members of the administrative or management body of a firm of auditors must be natural persons or firms of auditors who satisfy at least the conditions imposed in Articles 3 to 19; the Member States may provide that such

Art.	1978 Draft	1979 Draft	Art.	Final Version
				natural persons or firms of auditors must also be approved. Where such body has no more than two members, one of those members must satisfy at least those conditions.
-	that the confidentiality of audit reports produced by the auditors and all documents relating thereto is protected and that these are withheld from knowledge of the abovementioned persons.	that the confidentiality of audit reports and all documents relating thereto is protected.		[no equivalent]
(b)	The natural persons who are responsible for the audit and certification of annual accounts carried out under the auspices of the professional company or association in the Member State in which approval is sought, shall satisfy at least the conditions specified in the following Articles.	unchanged	1(b) (i)	the natural persons who carry out statutory audits of the documents referred to in Article 1 on behalf of firms of auditors must satisfy at least the conditions imposed in Articles 3 to 19; the Member States may provide that such natural persons must also be approved;
	[no equivalent]	[no equivalent]	1(b)	Without prejudice to Article 14 (2), the approval of a firm of auditors must be withdrawn when any of the conditions imposed in (b) is no longer fulfilled. The Member State may, however, provide for a period of grace of not more than two years for the purpose of meeting the requirements imposed in (b) (ii) and (iii).
	[no equivalent]	[no equivalent]	2	For the purposes of this Directive, the authorities of the Member States may be professional associations provided that they are authorized by national law to grant approval as defined in this Directive.

PART V

IASC HARMONIZATION

British Accounting Review (1990) **22**, 41–49

COMPLIANCE BY US CORPORATIONS WITH IASC STANDARDS

CHRISTOPHER W. NOBES*

University of Reading

This note examines the direct effects of IASC standards on listed US corporations. Three areas of disclosure are identified where there are IASC requirements but no US GAAP. In each case, compliance by a sample of companies is found to be significantly less than 50%. There is evidence that any compliance is co-incidental. There seems to be no effect of a listing on the London Stock Exchange.

INTRODUCTION

The success of the International Accounting Standards Committee (IASC) has been examined from a variety of angles. In particular, Tay & Parker (1990) distinguish between *de jure* international harmonisation (that of rules, standards, etc.) and *de facto* harmonisation (that of corporate financial reporting practices). Nair & Frank (1981) look at *de jure* harmonisation between 1973 and 1979. They arrive at no stronger a conclusion than that 'the period of the IASC's existence has coincided with a growing harmonization of accounting standards'. Evans & Taylor (1982) find little *de facto* compliance with IASC standards in a small sample of ten companies from each of five countries. However, in addition to the problem of having a very small sample, they do not separate out the IASC's direct effects on *companies* as opposed to its effects through changes to domestic *standards*. Doupnik & Taylor (1985) purport to 'examine the extent to which countries of Western Europe are conforming to . . . IASC standards . . .' (p. 32). However, they confuse *de jure* and *de facto* elements and they use doubtful data (Nobes, 1987). McKinnon & Jannell (1984), on *de jure* harmonisation, conclude that 'the IASC has not succeeded in changing existing standards or setting new standards'. Nobes (1985) seeks to define 'success' in the context of the work of the IASC, and suggests places where it might be found. Success by the IASC might be looked for in the nine following areas.

1. *De jure* effects in countries:
   (a) congenial to the IASC (e.g. English-speaking countries);

* The author gratefully acknowledges a grant from the Institute of Chartered Accountants in England and Wales to support this research. He also acknowledges useful comments from participants in a seminar at the University of Washington.

Address for correspondence: Prof. C. W. Nobes, Department of Economics, Faculty of Letters & Social Sciences, University of Reading, PO Box 218, Whiteknights, Reading RG6 2AA.

0890–8939/90/010041+09 $03.00/0

42   C. W. NOBES

    (b) uncongenial to the IASC (e.g. West Germany, where rules are
        numerous but essentially unlike Anglo–American rules);
    (c) where there were, or are, few rules (e.g. developing countries
        like Nigeria or Malaysia).
  2. *De facto* effects that result from *de jure* effects in countries (a), (b) or
(c) above,
  3. *De facto* effects directly on *companies* in countries (a), (b) or (c).

Clearly, it is not possible for one paper to address all these areas; and
other papers have already addressed some. This note is designed to add to
the overall evidence by looking at effects in area 3(a). Presumably, the
IASC expects there to be effects at level 3, otherwise its standards might
as well be addressed to standard setters only.

Of the companies examined here, SEC enforcement is obviously the
power behind GAAP. The reasons for any direct compliance with IASs
(where these are different from GAAP) are not so clear, but are briefly
addressed later.

SEEKING A TEST

Because US GAAP is generally more detailed than IASC Standards in any
particular area, the issue of whether IASC Standards are *mandatory* in the
US has not been important on most issues. The IASC originally hoped
for mandatory status. However, now even the revised Preface (IASC,
1983) to the IASs calls only for companies that *observe* the standards to
disclose this fact. Nevertheless, for a US company that is obeying GAAP,
it is very difficult for it not to comply with IASC standards. The only
way of testing for direct compliance is to identify small differences of
content, or timing of implementation between GAAP and IASC
standards. The areas chosen (see Table 1) are those *where there is no GAAP*,
so that it is possible to observe whether companies follow IASC standards
when they do not have to but are easily able to do so. The areas chosen here
are aspects of major accounting issues (depreciation and consolidation), and

TABLE 1

Some differences between IASs and US GAAP

  (i)   IAS 3's requirement to show minority interests separately in consolidated balance
       sheets.
 (ii)   IAS 4's requirement to show lives of depreciable assets, and rates of depreciation.
(iii)   IAS 22's requirements to disclose the amounts of assets transferred in poolings, the
       percentages of voting shares involved, and the effective date of pooling.

they represent arguably the most important matters which are capable of being tested because of differential GAAP/IASC requirements.

A survey was conducted of the 1985 Annual Reports of 200 randomly chosen listed corporations[1] (representing approximately 16% of the total NYSE and AMEX listings). The asset life and minority interest questions (see Table 1) were investigated for this sample. For poolings, a different selection method was necessary because of their infrequency (see below).

The hypotheses to be tested are the following:

H1. Most listed US companies do not comply with IASs where their requirements are not covered by GAAP.

H2. IASs have no direct impact on the financial reporting of listed US companies. This is a more vague hypothesis which cannot be formally tested.

MOTIVATION FOR COMPLIANCE

This note is designed to examine the effects of the IASC in only one area, so it does not attempt to examine in detail all the direct and indirect costs of the IASC. Neither is the purpose of this paper to establish a theory relating to the causes of compliance with standards. Nevertheless, a word on the motivation of companies may be suitable.

The *costs* of complying with the disclosure requirements listed in Table 1 are small. The information will be known to the accountors, and it would take up a small space in an annual report. It is hard to see that competitors would gain from the disclosures. The benefits from complying might be that the company signals its willingness to be open; it could state (as a few US corporations do, e.g. General Electric) that it is volunteering to obey a set of internationally agreed rules. The motivation for this might be strongest for those companies that seek to raise finance internationally. Hence, in a later section of this paper, there is an analysis of the effect of a listing on the London Stock Exchange.

A residual explanation for non–compliance may be that companies feel that there are sufficient SEC and FASB rules so that they do not wish to volunteer for any more. It may also be the case that, unless the SEC, FASB or their auditors point out the existence of IASs, directors may be unaware of them.

THE TEST

The three areas identified for testing above and in Table 1 are now examined.

44   C. W. NOBES

(a) *Minority interests*

Promulgated GAAP does not extend as far as rules on the disclosure of minority interests in financial statements. This may be partly due to the controversy over the nature of minority interests; for example, it depends on whether one takes a parent or entity view of consolidation. However, IAS 3 is clear that:

> The minority interest in the equity of consolidated companies should be classified in the consolidated balance sheet as a separate item and should not be shown as part of shareholders' equity. The minority interest in the profits or losses of such companies should be shown separately in the consolidated income statement. (para. 43)

In order to investigate the effects of IAS 3 on US companies, the following steps were necessary and are examined below:

(i) Do companies disclose minorities in both financial statements? (If so, they comply with IAS 3.)

(ii) In companies that do not, is it clear whether they have any significant minorities?

(iii) For unclear cases, a questionnaire survey of financial controllers is necessary to discover whether minorities exist.

(iv) Were the full disclosers already disclosing before IAS 3?

For the 200 US annual reports discussed above, disclosure of minority interests was as shown in Table 2. Part (a) shows the numbers of companies reporting various types of subsidiary relationships; part (b) combines the data in order to show the percentages of companies with and without minorities: 43% clearly had no minority interests, 16·5% clearly had minorities, and 40·5% of cases were unclear from the annual reports. A questionnaire survey of this latter 40·5% (i.e. 81 companies) (with a 51% response rate) suggested that 66% of these unclear cases had 'no minorities', 19% had 'no significant minorities', and 15% (i.e. 12 companies out of the 81) did have significant minorities. In conclusion, only 15 companies (see Table 2a) disclosed minorities in both financial statements out of an estimated 45 (i.e. 28+5+12) that had significant minorities. This is 33·3% compliance (significantly less than 50% compliance, at the 95% level of confidence).

It is obvious that immateriality cannot be used as an explanation for non-disclosure. The surveyed companies included in the 45 above had admitted 'significance', and all the 13 companies who disclosed in only *one* financial statement (see Table 2a) are unlikely to have thought that immateriality only applied to one statement. It seems fair to conclude that there is noticeable non-compliance with IAS 3.

The next step was to look at those 15 companies that did produce financial statements in conformity with IAS 3 to see if they were 'con-

TABLE 2

Existence and disclosure of minority interests, 1985

	Number	Both statements	Balance sheet only	Income statement only
(a)				
No subsidiaries	8			
'Wholly owned'	78			
'Subsidiaries'	71			
'Majority owned'	10			
Obvious minority*	5			
Minority disclosed	28	15	12	1
Total	200			

(b)	% of Companies in (a)
No minorities	43·0
Unclear	40·5
Minorities	16·5
	100·0

* Existence of minority is clear from various comments in notes.

forming' *before* IAS 3 was introduced. For this purpose, the 1976 annual reports of these 15 companies were examined. Table 3 shows that 47% of the companies were already fully disclosing minorities in 1976, and that *all* the others had good reasons for not doing so (i.e., they were not SEC-registered, they had no subsidiaries or no minorities). Thus, it appears that no company began to disclose minorities as a result of IAS 3. Companies are presumably following well-established textbook practice and the preferences of their auditors, rather than consciously complying with IAS 3.

TABLE 3

Status in 1976 of companies fully disclosing by 1985

Type of Company	%
Not SEC-registered	13
No subsidiaries	13
No minorities	27
Already fully disclosing	47
Total	100

46   C. W. NOBES

TABLE 4

Disclosure of asset lives by US corporations

Statement that 'useful lives' were used	117
Maxima disclosed	1
Ranges of lives by asset types	78
Details disclosed	4
Total	200

(b) Asset lives
Promulgated US GAAP does not require the disclosure of asset lives or
rates of depreciation, whereas IAS 4 requires that:

> the following should be disclosed for each major class of depreciable asset. . . .
> (b) the useful lives or the depreciation rates used . . . (para. 18).

For a 'class' of assets, the best that can be expected is a range of lives or
rates. In nearly all cases, the details provided were given in terms of lives
not rates. Table 4 shows the disclosures for the 200 corporations. The
majority of sample corporations (59%) gave no details of asset lives, usually
mentioning only that 'useful lives' were used. The rest provided details,
mostly ranges of lives by class of asset. This is significantly higher than
50% non-compliance, at the 95% level of confidence.

Clearly, there is majority non-compliance with IAS 4. The explanation
for the disclosures by the minority may be auditor pressure. For example,
some firms of auditors may include this disclosure as standard, as proposed
by some State CPA Societies.[2]

(c) Poolings
As Table 1 records, the disclosure requirements of IAS 22 go beyond those
of US GAAP. The IAS requires disclosure in the first financial statements
following the combination, of:

> para. 50: (b) . . . effective date of the combination for accounting purposes;
> para. 52: (a) . . . the percentage of each enterprise's voting shares exchanged to effect
> the combination;
> (b) . . . amounts of assets and liabilities contributed by each enterprise.

IAS 22 applies to business combinations effected on or after 1 January
1985. As a test of compliance, examination of 1985 year-end financial
statements was undertaken. To see whether any apparent compliance
might be due to other factors, 1983 and 1984 statements were also examined.

Given the relative scarcity of cases of pooling in any one year, it
seemed unsuitable to conduct a random sample of annual reports. Instead,

information was obtained from- the authors of *Accounting Trends and Techniques* as to the identity of the pooling companies in their survey of 600 companies for 1983, 1984 and 1985 year-ends (AICPA, 1984; 1985; 1986). This yielded a population of 61 annual reports of listed companies, all of which were examined. In some cases, a company appeared in the population in more than one year.

Table 5 shows the disclosures for 1983/4 and 1985. Using the order of additional disclosures described above the following can be noted.

(i) The effective date was disclosed in 50% of 1985 reports and 75% of 1983/84 reports.

(ii) The percentage of *issuer's* shares was not directly disclosed in any case, but the number of shares was disclosed in all cases, enabling a percentage calculation. The percentage of the *investee* bought was disclosed in those cases where 'all shares' was mentioned: 38% of 1985 reports and 51% of 1983/84 reports.

(iii) The amount of assets and liabilities contributed was not disclosed in any year by any company.

In summary, of the three disclosures, there was 50%, minority and zero 'compliance', respectively, in 1985 annual reports. Further, 'compliance' *fell* in this year for which IAS 22 first applied. This strongly suggests that IAS 22 had no positive effect on poolers. (It should be remembered that this is not a random sample, but represents *all* the poolers in the 600 companies.)

TABLE 5

Disclosure by poolers

	1983	1984	1983/84 (%)	1985	1985 (%)
No data	8	3	24	6	37
Date of pooling only	4	7	24	4	25
Statement only that 'all' shares bought	–	–	–	2	13
Date and 'all'	8	11	42	4	25
Date, 'all' and ratio	3	1	9	–	–
Total	23*	22†	99	16‡	100

* In *Accounting Trends and Techniques* (ATT), there was also one OTC company, one company where the existence of pooling was unclear, and one company recorded twice. These were excluded.

† In ATT there was also one OTC company. This was excluded.

‡ In ATT there were also four OTC companies, two cases where the existence of pooling was unclear, and one company recorded twice. These were excluded.

TABLE 6

Relevance of London listing

	Some disclosure		No disclosure	
	No.	Listed	No.	Listed
Minority interests (from Table 2)	15	7%	?*	?*
Depreciation (from Table 4)	83	2%	117	4%
Poolings [(from Table 5), all years]	44	7%	17	18%

*A percentage for non-disclosure is not clear, because the exact companies that have minorities is unclear.

LONDON STOCK EXCHANGE

One explanation for such compliance as there is might be international finance-raising by US corporations. The most obvious form of such finance-raising is a listing on the London Stock Exchange. For this purpose, US corporations do not have to follow UK Standards, but do they tend to follow IASs if they are listed on London?

The evidence here relates to the three topics of investigation earlier in the paper. The number of disclosing and non-disclosing companies and the proportions of them that are listed on London is shown in Table 6. For each of the three topics, the proportion for disclosing companies is less than 10%. For the two topics where the non-disclosing proportion is clear (depreciation and poolings), the percentage of companies that are listed on London is actually *larger* among the non-disclosers, although the differences involve very small numbers of companies. In conclusion, there is no evidence that a London listing is an explanation for 'compliance' by US corporations with IASC disclosure requirements.

CONCLUSION

This paper seeks to identify one aspect of the potential effects of IASC standards on listed US corporations: direct compliance. The only way to test for direct compliance is by identifying areas of *difference* between GAAP (which must be obeyed by the companies surveyed here) and IASs. These testable areas of difference (where there is no GAAP) are fairly few, but three of the most important are examined here. There are three types of disclosures required by IASs, but not by GAAP; and they are reported on in Tables 2, 4 and 5.

For minority interest disclosures, compliance was 33.3%. However, in *no* case did a company clearly move towards compliance since the introduction of the international standard. For depreciation disclosures, compliance was only 41%. For minority and depreciation disclosures, which were based on samples of 200 companies (about 16% of listed companies), non-compliance was significantly higher than 50%, at the 95% level of confidence. For pooling disclosures, compliance was 50%, 38% and 0% for the three requirements; compliance actually *fell* on the introduction of the IAS. For poolings, *all* examples in three years of the AICPA's survey were examined.

The strong suggestion from this evidence is that H1 (differential requirements of IASs are not obeyed by most listed companies) can be accepted. Also, there is sufficient evidence to be fairly confident about accepting the informal H2 (IASs have no direct impact). This implies that any apparent 'compliance' is the result of other factors, such as pressure from auditors or users of financial statements. One factor that seems not to explain compliance is a listing on the London Stock Exchange.

The evidence here does not suggest that the IASC has no influence or importance, but that one would have to look elsewhere than at direct compliance by US corporations.

Notes

1. From microfiche of Q-Data Corporation, NYSE/AMEX stocks. Regulated companies and real estate companies were excluded.
2. See, e.g. *Guide to Financial Statements*, Washington Society of CPAs (1979).

References

AICPA, 1984–86. *Accounting Trends and Techniques*, AICPA.

Doupnik, S. & Taylor, M. E. (1985). 'An empirical investigation of the observance of IASC standards in Western Europe', *Management International Review*, Vol. 1, pp. 27–33.

Evans, T. G. & Taylor, M. E. (1982). 'Bottom line compliance with the IASC: A comparative analysis', *International Journal of Accounting*, Fall, pp. 115–128.

IASC (1983). *Preface to International Standards*, IASC.

McKinnon, S. M. & Jannell, P. (1984). 'The International Accounting Standards Committee: A performance evaluation', *International Journal of Accounting*, Spring, pp. 19–34.

Nair, R. D. & Frank, W. G. (1981). 'The harmonization of international accounting standards', *International Journal of Accounting*, Fall, pp. 61–77.

Nobes, C. W. (1985). 'Is the IASC successful?', *Accountant*, August, pp. 20–21.

Nobes, C. W. (1987). 'An empirical investigation of the observance of IASC standards in Western Europe: A comment', *Management International Review*, Vol. 4, pp. 78–79.

Tay, J. S. W. & Parker, R. H. (1990). 'Measuring harmonisation and standardisation', *Abacus*, March.

Washington Society of CPAs. (1974). *Guide to Financial Statements*, p. 25.

Dates: Received 1 December 1988; final version received 19 May 1989.

*C. W. Nobes**

An Empirical Investigation of the Observance of IASC Standards in Western Europe: A Comment

Doupnik and Taylor (1985) purport to examine compliance with IASC standards over time and across regions. For data on practices in 1979 they rely on a Price Waterhouse survey; for 1983 they conducted their own questionnaire to Price Waterhouse offices, receiving 50 country responses. Their conclusions are not credible in some respects, particularly because they do not recognise the limitations of the data.

It has been pointed out that Price Waterhouse data are unreliable and unsuitable for classification purposes (Nobes, 1981). It is also unsuitable for the purposes of Doupnik and Taylor, who perpetuate the problems in their own questionnaire. For example, the response category "Required – application ... is required by a pronouncement of a professional accountancy body or by law" is highly misleading. To take one instance, the 1979 data shows that only

France had a score of 4.00 in 1979, indicating full compliance with the 53 propositions ... There are no countries exhibiting full compliance in 1983.

This apparent full compliance rests on the 1979 Survey giving scores of "required" for France on the basis that IASC standards had been issued in France. However, French law, French standards and French companies did not fully comply with IASC standards in 1979. As just one example of this, data from the Commission des Opérations de Bourse (1980) show that only about half of even the listed French companies prepared consolidated accounts (as required by IAS 3) in 1979. The "full compliance" of France in 1979 is total fiction, but this is merely the most obvious case. The apparent fall in compliance from 1979 to 1983 results from a change in response not a change in reality.

A less important case, but one that further illustrates the problem, is that, for 1983, Jersey gets a score of 3.53 which is only possible if over half the propositions are "required". In fact, there is no relevant law in Jersey, and UK standards are merely voluntarily followed (presumably about half of the propositions coincide with those UK rules used in Price Waterhouse's Jersey office).

The clear-cut errors for France and Jersey suggest that there are also many subtler problems with the scores for other countries. The most obvious cause of error is that a "pronouncement of a professional accountancy body" can range from one that is legally enforced (e.g. Canada), to one that is usually obeyed and is binding on auditors (e.g.

---

* Professor Christopher W. Nobes, Department of Economics, Faculty of Letters and Social Sciences, University of Reading, Whiteknights, Reading, England. Manuscript received April 1987.

MIR Vol. 27, 1987/4

UK), to one that is persuasive (e.g. the Netherlands), to one that is unimportant (e.g. domestic pronouncement of the accountancy body in West Germany), to one that is largely unknown to companies or auditors (e.g. an IASC standard in Frace, although referred to by the Price Waterhouse survey).

This suggests that, at least in some cases, Doupnik and Taylor's detailed discussions of increases and decreases in country scores bear little relationship to reality. In passing, it should be noted that the score for the UK is shown to rise in Table 2, whereas its components fall in Table 4. This is numerically impossible.

On another point, the authors' suggestion that the harmonization efforts of the European Communities "possibly have helped to improve the overall quality of financial reporting" seems unlikely to be an important factor. This is because only two countries out of the ten had brought the earliest accounting Directive into force (only Denmark and the UK had implemented the Fourth Directive by 1. 1. 83, although there may have been some effect of partial anticipations, e.g. in Belgium).

In summary, the data are too weak to support the detailed numerical analysis, descriptions and conclusions of Doupnik and Taylor. Even if this were not the case, the paper's frequent reference to "compliance with IAS standards" would be quite misleading since no evidence is offered to suggest causality.

References

Commission des Opérations de Bourse (1980): *Annual Report.*
Doupnik, S. and M. E. Taylor (1985): "An Empirical Investigation of the Observance of IASC Standards in Western Europe", *Management International Review,* Vol. 25, 1, pp. 27–33.
Nobes, C. W. (1981): "An Empirical Analysis of International Accounting Principles: A Comment", *Journal of Accounting Research,* Vol. 19, 1, pp. 268–270.

Name index

Abdel-Karim, R.A.A. 87
Abdel-Khalik, A.R. 118, 119
Accountancy 152, 156, 203, 210
AICPA 101,194, 231
Alexander, D. 171
Aliber, R.Z. 107
American Accounting Association 17, 47, 106, 107, 108
APB 107
Arden, M.H. 148, 164
Armstrong, J.S. 32
Arnold, J. 118
Aron, P. 120
ASC 146, 148
Ashton, R.H. 118

BADC 114
Balassa, B. 107
Ballon, R.J. 31
Barth, K. 141
Bartholomew, E.G. 154, 203, 204, 205
Baumbach, A. 158
Baxter, W.T. 104
Baydoun, N. 81, 86
Beaver, W.H. 78, 118, 184
Beeny, J.H. 31, 36, 37
Belkaoui, A. 73
Benston, G.J. 31
Biddle, G.C. 119
Biener, H. 71
Bigwood, G. 4, 6
Bird, P. 170
Bittker, B.I. 64
Botosan, C.A. 78, 90
Bourgeois, J.C. *see* da Costa
Brayshaw, R.E. *see* Samuels
Breton, G. 118, 120, 122, 134
Brierley, J.E.C. 20, 84, 199, 214
Briggs, J. 177
Briston, R.J. 81
Brooks, J. 7, 69
Buckley, A. 155
Busse von Colbe, W. 120, 134, 158, 167, 184

Cable, J. 77
Cairns, D. 46
Camfferman, K. 85, 87, 168, 170, 186
Carsberg, B. 19, 31, 54
Casanovas, I. 172

Cauvin Angleys 71, 68
Chadwick, L. *see* Pike
Chastney, J.C. 31, 164
Chau, G.K. *see* Chow
Chaveneau, J. 168
Choi, F.D.S. 31, 40, 41, 44, 73, 107, 112, 113, 114, 120, 121, 122, 131, 158
Choudhury, N. 12
Chow, L.M. 80
Christiansen, M. 71, 165, 186
Clarke, F.L. 87, 108
Clarkson, G.E.P. 121
CNCC 167
Cochrane, J.L. 133
Coenenberg, A.G. 168
Colombo, G.E. 169
Connor, J.E. 104
Cooke,T.E. 84, 114
Cooper, J.C.B. 118
Coopers & Lybrand 114
Corre, J. 68
Craig, R. 87
Craner, J.M. *see* Samuels

da Costa, R.C. 17, 19, 32, 36, 54, 75
Dahl, R.A. 178
Dale, B. 31
Darrat, A.F. 118
David, R. 20, 84, 199, 214
Davidson, R.A. 91
Day, J. 118, 121, 122
de Decker, P. 4
de Long, J B 119
de Roover. R. 3, 4, 9, 12
de Ste Croix, G.E.M. 12
Dean, G.W. 87
Dicksee, L.R. 103
Donaghy, P.J. 31
DOT 140
Doupnik, T.S. 44, 48, 73, 95, 225, 234
DTI 199, 206, 213
Duffy, W. 20
Dunne, K.M. 115

Easterguard, A. 19, 31
EC Commission 141, 142
Edey, H.C. 141
Edwards, J.R. 142, 145
Emenyonu, E.N. 120